DICTIONARY OF

Genealogical Sources

IN THE PUBLIC RECORD OFFICE

DICTIONARY OF

Genealogical Sources

IN THE PUBLIC RECORD OFFICE

STELLA COLWELL

WEIDENFELD AND NICOLSON
LONDON

FOR SARAH

Copyright © Stella Colwell 1992

First published in 1992 by
George Weidenfeld & Nicolson Ltd
91 Clapham High Street, London SW4 7TA

British Library Cataloguing in Publication Data
A catalogue record for this book is available from the
British Library

ISBN 0 297 83140 2

Typeset in Compugraphic Galliard by
BP Integraphics Ltd, Bath, Avon
Printed and bound in England
by The Bath Press, Avon

Contents

Acknowledgements

In compiling the Dictionary I have made liberal use of the existing guides and class lists to the contents of the Public Record Office, and for the Glossary, the Guides, Osborn's *Concise Law Dictionary* and the *Oxford English Dictionary*. I am grateful to the Public Record Office for permission to use in the Glossary some of the descriptions of terms which have appeared in successive published Guides to the Contents of the Public Record Office. I should like to thank the following friends and neighbours who gave their assistance in a variety of ways, unscrambling my word processor, keeping me going and promising things would improve: Douglas and Pat Brown, Julian Duffus, Catherine Jones, Terri Moeller, and especially Sarah Newens, Vanessa Thompson-Royds, Alf and Maureen Smeeth and Stanley West, whose supportive contributions I can never repay; Richard Palmer, the Librarian and Archivist of Lambeth Palace Library, supplied information on Lambeth degrees, and Nicholas Cox, of the Public Record Office, agreed to scan the text, and made numerous suggestions; lastly thanks to Emma Way, my editor, for her patience and encouragement.

Introduction

This book is written by a record-user and is intended to be a key to the hundreds of thousands of documents in the Public Record Office which await the bewildered family historian as he tries to reconstruct his personal heritage. Many must be the time that an enthusiast has gone there expecting his task to be straightforward, only to find that he does not even know where to begin: the documents he examines do not contain the names he seeks, or he has little idea of what records he should be looking for. How does he find his way through the maze?

Since 1838, the Public Record Office has been the custodian of the enrolments of administrative, financial and judicial business conducted since the Norman Conquest by the King's Court and its offshoots, of records from the Duchies and Palatinates, of State Papers from the reign of Henry VIII to the late eighteenth century, of material emanating from later government departments and numerous public bodies, and of disparate collections of gifts and deposits, most of which were housed until 1977 in an imposing Gothic building situated on the Rolls Estate in Chancery Lane, London, WC2. The ever-increasing accumulation of preserved papers and lack of adequate storage space led to the opening in that year of another futuristic octagon-shaped repository at Kew, near Richmond in Surrey, to which were transferred modern governmental archives dating mainly from about 1782, but including Colonial and Audit Office, Treasury and Service records from at least a century earlier, and it is to this institution that current governmental deposits are now made. A recommendation in the 1990 Scrutiny Report of the Lord Chancellor's Department was that all the public records should be brought together in one place, and this is likely on completion of a new structure at Kew later this decade, though it is hoped that accommodation will be found in central London for microfilm copies of certain classes of record, a bookshop, and other facilities. Since 1 April 1992, the Public Record Office has been an executive agency.

At present there are five types of guide to the contents of the Public Record Office. The first, still useful, is the indexed two-volume *Guide to the Manuscripts Preserved in the Public Record Office*, edited by M.S. Giuseppi, and published in 1923–4, and now obviously out of date owing to the huge number of later accessions, classification and rearrangement of existing material. The second, is the indexed *Guide to the Contents of the Public Record Office*, published in two volumes in 1963, describing documents deposited up to 31 August 1960, and the third volume, published in 1968, relating to transfers up to 1966, and correcting errors and omissions in the earlier volumes, all now out of date because of later receipts and subsequent heavy weeding, destruction or removal of some of the classes they describe. The third, the *Public Record Office Current Guide*, a massive and ongoing project, is divided into three parts, the first being administrative histories of the various courts, departments and bodies depositing their records, the second forming class descriptions, arranged alphabetically by class letter code and serial class numbers, setting out the total number of pieces in each, its time-span and any restriction on access, a rather perfunctory summary of the contents, and where held, whilst the third is a subject index listing the class letter code and class numbers in which a particular subject may be found, and which serves as a finding-aid to the other parts. However, it has to be said that it is incomplete, incorporates groups of records not yet received into the Office, or which have been withdrawn, or for periods not yet accessible to the public, which can prove a hindrance to the bemused searcher. There are microfiche copies of the *Guide* available for purchase, and like the previous *Guides*, they can often be consulted locally in county record offices or other major libraries, giving at least a clue to the classification of records dealing with a specific subject. The fourth type of guide are the often overlooked Appendices to the *Annual Reports of the Keeper of Public Records*, which summarize recent acquisitions, records made accessible during the year, and contain index compilations sifted from a single class or a collection of classes covering a particular topic; and finally, the burgeoning and welcome series of Information Leaflets, Records Information, General Information, Family Fact Sheets, and Source Sheets, devoted to subjects attracting most attention by readers, though not directed entirely at the family historian, and which will instil some knowledge of the history and purpose of the preserved records, the classes in which useful information will be found, and the years covered. Copies of all of these can be picked up, free of charge, at both repositories, and there is a subject index available to the numbered topics dealt with so far or in progress. Searchers are also recommended to peruse the free twice-yearly Readers' Bulletin, which embraces reading room news, staff re-organization, projects and future plans, recent additions to the records, and work on finding-aids; the Friends of the Public Record Office, a small but growing and active charity, sponsors voluntary work in indexing and producing new finding-aids, monthly lectures, Readers' Forums and occasional Study Days on a wide spectrum of subjects, and issues its own twice-yearly journal.

The searcher's first disappointment may be that the opening hours are limited at present to 9.30 am until 5.00 pm, Monday to Friday, though an experimental Saturday morning opening of the Census Rooms in Chancery Lane will commence in mid-1992, with a view to similar extensions elsewhere in the Office if this proves popular. The Office is also closed on Public Holidays and for stocktaking during the first two weeks of October. Only three documents at a time may be ordered by readers, though these can be placed in advance of a visit, so that they are ready for collection on arrival and the next requisitions made. Last requests for productions the same day must be made by 3.30 pm, though self-service microfilms may be removed up to 4.30 pm in Chancery Lane, and 4.15 pm at Kew. Records not collected the same day are generally held over a further three days before being returned to storage. Because the waiting period for document productions is on average fifty minutes in Chancery Lane, and slightly less than half this at Kew, time is at a premium, and it is vitally important to maximize time by knowing where and what to look for. Another disappointment may be that many records are closed for thirty years or an even longer interval, may be held at the repository at Hayes and will therefore involve a time-delay of several days before being produced, may be subject to restricted access, or may have been weeded leaving only a small representative sample of what was originally there, or survive only in the form of a personal name index. The new reader will also be quickly confronted by the fact that there is no union personal name index, rather a scattered series of card, or volume compilations, or integral indexes, extending over part or the whole of a particular class; nor is there a research service offered, so that he has to use his own initiative, or give up and hire one of the professional outside record agents listed by the Office. The documents come in an assortment of shapes and sizes, bundled and strung up in boxes, in sacks, in rolls, files, volumes, or individually. Each one will pose its own problem of handwriting style, abbreviation, language, dating system, and terminology peculiar to the period, court or department generating it. Many of the archives, certainly those of the common law courts, manorial courts, and governmental enrolments of grants, fines, fiscal business and land transfers, will be written in Latin until 1733, whilst some may be in Anglo-Norman, though English began to be used from the late-fifteenth century, and was the language of all documents during the years of the Interregnum (1651–60). This means that they could lie beyond the reach of many researchers, but for the fact that their contents frequently follow a distinctive pattern, written in doggerel rather than classical Latin, and most importantly, have long attracted translators with a view to publishing a précis of them in *Calendars*, to which there are excellent general indexes, though most have been treated only up to the sixteenth century, and they are summaries rather than exact transcripts of the records. Government Publications, Sectional List 24, *British National Archives*, last issued in 1984, identifies those classes for which printed *Calendars* have been prepared, while the two compilations by E.L.C. Mullins, *Texts and Calendars, an Analytical Guide to Serial Publications*, 1958 (reprinted in 1978), and *Texts and Calendars*, 1983, note which local societies have been instrumental in publishing public records for their own area or sphere of interest, a number of which may be found on open access in the Office. Consultation of these is an important means of learning the format employed by the clerks who wrote the documents, so that a reader can predict where names, places and dates are likely to occur in a similar document. For the voluminous collection of records belonging to the common law and equity courts, contemporary indexes and lists were constructed by officers who needed to refer to them as working documents, though to the modern reader they may seem primitive, yet they can be sufficient to identify a person or place. Later nominal, topographical or subject indexes have also been produced from time to time for the benefit of record-users, a number of which have been published as *Lists and Indexes*, or reproduced by the List and Index Society.

The public records are arranged into classes and assigned letter codes representing the court or department to which they belong, for example C for Chancery, E for Exchequer, HO for Home Office, but the system becomes less obvious with more recent additions, reflecting no doubt the proliferation of public bodies and government departments over the last hundred years, so now we have DT for records of the General Nursing Council, PIN for those of the Ministry of Pensions and National Insurance, and ZJ for *The London Gazette*. The class letter codes are divided into serial class numbers, each bearing a title related to its contents, and extending over a particular period, geographic area or type of enrolment, and further broken down into chronological, alphabetical or topographical piece-numbers, sometimes with the addition of sub-numbers. The searcher needs to know the class letter code, class number, piece-number and any sub-number of a document to enable him to requisition it.

Access to the records is by Reader's Ticket, obtainable on production of sufficient personal identification such as a driving licence, or a passport for overseas visitors, and this must be shown on each successive visit, and its number quoted in requesting documents. The only exception is for users of the Census Rooms in Chancery Lane, who sign a daily Visitors' Book and receive a pass allocating a seat number.

On arrival at the Public Record Office, all entrants must submit to a security check of their bags; briefcases and bags over a certain size must be stored in lockers, coats and umbrellas left in cloakroom space, and only papers and pencils taken into the reading rooms. In Chancery Lane, there are three reading rooms in addition to the Census Room complex in the basement; two, the Round Room and Long Room, are on the ground floor, and the Rolls Room is one flight up, access being through the Long Room. The reader first passes a small museum containing a selection of public records on display, then the bookshop which sells a variety of handbooks on local and national records, before signing his name in the Visitors' Book. On entering the Round Room or Long Room, the reader is faced by the banks of shelves lining the walls. In the Round Room, each press or bookcase is identified by number and the volumes cramming its shelves bear on the spine the press number and a shelfmark; in the Long Room the presses are given letters, the book spines being similarly marked. The key to what they contain lies in the drawers of card catalogues directly opposite the door in the Round Room, or at the officer on duty's desk in the Long Room. The cards are organized alphabetically by class letter code and serial class number which are written on the top left-hand side in the Round Room, on the top right in the Long Room, whilst the press and shelfmark of the book giving more information about the class is written on the opposite corner. The presses hold the numerical class lists, which set out in the left margin the piece-numbers and sub-numbers within each class, an indication of the period or area covered, and whether integrally indexed or with index volumes; sometimes the lists will be more expansive descriptive lists, providing a better idea of what each piece encompasses. The cards will refer to any contemporary nominal or topographical indexes, to printed indexes, transcripts of part or all the class, a catalogue in which it might be mentioned along with material of a similar nature extracted from other classes, or calendars summarizing the class contents. Many of the lists can be found in both rooms, though some are unique to one, and the cards in the Long Room usually give press and shelfmark references to volumes in the Round Room, though not vice versa. The cards may refer the reader to the Catalogue of Indexes, a bound volume placed next to the drawers of the card catalogue in the Round Room, and in press A in the Long Room. This runs alphabetically by class letter code and serial class number, and details the exact nature of and time span covered by any surviving indexes, and how they may be consulted, either on open access, or as INDEX volumes, requisitioned as documents. Most of the older class lists have a sample requisition ticket pasted in at the front, showing how documents in the class may be ordered, and later lists contain a short prefatory description of the background history, purpose and organization of the records in each class, drawing attention to any indexes, or range of piece-numbers covering a particular topic. Having extracted references to the documents he wishes to examine, the reader then proceeds to the Document Ordering Room, almost opposite the Round Room. Here he feeds into one of the computer terminals his ticket number, reading room title, class letter code, serial- and piece-number of each document. Once the first batch of three documents has been collected from the appropriate distribution counter, he can place another order, and when a search is completed the documents are returned to the counter.

During the wait for document delivery, time can be well spent scanning the presses which also house, for instance, volumes of the *Victoria County History*, printed transcripts of the Domesday Book, *Statutes of the Realm*, printed *Calendars* of the public records, biographical compendiums, dictionaries, chronologies, palaeography guides, handbooks of dates converting regnal into calendar years and ecclesiastical feast days into dates of the year, topographical dictionaries identifying the hundred or wapentake to which any given place belonged, compilations and indexes produced officially and unofficially by institutions, societies and individuals, and other ancillary sources, ranged as closely as possible to the lists of classes from which they derived their information.

The Rolls Room, on the first floor, hosts drawers of microfilms of certain classes, such as some of the State Papers, the registered wills and administration grants of the Prerogative Court of Canterbury, indexes to most of the Death Duty registers, to miscellaneous returns of births, marriages and deaths overseas, and deposited non-parochial registers, with attendant class lists, annual registers of the above wills and administrations, and typescript and printed indexes to them and to other probate material, plus serial publications relating to wills proved in local courts; there are also card index drawers of nominal and topographical entries drawn from surviving probate inventories, plus stacked volumes containing the latest purchased edition of the microfiche of the International Genealogical Index. Some documents have to be requisitioned, using the room's computer terminal, while other material, such as later Death Duty registers or original wills, have to be ordered by manual ticket and a few days' delay is endured before they are transported from Hayes. Once delivered, they will be held for several days before being returned.

The Census Room complex, in the basement, operates a system whereby the reader locates a microfilm for a specified place by reference first to a place-name index of one of the decennial census years, which highlights its registration district number; the reader then scans the relevant Relsgistration District volume in order to elicit a microfilm number. The entry will also indicate if there is a personal name or street index available. He helps himself to the appropriate film from one of the cabinets in the reading rooms, putting in its place a numbered block corresponding to his seat number. For the 1891 census there are both microfiche and microfilms on open access. Prints can be made from the microforms by readers, using tokens supplied by the officers on duty.

In the Reference Room, off the Document Ordering Room, is a duplicate set of class lists to sources held at Kew, which afford a tremendous time-saver for searchers faced with a long journey into London and then out to the Surrey repository, as he can arm himself with document references, order them in advance and then collect them on arrival. The arrangement of the volumes is alphabetically by class letter code and then sequentially by class number. Some of the classes will be found to be indexed or coded, or 'registers' or 'digests' to others in the same class code, whilst one volume within a class may be the key to the rest in coded form under their original departmental references, to which are appended their new references in the class list; other classes may be split up into periods, organized alphabetically by subject within these, or divided into codes, each devoted to specific subjects, often making it difficult for the hapless newcomer (or experienced searcher at times) to understand let alone manipulate them, when what he wants is a clear, not too sophisticated, list. The lists usually contain brief introductory remarks about the history and purpose of each class, and refer the reader to related classes. Some lists incorporate nominal or subject indexes, while others will be in the form of descriptive lists, or devoid of any details other than date and title.

At Kew, having signed the Visitors' Book in the Reception Area, where he will also see the restaurant and small bookshop, the reader will mount the stairs to the first-floor reading room (the Langdale Room). He will go first to the distribution counter on his left to collect a bleeper displaying his seat number and letter, and which in due course will tell him by flashes and intermittent aural signal that his three documents are ready for collection from the counter. He can carry the bleeper around with him anywhere in the building. The adjacent Reference Room is banked with two sets of class lists, and there are further sets in the foyer outside and in the Map Room on the second floor, from which references to documents are extrapolated and then fed into the computer terminals, together with Reader's Ticket number, and seat number and letter. The computer may advise that the record is available on microfilm, in which case the reader passes through to the Romilly Room and helps himself to the appropriate film from one of the ranks of drawers. There is a self-service printer in this room like the one in Chancery Lane. If the document is a large one, it may have to be ordered manually by ticket in the Map Room, and once produced it is delivered to one of the cumbersome and rather high map cabinets, and it is the reader's responsibility to locate it with his name and seat reference placed on top, and to return it to the distribution counter. The computer may record that a special permit is required to examine certain classes, or that a signed undertaking must be made concerning the purpose of the search; in such cases the advice of the officers on duty in the Reference Room should be sought, and similarly in situations where the document is already out to some other user, for a quick check by the staff will reveal the reader's location, or the document's other whereabouts.

In the Reference Room will be found books drawing on or amplifying a number of sources held at Kew, such as extensive runs of printed *Army Lists*, *Navy Lists*, *Royal Air Force Lists*, *Foreign Office Lists*, registers of British shipping, of Foreign Office and Treasury material, indexes to registered companies, nominal indexes to a variety of classes, either partial or complete, and subject indexes to immense deposits such as the records of Railway Companies, in card or book form; the Romilly Room houses printed volumes relating to emigrants and countries overseas; the Map Room holds bound volumes of maps; the foyer bookcases contain printed *Calendars* of material held at Kew, and other works.

* * *

Wherever possible in the text I have mentioned the above and other items which may be of relevance to the family historian looking for biographical profiles, inter-generational links, kinship networks or locative references to his forebears. I have arranged under subject details about the records I have been able to establish as containing such information, to make these sources user-friendly and less formidable, and perhaps to point the reader in new directions. There will inevitably be material I have not included which readers have found particularly informative, reflecting the enormity of the task of knowing what is there and where, though I have tried to make the survey as thorough and accurate as I can. Each entry has a potted explanation, an outline of what records are available, in which classes, for what period, and what they contain, whether indexed or otherwise made easier of access, are subject to any closure rules, and ends with a reference to other related entries in the book. Having pored over the text, and identified a promising source, the reader can look at the prefatory list showing the disposition of the records, and then approach the class lists with confidence. The Glossary explains the meaning of some of the words used to describe the contents of certain classes, and terms with which the reader may not be familiar.

Although the book is not illustrated, it may be seen as a companion volume to *Family Roots*, for which it was originally destined to be the middle section, and this contains photographs of a number of sources cited here, together with over a dozen case studies showing the documents at work. If he wishes to compile his own dossier of copied material, both Offices offer a copying service, the type of process being at the discretion of the Reprographic Section, and depending on the size, nature and condition of the document.

Finally, it should be emphasized that once the documents are before him, the reader should appreciate their age and uniqueness, and treat them with respect, which means not taking notes or leaning on top of them, not marking them in any way, or dampening fingers in order to turn a page, or roughly handling them, so that they can be preserved for future generations to enjoy and be informed by. Documents should always be replaced in the same order, rolls rewound with care, and loose papers returned without their edges dangerously exposed, and large documents should be kept flat with the paper-weights provided, large rolls draped over the stand, books placed on the book supports, and each of them touched as little as possible; similarly the class lists should be replaced where they came from, not inserted in some other convenient spot, or lodged behind, on top of or squeezed perilously between their neighbours, ready to disappear or bring the rest of the volumes down with them when the next reader comes along. This may seem trite and obvious, but I have often winced at the way obviously intelligent readers have behaved towards these treasures; if we want to have access to original sources rather than microform copies of them, and can perceive their increasing popularity, we must all play our part in ensuring the archives' continuing health.

STELLA COLWELL 1991

The reader wishing to know more about the history of the public records and their contents, may like to read:

The Public Record Office, 1838–1958, J.D. Cantwell, 1991
The Records of the Nation, eds. G.H. Martin and P. Spufford, 1990
Tracing Your Ancestors in the Public Record Office, A. Bevan and A. Duncan, 1991
Family Roots, Discovering the Past in the Public Record Office, S. Colwell, 1991
Record Sources for Local History, P. Riden, 1987

The Records

Current disposition of classes of records by letter code mentioned in the text

Chancery Lane, London

A	Alienation Office	LO	Law Officers' Department
ASSI	Clerks of Assize	LR	Exchequer Auditors of
B	Court of Bankruptcy		Land Revenue
C	Chancery	LRRO	Land Revenue Record
CHES	Palatinate of Chester		Office
CP	Court of Common Pleas	LS	Lord Steward's Department
CRES	Crown Estate Com-	PALA	Palace Court
	missioners	PC	Privy Council Office
CRIM	Central Criminal Court	PCAP	Judicial Committee of the
DEL	High Court of Delegates		Privy Council
DL	Duchy of Lancaster	PEV	Court of the Honour of
DPP	Director of Public Prosecu-		Peveril
	tions	PL	Palatinate of Lancaster
DURH	Palatinate of Durham	PRIS	King's Bench Prison
E	Exchequer	PRO 30/5	18–19, 21, 23–26, 28, 34,
HCA	High Court of Admiralty		38, 41, 44, 47, 49, 50, 53
HO 107	Home Office		and 80, Gifts and Deposits
IND	INDEX Volumes	PRO 31	Transcripts, except
IR 26–IR 27	Board of Inland Revenue		PRO 31/20 Gifts and
	(Death Duty Registers and		Deposits
	Indexes)	PROB	Prerogative Court of
J	Supreme Court of Judica-		Canterbury
	ture	PSO	Privy Seal Office
JUST	Justices Itinerant	QAB	Queen Anne's Bounty
KB	Court of King's Bench	REQ	Court of Requests
LC	Lord Chamberlain's	RG	4–12, 18, 19, 27, 30–37,
	Department		43 General Register Office

SC	Special Collections	LCO	Lord Chancellor's Office
SO	Signet Office	LT	Lands Tribunal
SP	State Paper Office	MAF	Ministry of Agriculture, Fisheries and Food
STAC	Court of Star Chamber		
TS	Treasury Solicitor	MEPO	Metropolitan Police Office
WALE	Principality of Wales	MH	Ministry of Health
WARD	Court of Wards and Liveries	MINT	Royal Mint
		MT	Ministry of Transport
Ruskin Avenue, Kew		NDO	National Debt Office
		OS	Ordnance Survey Department
ADM	Admiralty		
AIR	Air Ministry	PCOM	Prison Commission
AO	Exchequer and Audit Department	PIN	Ministry of Pensions and National Insurance
AST	National Assistance Board	PMG	Paymaster General's Office
BT	Board of Trade	PREM	Prime Minister's Office
CAB	Cabinet Office	PRO	Gifts and Deposits (except PRO 30/5, 18–19, 21, 23–26, 28, 34, 38, 41, 44, 47, 50, 53 and 80)
CAOG	Crown Agents for Overseas Governments and Admin- istrations		
CO	Colonial Office	RAIL	British Transport Historical Records
COPY	Copyright Office		
CSC	Civil Service Commission	RG	General Register Office (except RG 4–12, 18, 19, 27, 30–37, 43)
CUST	Board of Customs and Excise		
DO	Dominion Office and Commonwealth Relations Office	STAT	Stationery Office
		T	Treasury
		TITH	Tithe Redemption Commission
DT	General Nursing Council		
ED	Department of Education and Science	WO	War Office
		WORK	Ministry of Public Build- ings and Works
F	Forestry Commission		
FEC	Commissioners of Forfeited Estates	ZHC	House of Commons Sessional Papers
FO	Foreign Office	ZHL	House of Lords Sessional Papers
HO	Home Office (except HO 107)		
		ZJ	*The London Gazette*
IR	Board of Inland Revenue (except IR 26–27)	ZLIB	British Transport Historical Records Office Library
		ZPER	

The telephone number for both Offices is 081–876 3444

DICTIONARY

Note: Details of births, baptisms, marriages, deaths and burials of Britons overseas are listed under the appropriate country; in some cases they appear also under the country which at the time had control or jurisdiction over them, reflecting the way in which the Public Record Office class lists are organized.

Abbreviation: temp.: tempore (in the time of)

Aa

Administration, Letters of When a person dies without leaving a will the next of kin, or failing that, an interested party, can apply to the appropriate probate court for letters of administration to be granted to them so that the estate can be administered. Grants concerning estates of public officers, 1622–1834, E 406, indexed, and 1784–1804, E 407/106/4; grants relating to assigned board wages in the Office of the Clerk of the Kitchen in the Royal Household, 1712–26, LS 13; registration of grants to enable share transfers and annuities arising out of 1677 London Bankers' Loan to the Crown, 1677–1704, E 406/27–44, indexed. Certificates sent by the Navy Pay Office to the High Court of Admiralty to enable intestate seamen's next of kin to obtain a grant, 1795–1807, HCA 30; letters of administration relating to members of the Armed Services, 1836–1915, PMG 50. Alphabetical list giving date of grant, of cases brought before the Court of Chancery, 1669–1799, C 100; 7% sample of contentious cases, arranged by year, then alphabetically by suit title, 1858–1960, J 121; pedigrees in the Chancery Division of the High Court filed since 1946, indexed by name of the first person on them, and the date of death, and under the names of parties to the suits, 1852–1974, J 68 (closed 30 years); selected letters of administration in *bona vacantia* cases, where a person died without lawful heir, or was guilty of treason, with a nominal list giving date of grant and amount estate sworn under, 1808–57, TS 17, and 1517–1953, TS 18 to which there is a nominal card index via TS 33, which gives references to TS 18 material (some closed 75 or 100 years); administration cases of the Treasury Solicitor and Procurator General, 1584–1852, TS 11.

see *Canterbury, Prerogative Court of, Chancery (Equity), Court of, Death Duty, Delegates, High Court of, Estate Duty, Succession Duty*

Admiralty, High Court of This was originally established to deal with cases of piracy and booty, but came to hear all matters relating to the high seas and business abroad. The Court of Chancery also served in a similar capacity until the early sixteenth century. The Court's jurisdiction was divided into two: Instance Court (civil cases of commercial disputes, wages, collisions and salvages, and criminal cases of murder and piracy), and Prize Court (cases arising from prizes taken from the enemy in warlike operations). At first the two Courts were combined, but separated after 1660; the cases were heard by doctors in civil law, from 1675 based in Doctors' Commons. Criminal cases in the Instance Court came before the sessions of oyer and terminer and gaol delivery for the Admiralty of England, at the Old Bailey from the seventeenth century, and from

1834 the Central Criminal Court. Appeal lay from the Instance Court to the Court of Chancery until replaced by the High Court of Delegates in 1535, which in turn was superseded by the Judicial Committee of the Privy Council in 1834. The Vice-Admiralty Courts were set up in the colonies and maritime counties of England and Wales to deal with cases occurring locally. In 1875 the Court was merged into the High Court of Justice as part of the Probate, Divorce and Admiralty Division. The following sources concentrate on the Instance Court, though many contain similar information on the Prize Court: Acts, recording daily business with brief summaries of proceedings, 1524–1786, HCA 3; Assignation Books, 1786–1810, HCA 6, 1810–64, HCA 7 summarize proceedings, and from 1786 there is an index of ships' names in each volume. Indexes to HCA 6 and HCA 7 are in HCA 56; Instance papers, including original pleadings, affidavits and exhibits, 1629–1778, HCA 15, 1772–1806, HCA 16, 1807–39 in HCA 17, 1840–59, HCA 18, 1860–74, HCA 19, 1875–1943, HCA 20; from 1860–1918 reference to these records is via the Minute Books, HCA 27, which contain brief notes and reference numbers to cases, with an index of ships' names; indexes, 1772–1946, are in HCA 56, relating to HCA 16, HCA 17 and HCA 27. Libels, 1519–1739 (Instance Court), 1519–1814 (Prize Court), contain libels commencing suits, allegations and other pleadings, decrees and sentences, and exhibits up to 1739, HCA 24; interrogatories, 1541–1733, HCA 23; examinations and depositions, 1536–1826, with integral indexes, 1653–1749, and including answers to libels, 1577–1770, HCA 13. Oyer and terminer, and gaol delivery proceedings in Doctors' Commons, 1535–1834, with an index to persons and to ships, HCA 1 (from 1834 see **Central Criminal Court**); Old Bailey sessions, 1807–8, indexed, PCOM 1; warrants for execution on conviction of a capital offence, 1802–56, respites of execution, 1802–20, and warrants for arrest, jail or movement of officers and seamen for breaches of naval or criminal law, 1805–56, HCA 55; warrant books for arrest of ships, 1541–1772, HCA 38. Some Vice-Admiralty proceedings in the colonies to 1834, HCA 1, with a nominal and ship index; proceedings in foreign courts or languages, 1550–1778, and Vice-Admiralty Courts, 1740–1860, HCA 30. Notes of proceedings on appeal from Instance, Prize and Vice-Admiralty Courts, 1827–78, TS 15. Appointments and admissions of proctors, 1727–1841, warrants for appointments, 1604–1853, bail bonds, 1741–1829, HCA 30; appointments of court officers in High and Vice-Admiralty Courts, temp. Elizabeth-1873, HCA 50, indexed in HCA 51.

see **Appeal, Court of, Central Criminal Court, Chancery (Equity), Court of, Delegates, High Court of, Privy Council, Judicial Committee of, Marshalsea Prison, Probate, Divorce and Admiralty Division, Vice-Admiralty Courts**

Advance of Money, Committee for

This was the earliest Parliamentary committee, embodied by Order in Parliament in 1642, to receive loans of money or plate to be put to public use in return for a fixed annual interest. It was intended for inhabitants within twenty miles of London, though counties further afield were held to account if they failed to subscribe. In 1650 it was amalgamated with the Committees for Sequestration and for Compounding with Delinquents. Order books, assessments, cases and general papers, 1642–56,

SP 19, summarized in *Calendar of Proceedings for the Committee for Advance of Money*. see **Delinquents, Committee for Compounding with**

Advowson, Grants of The perpetual right of presentation to a living, being a rectory or vicarage, is deemed real estate. Patent Rolls, 1201–1962, C 66, to which there are printed *Calendars* to 1582, and 1584–7.

African Company, Royal This had a monopoly over the slave trade between Africa and the West Indian and American colonies. Instruments of appointment, 1707–22, receipts for payment of wages and salaries, 1717–20, pay orders, 1717–20, some wills, 1710–21 (indexed), Registrars' accounts concerning deceaseds' estates, 1714–18, receipts, 1711–20, bonds and letters of attorney, 1711–22, C 113; Company stockholders, 1713–40, details of probate and other documents necessary to effect share transfers, 1721–52, share transfer books, 1720–27, Company servants, including passenger lists and salaries, 1702–38, lists of living and dead at the forts, 1673–1746, register of all servants and officers, 1750–1815, indentures, covenants and deeds, 1719–49, agreements by Company servants on appointment, 1712–16, 1721–30, dead men's effects at Cape Coast Castle (including wills, inventories, accounts of sales of effects, 1718–22, and buyers with items purchased, 1780–7), list of Company freemen, 1720, freemen in the Cities of London, Bristol and Liverpool, 1750, 1758, 1788, register of payments of £2 entry fee as freemen in the above Cities, 1750–1819, all in T 70; Accounts and Invoice Books, Outwards, 1683–1816, T 70/913–35, Inwards, 1673–1743, T 70/936–61, recording sales of

shiploads of slaves in the West Indies, Virginia and South Carolina, giving the ships' names, captains, dates and places of sales, purchasers' names and number of slaves and their cost; pensions, 1825–34, E 404/592; petitions, memorials and letters concerning the Third African Company, 1771–89, listed by country, BT 6/1–19.
see **Slaves**

Age, Proofs of These were required to show that the next heir to lands held directly from the Crown as a feudal tenant-in-chief had attained his majority, so entitling him to take possession (livery of seisin) of them and enjoy their profits, and thus end the period of wardship. Feudal tenure was abolished in 1660. The proofs include statements made by relatives, servants, employees or people in the neighbourhood at the time the heir was born, and which record details of their ages, occupations and other autobiographical information. Inquisitions post mortem, temp. Henry III (thirteenth century)–1660, C 132–C 142, printed to 1405, and for the reign of Henry VII, 1485–1509; also found in inquisitions post mortem in the Court of Wards and Liveries, 1541–1660, WARD 7, indexed by reign, and inquisitions post mortem in the Palatinate of Chester, 1272–1642, CHES 3.
see **Inquisitions post mortem, Wards and Liveries, Court of, Wardship**

Agricultural Returns Parish lists, giving names and addresses of occupiers of agricultural holdings, reference numbers, amount of land worked and changes in ownership, and size of holding, 1941, MAF 65 (access only by consent of Ministry of Agriculture); MAF 65/81 is an alphabetical parish list, giving page references.

Agriculture, Fisheries and Food, Ministry of Staff lists, ranks and salaries, 1892–1947, registers of service, Establishment staff, 1854–1929, and temporary staff, 1893–1920, lists of officers serving with the Forces, 1914–18, 1939–45, including honours and casualty lists, recommendations of the Promotion Board, MAF 39; lists of Established officers, ranks and salaries, 1948–55, MAF 184.

Aids These were originally feudal in nature or Gracious Aids on knights' fees raised by the King to pay for his government at home and policy abroad, and range in date from temp. Henry II (twelfth century) until the reign of William and Mary (late seventeenth century). Lists of assessments, giving names of payers, are arranged by county, chronologically by regnal year, and then by hundred, township or vill, or by borough, ward and parish, E 179; many have been printed in *Feudal Aids, 1284–1431*; later aids of the reign of William and Mary only are in E 182, organized in county bundles, by calendar year, then by hundred and parish; Receivers' accounts, arranged in similar fashion, give parish totals and names of collectors, together with defaulters, those against whom no distress could be brought owing to lack of sufficient goods to sell to pay the tax, death or absence, and names of Papists, E 181.

Air Force, Royal Formed on 1 April 1918 from the Royal Flying Corps and Royal Naval Air Service. Muster, 1 April 1918, AIR 1/819, and AIR 10/232–37; *Confidential Royal Air Force Lists*, 1939–54, AIR 10. Submissions for appointments, promotions, awards of medals giving details of the circumstances giving rise to the recommendation, 1918–55, and petitions in courts martial cases, 1924–59 AIR 30; commissions, appointments, promotions, resignations, despatches, casualties, 1918–86, in *The London Gazette*, ZJ 1, with annual subject indexes. Correspondence with officers, recommendations for awards and promotions, combat and other reports, with subject indexes, 1918–59, AIR 1. Medals for World War I, 1917–26, indexed by name, giving reference to the Medal Roll, for which WO 329/1 supplies the old volume number, and the class list the current requisition number, WO 329, disablement pensions and gratuities, 1918–20, PMG 42/1–12, arranged alphabetically; pensions to relatives of deceased officers, 1916–20, PMG 44; war casualties, 1915–18, AIR 1/2395–96; prisoners of war in German hands, 1944–5, AIR 20/2336, in Japanese hands in Horoshima Camp, 1942–6, Royal Air Force Nursing Service in Japanese hands, 1943–51, AIR 49/383–85; aircrew log books, Battle of Britain, 1940, AIR 4; extracts from pilots' reports, August–September 1940, AIR 20/2290; aircrew casualties, July–October 1940, AIR 16/609; recommendations for honours and awards, Battle of Britain, AIR 2/4086, 4095, 8351, 9468; casualty returns, January 1940–April 1945, AIR 16/888–90, and daily summaries of casualties, 1939–43, AIR 22/99–100.

see *Flying Corps, Royal, Falklands War, Korean War, Medals, Naval Air Service, Royal, Prisoners of War, British, World War II*

Albert Medal Instituted in 1866 for merchant seamen, and from 1877 for those committing acts of bravery on land in mines, on the railways or at fires, in October 1971 all surviving holders exchanged the Medal for the George Cross. List of recipients, 1866–1913, and photograph

album, 1866–79, BT 97; recommendations for the award, 1866–1953, MT 9, Code 6; warrants for the award, 1866–1950, in HO 45; citations published in *The London Gazette*, 1866–1971, with annual or half-yearly subject indexes, ZJ 1.
see *George Cross, Medals, Merchant Seamen*

Alderney Rentals of Crown lands, 1832–1961, LRRO 12 (most closed 100 years), indexes 1817–1902, LRRO 65.
see *Channel Islands*

Alehouse Recognizances These were annual bonds, with the names of sureties, made by alehouse keepers to justices of the peace to observe prevailing regulations. A statute of 1552 required all alehouse keepers to be licensed on bond with a jail penalty, and was intended to regulate good behaviour and to control and limit the increasing number of alehouses. Later statutes refined this and there were regional variations. Palatinate of Chester recognizances, 1580–1640, CHES 38; Palatinate of Durham, 1583–4, DURH 8.
see *Victuallers' Recognizances*

Algeria Deaths, 1840–1958, RG 35/14–15, 20–44, indexed in RG 43.

Alienage, Declarations of Renouncing British nationality, under the Naturalization Act 1870, 1871–1914, and under British Nationality and Status of Aliens Act 1914, 1915–49, HO 334. Both have nominal indexes.

Alienation In order for a feudal tenant-in-chief of the Crown to gift or sell his land a licence had to be obtained from the Crown; applications were followed by enquiries to establish whether the grant of a licence would prejudice the King's financial interests or those of others. Inquisitions *ad quod damnum*, temp. Henry III (thirteenth century)–Richard III (fifteenth century), C 143, and temp. Henry III–Henry VI (fifteenth century), E 151, temp. Henry VII–Charles I, 1485–1642, C 142, E 150, contain details of the enquiries made by sworn local juries before the King's escheators, and include applications for licences in mortmain. Fines for a licence, or pardon for alienation without a licence were payable to Chancery from 1327, before which date lands transferred without a licence were subject to forfeiture to the Crown; Escheators' files, temp. Henry III–Richard III, E 153, include inquisitions into lands alienated without a licence. Entry Books of licences and pardons for alienation, giving names of parties, properties and fines, 1571–1650, A 4; payments for licences are recorded on the Fine Rolls, 1272–1648, C 60, for which there are printed *Calendars* up to 1509; licences and pardons for alienation without a licence are on the Patent Rolls, 1216–1660, C 66, with printed *Calendars* to 1582, and 1584–7. The Alienation Office was created after the fines were farmed out to the Earl of Leicester in 1576, in return for a percentage of the yield. After his death in 1588 short leases were given to Exchequer officers and from 1689 power was vested in the Treasury, and it was finally abolished in 1834; extracts from writs of covenant when land was conveyed by final concord (agreement) and including county, parties, details of the premises, and an approximate valuation, with a note of the pre-fine, 1576–1661, are in A 7; post-fines, 1595/6–1660, E 374; Receivers' accounts of fines on alienations, 1601–60, E 104; on the abolition of feudal tenure in 1660 fines and pardons became moribund.

Aliens Taxation of aliens, fifteenth–seventeenth century, being singled out for imposts in 1440, 1442, 1449, 1453–61, 1482 and 1487, and from 1523 until the reign of William and Mary included in the lists of other taxpayers, E 179, arranged by county, chronologically by regnal year, then by hundred, township or vill, or by borough, ward and parish; as they were subjected to double tax rates or to a poll tax from 1523, they may be listed separately; from 1571 alien denizens also attracted the same rates as aliens; returns of the reign of William and Mary only are in E 182, and in Receivers' accounts of the same reign, E 181, in county bundles, by calendar year, and then by hundred and parish. Lands of aliens forfeit to the Crown, 1640–1883, C 205, extents of possessions of foreign subjects seized during the Wars with France, 1293/4–1482, E 106; alien returns, 1547–53, SP 10; passes issued to foreign subjects allowing them to leave English ports for the Continent within a prescribed period, giving name, country or place of residence, status or occupation, port of departure and destination, 1697–1784, SP 44/386–413; passes issued by Customs officers giving date, name, occupation, principal residences over the previous half-year, and pass to a specific destination, 1792–1837, HO 1; aliens arriving in English ports, 1810–11, FO 83/21–22; certificates of arrival, arranged by port of arrival, stating nationality, profession, date of landing, last country visited, and bearing a signature, 1836–52, HO 2, indexes 1826–49, HO 5/25–32; returns and papers, listing immigrants, made by ships' masters, giving similar information, arranged chronologically by date, 1836–69, HO 3; out-letters relating to aliens, 1794–1870, HO 5, 1871–3, HO 136, 1874–1904, HO 43, from 1905 onwards in HO 162; lists of persons in foreign embassies or under their protection, 1571–1783, SP 104, 1791–1821, FO 95, 1822–46, FO 91; registers of protections against impressment into the Royal Navy, 1761–2, 1795–1806, ADM 7; registers of Foreign Protestant Churches in England, 1567–1840, RG 4, and 1646–1921, RG 8.

see *Bouillon Papers, British Nationality, Declarations of, Denization, Foreign Churches in England, Naturalization, Refugees, Safe Conduct, Letters of*

Almsmen Petitions from disabled soldiers seeking a place in a royal almshouse, setting out cause of disablement, present financial and other circumstances, 1660–1750, SO 5/31, 1688–1784, SP 44, 1784–1898, HO 56; appointments, 1792–1833, HO 44/50, 1828–1969, indexed, HO 115; warrant book of appointments, 1750–1960, HO 118; appointments of almsmen at Westminster Abbey, 1903–10, HO 144; correspondence and papers, 1841–1950, HO 45.

see *Charterhouse, Poor Brothers of the, Windsor, Poor Military and Naval Knights of*

America Colonial Papers, General Series, 1574–1757, CO 1, and Original Correspondence, 1606–1822, CO 5, both printed up to 1738, in *Calendar of State Papers, Colonial, America and West Indies*. From 1689, CO 5 is more useful, and is arranged under colony, containing information on early settlers, their elected Councils, charters, petitions, grants of land and offices. Association Oath Rolls of Burgesses of St James' City, Virginia, 1696, C 213/468, and of the Mayor, Recorder and Commonalty of New York City, C 213/470; hospital muster of patients in New York Military Hospital, 1777, ADM 102/583; list of provincial Army officers, 1782, T 64.

see *American Loyalists' Claims, America, United States of, Land Grants, Colonial*

America, British North Emigration registers, 1850–63, CO 327/1–2, 1864–8, CO 328; Original Correspondence, emigration, 1817–96, CO 384; Original Correspondence, 1816–68, CO 6; settlers, mainly British troops already stationed there and applying for land grants, giving personal details of age, career, marital status, children, purpose of application, and bearing signatures, 1837–8, CO 384/51.

see *Canada, Emigrants*

America, United States of Aberdeen, Washington State, British Consular returns of births, 1916, deaths, 1914, FO 700/22–23; Boston, Massachusetts, births, 1871–1932, deaths 1902–30, FO 706/1–3; Cincinnati, Ohio, births, 1929, 1943–8, 1951–8, deaths, 1947, 1950–55, FO 700/31–35; Cleveland, Ohio, births, 1914–30, 1944–69, deaths 1948–69, FO 700/36–43; Dallas, Texas, births, 1951–4, deaths, 1951, FO 700/24–25; Detroit, Michigan, births 1910–69, marriages, 1936–7, deaths, 1931–43, 1949–68, FO 700/44–53; El Paso, Texas, births, 1916–30, deaths, 1914–26, FO 700/26–27; Galveston, Texas, births, 1838–1918, deaths 1850–1927, FO 701/23–24; Honolulu, births, 1848–93, FO 331/59, registers of British subjects, 1895–1944, claims of British subjects against the American government for indignities inflicted by Hawaiian authorities, 1895, FO 331, marriages, 1850–53, RG 33/155, indexed in RG 43/7; Kansas City, Missouri, births, 1904–22, 1944–66, marriages, 1958–61, deaths, 1920–26, 1943–9, 1952–65, FO 700/54–60; New Orleans, Louisiana, births, 1850–1932, marriages, 1852–81, deaths, 1850–1932, FO 581/15–19; Omaha, Nebraska, births, 1906, FO 700/61; Pensacola, Florida, births, 1880–1901, deaths, 1879–1905, FO 885/1–2; Pittsburgh, Pennsylvania, births, 1954–6, FO 700/63; Portland, Oregon, births, 1880–1926, deaths, 1929, FO 707/1–2; Providence, Rhode Island, births, 1902–30, deaths, 1930, FO 700/8–9; St Paul, Minnesota, births, 1943–66, deaths, 1944, FO 700/71–74; Tacoma, Washington State, births, 1896–1921, deaths 1892–1907, FO 700/20–21. Claims made under the Treaty of Amity 1794, concerning the North-East Frontier, 1796–1812, awards, 1802–4, register of awards, 1796–8, reports of assessors, 1798–1803, claims, A–W, FO 304; British and American claims under the Treaty of Ghent 1814, 1816–17, 1820, FO 303; other claims in FO 5 under both treaties; claims and awards, 1871–5, under the Treaty of Washington 1871, and an index to claimants, FO 305. New York Consular correspondence and papers concerning the slave trade, 1834–42, and extradition, 1893–1901, FO 285.

American Loyalists' Claims After the War of Independence, the Treaty of Peace 1783, provided for settlement by the United States of America of claims of those suffering losses in the former British colonies because of their loyalty to the British Crown. During subsequent delays and negotiations the British Government paid out pensions, allowances and compensation. Under the Treaty of Amity 1794, it was agreed that all debts contracted with and due to British subjects before 1783 should be settled. After secession in

1799 a new Convention was signed in 1802 by which both countries were committed to pay. General Correspondence, United States of America, Series I, 1782–95, FO 4, includes claims arising out of the War; accounts of Commissioners, 1776–1826, AO 1; compensation to Loyalists and other refugees, 1788–1837, AO 3/276; temporary allowances, 1781–1831, and quarterly pension lists, 1788–1839, T 50; Claims, Series I, 1776–1831, AO 12, Series II, 1780–1835, AO 13: Series I contains evidence of witnesses, reports, examinations and decisions, and lists of claimants, whilst Series II contains the original claims and papers; both have nominal indexes; Claims Commission Minute Books and reports, and including British merchants, 1777–1841, T 79.

Analysts, County Correspondence with the Local Government Board on public health matters, 1872–1904, arranged alphabetically by county, MH 30; registers of correspondence, 1867–1920, MH 31, being the key.

Angola Luanda, British Consular returns of births, 1865–1906, marriages, 1871–1928, deaths 1859–1906, FO 375/1–4.

Annuities Offering a series of payments at equal intervals throughout a given term or for the life of a specified nominee or nominees, in return for a capital investment. The life might be that of the purchaser or some other person nominated by him, perhaps a relative or friend. Three State Life Annuities, 1745, 1746 and 1757, also offered lottery tickets as an inducement to people investing more than a certain sum; there are ledgers, arranged by number and providing date of purchase, name and address of proprietors, premium paid and name of contributors, number of lottery tickets, annual yield and the name and address of the nominee, age at time of purchase and eventual date of death, or when the last annuity was paid out: NDO 1/1–3; NDO 1/1 relates to 1745, for which there is a printed index to nominees, with details of any transfers of annuities; no names of contributors are mentioned in 1746, ledgers for which are in NDO 1/2 and 2A, while the 1757 Annuity gives names of parents of the nominees, NDO 1/3; assignment ledgers give details of wills, grants of letters of administration, marriage settlements and deeds, as well as assignments, arranged chronologically, and recording the original debenture number and annuity paid, NDO 1/4; Tontine and Annuity Dead Orders sometimes include death certificates of nominees, NDO 1/128–50; ledgers for the 1778 State Annuity are in NDO 2/4, and for 1779 in NDO 2/6; in 1778 life annuities or annuities for thirty years were offered, plus entry into a lottery, while in 1779 offers were extended of life annuities or annuities of twenty-nine years, plus a lottery; a book of endorsements lists nominees, their dates of death, and assignments, NDO 2/8. Other annuities include those offered in 1698 to original subscribers to the 1693 State Tontine, and others, for a period of ninety-six years, the lists of names recording nominees and their relationship to the proprietors, E 403/2379; purchasers of annuities, 1704, and dividend payments to 1709, recording names and sums, annuities payable from lottery orders, 1706–9, 1805, 1807, 1810, E 351/53–56; receipts for annuities, 1706–1832, E 404; payments of annuities, 1527–33, E 403/2444; registers of grants of annuities, 1558–1650, E 403/2371; grants and registers of payments of annuities, some giving offices held, 1558–1698, E 403/2362–70; in-

dexed registers of assurances and wills, 1681–1720, E 403/2372–78; acquittances and signed receipt books of annuitants, 1629–32, 1693–1706, E 407/10–11; indexed bankers' annuities, 1706–14, granted under a statute of 1701, E 403/2129–43; indexed Assignment Books of annuities granted to Goldsmiths of the City of London in return for a loan, 1677, 1676–1713, E 406/1–26; deeds, wills, and administration grants effecting share transfers in the interest on the loan, 1677–1704, E 406/27–44, indexed; assignments of orders on bankers' annuities, 1704–17, E 407/16–17; annuities for ninety-nine years from 25 March 1708, E 403/2144, and annuities on duties on wrought silver, 1721–39, E 403/2145; names of contributors to loans, 1696 and 1698, E 401/2591–92, contributors to loans, 1709, 1710, 1757, 1841 and 1847, E 401/2594–98; payments to reduce the national debt, giving numbers, names and amounts, 1808–37, AO 3; list of subscribers to the Scottish Fund, 1780–1852, AO 3/947–48; Adventure of £2,000,000, 1711, E 401/2600, and Classis Lottery, 1712, E 401/2599, giving lists of beneficiaries under class, according to date of purchase, ticket number, name and abode of proprietor, sum, annuity, and unclaimed premiums used as prizes; memorials of deeds, bonds, instruments or assurances granting life annuities or rent charges enrolled within twenty days on the Close Rolls, 1777–1812, and designed to protect infants against purchases by them and to overcome secret transactions, C 54, enrolled within thirty days, 1813–54, C 63; there are indexes to grantors and grantees for both; grants of annuities in the Duchy of Lancaster, temp. Henry VII, DL 37.
see *Lotteries, Million Bank, Tontines*

Antarctic Expedition, British Annuities, 1910–12, PMG 28.

Antigua Baptisms, 1733–4, 1738–45, marriages, 1745, burials, 1733–4, 1738–45, CO 152/21, 25. Registers of slaves, 1817–32, T 71.

Appeal, Court of Set up in 1875 to deal with appeals from the civil courts, and from 1966 has heard criminal appeals. Some judgments in Chancery actions, included in Entry Books of decrees and orders, 1876–1955, J 15, to which 'A' and 'B' books (1876–1955), on open access, give folio reference, and which are arranged chronologically within legal term by date of filing or entry, by initial letter of plaintiff's name; final and interlocutory appeals, 2% sample from King's Bench Division, including County Courts from 1935: Motions (final appeals), 1918–26, (interlocutory appeals), 1921–6, (final and interlocutory appeals), 1927–61, J 69 (some closed 75 years); Rule Books of appeals, including some from the Exchequer Division, and some with integral indexes from 1880, 1875–1906, KB 25; Final and Interlocutory Order Books, from King's Bench Division, 1907–26, J 70, the numbers corresponding to those in J 69.

Apprentices Tax on apprentices, under Statute of 8 Anne C.5, 1710: Apprenticeship Books, 1710–1811, IR 1, arranged under City or Town Registers from October 1711–January 1811, for payments made in London, and Country Registers, May 1710–September 1808 for payments made to provincial agents; the volumes give chronologically by date when duty was paid, the name, address, and occupation of the master, the name of the apprentice (and up to *c.*1752 the father or guardian, and his address), the date of the indenture of apprenticeship, term of years, premium paid, and duty calculated; charitable and parish apprentices were exempt; indexes to apprentices, 1710–62, 1763–74, IR 17, and to masters, 1710–62, IR 17; registers of protections from impressment into the Royal Navy, 1740–59, 1761–2, 1795–1806, ADM 7; five-yearly samples of merchant marine apprenticeship indentures, 1845–1950, BT 151, indexed, giving name, age, date and period of apprenticeship, master's name, and later the port where the boy signed on and name of his ship, 1824–1953, BT 150; register of apprentices to fishermen at Colchester, 1639–44, HCA 30/897, five-yearly specimens of indentures, 1895–1935, BT 152; children apprenticed to the sea from Christ's Hospital, 1766, T 64/311.

Argentine Republic Buenos Aires, letters and papers relating to claims of British subjects, 1832–78, marriage declarations, estates, wills, 1826–1900, FO 446/3–6, 28–30; claims by and against Britain, 1882–4, FO 307.

Armorial Bearings, Tax on, 1793–1882.
see *Land Tax and Assessed Taxes*

Arms, Coats of Some original grants, 1547–53, SP 10, with a printed *Calendar of State Papers*; heraldic notes and drawings, made by Sir Joseph Williamson, Keeper of State Papers, and including some original grants, 1661–1702, SP 9; petitions relating to false use of arms, 1660–1782, SP 44/235–66B; funeral certificates where officers of the College of Arms presided at interments, and mainly relating to Wales, 1625–49, SP 17; applications for grants or augmentations of arms, and for change of name and arms,

listed chronologically under subject headings, 1841–1950, HO 45; indexed warrants for change of name and arms by royal licence, 1782–1868, HO 38, March 1868–1969 (gaps 1922–30, 1957–61), with integral indexes, HO 142.

Arms, College of Association Oath Roll of officers, 1696, C 213/398; Heralds' Warrant Books, 1792–1854, LC 5/176; reports to the Home Office concerning peerage claims, and petitions for changes of name by royal licences 1783–1837, HO 54.
see *Lord Chamberlain's Department, Name, Change of*

Army, British

(1) *Commissioned Officers* Manuscript Army Lists giving officers' names and dates of commissions, arranged under regiment, 1702–52, and an alphabetical list, 1751–1823, WO 64; printed annual *Army Lists*, with manuscript corrections, 1754–1879, and including regiments in North America, 1782, British American half-pay officers, 1783, and Foreign Corps, 1794–1802, WO 65; quarterly *Army Lists*, containing birth dates and seniority lists, and from April 1881 war service details, 1879–1900, WO 66; incomplete series are on open access from 1754; Hart's *Army Lists* are unofficial quarterly and annual lists of officers, with annotations and extra service information, 1839–1915, WO 211. Commissions of cavalry and infantry officers, 1679–1782, SP 44/164–703, 1758–1855, HO 51; Commission Books, 1660–1873, WO 25/1–88, 1728–1818, WO 25/89–111, 119, 1704–1858, WO 4/513–20, WO 25/122–203; Army purchase commission papers, including registers of service and the estimated value of each commission at 1 November 1871,

when commissions by purchase were abolished, giving the date, length of service, sum allowed, notes on retirement and the sum received, 1861–1908, WO 74; appointments and later transfers and promotions, under regiment, 1754–1808, WO 25/209–20, and by date, 1773–1807, WO 25/221–29; applications for commissions, appointments, promotions and resignations, arranged chronologically by regiment, 1793–1870, WO 31; birth, baptism, marriage and death certificates, 1755–1902, WO 42, marriages, 1811–72, deaths 1835–88, WO 32/8920, official notifications of marriages, 1799–1882, WO 25/3239–45; staff appointments, 1809, 1871–1902, WO 103, unattached pay, 1835–53, WO 25/3230–31, and pay ledgers, 1814–96, PMG 3; alphabetical registers of officers on unattached pay, 1872/3–1879/80, WO 23/66–67, and some commissions, 1780–1874, WO 43/1059; service records of commissioned officers, arranged alphabetically, 1809–10, WO 25/744–48, of officers on half-pay or retired, organized alphabetically, giving age on commission, date of marriage and children's births, as well as promotions and periods and areas of service, 1828, WO 25/749–79, of serving officers' services, arranged under regiment, including date and place of birth, 1829, WO 25/780–805, alphabetical returns of service of retired officers, 1847, WO 25/808–23, of serving officers, 1870–72, with some later entries, listed by year and regiment, WO 25/824–70; nominal index on open access; regimental records of service, 1755–1954, WO 76, partial index on open access. Selected personal files, from 1830, WO 138 (closed 75 years); inspection returns, 1750–1857, WO 27/489, and monthly station returns, noting presence or absence from regiments, 1759–1865, WO 17; Entry Books of Royal Warrants,

granting leave of absence out of the United Kingdom, 1752–63, PMG 14; confidential reports on officers, 1872–1905, WO 27. In 1641 half-pay was instituted for officers of reduced or disbanded regiments: alphabetical registers, giving rank and regiment, date of commencement of half-pay, the rate, and when paid, are amplified by dates of death, 1858/9–1879/80, WO 23/75–78, 1880/1–1893/4, WO 23/68–74; ledgers of half-pay, 1737–1921, up to 1841 being arranged under regiment and thereafter alphabetically by name, and including deaths, assignments of pay, and commission sales, and from 1837 addresses to which payment was sent, with dates of birth, PMG 4; half-pay to commissariat officers, 1834–55, PMG 5; Entry Books of Royal Warrants for half-pay, 1720–1817, PMG 14, 1763–1856, WO 25/2979–3002, arranged chronologically with a list of regiments, and some bearing officers' signatures, ages, number of years in the Army, and service overseas; lists of those entitled to half-pay, organized by regiment, 1713–1809, and recording the daily rate, rank, and those officers not yet provided for elsewhere, WO 24/660–747, to British American troops, 1783–1813, WO 24/748–62; half-pay and retired pay lists, 1712–1870, WO 25/3003–08, 3013–19; replies to 1854 circular about fitness for service of half-pay officers, WO 25/3009–12; awards to officers on retirement, full and general officers' pay and allowance registers, 1813–96, WO 23/66–82, and ledgers of payment, 1813–1920, PMG 3; civil officers, artificers, etc, superannuations, 1814–56, PMG 9, 1857–1920, PMG 57. Pensions for wounds, 1812–92, WO 23/83–92, payment ledgers, 1814–1920, PMG 9; commissariat officers' pensions for wounds, 1834–55, PMG 5; disability and retired pay and gratuities during and after World War I,

1917–19, arranged alphabetically, PMG 42/1–12, and supplementary allowances and special grants to officers, widows and dependants, 1916–30, PMG 43; widows' pensions, 1815–92, including payments of Drouly Annuities from 1818 to fifteen widows of officers whose annual income was less that £30, WO 23/88–92, 105–13; payment ledgers, 1713–1829, WO 24/804–83; Drouly Annuities, April 1870–March 1882, Compassionate List and Royal Bounty payment to officers' widows, 1812–1916, PMG 10; Drouly Annuities, 1827–March 1870, and April 1882–1920, and widows' pensions, 1810–1920, PMG 11; commissariat officers' widows' pensions, 1810–55, PMG 5; pensions to widows of officers killed in World War I, PMG 45; payments of Children's and Dependent Relatives' Allowances out of the Compassionate Fund and Royal Bounty, registers, 1815–94, WO 23/113–23, payment ledgers, 1812–1916, PMG 10; allowances and pensions to relatives and dependants of officers reported missing in World War I, 1915–20, PMG 47; pensions to relatives and dependants of deceased officers, 1916–20, PMG 44; children's allowances, 1916–20, PMG 46. Entry Books and registers of powers of attorney, 1721–1841, PMG 14, 1825–99, PMG 51; letters of attorney registers, including grants of letters of administration to officers' widows, 1755–83, WO 30/1.

(2) *Warrant Officers* Pensions to non-effectives, 1813–1920, PMG 3, 1909–28, including schoolmasters, PMG 33; pensions and rewards for Distinguished Services, 1873–1941, PMG 35, for Distinguished or Meritorious Services, 1909–28, PMG 36, 1917–21, PMG 34/3.

(3) *Other Ranks* Monthly station returns record regiments at particular places and can be of use where only a soldier's whereabouts are known, but not his regiment, 1759–1865, WO 17, 1859–1938, WO 73; Soldiers' Documents, 1756–1872, 1873–82, 1883–1913, of soldiers discharged to pension, the first series arranged alphabetically within each regiment, the second by cavalry, artillery, infantry and corps, and the last alphabetically regardless of regiment and including those discharged for other reasons than a pension; information on age, birthplace, trade, physical appearance, ranks and dates, service, conduct, and dates and places of enlistment and discharge, intended place of abode, are accompanied by a medical report, and from 1883 the names of next of kin, WO 97; general register of discharges of invalid and veteran battalions, 1782–1833, WO 121/137–222, 1871–84, WO 121/223–57; Description Books, arranged alphabetically by regiment, giving age, birthplace, trade, service and physical description, 1756–1900, WO 25/266–688, and for Depots, 1768–1908, WO 67; returns of service of those liable to serve abroad, alphabetically within regiment, 24 June 1806, WO 25/871–1120; soldiers discharged and not known to be dead or totally disqualified from service, 1783–1810, by regiment, WO 25/1121–31. Pay lists and musters, arranged by regiment, and then by rank, 1673–1810, AO 16, 1732–1878, WO 12, 1878–98, WO 16, and from 1868 includes names of wives and numbers and ages of children in married quarters; the quarterly musters record ages of new recruits at the end, together with birthplaces, trades, dates of enlistment and reasons for discharge of non-effectives; pay lists of commissariat staff, 1791–1876, WO 61/94–135; hospital muster of patients in the Military

Hospital, Malta, 1802–4, ADM 102/555, and at New York, 1777, ADM 102/583. Casualties and deserters in monthly and quarterly returns, under regiment, 1809–72, WO 25/1359–2410, WO 25/3251–60, indexed in WO 235/2411–2755, and WO 25/3261–3471 respectively; Entry Books of casualties, giving rank, birthplace, trade, date, place and nature of casualty, plus debts and credits and the name of the next of kin or residuary legatee, 1797–1817, WO 25/1196–1358; registers of authorities to deal with effects, 1810–22, WO 25/2966–71, and an index of soldiers' effects, 1830, WO 25/2974, register of effects and credits, 1830–44, WO 25/2975; registers of deserters, arranged by regiment, giving a physical description, age, date and place of enlistment and desertion, 1811–52, WO 25/2906–34; registers of captured deserters, 1817–48, with an index for 1833, WO 25/2935–54; deserter bounty certificates recording reward of twenty shillings from parish Land Tax receipts to informers causing their apprehension, c.1716–c.1830, to which there is a nominal card index under Bedfordshire, Berkshire, Buckinghamshire, Cambridgeshire, Cheshire and Middlesex, with another card index of regiments, E 182; Entry Books of deserters, 1744–1813, 1848–58, mostly indexed, WO 4/591–654; lists of deserters published in *The Police Gazette*, 1828–45, giving age, birthplace, trade, physical description, apparel and place of desertion, HO 75/1–18. In-pensioners, Royal Hospital, Chelsea, 1702–89, WO 23/124–31, 1795–1813, WO 23/134, 1864–65, WO 23/132, alphabetical register, 1837–72, WO 23/146; Admission Books and Rolls, arranged chronologically, and giving regiment, age, service record, cause of discharge, date of admission, pension

and former address, 1824–1917, WO 23/162–72, 174–80, indexed 1858–1933, WO 23/173; Appeal Minute Books, relating to appeals against decisions of the Board relating to eligibility and pension rate, 1823–1915, WO 180/53–78; baptism, marriage and burial registers of the Hospital, 1691–1856, RG 4/4330–32, 4387; Admission Books to out-pensions, recording details of disability and pension, 1715–1882, WO 116; details of medical examination, service record, birthplace, physical description and disability, 1830–44, with intended residence, WO 23/1–16; certificates of service of Chelsea out-pensioners, 1787–1813, listed chronologically, WO 121/1–136; certificates of service of those awarded deferred pensions, arranged alphabetically, 1838–96, and a nominal roll, 1839–96, WO 131; out-pensioners of Royal Kilmainham Hospital, Dublin, 1783–1822, arranged by discharge number, WO 119, located in records of out-pension admissions, 1704–1922, WO 118. Length of service pensions, 1823–1902, WO 117; regimental pension registers, arranged chronologically from 1845, and giving date of admission to pension, age and birthplace, service record, pension paid, disability and physical description, c.1715–1857, indexed 1839–43, WO 120, 1858–76, annotated with dates of death and addresses for payment, WO 23/26–65; pension returns, 1806, WO 23/136–40, 1842–83, giving regiment, rank, pension rate, date of admission and address, under district and including Great Britain and Ireland, 1842–62, the Channel Islands, 1842–52, Jersey and the Isle of Man, 1852–62, Ireland, 1882–3, South Australia, 1876–80, New Zealand, 1845–78, Canada, 1845–62, Cape of Good Hope, 1849–58, 1876–80, Bengal, 1845–80, Bombay,

1855–80, and black persons, 1845–80, WO 22; list of out-pensioners serving in tropical climates and discharged with extra pensions, and superannuations to civilian employees, 1820–92, arranged alphabetically, 1868–92, WO 23/93–104; selected pensions from Chelsea Hospital, 1799–1892, and Kilmainham Hospital, 1798–1817, with a nominal list, giving regiment, WO 900; selected pensions to widows, and to disabled soldiers, awarded prior to 1914, listed in alphabetical order of applicant, under widows, or disabled, and giving the effective dates of the pension, while the files record an account of the death or injury giving rise to the original claim and any later papers, details of age, birthplace, physical description, parentage, parental status, siblings, address, last rank and regiment of the casualty, medical and conduct records, date of award and amount of original pension, employment, marital status, annual income, and signature, 1854–1977, PIN 71.

(4) *Royal Artillery, Royal Horse Artillery, Engineers and Ordnance* Manuscript Army Lists of officers, 1702–52, WO 64, printed *Army Lists*, 1754–1879, WO 65, quarterly *Army Lists*, 1879–1900, giving birthplace and promotions in a seniority list, and from April 1881, details of war service, WO 66; Hart's *Army Lists*, 1839–1915, are quarterly and annual unofficial compilations of officers often with additional details of service, WO 211; printed *Army Lists* from 1754 are on open access; commissions, appointments and warrants, 1758–1855, HO 51, fees for commissions, 1782–1880, HO 88; incomplete set of Commission Books for Royal Artillery and Engineers, 1740–1852, WO 54/237–47; lists of artillery officers, 1727–51, artillery and engineer officers, 1793, WO 54/684, 701; appoint-

ment papers, 1809–52, WO 54/908–26, original patents and warrants of appointment, 1670–1855, WO 54/939–45; records of artillery and ordnance officers' services, 1727–51, WO 54/684, 1777–1870, WO 76 (to which there is a partial index on open access); engineer officers' services, 1786–1850, WO 54/248–59, 1796–1922, WO 25/3913–19 (partial index on open access); registers of officers in the Field Train, 1809–49, applications and testimonials, 1819–38, WO 54; confidential reports on engineer lieutenants at the School of Military Engineering, Chatham, 1858–1914, WO 25/1945–54; records of services of officers, giving age, birthplace, description and dates of marriage and death, and indexed, 1765–1906, for Royal Artillery, 1791–1855, Royal Horse Artillery, 1803–63, WO 69; artillery and engineer officers' half-pay, c.1810–c.1880, WO 23/82; service of ordnance and artillery officers, non-commissioned officers and men (mid-nineteenth century), WO 44/695–700, services of deceased officers in the Engineers and Ordnance (mid-nineteenth century), WO 44/684–94, and pensions, 1825–37, WO 44/653–76; ordnance officers' half-pay and pensions for wounds, 1836–57, PMG 12; allowances and pensions paid to relatives and dependants of officers reported missing in World War I, 1915–20, PMG 47, pensions to relatives of deceased officers, 1916–20, PMG 44. Soldiers' documents of those going to pension, c.1756–c.1913, arranged alphabetically from 1883, and all containing particulars of age, birthplace, trade, dates of enlistment and discharge, service and conduct record, medical condition, and from 1883 the name of the next of kin, WO 97; Description Books of other ranks in the Royal Artillery and Royal Horse Artillery, 1749–1863,

WO 54/260–309, 1773–1876, WO 69/74–80, Royal Irish Artillery, 1756–74, WO 69/620, Royal Sappers and Miners, Artificers, etc, 1756–1833, WO 54/310–16, all giving details of age, birthplace, physical description, trade, and service record, and including non-effectives 1830–82, indexed; service records of non-commissioned officers in the Royal Artillery, 1791–1855, Royal Horse Artillery, 1803–63, by unit in which the soldier last served, and setting out age, birthplace, physical description, trade, service record, marriage and date of death or discharge, WO 69/779–82, 801–39; registers of baptisms and marriages, Royal Artillery, 1817–77, Royal Horse Artillery, 1848–83, WO 69/63–73, 551–82. Musters and pay lists, Royal Artillery, 1708–1878, WO 10, Royal Sappers and Miners and Engineers, 1816–78, WO 11, Artillery and Engineers, 1878–98, WO 16; miscellaneous pay lists, Artillery and Engineers, 1692–1871, WO 54/672–755; quarterly lists of salaries, wages and pensions to civil and military Ordnance Establishment, 1594–1837, returns of persons employed in Great Britain, Ireland and Foreign Stations, arranged alphabetically by station and giving age, abode, occupation, marital status, number of children, service details and salary from the Ordnance Department, 1811–47, WO 54/388–493; half-pay, superannuations, widows' pensions and children's allowances, 1836–75, PMG 12; salaries and pensions of the Royal Artillery, 1802–44, giving abodes between 1816–33, pension returns, 1822–44, including widows' pensions, 1802, 1832–6, and letters of attorney, 1699–1857, WO 54; pensioners of Ordnance, Artillery and Engineers, 1834, WO 23/141–45; admission registers to disability and long service pensions, Royal Artillery, 1833–1913, WO 116/125–85;

deferred pensions, 1838–96, arranged alphabetically, WO 131; discharges, transfers, and casualties of the Artillery and Engineers, 1740–1859, WO 54/317–37; incomplete registers of deceased Artillery, 1821–73, WO 69/583–97; deaths and lists of effects of Artillery and Engineers, 1824–59, WO 25/2972–73, 2976–78; selected pensions to disabled men, and widows, awarded before 1914, and giving full particulars of circumstances of claim, age, birthplace, address, date of discharge or death, rank at retirement, later employment and annual income, marriage, and bearing signature of claimant, and listed alphabetically by applicant, giving effective dates of pension, 1854–1977, PIN 71.

(5) *British Army in the Colonies* Royal Garrison Regiment officers' services, including details of marriage and issue, 1901–5, casualties, 1904–6, posting book of officers transferred to other regiments, 1903–6, WO 19. Musters of infantry and cavalry regiments in India, 1883–9, WO 16/2751–2887, discharges located in musters of Royal Victoria Hospital, Netley, 1863–75, WO 12/13077–105, at the discharge depot at Gosport, 1875–89, WO 16/2284, 2888–915; pensions to the British Army in India, 1849–68, WO 23/17–23; admission books of pensions paid in the colonies, by district, and recording regiment, rank, and any transfer elsewhere, and date and place of death, 1817–1903, WO 23/147–60, pension returns, 1842–83, WO 22; lists, registers and admission books of negro and Cape Corps pensioners 1837–79, WO 23/153–59.

(6) *Foreign Troops in the British Army* Manuscript additions to printed annual *Army Lists* of officers, 1794–1802, WO 65; half-pay to officers, 1858–76, WO 23/79–81, payment ledgers, including pensions and

allowances and widows' pensions, 1822–85, PMG 6, 1843–62, PMG 7. Musters and pay lists, 1776–1816, AO 3, of French emigrant Artillery and Engineers, 1795–1802, WO 54; muster rolls, nominal rolls, records of service and attestations of British German and British Swiss Legions, 1854–6, WO 15; French Royalist Forces in British pay during the Napoleonic Wars, HO 69; King's German Legion pensions, 1801–15, WO 23/135; Royal Chelsea Hospital out-pensions to Foreign Corps at Hanover, 1844–77, PMG 8; pensions for wounds, 1814–1921, PMG 9; disability pensions, 1917–20, PMG 42; some lists of foreign nationals and Poles in the British Army, 1945–7, WO 315/23.

(7) *Miscellaneous* Census returns of barracks and depots in England and Wales, 1851, HO 107, 1861, RG 9, 1871, RG 10, 1881, RG 11, 1891, RG 12. Births, marriages and deaths of families of Army personnel overseas, 1627–1958, RG 33, indexed in RG 43; deaths of British soldiers in French and Belgian hospitals, 1914–21, RG 35/45–69; deaths in Hong Kong and the Far East, 1941–5, RG 33/11, 132, indexed in RG 43/14; baptisms of children of Palestine Forces, 1939–47, banns of marriage, 1944–7, WO 156/6–8. Soldiers taking the Oath of Allegiance before going to the Low Countries, 1613–14, 1616–21, 1623–5, 1631, 1632–5, to Utrecht, Vienna and elsewhere, March 1631, E 157. Petitions of disabled soldiers for places as almsmen, 1660–1750, SO 5/31. Military expeditions abroad, 1695–1763, SP 87. Despatches, 1794–1855, WO 1, and in *The London Gazette* up to 1986, ZJ 1, with subject indexes sporadically from 1790 and invariably from 1848, and including citations and publications of

awards and decorations, and of casualties. Warrants for grants of probate to executors or for letters of administration, giving rank, regiment, marital status, date and place of death, name and relationship of applicant or attorney, and estate value, 1666–1858, PROB 14.

(8) *Medals* Campaign and War Medals, 1793–1935, arranged by war or campaign, then by regiment, rank, number and name, and including a note of any bars to which entitled, and indexed, WO 100; Waterloo Medal Book, 1815, naming officers and men, by regiment, MINT 16/116; medals for World War I, indexed by name, giving unit and service number and reference on the Medal Roll, 1917–26, WO 329 (WO 329/1 provides the old volume reference, and the class list the current requisition number); Gallantry Medals, 1854–1983, WO 32 Code 50M; Distinguished Conduct Medal submissions, 1855–1909, WO 146; Boer War, 1899–1902, WO 108; Meritorious Service Medal, 1846–1919, WO 101; Long Service and Good Conduct Awards, 1831–1953, WO 102, annuities, 1846–79, WO 23/84. Medals and discharges, out-letters, 1854–7, WO 3; card indexes to entitlement to Distinguished Conduct Medal, to Meritorious Service Medal and Military Medal, arranged alphabetically and giving initials or forename, unit, rank and number, and date of relevant issue of *The London Gazette*, 1919, ZJ 1; register of Royal Red Cross Medals awarded to military nurses, annotated with dates of death to 1952, 1883–1918, WO 145/1; Commemorative Medals, 1911–35, WO 330. Correspondence about medals, 1805–1948, MINT 16.

(9) *Courts Martial* District courts martial, 1829–1919, WO 86, those held in London, 1865–75, WO 87, in India,

1878–1945, WO 88; General courts martial held abroad, 1796–1917, and in India, 1879–1920, WO 90 (closed for 75 years), registers, 1666–1704, 1806 onwards (closed 75 years), WO 92, with an index for 1806–33 in WO 93; Field General courts martial and military courts, giving name, rank, regiment, place of trial, nature of charge, verdict and sentence, 1909–63 (closed 75 years), WO 213, in the Crimea, 1854–6, WO 28. Original proceedings, 1666–97, 1758–60, WO 89/1–3, 1668–1851, WO 71; Entry Books of proceedings, 1806–1904, WO 91, with nominal indexes in WO 93/1A–1B; trials of officers, 1806–1904, nominal rolls of courts martial of Australian Imperial Forces, 1915–19, Canadian Expeditionary Force, 1915–19, and No. 1 POW Camp, Changi, Malaya, 1942–4, WO 93.

see *Boer War, Crimean War, Falklands War, Korean War, Medals, Prisoners of War, War Pensions, Waterloo, Battle of, World War I, World War II*

Ascension Island Births and baptisms, 1858 onwards, RG 32, deaths from *c*.1858, RG 35, both indexed in RG 43.

Assessments, Weekly and Monthly Raised to pay for Parliamentary and Commonwealth expenses, and including loans and contributions, listed alphabetically by county, then by hundred and parish, 1642–60, SP 28/148–204; for 1689–1697, SP 33 Cases B-D, listed in *Calendar of State Papers (Domestic Series) of the reign of William and Mary.*
see *Subsidy, Lay*

Assizes Up to 1875 there were six English circuits composed of contiguous counties, which were subsequently reorganized and finally abolished in 1971.

The most useful records are the Minute Books, covering perhaps several years at a time, which before 1805 are the key to the bundles of indictments for each sitting; however, the Books are often scrawled and abbreviated, but record the names of all indicted persons, with the charges against them, the plea and verdict and any sentence; the indictments set out a more extensive account of the alleged offence, and are endorsed with the names of people called as witnesses; very few of their depositions survive, unless they refer to manslaughter or murder, or to coroners' inquests. The records are in Latin until 1733. From 1805 the Annual Criminal Registers can be used to trace the court where a person was indicted: they are arranged alphabetically by English and Welsh county, then chronologically by court session, and give details of offence, verdict and sentence, and run up to 1892, HO 27; calendars of prisoners, giving number, name, age, occupation, degree of education, name and address of committing magistrate, date of warrant and taking into custody, the charge, when and where tried and the verdict, and sentence, are organized alphabetically under county, 1868–1915, HO 140 (closed 75 years).

(1) *Home Circuit* (Essex, Hertfordshire, Kent, Surrey and Sussex) 1558–1875, thereafter part of the South Eastern Circuit: Minute Books, 1783–1943, ASSI 32, Gaol Books, 1734–1863, ASSI 33, Agenda Books, 1735–1943, ASSI 31 (with an index, 1859–1911 in ASSI 40); Causes, 1763–68, Process Books, 1773–1822, posteas (giving a brief summary of proceedings), 1791–1856, indictments and depositions, 1559–1957, ASSI 34; depositions, 1813–1943, ASSI 36, pleadings, 1870–90, ASSI 37, estreats, 1770–1870, ASSI 38.

(2) *Norfolk Circuit* (Bedfordshire, Buckinghamshire, Cambridgeshire, Huntingdonshire, Norfolk and Suffolk) 1558–1875, though the last four counties became part of the South-Eastern Circuit from 1876, and between 1864 and 1875 Leicestershire, Northamptonshire and Rutland belonged to this Circuit, thereafter merging with Bedfordshire and Buckinghamshire as part of the Midland Circuit: indictments, 1653–98, ASSI 16, miscellaneous books of indictments, 1774–5, Causes, 1742–6, Process Books, 1831–63, posteas, 1829–62, ASSI 34.

(3) *Midland Circuit* (Derbyshire, Leicestershire, Northamptonshire, Nottinghamshire, Rutland and Warwickshire) 1558–1875; in 1864 Leicestershire, Northamptonshire and Rutland became part of the Norfolk Circuit, while Yorkshire was added to this Circuit. From 1876 until 1971 Bedfordshire, Buckinghamshire, Derbyshire, Leicestershire, Lincolnshire, Northamptonshire, Rutland and Warwickshire formed the Midland Circuit, while Yorkshire was part of the North-Eastern Circuit: Crown Minute Books, 1818–1945, ASSI 11, Civil Minute Books, 1929–44, ASSI 14, indictments, 1652–88, ASSI 80, 1860–1957, ASSI 12, depositions, 1862–1943, ASSI 13, miscellaneous papers, 1606–17, 1852–1919, ASSI 15, pardons, 1866–86, ASSI 81/14–103.

(4a) *Northern Circuit* (Cumberland, Northumberland, Westmorland, and Yorkshire) 1558–1875; after 1864 Yorkshire formed part of the Midland Circuit. From 1876–1971 the Northern Circuit comprised Cumberland, Lancashire and Westmorland, and Northumberland formed part of the North-Eastern Circuit: Minute Books, 1877–1915, ASSI 54, Order Books (certificates of criminal convictions), 1879–90, ASSI 53, Miscellaneous Books (judgments and postea books), 1810–76 ASSI 55, indictments, 1868, 1877–1957, ASSI 51, depositions, 1877–1945, ASSI 52.

(4b) *North-Eastern Circuit* (Durham, Northumberland and Yorkshire) 1876–1971: Minute Books, 1714–1889, 1921–44, ASSI 41, Gaol Books, 1658–1811, ASSI 42, Miscellaneous Books, 1730–1866, including posteas from 1830–60, ASSI 43, indictments, 1607–1890, 1924–57, ASSI 44, depositions, 1613–1890, 1924–41, ASSI 45, estreats, 1843–90, ASSI 46, miscellaneous 1629–1950, including special cases, 1629–1890, coroners' inquisitions, 1640–1890, ASSI 47.

(5) *Oxford Circuit* (Berkshire, Gloucestershire, Herefordshire, Monmouthshire, Oxfordshire, Shropshire, Staffordshire and Worcestershire) 1558–1971: Minute Books, 1803–88, ASSI 1, Crown Books, 1656–1949, ASSI 2, and of second Court, 1847–1951, ASSI 3; Miscellaneous Books, including posteas and processes, 1660–1888, ASSI 4, indictments, 1650–1957, ASSI 5, 1688 in PRO 30/80, depositions, 1719–1951, ASSI 6, pleadings, 1854–90, ASSI 8, estreats, 1746–1890, ASSI 9, pardons, 1944–58, ASSI 81/4–13.

(6) *Western Circuit* (Cornwall, Devonshire, Dorset, Hampshire, Somerset and Wiltshire) 1558–1971: Crown Minute Books, 1730–1953, ASSI 21, Civil Minute Books, 1656–1945, ASSI 22, Gaol Books, 1670–1824, ASSI 23, Miscellaneous Books, 1611–1932, including a Bail Book, 1654–77, Certificate Books, 1876–87, Estreat Book, 1740–1800, Postea Book, 1611–79, Process Books, 1717–1820, ASSI 24, indictments, 1729, 1801–1953, ASSI 25, depo-

sitions, 1861–1947, ASSI 26, pleadings, 1812–1957, ASSI 28, returns, 1740–1902, ASSI 30, pardons, 1948, ASSI 81/1–3, case papers, 1951–3, ASSI 82.

The Courts of Great Sessions for Wales included all the Welsh counties between 1543 and 1830; after its abolition, the North and South Wales Circuits embraced Chester, 1830–1875; from 1876–1945 this was further divided into the North Wales Division and South Wales Division, merging again between 1945 and 1971 to form the Wales and Chester Circuit.

Chester and North Wales Circuit (Chester, Flintshire, Montgomeryshire, Merionethshire, Carnarvonshire, Anglesey and Denbighshire) Crown Minute Books, 1831–1938, ASSI 61, Civil Minute Books, 1843–78, 1911–24, ASSI 57, Crown Books, 1835–83, being returns of prisoners tried, with offence, verdict and sentence, ASSI 62, Miscellaneous Books, 1694–1942, including fines and forfeitures, 1844–52, list of young persons employed in factories, 1846, ASSI 63; indictments, 1831–91, 1908–45, ASSI 64, depositions, 1831–91, 1909–44, ASSI 65, pleadings, 1840–1927, ASSI 59, coroners' inquisitions, mostly relating to Chester, 1798–1891, ASSI 66.

South Wales Circuit (Brecon, Radnorshire, Glamorgan, Carmarthenshire, Pembrokeshire, Cardiganshire and Haverfordwest) Crown Minute Books, 1844–1942, ASSI 76, Civil Minute Books, 1846–1943, ASSI 75, Miscellaneous Books, 1837–84, ASSI 77, indictments, 1834–92, 1920–45, ASSI 71, depositions, 1837–1942, ASSI 72, miscellanea, 1839–1937, ASSI 73, nisi prius pleadings, judgment rolls, 1841–2, ASSI 74.

Wales and Chester Circuit Crown Minute Books, 1945, ASSI 79, Civil Minute Books, 1945–6, ASSI 78, indictments, 1945–57, ASSI 83, depositions, 1945, ASSI 84, pardons, 1945, listed by name ASSI 84.

Palatinates
of Chester Gaol files, 1341–1830, CHES 24; from 1830–1945 it formed part of the North Wales Circuit, and from 1876–1945, the North Wales Division, thereafter to 1971 the Wales and Chester Circuit.

of Durham Minute Books, 1770–1876, DURH 15, Crown Books, 1753–1876, DURH 16, indictments, 1582–1876, DURH 17, depositions, 1843–76, DURH 18, miscellanea, 1472–1815, including jury panels, 1702–38, proceedings, 1662–1775, DURH 19. From 1876 Durham formed part of the North-Eastern Circuit.

of Lancaster Minute Books, 1687–1877, PL 28/1–12, indictments, 1424–1868, PL 26, depositions, 1663–1867, PL 27, miscellanea, temp. Richard II–Victoria, including outlawry rolls, temp. Richard II–Edward VI, and pardons, PL 28; Assize Rolls, 1401, 1402–1501, PL 15/1–93, 1524–1843, PL 25/6–317. In 1876 Lancaster became part of the Northern Circuit.

Assizes, Petty

(Also known as Possessory Assizes, and abolished in 1833) Proceedings were held by justices itinerant in eyre to 1285, and thereafter by justices sent to the shires up to three times a year, and concerned cases of novel disseisin (for recovery of land of which the suitor had allegedly been recently dispossessed), *mort d'ancestor* (for restoration of land of which the suitor had allegedly been deprived on the death of an ancestor) and darrain presentment (the advowson of a living interrupted by the intervention of a stranger); the records are in Latin: Rolls, 1248–1482, JUST 1, Files, 1248–*c*.1450, JUST 4.

Association Oath Rolls After the plot to assassinate William III in 1696, Parliament established an association for the defence of the King and in support of the Protestant Succession against the Pretender and the Papacy. The Rolls, 1696–7, are signed by Members of Parliament, C 213/1, freemen of London City Companies, C 213/171, military and civil officers holding commissions under the Crown, clergy, gentry and other subscribers or their proxies, and arranged under county, subdivided in some cases into towns and parishes; Cornish tinners, C 213/34, Doctors' Commons, C 213/164, Baptist Ministers, C 213/170, London dissenters, C 214/9, Quakers at Colchester, C 213/473, Trained Band officers, C 213/163, Inns of Court, C 213/165–67, College of Physicians and the Welsh counties, C 213/168, the Royal Household, C 213/365–72, serjeants at law and judges at Westminster, C 213/373, the Earl Marshal and heralds, C 213/398, nobility and gentry of Ireland now in England, C 213/402, clergy (arranged by diocese, archdeaconry and deanery), C 213/403–58; also included in C 213 are signed Rolls from Foreign Plantations, for example, the King's subjects in Holland, the Channel Islands, Scilly, Barbados and West Indies, the English Factory in Malaga, English merchants in Geneva, burgesses at St James' City, Virginia, the Mayor, Recorder and commonalty of New York City.

Asylums, Criminal Lunatic Out-letters relating to staff, 1899–1921, HO 145.
see *Idiots and Lunatics*

Attainder Was the extinction of all civil rights when judgment of death or outlawry was recorded for treason or felony, and involved forfeiture of goods and escheat of lands to the Crown, and cut off the line of inheritance to land or title. It was abolished in 1870. Inventories of goods and chattels of attainted persons, temp. John–1721, E 154; inventories and possessions of some attainted persons, temp. Henry V–1841, LR 2; commissions of enquiry into possessions, temp. Elizabeth I–Victoria, E 178; deeds relating to the estates of persons attainted during the 1715 Jacobite Rebellion, including claims concerning forfeited estates, proceedings, returns by clerks of the peace of names and estates of Papist recusants in England and Wales, arranged under county, rentals and particulars of estates sold, land held to superstitious uses, 1552–1744, with a descriptive list, FEC 1; registers of claims on forfeited estates, 1716–19, indexed, FEC 2.
see *Jacobite Rebellions, Outlaws, Superstitious Uses, Lands given to*

Attorney, Letters and Powers of These are a witnessed formal instrument whereby a person empowers another to act on his behalf. Grants concerning members of the Royal Household, 1547–1791, LC 5, registers in relation to royal and public officers' salaries, 1706–68, including some from Nevis and St Christopher, 1707–45, E 407/18–26, and assignments of annuities and pensions, 1622–1834, E 406/45–80; grants of powers of attorney accompanied by statutory declarations, or Queen's Bench or Chancery affidavits, verifying execution, 1882–1930, indexed, J 62; Entry Books and registers of the Army, 1721–1841, PMG 14, and *c*.1800–39 for naval, 1825–99 for military and civil officers and their dependants, PMG 51; in the Palatinate of Lancaster, 1409–70, PL 2; for members of the Royal African Company, 1711–22, C 113.

Attorneys Were persons admitted to practise in the superior courts of common law, representing suitors, who did not appear in person. Since 1875 they have been collectively called solicitors. From 1729 their training was by five years in articles to a practising attorney; on admission the new attorney took the prescribed oaths and his name was enrolled with the relevant court. Until 1838 if an attorney wished to transfer to another court, he had to be separately admitted there. From 1785 once qualified attorneys were required to apply to the appropriate court for an annual practising certificate. Appointments by sheriffs to serve in Chancery, temp. Edward I–1633, C 236; articles of clerkship, in the Court of Common Pleas, 1730–1838, admissions, 1729–1848, arranged alphabetically, CP 5; admission rolls, 1838–60, CP 8, Oath Rolls, 1779–1847, of Catholics, 1790–1836, Quakers' Affirmations, 1835–42, arranged by legal term and year, CP 10; rolls of attorneys, 1730–50, arranged in yearly rolls, alphabetically, and giving county, CP 11; indexed certificates of attorneys admitted in the Court of Chancery, 1730–87, C 203/7; affidavits concerning qualification, 1730–1836, and of due execution of articles of clerkship before 1800, and 1835, C 217/23–39; affidavits as to qualification, 1804–37 (with gaps), admissions, 1738–1818, C 217/183; admissions, 1815–42, affidavits as to qualification, 1800–39 (some gaps), C 217/186; books of attorneys, giving residence, date of admission or enrolment in the Exchequer of Pleas, 1830–55, E 4; Oath Rolls, 1830–

72, including Catholics, 1831–7, Quakers' Affirmations, 1831–5, E 3; affidavits of due execution of articles of clerkship in the Court of King's Bench, with details of parentage or guardianship of the clerk, and name and address of the attorney, 1775–1817, KB 105, 1817–34, KB 106, 1834–75, KB 107, with INDEX volumes, 1749–1845 to registers of articles, 1749–77, naming the attorney providing training, and the registered number, and indexes, 1749–1876 (gap, 1845–60), indexes to destroyed articles of clerkship, 1838–75, attorneys' residence books, 1790–1829, and rolls of attorneys, 1729–1875; articles of clerkship of persons previously admitted in other courts, 1843–67, Wales, 1830–4, and of those not admitted, 1831–48, KB 109; miscellaneous papers relating to transfers of articles, striking off the roll, litigation, and resignation, 1828–89, KB 111; Oath Rolls on admission to practise, 1750–1874 (gap 1841–60), KB 113; re-admissions, 1806–48, KB 101/27–34. Lists of attorneys and solicitors admitted to the Court of Bankruptcy, 1832–83, B2. Articles of clerkship and affidavits of due execution, temp. George II–William IV, admission rolls in the Exchequer Court, 1750–1806, the Great Sessions, 1697–1830, Oath Rolls, 1729, 1754, 1787–1830, all in the Palatinate of Chester, CHES 36. Admissions to the Court of Pleas, Palatinate of Durham, 1660–1723, and Oath Rolls, 1730–1841, DURH 3; affidavits of attorneys' clerks, 1750–1834, DURH 9, with an INDEX volume giving dates and residences, 1785–1842. Articles of clerkship and admissions, 1730–1875, Oath Rolls, 1730–93, Palatinate of Lancaster, PL 23. Specimens of articles of clerkship, 1838, 1840, 1850, 1859, 1870, 1875, 1876, 1880, 1890, 1904, and affidavits of due execution of articles, 1875, 1880, 1890,

1900, and 1903, applications for practising certificates, 1875, 1880, 1889, attorneys' certificate books of residence, 1785–1843, J 89. Tax on indentures of articles of clerkship, 1710–1810, IR 1, with indexes of apprentices, 1710–62, 1763–74, and of masters, 1710–62, IR 17.

see *Proctors, Solicitors*

Attorney, Warrants of A written authority by a defendant enabling another person to enter an appearance on his behalf in a court action and allow judgment to be entered against him, or to suffer judgment by default, usually where debts were involved, and qualified by the condition that if the debt was paid by a certain date it would not be put into force (the defeasance). 1745–87, 1801–29, E 406/81–88, 1875–85, indexed 1875–82, J 58.

Auditors, District Correspondence with the Highway Boards, 1879–1900, arranged alphabetically by Board, MH 21; registers of correspondence, 1879–1900, form the key to MH 21, MH 22.

Augmentations of the Revenues of the King's Crown, Court of Established by Henry VII and expanded by Henry VIII to deal with the lands and profits confiscated from dissolved monasteries and chantries, it merged with the Court of General Surveyors in 1547 and was dissolved in 1554, when it was annexed into the Court of Exchequer. Warrants for leases and grants of offices, temp. Henry VIII–Edward VI, E 300; particulars for leases, *c*.1501–*c*.1700, E 310; counterpart leases, made by the Court and the General Surveyors of Crown Lands, 1526–47, E 299; counterparts or transcripts of leases, temp. Mary–James I, E 311, leases surrendered to the Crown, temp. Henry

VIII–Philip and Mary, E 312; enrolments of leases, 1560–1601, E 309. Deeds (Cartea Miscellanaea), and cartularies, twelfth century–1730, E 315. Court rolls, *c*.1200–*c*.1900, SC 2, rentals and surveys relating to monastic and other possessions, temp. Henry VIII–William IV, SC 11 and SC 12, with descriptive lists. Entry Books of decrees and orders, 1536–54, E 315; proceedings, being bills, answers and other pleadings, with interrogatories and depositions, temp. Henry VIII–Philip and Mary, E 321; payments of salaries, pensions and annuities, 1538–53, indexed, E 403/2447–50.

see *Crown Lands, Land Revenue, Exchequer Office of the Auditors of*

Australia Chancery Master's Exhibits, including lists of shareholders of the Royal Bank of Australia, 1807–56, J 90/1328–1473. Original Correspondence relating to emigration, 1817–96, CO 384; register of correspondence on emigration, 1850–1, letters from the Secretary of State concerning bounties and loans to emigrants, 1831–2, CO 385; assisted passages of those born in Australia, now resident in the United Kingdom and applying to return, 1947–8, DO 35/3368; appointment of escorts to young boys aged 15–17, twenty-one going to Australia under the Big Brother Scheme, and to act as carers until aged 21, 1947–52, DO 35/3383. Records of naval officer casualties, 1914–20, ADM 242/1–5, with index cards setting out name, rank, date, place and cause of death, and the name and address of next of kin, alphabetical War Graves Roll, 1914–19, ADM 242/7–10. Courts martial of Australian Imperial Forces, 1915–19, WO 93.

see *Australia, South, Convicts, Transportation of, Emigrants, Evacuees, New South Wales, Tasmania*

Australia, South Register of emigrant labourers' applications for free passages, 1836–41, CO 386/149–51, with a partial index giving embarkation and certificate numbers. Peculiar Land Order Book, 1839, CO 386/146. Entry Books of Original Correspondence of South Australian Commissioners, 1833–94, CO 386. Register of Royal Chelsea and Greenwich Hospital out-pensions to military, naval and marine personnel, arranged by pay-district and supplying details of name, rank, regiment and number, date of commencement, amount and nature of pension, any transfers elsewhere, and date of death, 1876–80, WO 22/227.

Austria Baptisms of British subjects from 1867, RG 32, indexed in RG 43, deaths in Austria, *c*.1831–1920, RG 35/20–44; marriages at Vienna, 1846–90, FO 83, indexed in FO 802/239; marriages at Vienna, 1883–91, FO 120/697.

Awards and Decorations, British and Foreign Announcements to 1986 in *The London Gazette*, with annual or half-yearly subject indexes from 1848, ZJ 1; 1919–45, AIR 2 Code B 30, submissions, 1918–54, AIR 30, for the Royal Air Force. Correspondence, 1813–1905, arranged under country or by decoration, FO 83, selected correspondence, 1906–60, FO 371, to which there is a card index, 1906–19, and nominal index, 1920–51, in FO 409.

B*b*

Balearic Islands
see *Spain*

Bankers, City of London
see *Annuities*

Bankruptcy, Court of List of attorneys and solicitors admitted, January 1832–August 1883, B 2/8; registers of Town attorneys, January 1832–May 1883, B 2/9, and of Country attorneys, January 1832–August 1883, B 2/10–11.

Bankruptcy Department Set up in 1883, it is responsible for investigating, regulating and administering all insolvencies of individuals and firms for whom Receiving Orders have been made by English and Welsh courts; it also registers and has custody of deeds of arrangement and the accounts of the trustees appointed under them. It directs the work of the Official Receivers investigating the debtors' affairs and of the trustees. Selected files survive: registers of petitions in bankruptcy, 1884–1925, B 11, and Receiving Orders made against debtors and partnerships, and including administration orders against estates of deceased debtors, arranged in chronological order of filing of petition, and by initial letter; they include details of debtor's residence and occupation, date of the Receiving Order and name of the trustee in bankruptcy, 1884–6, B 11/1–3; registers of Receiving Orders, 1887–1925, indexed by subject, B 12; registers of deeds of arrangement, arranged alphabetically under debtor, 1888–1947, BT 39; ledgers, accounts, and registers of unclaimed dividends, registers of bankruptcies, resolutions at first meetings of courts and Special Orders of the Commissioners, 1844–1903, BT 40, including Bankruptcy Court in London, 1870–86, and County Courts, 1870–84, BT 40/25–52; many volumes are indexed; deeds of arrangement, 1897–1915, of assignment, 1899–1913, and Official Releases from bankruptcy, 1900–19, and case papers, 1884–1963, listed by date, name and file number, BT 221; cases relating to insolvent and deceased debtors under Receiving or Administration Orders, papers concerning applications by the Receiver, public examinations and committee proceedings, 1891–1914, with a card index, and 1915–30, a selection only, with a nominal list, BT 226; correspondence and papers, 1883–1956, BT 37, indexed in BT 38.

Bankrupts Between 1543 and 1861 traders who went bankrupt were subject to different legislation than debtors, but the definition of 'trader' was loosely applied; proceedings against them involved the creditors striking a docket issued out of Chancery, declaring their intention to render the trader bankrupt, which resulted in a commission (a fiat from 1832, an adjudication from 1849) issued by the Lord Chancellor, and after 1831 by the Court of Bankruptcy, and which was published in *The London Gazette*. The commission suspended the trader's business activities and fixed dates for three meetings between himself and his creditors at the second of which he was required to produce a statement of his financial affairs. The creditors appointed an assignee to collect in the assets and moneys owed to him, and drew up an inventory; affidavits were taken from relatives and business associates, and from the creditors to prove the debt claims. Either party could petition the Lord Chancellor for advice, or order for a trial of issue in the Court of King's Bench; proceedings could be ended by mutual agreement; otherwise once the assets had been quantified the creditors were paid dividends out of such funds as remained, and a certificate of conformity was issued discharging the bankrupt from any further liability. From 1876 bankruptcy proceedings took place in the Exchequer Division of the High Court, and were transferred to the Chancery Division in 1880. Commission Files, 1759–1911, B 3, Commission Docket Books, 1710–1849, B 4, Enrolment Books, containing enrolments of commissions, fiats and adjudications, appointments of assignees, assignments, examinations, depositions, and certificates of conformity, 1710–1859, B 5, index, 1820–70, in B 8; Bankruptcy Registers, 1733–1925, including Declarations of Insolvency, 1733–1835, B 6; Bankruptcy Minute Books, 1714–1875, B 7; Order Books, 1710–1877, including Orders made by the Lord Chancellor, 1710–1832, by the Court of Review, 1832–47, Court of Bankruptcy and Vice-Chancellor, 1847–61, Orders on Appeal by the Lord Chancellor of

Lords Justices, 1832–74, indexed under bankrupt's name and petitioning creditors, B 1; Bankruptcy Books, consisting of journals, ledgers, balance and deposit books held by the Bank of England, 1832–6, 1851, AO 18. Registers of petitions for protection from process (proceedings), giving petitioners's name, address, occupation and Court and amount of debt, 1854–1964, LCO 28 (these mainly relate to bankrupts under Bankruptcy Act 1883, and to some insolvent debtors, 1854–61, under County Courts Act 1854, and are arranged by initial letter). Commissions, fiats and adjudications, 1684–1986, sales by auction from 1712 announced in *The London Gazette*, some with subject indexes from 1790, invariably from 1848, ZJ 1. Papers and exhibits in bankruptcy proceedings, 1774–1830, C 217; gaolers' returns, 1861–9, B 2. Conveyances of bankrupts' estates are enrolled, 1572–1903, on the Close Rolls, indexed by bankrupt, and first Commissioner in Bankruptcy, C 54, thereafter in J 18; recognizances and bonds of Receivers to 1883, indexed under bankrupt, in C 54, thereafter to 1909 in C 68. Bankruptcy papers, Palatinate of Chester, 1760–1830, CHES 10.

Baptisms, marriages and burials Certificates of baptism, 1693–1826, marriage, 1744–1829, and burial, 1721–1831, from London parishes and a variety of counties, including some Jewish entries, listed, KB 101/26.

Barbados Licences to pass beyond the seas: registers of passengers, 1634–9 and 1677, printed in J.C. Hotten's *Original Lists of Persons Emigrating to America, 1600–1700*, 1874; 1715 census of white inhabitants, CO 28/16; baptisms and burials, 1678–9 (printed by Hotten),

CO 1/44, and RG 33/156; Association Oath Roll, 1696, signed by Governor and Council, clergy and officers of the Governor's Regiment, C 213/465–47. Registers of slaves, 1817–34, T 71.

Bargain and Sale, Deeds of Before the Statute of Uses 1536 bargains and sales of freehold land transferred it to the purchaser, usually as a trustee for some unnamed third party, while the vendor was regarded as the legal owner. The Statute recognized the purchaser as legal owner, so bargains and sales were arranged secretly making it difficult for an intending buyer to ascertain who was the real owner of the land; the Statute of Enrolments 1536 ordered the enrolment of all subsequent bargains and sales within six months at a central court of record or locally with the clerk of the peace of the county concerned; the statutes were repealed in 1845, though lawyers had long before evolved the device of lease and release to avoid enrolment. Enrolments centrally were effected on the Close Rolls, C 54, for which there are manuscript yearly initial indexes of grantees, and sometimes of places, to 1837, thereafter of grantors, and a second yearly index, of grantors, which between 1680 and 1842 is listed by four divisions, B, E, N and Y, made up of groups of counties (identifiable from the Catalogue of Indexes, on open access); an Act in 1563 extended enrolment to the Palatinates, for which enrolments may be found for the Palatinate of Chester, 1563–1830, CHES 29, Palatinate of Durham, 1563–1844, DURH 13, and Palatinate of Lancaster, 1563–1848, PL 15.

see *Church Lands, Crown Lands, Delinquents' Estates, Fee-Farm Rents, Leases and Releases*

Baronets Created in 1611 as an hereditary title to raise money for supporting the Army in Ulster, and open to landowners of estates worth £1,000 a year or more, and whose paternal grandfather was armigerous; from 1616–1827 it was possible for a baronet's eldest son to claim knighthood at twenty-one. Enrolment of letters patent of creation, 1611–1962, listed by regnal year, by initial letter, C 66; creations announced in *The London Gazette*, 1665–1986, with subject indexes sporadically from 1790 and invariably from 1848, ZJ 1; entries of patents and privy seals for payments on baronets' tallies, 1620–91, and accounts of sums paid for patents, E 403/2712–20; warrants for King's Bills of creation, 1783–1851, then for letters patent to 1921, indexed, HO 116; out-letters concerning creations and successions, 1806–1909, HO 117, 1910–21, HO 175; petitions, reports and letters concerning claims, 1661–1782, SO 44/235–66B, 1784–1898, HO 56, 1820–40, 1862–88, HO 80. Rolls of the Baronetage, 1901–10, 1915, 1931–51, and claims, correspondence, lists of creations and successions, 1841–1951, HO 45, with a descriptive list under subject.

Barristers Members of one of the four Inns of Court called to the Bar by the Inn and having an exclusive right of audience in the superior courts. Swearing or Oath Rolls, each roll covering a legal term and bearing the signature and Inn of the barrister, 1673–1906, 1910–44, with index volumes, 1910–85, KB 24, and superseded after the Promissory Oaths Act 1868, when the Oath of Allegiance was no longer compulsory; Rolls, giving the right on call to practise in the courts, 1868–1982, KB 4; Association Oath Rolls of the Inns of Court, 1696, C 213/165–67.

Bath, Most Honourable Order of the A chivalric Order, founded in 1725, with both Civil and Military Divisions. Sign manual warrants, 1777–1863, HO 37; recommendations and appointments, and investitures, 1815–94, WO 104; list of Military Members, 1919–45, AIR 2/1581–82; announcements in *The London Gazette*, 1725–1986, some with subject indexes from 1790, and invariably from 1848, ZJ 1.

Bedford Level Enrolments in Chancery of decrees made by county Commissioners of Sewers acting to sell lands of persons in default of payment of rates for repairing sea-banks and sea-walls, cleaning rivers and ditches etc, recording county, manor and names of parties, 1664–85, C 229, and IND 1/16815.

Belgium Death registers of Britons in Belgium, 1830–71, RG 35/1–3, deaths, 1870–1920, RG 35/20–44, incomplete returns of military deaths, 1914–21, RG 35/45–57; Antwerp, baptisms, 1817–52, marriages, 1820–49, burials, 1817–52, RG 33/1–2, indexed RG 43/1, 7 and 3 respectively; baptisms, 1831–42, marriages, 1832–8, 1841–2, burials, 1831–6, 1841–2, RG 33/155, indexed in RG 43/1, 7 and 3 respectively; baptisms from 1840, RG 32; Brussels, marriages, 1816–90, RG 33/3–8, indexed in RG 43/7; marriages, 1846–90, FO 83, indexed in FO 802/239; correspondence relating to marriages and deaths, 1927–51, FO 744; Ghent, marriages, 1849–50, RG 33/9, indexed in RG 43/7. History cards of Belgian refugees, arranged alphabetically, recording name, age, relationship within the family, wife's former name, allowance paid, and to what address, 1914–18, MH 8/39–92.
see *Refugees*

Benefices
see *Clergy*

Benevolences
see *Subsidy, Lay*

Bermuda Registers of baptism, marriage and burial of Naval Dockyard and Royal Marine churches, 1826–1946, ADM 6/434–6, 439. Case book of the Royal Naval Hospital, 1832–6, 1840–44, 1850–62, 1870–83, ADM 104. Registers of slaves, 1821–34, T 71.

Bethnal Green Protestant Dissenters' Burying Ground (also called Gibraltar Burying Ground) Burials, 1793–1826 (gap 1804–9), RG 8/305–11, index on open access.

Bills of Middlesex
see *King's Bench (Plea Side), Court of*

Births and Baptisms of Britons Abroad Miscellaneous returns, 1831–1958, duplicating some of the consular registers in FO classes, RG 32, indexed in RG 43/1–3, 7, 10–14, 20–21; 1627–1958 (though most date from the last century), and including the seventeenth-century English congregation at The Hague, African and Asian Protectorates, 1895–1957, and listed by country, RG 33, indexed in RG 43/1–3, 7, 10–14, 18, 20–21; African and Asian Protectorates, 1895–1950, RG 36/1–13, indexed 1904–40, in RG 43/18; the arrangement of the indexes of births and baptisms in various countries is as follows: 1627–1917, RG 43/1, 1627–1951, RG 43/3, births, 1831–1930, with an alphabetical list of countries, RG 43/2, births, 1921–45, RG 43/10–14, 1946–60, RG 43/20–21, baptisms, 1627–1958, RG 43/7.
see under individual countries, *Army, British, Merchant Seamen, Navy, Royal, Protectorates, British*

Births at Sea Registers of births to British passengers at sea, extracted from merchant ships' official logs, 1854–90, BT 158, 1902–12, BT 165, 1913, BT 99; births to British nationals reported to the Registrar General and passed on to English, Scottish, and Irish General Registration Offices, 1875–91, BT 160; miscellaneous returns from British and foreign vessels of births to British subjects, nationals of the colonies, Commonwealth and countries under British jurisdiction, 1831–1958, RG 32, indexed in RG 43/2, 3, 7, 10–14, 20–21; register of births to emigrants at sea, 1847–54, CO 386/169.

Births, Marriages and Deaths Correspondence and papers with the Registrar General, where local registrars or individuals sought advice, the law was infringed, or revision of legislation was considered, from 1874, RG 48 (some closed 50 or 75 years).

Bishops Letters to deans and chapters, recommending elections in English and Welsh sees, 1627–1872, SO 1, indexed 1643–1875, SO 2, and in printed *Calendars of State Papers (Domestic Series)* to 1704; others 1853–74, SO 3; warrants for patents, 1722–1875, C 201, patents enrolled, 1722–4, 1876–1962, C 66, 1725–1875, C 209; nominations and resignations announced in *The London Gazette*, 1665–1986, some with subject indexes from 1790, invariably from 1848, ZJ 1.
see *Clergy*

Blood Money Certificates On conviction of highwaymen and other felons, informers were given a reward, receipts for which, 1649–1800, are in E 407/27–30.

Boer War 1899–1902: Despatches, citations for awards, campaigns and casualties, in *The London Gazette*, ZJ 1, with annual or half-yearly subject indexes; local Armed Forces, enrolment forms, relating to units raised in South Africa, giving nationality, age, trade, date and place of enrolment, Oath of Allegiance, and date and place of discharge, arranged alphabetically by unit, 1899–1902, WO 126; alphabetical nominal rolls of units, giving date of enrolment and discharge, 1899–1902, WO 127; Imperial Yeomanry, Soldiers' Documents, giving details of age, birthplace, occupation and full service record, under regimental number, 1899–1902, WO 128, registers, 1899–1902, form indexes to them, WO 129/1–7 and include also casualty books, 1900–2, nominal roll of officers who served in South Africa, 1899–1902, WO 129; records of officers' services, WO 68; casualties, 1899–1902, WO 108/89–91, 338; recommendations for valour awards, 1901–2, WO 108; Field General and District courts martial, 1900–1, WO 92; registers of Boer prisoners, 1899–1902, WO 108/303–05; correspondence about Boer prisoners, 1899–1902, CO 537/403–09, 453, and on Dutch, German and French prisoners, 1899–1903, FO 2/824–26; selected claims by civilians for losses and requisitions of land or property, 1902–3, with an index to claimants, WO 148.

Bona Vacantia Division Deals with the estates of intestates where there is no-one entitled to it, and includes treasure trove and shipwrecks. Selected administration of estates case papers, 1818–1955, including letters of administration, 1808–57, with a nominal list giving date, and amount the estate was sworn under, pedigrees of intestates or those testators failing to dispose of residual estate or dying without a lawful heir, TS 17, 1517–1953, TS 18 (some closed 75 or 100 years). Pedigrees prepared by claimants or lawyers, arranged by date of compilation, and listed by the name of the earliest progenitor, detailing abode, date of birth, marriage or death, or period in which alive, and referring to any related papers in TS 18, 1794–1944, TS 33; joint card index to TS 18 and TS 33 on open access; Royal Warrants and Treasury authorizations for ex gratia payments and release of estates to lawful claimants, mainly from estates of intestates, 1807–1925, TS 30.

Border Papers Correspondence and reports of the Wardens of the Marches between England and Scotland, 1558–1603, SP 59, printed 1558–77 in *Calendar of State Papers, Foreign*, and *The Border Papers, 1560–1603*.
see *Scotland*

Borneo Births of British subjects, 1907, deaths, 1897–1907, FO 221/2–3; deaths from enemy action, 1941–5, RG 33/132.

Borneo, North (Sabah) Births, marriages and deaths of British subjects, 1923–c.1946, RG 36, indexed to 1940 in RG 43/18; deaths, 1941–5, RG 33/132, indexed in RG 43/14.

Both Kingdoms, Committee for One of the Parliamentary Committees. Books, 1644–50, and including Entry Books of letters and Order and Warrant Books of the Committee on Irish Affairs, SP 21, listed in *Calendar of State Papers (Domestic Series) of the reign of Charles I*.

Bouillon Papers Of Philip d'Auvergne, Prince de Bouillon, 1793–1815, and including papers of Charles Alexandre de Calonne, 1787–92, FO 95; Entry Books

of authorities in the Channel Islands charged with the relief of French emigrés, registers of refugees in Jersey, 1793–6, FO 95/602–03; memorials, reports, muster rolls, etc, and letters to Philip d'Auvergne, 1779–1809, HO 69; letters to Calonne, 1777–1814, PC 1, 1794–1816, WO 1, all with descriptive lists.
see *Aliens, Channel Islands, Refugees*

Brazil Papers relating to property of deceased British subjects, 1875–1915, FO 272; British and Brazilian claims after Brazilian independence, 1858–77, FO 306. Bahia, marriages, 1816–20, RG 33/155, indexed in RG 43/7; Maranhao, marriages, 1844, RG 33/155, indexed RG 43/7; Morre Velho, indexes to marriages, 1851–67 (the registers are at the General Register Office in London), RG 43/7; Para, births and deaths, 1840–41, RG 33/155, indexed in RG 43/1 and 3; Rio de Janeiro, baptisms, 1850 onwards, RG 32, marriages, 1809–18, RG 33/155, indexed in RG 43/7, from c.1850 onwards, RG 34, burials, 1850 onwards, RG 35/20–44, all indexed in RG 43, registers of births, 1850–59, FO 743/11, marriages, 1870–90, FO 83, indexed in FO 802/239.

British Empire, Most Excellent Order of the Instituted in 1917, with a Military Division from 1918. Announcements, 1917–86, in *The London Gazette*, with subject indexes, ZJ 1; out-letters, 1902–21, HO 180.

British Guiana Newspapers, often with birth, marriage and death notices, 1835–56, grants of land in Berbice, 1735–55, Poll Tax and Church Tax returns, 1765–94, CO 116. Registers of slaves in Berbice, 1813–34, and Demerara, 1817–32, T 71.

British Lying-In Hospital, Endell Street, Holborn, London Where poor married women, usually of servicemen, were admitted for their confinements on personal recommendation. Hospital records of admission give husband's abode or place of settlement, occupation (and from 1849 the place of marriage), the wife's age on admission and on what date, the date of birth and baptism of the infant, and date of discharge or death, plus the name of the person recommending admission, 1749–1868, RG 8/52–61; births and baptisms, 1749–1830, and recording addresses from 1814, RG 8/62–66.

British Nationality, Declarations of Renouncing nationality elsewhere, under the Naturalization Act 1870, 1870–72, declarations made under the Burma Independence Act 1947, 1948–50, both indexed, declarations of alienage, renouncing British nationality, 1871–1914, all in HO 334.

Brunei Births to British subjects, 1932–50, RG 36, indexed in RG 43/11–14, 20.

Bulgaria Philoppopolis (Plovdiv), registers of births to British subjects, 1880–1922, deaths, 1884–1900, FO 868/1–2; Rustchuk (Ruse), births, 1867–1908, deaths, 1867–1903, FO 888/1–2; Sofia, births, 1934–40, FO 864/1; Varna, births, 1856–1939, deaths, 1851–1929, FO 884/1–5.

Bunhill Fields Burial Ground A cemetery for Protestant dissenters. (City Road, London) authenticated registers of burials, 1713–1854, RG 4/3974–4001, 4288–91, 4633, indexed 1713–1838 in RG 4/4652–57; (Golden Lane Cemetery, London) unauthenticated burial registers, 1833–53, RG 8/35–38.
see *Bethnal Green Protestant Dissenters' Burying Ground, Dissenters, Protestant*

Burma Rangoon, marriages of British subjects, 1929–42, RG 33/10, indexed in RG 43/11–13.

Business Names, Registration of Required in the United Kingdom under Statute from 1916, where business names varied from those of their owners, or had a corporate name, or where the name of any individual changed, where business was conducted by an agent or nominee for overseas firms; it was abolished in 1981. Samples from registers, giving name and nature of the business, its address, and date of registration, with the names of owners, 1916/7, and ten-yearly samples from 1921, arranged in numerical order.

Cc

Canada Out-letters from the Treasury, 1763–1838, T 28. List of Scottish settlers, 1815, CO 385/2, and in AO 3/144; militia and volunteer musters, 1837–43, WO 13/3673–3717; Royal Chelsea and Greenwich Hospital pensions, arranged by district and giving name, former rank, and details of any transfer elsewhere, and date and place of death of retired military, naval and marine personnel, 1845–62, WO 22/239–42, for West Canada, 1852–62, WO 22/204; naval officer casualties, 1914–20, ADM 242/1–5, with a card index giving date, place and nature of casualty, and name and address of next of kin, and alphabetical War Graves Roll, 1914–19, ADM 242/7–10; nominal roll of courts martial of Canadian Expeditionary Force, 1915–19, WO 93.

see *America, British North, Emigrants, Prisoners of War, British, Commonwealth and Dominion, World War I, World War II*

Canterbury, Prerogative Court of Up to 11 January 1858 the superior probate court of England and Wales, and for those dying overseas leaving property here. During the Commonwealth, 1653–60, it was suspended along with all other ecclesiastical probate courts and was used as the sole court of probate for England and Wales as a court of Civil Commission.

(1) *Wills* Relate to the real estate of the deceased, and the testament to the personal estate, both taking effect after his death. Probate Act Books, giving date of grant, name, parish and diocese of the deceased, 1526–1858, limited probates, 1552–1780, PROB 8, 1740–1858, including dates of death, 1819–57, PROB 30, limited probates, 1781, 1800, 1802–4, 1806–58, PROB 9; published indexes, 1383–1700, in progress 1750–1800. Commissions for wills, containing oaths sworn by executors to carry out the testator's instructions, 1796–1857, PROB 52, Warrants, being the applications and authorization by the Court for the executors to act, 1666–1858, and from the mid-eighteenth century recording date and place of death and estate valuations where the amount was under £5, PROB 14. Wills of famous people, 1552–1854, indexed, PROB 1; original wills, 1484–1858, though most before 1600 are actually Court copies, PROB 10; registered copy wills endorsed with details of probate grant, which is in Latin to 1733, 1383–1858, PROB 11, listed in yearly Register Books, 1383–1858, PROB 12, which also relates to PROB 9 and PROB 10, and duplicates, 1384–1800, PROB 13, 1655–1858, PROB 15; published indexes outlined above, giving quire references.

(2) *Administration, grants of Letters of* When a person died intestate (without

33

making a will), the next of kin, or failing which a creditor, could apply to administer the estate; the grant authorized the administrator to act, in return for which he entered a bond with the court to administer the estate according to law; the bond usually offered security of double the estate's estimated value. Act Books, 1559–1858, including estate valuations from 1796, PROB 6, limited administrations, 1559–1858, PROB 7; both contain the name and abode of the deceased, and of the administrator, and relationship between them, and the date of the grant; yearly Register Books, indexed by initial letter form the means of reference to both classes, 1383–1858, PROB 12, on open access, and duplicates, 1384–1800, PROB 13, 1655–1858, PROB 15. Further limited administrations, 1740–1858, PROB 30. There are published indexes, 1559–1660, 1853–8. Warrants before the affidavit or application for an ordinary grant, giving estate value especially when less than £5, and from the mid-eighteenth century the date and place of death of the intestate, 1666–1858, PROB 14. Administration bonds, concerning probate cases brought before the Court, 1713–44, give the name and addresses of the parties to the bond, and a rough estate valuation, and are listed chronologically, PROB 46; bonds, 1550–1600, PROB 51, 1714–1858, including some undertaken by administrators in the absence of a valid will, or where there was no executor to pay the debts and legacies, PROB 45. Court Orders for distribution of an intestate's estate, recording moneys paid out to beneficiaries, are in the Muniment Books, 1611–1858, which have integral indexes, PROB 16.

(3) *Inventories* Taken of the personal goods and chattels of the deceased soon after death, and no longer necessary after 1782 unless an interested party called for it, and including leases and debts owed. Series I, 1417–1660, PROB 2, Series II, 1702, 1718–82, PROB 3, office copies, 1660–c.1720, PROB 4, originals, 1661–c.1725, PROB 5; there are card indexes to PROB 2, PROB 3 and PROB 5, and a partial index (including a topographical index) to PROB 4.

(4) *Disputes* The ecclesiastical courts had authority over personal estate, the Court of Chancery over realty, and over the validity of testaments and wills, respectively. The yearly Register Books, 1383–1858, often have marginal notes against the name of the deceased indicating by 'sentence' or 'decree' that the will or administration was the subject of litigation, PROB 12, while the registered copies of them may also contain a brief summary of the date of the suit, and names of suitors, PROB 11, PROB 6. Supplementary wills where there was litigation, Series I, 1623–1838, with a typescript nominal index, PROB 20, Series II contains Court copies of wills where the original was exhibited in another court of law, 1623–1857, PROB 21, Series III, 1827–57, PROB 22, Series IV, 1629–1827, and which from 1660 include wills from lesser probate courts cancelled by the Prerogative Court, or administrations with will annexed, PROB 23. Action commenced with the complainant filing a caveat suspending a grant of probate or of letters of administration. Caveat Books, 1666–1858, indexed by name of deceased, PROB 40, Court Caveat Books, 1678–1857, PROB 41; Acts of Court Books, with integral indexes and recording the proceedings and including the date of testator's or intestate's death, 1536–1819, PROB 29, 1740–1858, arranged

alphabetically by name of deceased in monthly bundles, and including renunciations of executorship, appointments of guardians for minors, and acts to lead decrees, limited grants of probate and administration, with a card index of names and places, PROB 30; appointment of proctors to act as proxies in court, sixteenth century, PROB 55, 1674–1718, PROB 19; processes, some containing excommunications of defaulting executors and administrators, 1666–1857, PROB 48, and which with PROB 40 and PROB 41 can be used to fill in gaps in PROB 29; card index to Causes, 1666–1713, arranged by deceased and under plaintiff, PROB 45/2; early sixteenth-century proceedings, PROB 53; probate cases, 1845–1878, TS 15. Allegations made by plaintiffs, 1661–1858, with a card index to deceased and plaintiffs, PROB 18; answers filed by defendants, 1664–1854, indexed to 1787 under plaintiff, PROB 25; Town depositions by witnesses at Doctors' Commons, 1657–1809, most with integral indexes to plaintiffs, the rest located via a typescript index of plaintiffs, cross-referencing names of the deceased, PROB 24; depositions bound by suit, and some exhibits, 1826–58, most integrally indexed, and with a typescript index to both deceased and plaintiffs, PROB 26. The depositions record age, birthplace, occupation, annual income and relationship to the deceased and contesting parties of each witness. Exhibits, 1529–86, PROB 35, 1653–1721, with a typescript index to deceased and plaintiffs, PROB 36, 1722–1858, PROB 31, indexed by year, and initial letter of deceased's surname, listing wills, revoked wills and codicils, and topographical index on open access, 1683–93, and 1721–1858, in PROB 33; supplementary exhibits, 1575–1857, indexed, PROB 42;

filed exhibits, mostly London and Middlesex, 1662–1720, with a nominal index, PROB 32. Orders of Court, 1817–57, integrally indexed under deceased, and containing estate valuations, PROB 38, duplicates in PROB 30. Probate cases referred to Procurator General, 1845–57, indexed, TS 15.

(5) *Renunciations and guardianship* Renunciations as executor or administrator, and appointments of guardians for children of deceased who were infants or minors, 1536–1819, most with integral indexes to parties, and from the eighteenth century to the deceased, PROB 29, 1740–1858, PROB 40.

(6) *Probate Accounts* Once all the debts owing to and by the deceased had been quantified, a final valuation of his estate was possible, setting out his expenses and income and totalling the final balance left for distribution according to the will or letters of administration. Some may be found, 1662–1720, with a nominal index, PROB 32, 1722–1858, among Court exhibits, PROB 31, to which there is a card index of names and places in PROB 33; Death Duty Registers, wills and administrations, 1796–1858, IR 26/1–286, 535–2158, indexed in IR 27/1–16, 140–323 (wills), IR 27/17–66 (administrations), and in selected death duty accounts, 1805–1908 (the Registers were kept open for fifty years), IR 59, and Legacy, Succession and Probate Duty case books, 1853–66, IR 67.

see *Chancery (Equity), Court of, Death Duty, Delegates, High Court of, Privy Council, King's Bench (Crown Side), Court of, Testamentary Causes*

Cape Colony (Cape of Good Hope)

Original Correspondence, 1807–1910,

including letters from settlers, grants of land, 1814–25, CO 48, and alphabetical lists of settlers in 1819, CO 48/41–46, 1820, CO 48/52–53, and 1827, CO 48/57; Entry Books of correspondence, 1795–1872, CO 49. Slave registers, 1816–19, including personal and plantation slaves, indexed, T 71; registers of suspected slavers in Cape Town, 1843–70, FO 312. Registers of pensions to military, naval and marine personnel paid by Royal Chelsea and Greenwich Hospitals, arranged under district, and giving former rank, regiment, date of commencement, amount and nature of pension, any transfer elsewhere, and details of death, 1849–58, 1876–80, WO 22/243–44.

see *Slaves, South Africa*

Carriages, Duty on 1747–82: yearly lists of persons paying, including defaulters, 1753–66, T 47/2–4, and payers in Scotland, 1756–62, T 36/7.

Carucage (or Hidage) Levied between 1194 and 1224 on each carucate or hide of land, based on the Domesday Book, and listed by county, chronologically by date, and then by hundred, township or vill, E 179. Printed in *The Book of Fees* (Testa de Nevill), 1198–1293, 3 volumes, 1921–31, including an index volume.

Census A ten-yearly listing by household of all people in the United Kingdom on a particular night, arranged by registration and enumeration district (recommended to be no more than 200 households), and then by household schedule number. The 1841 returns give name, age down to nearest five for those over fifteen, exact ages of those below this, occupation, and whether born in the county where recorded on census night with provision for whether born in Scotland, Ireland or Foreign Parts; from 1851 onwards, relationship of each person to the head of the household, marital status, alleged exact age, farming acreage and details of employees are given, plus place and county of birth and whether a person was blind, or deaf and dumb; to this particulars of whether a person was an idiot, imbecile or lunatic were added from 1861 onwards. In 1891 enquiries were made about the number of occupied rooms if fewer than five, employment status (employer, employed, or neither employer nor employed), and in the Welsh returns an indication of language spoken. Returns for England, Wales, Channel Islands and the Isle of Man, 6 June 1841, and for 30 March 1851, HO 107, 7 April 1861, RG 9, 2 April 1871, RG 10, 3 April 1881, RG 11, 5 April 1891, RG 12, indexed by place and then by registration district number. Reference maps, showing registrars' districts and sub-districts, 1861–1921, including two complete sets for London and England and Wales, 1891, three incomplete sets for London, 1861, 1891 and 1921, two individual maps of municipal wards and ecclesiastical parishes in the City of London, c.1911, and two incomplete sets for England and Wales, 1870 and 1921, RG 18. Royal Naval and British Merchant shipping in home waters and home ports, 1861, located at the end of RG 9, Royal Naval ships in port, filed at the end of the registrar's district covering the port, 1871, RG 10, 1881, RG 11, 1891, RG 12; merchant ships are listed likewise, but relating to vessels arriving in port over a time-scale extending to a month after census night, and those absent from port on census night in 1891 are omitted; fishing vessel crews already in port or arriving within a fixed period thereafter, are also listed between 1861 and 1891; people on the canals and inland waterways are found at the end of the appropriate enumeration district, 1861–91. Clergymen's returns, 1831, arranged by county and parish, list the total number of baptisms, marriages and burials from 1820–30, and the number of illegitimate children born in 1830, HO 71. Ecclesiastical returns, 1851, record total attendances at church or chapel on Sunday 30 March, and average attendances over the previous year, arranged by registrar's district, HO 159. Correspondence and papers relating to the 1900, 1910 and 1920 Census Acts, RG 19.

Census Staff In- and out-letters between the Registrar General and local officials, 1836–1917, concerning the 1891 census, and private correspondence of the Registrar General, 1837–50, concerning the 1851 census and staff requirements, RG 29.

Central Criminal Court Superseded the Old Bailey Sessions in November 1834, to try indictable offences in the metropolitan and adjacent areas, and also to hear matters concerning crimes on the high seas or abroad, formerly tried in the High Court of Admiralty at the Old Bailey, and cases transferred from other courts to ensure a fair trial and avoid delay. Returns of committals for trial, 1834–49, giving charges and the trial outcome, HO 16; annual criminal registers, 1834–49, setting out chronologically the date of trial, charge, verdict and sentence, and details of age, and educational level, HO 26, 1850–92, without education details, HO 27; sessions papers, 1834–1904, including parts of Essex, Kent and Surrey, as well as the City of London and Middlesex, PCOM 1; Court Books, 1834–1949 (some closed 75 years), CRIM 6, minutes of evidence, 1834–1912, CRIM 10. In-

dictments, 1834–1957, CRIM 4, with Calendars of indictments, 1833–1971, arranged by session, and initial letter of surname, CRIM 5. Depositions of general or historical interest, with 2% random sample of the rest, 1835–1949 (some closed 75 years), and including pardons, CRIM 1, Calendars of depositions, 1923–40, CRIM 2. After-trial Calendars of prisoners, 1855–1949 (some closed 75 years), containing details of prisoners, committing magistrates, offences and trials, verdicts and sentencing, CRIM 9. Salary Book, 1889–95, letters about salaries, pensions, and staff appointments, 1918–71, CRIM 13.
see *Old Bailey Sessions*

Ceylon Registers of slaves, 1818–32, including personal and plantation slaves, with an incomplete index for 1819, T 71.

Chancery (common law), Court of Merged into the Chancery Division in 1875, it dealt with proceedings for the repeal of letters patent, and personal actions by or against officers of the Court, and formerly for traverses (disputes) relating to inquisitions post mortem, and writs of partition of lands in co-parceny, or for dower; its officers were responsible for the issuing of common law writs, and enrolment of deeds. The records are in Latin to 1733. Pleadings, under writ of *scire facias*, temp. Edward I (thirteenth century)–Richard III (fifteenth century), C 44, temp. Henry VII–James I, C 43, temp. Elizabeth–Victoria, C 206.

Chancery (Equity), Court of Established in the reign of Richard II to deal with cases for which there was no remedy by common law writ, it soon came to deal with the rights of one person as against another's, particularly in relation to trusts, wills, marriage and business settlements, tithe matters, and mortgages. The proceedings were originally delivered orally, but by the end of the fourteenth century they took the form of written bills, in English, the plaintiff being described as the 'Orator'. The outcome was determined by interlocutory orders leading to the final decree. In 1842 it absorbed the Equity side of the Court of Exchequer, and in 1875 it was merged into the Chancery Division of the High Court. Appeal lay to the House of Lords. Early proceedings, consisting of bills, answers and depositions, temp. Richard II (fourteenth century)–Philip and Mary, C 1, Series I, Elizabeth–Charles I, C 2, Series II, Elizabeth–Commonwealth, C 3, all undated, but descriptive listing by initial letter of plaintiff's surname, within bundles representing the period in office of the Lord Chancellor to whom they were addressed, gives the names of defendants, and the subject under dispute; supplementary Six Clerks' Series, late-fifteenth–mid-seventeenth century, mainly being answers, with a calendar and index to plaintiffs and index of defendants, C 4. From the mid-seventeenth century the Six Clerks served to receive pleadings, each maintaining separate Bill Books and files of subsequent answers, replications and rejoinders, some of which may be found scattered among different classes rather than attached to the original suit to which they relate, making them difficult to reconstruct. Proceedings, 1649–1713, Bridges Division, C 5, Collins Division, C 6, Hamilton's Division, C 7, Mitford's Division, C 8, Reynardson's Division, C 9 (with a rather poor published index to surnames of plaintiffs and defendants), Whittington's Division, C 10; manuscript calendars to these classes record chronologically within initial letter of the surname of the first

plaintiff and including as part of the entry up to three others, the names of the first two or three defendants, then the date of the appropriate document, nature of the case and type of document on file; proceedings, 1714–1842, are amalgamated in a union series, and include Country depositions: 1714–58, C 11, 1758–1800, C 12, 1800–42, C 13, but sub-divided into the respective divisions, and the class lists are chronological by year of filing under initial index of the names of plaintiffs, and record surnames only of both sides, the date of filing and the number and type of documents. Modern pleadings, 1842–75, were commenced by a statement of claim, followed by a defence or counterclaim, and again include Country depositions, and Town depositions from 1854: 1842–52, C 14, 1853–60, C 15, 1861–75, C 16, the class lists being organized alphabetically under plaintiff's surname in yearly volumes and noting the surname of the defendant. Miscellaneous proceedings, 1664–Victoria, includes nineteenth-century printed copies of proceedings, affidavits, notes on cases, depositions and fee books, C 18. Action concerning administration of estates and other summonses, 1852–5, including depositions, C 17; index to Causes, and to Matters, IND 1/2228–36; from 1856–75 this information is in C 15 and C 16 with the proceedings. Country depositions, taken in the provinces on Commission, giving the name, age, abode and occupation of witnesses, and signed at the end of the numbered answers to interrogatories put to them on behalf of the suitors, Series I, temp. Elizabeth–Charles I, C 21, Series II, 1649–1714, C 22, both indexed under plaintiff and giving names of defendants; unpublished depositions, procured but not used, Elizabeth–Victoria, C 23; Town depositions, taken in London by examiners of the Court, 1534–1853, arranged alphabetically by plaintiff, by term, C 24; there is a microfilmed index of names of deponents up to the end of the reign of Charles I, thereafter 8% sample of Country deponents' names and a complete index to Town deponents up to 1800, at the Society of Genealogists, in London; interrogatories, 1598–1852, C 25, arranged by year, and most concerning Town depositions in C 24. Affidavits, 1611–1875, up to 1819 organized chronologically by term, thereafter by term and alphabetically by title of Cause of Matter, C 31; between Trinity 1828 and Michaelmas 1855 the Causes and Matters are separated, and there are indexes, 1611–1800, IND 1/7245–93, 1781–1875 in IND 1/14545–14684; registers of affidavits, 1615–1747 (including some missing from C 31), C 41, while the indexes to C 31 identify the registered entries. Lord Chancellor's petition books, 1756–1858, which to 1800 give fairly full abstracts, the later ones only brief notes, on a daily basis, with indexes up to 1845, C 28. Cause (Bill) Books, 1842–75, recording the names of parties, their solicitors, the dates of entry of all appearances, and all filed records, giving reference to any orders and decrees, reports and certificates, C 32, to which there is a typescript list and index to plaintiffs, with the date and cause number and name of the judge, 1860–75. Entry Books of decrees and orders, 1544–1875, C 33, access to which is via the 'A' and 'B' Books on open access: the 'A' Books commence in 1544 and up to Trinity Term 1629 note all decrees and orders, chronologically by date of filing or entry, by initial letter of the plaintiff's surname, and including the surname of the defendant, arranged by the four legal terms, but thereafter relate only to plaintiffs with surnames between A and K. The annual 'B' Books start in 1547, and to Trinity 1629 duplicate the 'A' Books, thereafter they record cases in which the surnames of the plaintiffs were between L and Z. To 1859 the yearly volumes start at Michaelmas, being the beginning of the new legal year, after which they are organized by calendar year. Decree Rolls, 1534–1875, which are formal enrolments of the decrees and orders in C 33, and of dismissals, setting out the full claims by each side, and the final judgment, and which rendered the original rulings more solemn and authoritative, C 78; supplementary series, 1534–1875, C 79; enrolment took place within six months in one of the six divisions, or with special leave, up to five years later, and there is a nominal and topographical index to the first five divisions; the original dockets setting out the preliminary proceedings and drawn up prior to enrolment of a decree, 1535–1875, C 96. Reports by Masters in Chancery, of investigations and opinions commissioned by the Court and arranged alphabetically by surname of plaintiff by term, 1544–1842, C 38, with a supplementary series, 1700, 1703–99, C 39, and to which there is a printed initial index of surnames of plaintiffs, 1606–1875; exceptions to reports, made by parties to the suits, with alphabetical indexes, 1756–1859, C 40; Masters' documents, containing affidavits, examinations of witnesses, documents and reports, seventeenth–nineteenth centuries, C 117–C 126, with descriptive lists of cases, dates and documents; deeds and evidences, 1597–1648, C 171, with a descriptive list; Masters' exhibits of title deeds, court rolls, and other unclaimed evidences deposited with the Court, filed under names of plaintiffs and giving the names of defendants and the date, c.1700–1918, ranging in period from 1150–1875, C 103–C 116, and c.1700–1875, J 90 (to which there is an index of cases and a place-name index); Duchess of Norfolk's deeds, including rentals and court rolls, c.1150–c.1850, C 115; court rolls, 1294–1808, in C 116, both indexed by county, then manor. Awards and agreements, where actions were concluded by arbitration or agreement and including bonds to abide by the decision, and which were usually made orders of the Court, 1694–1844, C 42, with some relating to early enclosures in C 54, to which there is a typescript list. Appeal petitions, 1774–1869, with a typescript alphabetical list of appellants, ordinary petitions, 1834–75, indexed chronologically by initial letter, C 36. Returns of prisoners, 1860–75, J 93.

Chancery Division of the High Court of Justice On its creation in 1875 it absorbed the Court of Chancery, and from 1880 the Revenue Side of the Exchequer Division, while since 1970 it has dealt with probate matters formerly in the Probate, Divorce and Admiralty Division. Its business concentrates mainly on the administration of estates, trusts, wardship of infants and care of infants' estates, mortgages, deeds, contracts concerning land sales, business partnerships, winding-up of companies, bankruptcies, landlord and tenant disputes, and since 1959 has been the Court of Protection for mental patients. Entry Books of decrees and orders, 1876–1955, including some Court of Appeal and House of Lords judgments in Chancery actions, J 15 (which continues C 33, see under *Chancery (Equity), Court of*); yearly indexes to 1955, 'A' and 'B' Books, arranged chronologically by initial index of case, by legal term, on open access. Decree Rolls, 1876–1903, C 78, supplementary series, 1876–1903, C 79. Cause Books, recording the names of par-

ties, their solicitors, dates of entry of appearance by the defendant, all filed papers, and with reference to the decrees and orders, and any reports, and with a typescript list and index to plaintiffs, giving date, number of cause and name of the judge, 1875–80, C 32, ten-yearly samples, 1880–1930, giving under each year the letter and number of each cause and the names of parties, their solicitors, and entry of appearance with date of filing of pleadings, J 89. Common law pleadings, 1876–1942, arranged under date of filing, alphabetically by plaintiff in quarterly divisions of the year, and including statements of claim, defence and counterclaims, J 54; Masters' miscellaneous books, including exhibits, registers of claims, orders, notes on proceedings, 1850–1911, J 23; Masters' papers and pedigrees, mid-nineteenth century–1974, indexed under the name of the progenitor, giving date of birth, marriage or death or when living, and index to case titles, J 46, J 63, J 64, J 66 and J 67, and 1852–1974, J 68, all mainly relating to will and administration disputes and to intestacy. Affidavits, 1876–1945, indexed, J 4; depositions, 1880–1925, 1960–63, including some exhibits, and with an index of case titles, 1880–1925, J 17; exhibits, c.1700–1918, with a case title and place-name index, J 90; miscellaneous papers, 1517–1953 (some closed 75 or 100 years), TS 18, with a descriptive list arranged under subject, and to which there is a nominal card index covering TS 33 giving reference to related material in TS 18, on open access. Returns of prisoners, 1875–81, and committal warrants, 1904–61, J 93.

Channel Islands Births, marriages and deaths, 1831–1958, RG 32, indexed in RG 43. Census returns, 6 June 1841, 30 March 1851, HO 107, 7 April 1861,

RG 9, 2 April 1871, RG 10, 3 April 1881, RG 11, and 5 April 1891, RG 12; ecclesiastical returns, giving church and chapel attendances on 30 March 1851 and average attendance over the previous year, HO 129. Association Oath Roll of Jersey and Guernsey, 1696, C 213/462–63. Royal Chelsea and Greenwich Hospital quarterly out-pensions paid to military, naval and marine personnel, giving address, rank at retirement, any transfer to a different pay-district, date of commencement, amount and nature of pension and date of death, 1842–52, WO 22/205. Entry Books of the authorities charged with the relief of French emigrés, 1793–1812, FO 95, 1779–1809, HO 69, 1777–1814, PC 1, 1794–1816, WO 1, and a register of refugees in Jersey, 1793–6, FO 95/602–03, all with descriptive lists. Correspondence, 1671–1782, SP 47, printed in *Calendars of State Papers* of the period (see *State Paper Office*), and between 1760–75 in *Calendar of Home Office Papers of the reign of George III*. General letter book, 1748–60, SP 111.

see **Alderney, Bouillon Papers, Guernsey, Jersey**

Chantries Were provision of services for the dead in a parish church, usually made and paid for by the benefactor's will, and sometimes providing for the erection of a chantry chapel and payment of a chantry priest. In 1545 and 1547 chantry surveys were made by Crown Commissioners, and certificates recording chantry land valuations and inventories of goods, plus the name of each founder, were produced to the Court of Augmentations, which then took control of the lands, and in 1547 chantries were abolished. Certificates from both surveys, E 301, and for the Duchy of Lancaster, DL 38; particulars for sale of chantries, temp. Henry VIII and Edward VI, E 315 and Duchy of Lancaster, DL 14; warrants for pensions of dissolved chantries, 1548, E 101.

see **Augmentations of the Revenue of the King's Crown, Court of**

Chapels Royal Births and baptisms of members of the Royal Household, 1755–1875, marriages, 1761–1880, PRO 30/19/1, marriages, 1647–1709, indexed, RG 8/110, and marriage licences, 1687–1754, 1807, RG 8/76–78.

Charities Memorials of deeds establishing charities and appointing trustees, 1812–75, with a descriptive list, arranged by county, J 19, and 1841–1953, TS 18, with a descriptive list arranged under subject.

Charterhouse, Poor Brothers of the Petitions for admission, 1661–1782, SP 44, admissions, 1782–1877, indexed, HO 38.

see **Almsmen**

Charter Rolls Enrolments of original and confirmatory royal grants of lands, liberties and privileges, executed in the presence of witnesses and addressed to 'Archbishops, bishops, abbots, priors, earls, barons etc'. The charters of confirmation or inspeximus (exemplification or copy) may recite the original grant in full, perhaps adding new clauses, or without repeating the contents. They are in Latin, 1199–1517, C 53, and the entire series has been published in *Calendars*. Later grants were enrolled on the Patent Rolls, C 66, to which there are printed *Calendars* 1216–1582, 1584–7, and then manuscript indexes arranged under divisions of each regnal year, by initial alphabet. Some confirmations before 1483 are enrolled on the Patent Rolls, C 66, thereafter they are enrolled on the Confirmation Rolls up to

1626, C 56, included in *Calendar of Letters and Papers (Foreign and Domestic) of the reign of Henry VIII, 1509–47*, and subsequently on the Patent Rolls.

Charters Payments made for grants or renewals of grants are recorded in Latin on the Fine Rolls, C 60, with printed *Calendars*, 1272–1509. Certificates of surrenders, 1660–1689, C 203. Enrolments of charters in the Palatinate of Chester, 1307–1830, CHES 2; original charters in the Duchy of Lancaster, temp. Henry I (twelfth century)–1625, DL 36.
see *Charter Rolls*

Chatham Chest Established in 1581 to relieve sea officers and men hurt or wounded in service, and maintained out of monthly deductions of sixpence from seamen's wages, administration of the fund was in 1803 transferred to the Royal Hospital at Greenwich, and in 1814 ceased to be independent. Admission papers, certificates as to wounds, 1617–1807, indexes of warrant officers, ratings, dockyard workers and their widows, giving details of injuries and the vessels in which they were sustained, and annual payments, 1744–97, payments, 1653–7, 1675–1799, the latter listing alphabetically recipients paid each Lady Day, ADM 82, 1831–7, ADM 22/52–55.
see *Greenwich Hospital, Royal*

Chelsea Hospital, Royal Founded in 1681 for the relief of old, lame and infirm soldiers, in 1686 provision was made for pensions, and from 1708 pensions were awarded for officers killed in action. Pensions for wounds were introduced in 1812. Names of in-pensioners may be found in musters covering 1702–89, WO 23/124–31, and 1864–5, WO 23/132, in a list of inmates, 1795–1813,

WO 23/134, and there is an alphabetical register, 1837–72, WO 23/146. Admissions, 1824–1917, arranged chronologically, record regiment, name, age, service, pension rate, cause of discharge, and date of admission to pension, plus an address, WO 23/162–72, 174–80; there is an index of soldiers admitted between 1858 and 1933, WO 23/173; appeals against Board decisions for admission, 1823–1915, in Board Minute Books, WO 180/53–78; ledger of in-pensions, 1836–46, and orders for payments, PMG 14; registers of births, marriages and burials, 1691–1856, RG 4/4330–32, 4387; services between January 1878 and December 1910 of nurses appointed at the Hospital, 1857–1909, WO 23/181. Out-pensioners may be traced in Admission Books, relating to disabled soldiers, 1715–1882, arranged chronologically by date of medical board and giving name, regiment, regimental number, ranks, birthplace, physical description, cause of disability, and brief service record, WO 116, with similar information about those going to pension after long service, 1823–1902, WO 117. Registers, 1830–44, record also the soldier's intended abode, and are indexed, 1838–44, WO 23/1–16; regimental registers of pensioners, *c*.1715–1843, organized chronologically under each regiment, give admission date, age, summary of service, pension rate, disability, birthplace, and physical description, and from *c*.1812 the date of death, and are indexed, 1806–43, WO 120/1–51; pensions paid, 1845–57, record admissions before 1845 according to rate of pension, and later ones chronologically by date, and include details of date of admission, abode, payment district, and date of death, WO 120/52–70, 1805–95, in WO 23; out-pensions paid in 1806, WO 23/136–40; pension returns, giving name, regiment, rank at retirement, nature of and pension rate, date going to pension, and arranged by pay-district, including Ireland, with a note of any transfers, and date of death, 1842–62, WO 22/114–203, and Ireland, 1882–3, WO 22/209–25; out-pensions paid overseas, by colony, and then by pay-district, and recording similar information, 1845–80, WO 22/204, 227–44, 276–91, and to black persons, 1845–80, WO 22/231–36; other pensions paid in the colonies may be located, 1817–1903, WO 23/147–60, and a nominal list of pensioners entitled to an additional pension for having served in tropical climates, 1821–9, WO 23/25; out-pensions paid to Foreign Corps at Hanover, 1844–77, PMG 8. Out-pensions to wounded officers, 1812–92, WO 23/83–92, correspondence concerning claims, 1812–55, WO 4/469–93, and 1809–57, WO 43, to which there is a nominal card index on open access; payments of pensions, 1814–1921, PMG 9, and to Ordnance officers, 1836–75, PMG 12. Payment of pensions to warrant officers, 1873–1941, PMG 35; selected pensions, 1799–1892, listed by name and regiment, WO 900.

see *Army, British*

Chester, Palatinate of Enrolments of charters, letters patent, fines, deeds and wills, 1307–1830, CHES 2; manorial court rolls, *c.*1200–*c.*1900, to which there is a descriptive list and index, SC 2, rentals and surveys of manors, temp. Henry III (thirteenth century)–William IV, SC 11 and SC 12, with descriptive lists; Ancient Deeds, Series F, temp. Edward I (thirteenth century)–Elizabeth I, WALE 29, *c.*1507–1633, WALE 30, Modern Welsh Deeds, temp. James II–nineteenth century, WALE 31. Feet of fines and common recoveries of land, 1280–1831,

CHES 31, with enrolments, 1585–temp. Anne, CHES 32, and 1255–1831, CHES 29. Inquisitions post mortem, including inquisitions *ad quod damnum*, inquisitions as to lunatics and idiots, proofs of age, assignments of dower, extents of land and writs of livery, temp. Edward I–Charles I, CHES 3, with nominal and place-name indexes. Judicial records (1) *common law*: Chester Eyre Rolls, 1306–1500, CHES 17, Sheriff's Tourn Rolls, temp. Edward III–Henry VIII, CHES 19; Chester Sessions Calendar Rolls, naming indicted persons, fourteenth–sixteenth centuries, CHES 20; gaol files, including coroners' inquisitions, indictments, and jury panels, 1329–1831, CHES 24; coroners' inquisitions, temp. Edward III (fourteenth century)–Victoria, with later ones including signatures of the jurors, CHES 18; Indictment Rolls, 1293–1497, CHES 25; Mainprise Rolls, of entries of bails before the justices at Chester, 1344–sixteenth century, CHES 26; Outlawry Rolls, giving names and reason for judgment in outlawry, 1461–83, CHES 27; Crown Books, 1533–1830, including lists of Welsh recusants, CHES 21; sequestrations of real and personal estate, temp. James I–Charles II, and significations of excommunications, 1378–98, 1551, 1663–8, 1671–90, CHES 38. Plea Rolls for civil actions, 1255–1831, CHES 29.

(2) *Equity* Exchequer decrees and orders, 1559–1790, CHES 13; Entry Books of decrees and orders, 1562–1830, CHES 14; pleadings, temp. Henry VIII–George IV, CHES 15, with a calendar and index up to the reign of Philip and Mary; papers on Causes, including bills, answers, depositions, decrees and orders, 1501–1830, CHES 9; unpublished depositions, temp. Elizabeth–Victoria, CHES 12;

exhibits, temp. Henry III–Charles II, CHES 11. (3) *Common law Court of Exchequer* Pleadings relating to debt and personal property, 1559–1762, CHES 16; papers in bankruptcy, 1760–1830, CHES 10. (4) *Pentice* (dealing with personal actions in the City of Chester, tried by the Sheriff), *Portmote and Crownmote Courts* (both tried all criminals except traitors, and heard civil actions, presided over by the Mayor and Recorder) Transcript of proceedings, 1551–1762, CHES 8. Articles of clerkship of attorneys and solicitors, and affidavits of their due execution, eighteenth–early-nineteenth century, Admission Rolls in the Great Sessions, 1697–1830, in the Exchequer at Chester, 1750–1806, Oath Rolls, 1729, 1754, 1787–1830, CHES 36; patents for justices of the peace, 1797–1825, CHES 38; sacrament certificates, 1673–1768, CHES 4; alesellers' recognizances, 1580–1640, CHES 38.

see *Assizes, Wales, Principality of*

Chile Receipts of payments under wills of people dying in Punta Arenas, 1901, FO 162.

China Title deeds, trust deeds, agreements, wills, powers of attorney of Britons, 1837–1959, FO 678; registers of deeds, 1853–1953, FO 679; consular land registers, 1854–1942, FO 680; deeds, and material relating to missionaries in China, 1765–1951, FO 682. Marriages of Britons in China, 1873–89, FO 97/503; Amoy, registers of births, 1850–1950, marriages, 1850–1949, and deaths, 1850–1948, FO 663/85–95, births, marriages and deaths, 1869–76, FO 681/1; Canton, births, 1864–5, 1944–50, marriages, 1865, 1943–9, deaths, 1944–50, FO 681/2–9, births, marriages and deaths, 1869–76, FO 681/1; list of British subjects, 1844–1951, FO 694; Changsha, births, 1905–41, marriages, 1906–36, deaths 1906–33, FO 681/10–12; Chefoo, births, 1861–1943, marriages, 1872–1940, deaths, 1861–1942, FO 681/13–22; Chengtu, births, 1902–15, marriages, 1904–24, deaths, 1904–26, FO 664/3–5; Chinanfu (Tsinan), births and marriages, 1906–35, deaths, 1906–31, 1937, FO 681/23–27; probates, inquests, and court cases, 1907–37, FO 693; Chinkiang, births, 1865–6, 1899–1926, marriages, 1865–6, 1896–1919, deaths, 1865–6, 1889–1927, FO 387/4–5, 7–11, births, marriages and deaths, 1869–76, FO 681/1; registers of British subjects, 1890–1916, FO 387/1–2, and copies of powers of attorney, 1895–1924, FO 387/3; Chunking, births, 1888–1951, marriages, 1891–1949, deaths, 1891–1950, FO 681/28–34; Darien, births and marriages, 1907–40, deaths, 1910–40, FO 681/35–88; Foochow, births, marriages and deaths, and lists of British subjects, 1846–1946, FO 665/3–8, births, marriages and deaths, 1869–76, FO 681/1; Hankow, births, marriages and deaths, 1863–1951, FO 666/2–22, births, marriages and deaths, 1869–76, FO 681/1; Hong Kong, deaths, 1941–5, RG 33/11, indexed in RG 43/14; Ichang, births, 1879–1938, marriages, 1881–1937, deaths, 1880–1941, FO 667/2–6; Kuikiang, births, 1866–1929, marriages, 1872–1928, deaths, 1863–1929, FO 681/39–45, births, marriages and deaths, 1869–76, FO 681/1; Kunming, births, marriages and deaths, 1945–51, FO 668/2–3; Kwelin, births, 1942–4, deaths, 1943, FO 681/46–47; Mukden, births and deaths, 1949, marriages, 1947–8, FO 681/48–49, 79–80; Nanking, births, 1930–48, marriages, 1929–49, deaths, 1930–47, FO 681/50–53; Newchang, births, marriages and deaths, 1869–76, FO 681/1; Ningpo, births, 1858, marriages and deaths, 1856–8, and lists of British subjects, 1849, 1856, 1858, FO 670/2–7, births, marriages and deaths, 1869–76, FO 681/1; Peking, births, 1911–14, marriages, 1909–26, deaths, 1911, 1913, FO 564/13, 1–6, 14, births, marriages and deaths, 1869–76, FO 681/1; marriages, 1870–90, FO 83/1147, indexed in FO 802/239; registers of British subjects, 1921–2, passports, 1874–94, passport applications and military registration papers, 1874–1926, FO 564; Shanghai, births, 1856–64, marriages and deaths, 1851–64, FO 672/1–3, marriages, 1852–1951, RG 33/12–32, indexed in RG 43/7, 9–14, births, marriages and deaths, 1869–76, FO 681/1; Supreme Court probate records, 1857–1941, arranged chronologically and alphabetically by surname, FO 917; Shantung, marriages, 1912–42, RG 33/33; Swatow, births, 1864–5, 1947–9, marriages, 1865, deaths, 1864–5, FO 681/54–56, births, marriages and deaths, 1869–76, FO 681/1; Taiwan, births, marriages and deaths, 1869–76, FO 681/1, deaths, 1873–1901, FO 721/1; Taku, births, 1862–76, deaths, 1871–5, FO 673/9–10; Tamsin, births, marriages and deaths, 1869–76, FO 681/1; Tengyueh, births, 1904–41, marriages, 1913–41, deaths, 1906–41, FO 681/60–62; Tientsin, births, 1864–1939, 1941–5, 1915–51, marriages, 1863–1952, deaths, 1862–1952, FO 674/297–327, and deaths of Army personnel and their families, 1909–38, FO 674/316, births, marriages and deaths, 1869–76, FO 681/1; Tsingtao, births, marriages and deaths, 1911–51, FO 675/7–10; Weihaiwei, births, 1899–1929, marriages, 1905–40, deaths, 1899–1929, 1938–41, FO 681/63–71, births, marriages and deaths, 1899–1930, RG 33/34, indexed (births from 1899, marriages from 1904 and deaths from 1900) in RG 43/19; Whampoa, births and deaths, 1865, FO 681/72–73, births, marriages and deaths, 1869–76, FO 681/1; Yunanfu, births, 1903–48, marriages, 1904–49, deaths, 1903–50, FO 681/74–78.

Chivalry, Court of Held at the College of Arms under the auspices of the Earl Marshal of England, to determine disputes concerning coats of arms. Appeals from the Court went to the High Court of Delegates to 1834.
see *Arms, College of, Delegates, High Court of*

Christ's Hospital Children apprenticed to the sea, 1766, T 64/311.

Church Lands Bargains and sales of lands during the Commonwealth, 1650–60, are enrolled on the Close Rolls, C 54, with a manuscript calendar and place-name index.

Churchwardens
see *Sacrament Certificates*

Civil Defence Gallantry awards and recommendations, 1940–49, HO 250 (some closed 75 or 100 years); announcements in *The London Gazette*, to 1986, with subject indexes, ZJ 1.

Civil Engineers, Institution of Indexed proceedings of meetings, 1837–1926, lists of members, 1893, 1896 and at two-yearly intervals to 1914, 1920, ZLIB 21.

Civil Disturbances
see *Riots and Civil Disturbances, Suffragettes*

Civil Servants In 1855 the Civil Service Commission was established, but relied on patronage in making appointments until entry by open competition was introduced in 1870. Some Establishment lists and royal warrants relating to Great Britain and Ireland, 1836–66, AO 21; Commissioners' Minute Books of examinations for employment in the United Kingdom, 1855–1962, and Indian Civil Service up to 1947, the early volumes giving names of candidates and records of certificates of qualification, promotions and appointments, CSC 8; lists of certificated candidates, and tables of marks in limited and open examinations, 1856–72, 1879–81, 1884–90, CSC 4; examination marks and results, by grade, 1876–1962, CSC 10; salaries, retired allowances, superannuations, and pensions payable after ten years' service, in monthly payment records, giving date of death, name and address of next of kin, date of probate or administration grant, and names of executors or administrators, 1855–1924, arranged alphabetically by department from 1870, and with integral indexes, PMG 28; disciplinary cases, 1856–1920, arranged under department, T 1, and an alphabetical list in subject registers, 1876–1920, T 108.

Clements Inn Admission books of proctors, 1656–1883, Oaths of Supremacy taken before admission and bearing signatures of proctors, (?)1815–(?)1866, pension books, 1683–1781, deeds, 1661–1780, PRO 30/26.
see *Proctors*

Clergy Bishops' certificates of institutions to benefices, 1544–1912, E 331, with indexes (Institution Books), 1556–1660, 1661–1720, and 1721–1838, on open access, arranged under county, then by parish, and providing the name of the new incumbent, archdeaconry, date of institution, and name of patron, and after 1704 indicating in the margin whether the annual income was lower than £50; certificates of second admissions, 1561, 1661–93, granting exemption from payment of First Fruits and Tenths, E 333; bishops' certificates of church livings not exceeding £50 a year, 1706, E 332; lists of presentations to livings, June 1829–November 1950, giving their approximate values to 1877, with indexes from 1829–May 1843, C 247; church appointments, 1839–40, HO 44; presentations to Crown livings are enrolled on the Patent Rolls, 1536–1962, C 66, with printed *Calendars* 1536–82, and 1584–7; royal warrants of appointment and presentation, 1828–1969, with integral indexes, HO 115; reports on candidates, 1897–1905, T 64/409; Prime Ministerial patronage concerning appointments, 1907–67, PREM 5 (some closed 50, 75 or 100 years); draft presentations to benefices in the Duchy of Lancaster, temp. Edward III (fourteenth century)–Henry VII, DL 37, temp. Henry VII and VIII, DL 12, temp. Elizabeth I–George I, DL 16. Presentations to Scottish churches, 1724–1808, SP 56, and 1760–75, SP 44 (being included in *Calendar of Home Office Papers of the reign of George III*). Composition Books relating to payment of First Fruits and giving dates and names of sureties, 1535–1794, E 334; Controllers' State Books, 1688–1783, E 335, and Process Books, 1540–1822, both arranged under county, then the parish, listing incumbents, sums due and details of the method of payment, or the process taken for recovery of First Fruits, E 338; payments 1535–1839, QAB 1; Remembrancers' Account Books, show monthly receipts, 1616–26, and arrears, 1614–53 (gaps), of First Fruits, E 341; Remembrancers' Constat Books, listing livings and incumbents and their annual value less the Tenth, 1709–13, 1793–1838, E 340; arrears of Tenths, 1717–1822, showing when finally paid, E 342. Association Oath Rolls, arranged by diocese, archdeaconry and deanery, 1696, C 213/403–45; Oaths of Allegiance, 1789–1836, CP 37. Orders for a Loan, 1590, by diocese, recording names, parishes, and amounts given, SP 12/236. Incumbents listed in surveys of church livings, 1649, and during the Commonwealth, arranged by county and parish, and giving the value of the benefice, C 94; returns of benefices and incumbents, 1651–8, E 339. Acreage returns, 1801, arranged alphabetically by parish within each diocese and often signed by clergy, HO 67; clergymen's returns, 1831, giving total baptisms, marriages and burials each year from 1821–30, and the number of illegitimate children born in each parish in 1830, organized under county, HO 71; ecclesiastical returns, of total church and chapel attendances on 30 March 1851, and average attendance over the previous year, arranged by registration district, HO 129. Salaries of chaplains at the Chapels Royal, 1761–1854, LS 2. Committee for Plundered Ministers, orders and papers, 1642–53, recording yearly sums paid towards the maintenance of named ministers in benefices, out of tithes and revenues sequestrated from named delinquent impropriators, SP 22. Deeds of relinquishment of Holy Orders under the Clerical Disabilities Act 1870, allowing them to stand for Parliament, but barring them from acting as priests, 1903–87, with initial indexes, 1903–48, thereafter arranged chronologically by date, J 18; preferments and resignations of clergy, 1665–1986, in *The London Gazette*, with subject indexes

sporadically from 1790, invariably from 1848, ZJ 1. Emigrant ministers going to America, 1660–1791, E 407/82, 1667–1805, T 29, 1667–1857, T 52, 1676–1839, T 53, and 1685–1831, T 60.

see *Bishops, Navy, Royal, Plundered Ministers, Committee for, Queen Anne's Bounty, Sacrament Certificates*

Clerks of the Peace Officer appointed to keep county records and assist justice of the peace in Quarter Sessions. The post was abolished in 1972. Lists, including some in Scotland, *c*.1819–39, HO 94.

Close Rolls These are copies of sealed letters containing writs and orders under the Great Seal of England and addressed to individuals. To Tudor times they included instructions on a wide range of subjects, including orders to levy subsidies, pay salaries, repair buildings, deliver lands to heirs, for assignment of dower to widows, and the issue of writs of summons to peers to attend Parliament. Private deeds were enrolled on the dorse for safekeeping, especially from 1382, after the Revolt in 1381, and deeds of bargain and sale of freehold estates after the Statute of Enrolments 1536–1845, with occasional enrolments, including disentailing deeds relating to barred entails of land until 1903, when they were superseded by the Enrolment Books of the Supreme Court of Judicature, in J 18. After 1834 and especially 1875, it was the only central court of record used for enrolments of private deeds. Sales of lands of bankrupts from 1572, of those of Royalists (delinquents), of Crown and church lands effected during the Interregnum, and fee-farm rents, 1670–73, deeds of lease and release, conveyances in trust for chapels, schools and charitable purposes, conveyances of land under Queen Anne's Bounty Act 1703 to augment curacies, and surrenders of offices also found their way onto the Close Rolls; other enrolments are of Enclosure Awards, deeds poll for change of name, naturalization certificates, 1844–73, memorials of annuities from 1777–1812, specifications of inventions, 1712–1853, and disclaimers of patents, 1854–67, recognizances and bonds of Receivers and Official Liquidators of businesses and companies, and the deeds and wills of Papists from 1716. They are in a mixture of Latin and English, 1204–1903, C 54, with printed *Calendars* extending to 1509, and thereafter, manuscript initial indexes to grantees, and sometimes to places, running to 1837, under regnal year to 1648 and thereafter by calendar year, with a separate series for grantors, which between 1680 and 1842 is organized under four divisions, B, E, N, and Y, made up of groups of counties (identifiable from the Catalogue of Indexes, on open access), and from 1838 continues as the only index; a card index of deeds enrolled for safe custody, temp. William and Mary–George III is on open access; there is a place-name index to bargains and sales of church lands during the Commonwealth, to those of Crown lands and Royalists' estates similarly disposed of, and of fee-farm rents disposed of by the Trustees for Sale, 1670–73; there is a pasted-up topographical index to charitable trust enrolments 1736–1870, then a card index, 1870–1903, on open access; Close Rolls of the Palatinate of Lancaster, 1409–70, PL 2, 1354–1440, DL 37, both incorporating letters patent, writs and warrants, recognizances, letters of attorney and deeds, with a printed *Calendar*.

see under individual subjects

Coast Bonds Made by shippers engaged in the coastal trade, undertaking not to land goods except at declared ports, and certified by port officials, temp. Elizabeth–George III, E 209.

see *Port Books*

Coastguard Formed in 1822 from the Revenue Cruisers, Riding Officers and Preventive Water Guard, to which was added the Coastal Blockade in 1831, it came under the Board of Customs until 1856, when it was controlled by the Admiralty as a Shore Force, Permanent Cruiser Force and Guard Ships. Its purpose is to prevent smuggling, guard the coast and prevent the inland movement of smuggled goods, and has charge of wrecks, the Lifeboat Service, life-saving, lighthouses, and responsibility for searching for mines lost at sea, and wild birds and fish washed ashore. Registers of nominations for appointment, 1819–66, England, 1821–49, Ireland, Establishment Books, 1816–1918, England, 1816–69, Ireland, 1816–66, Scotland, ADM 175, both with indexes; Admiralty nominations to the Coastguard in England, ADM 6, and appointment book of boatmen, 1831–50, ADM 6/199; nominations for boatmen, 1851–6, discharges, 1858–68, indexes of chief officers, 1886–1922, ADM 175; appointments to Revenue Cruisers, 1816–31, ADM 6/56, and 1822–32, ADM 2/1127; Establishment of Revenue Cruisers, Michaelmas 1827–Christmas 1829, CUST 19/52–61; Coastguard Minute Books, 1833–49, CUST 29/40–42; Thames Coastguard salaries and incidents, 1828–32, CUST 39/173. Musters of Coastguard and Revenue Cruisers, 1824–57, ADM 119; return of officers and men appointed to the Preventive Boat Service, November 1816–March 1819, ZHC 1/693, names of commanders of Revenue Cruisers in Scotland, 1822–3, ZHC 1/773, names of men killed on the Kent and Sussex coasts in conflict between the Coastal Blockade and smugglers, 1821–5, ZHC 1/822; return of captains and commanders in the Preventive or Coastguard Service and Revenue Cruisers, 1 July 1833, ZHC 1/1092; return of name, age, date of appointment, gross pay and allowances, of all chief officers of the Coastguard with details of previous service, 1857, ZHC 1/2390; registers of protections from impressment into the Royal Navy, 1755–8, 1770–81, 1787–1811, ADM 7; pensions to Preventive Service, c.1818–25, CUST 40/28; pensions and allowances from Royal Greenwich Hospital to chief officers, 1866–1928, PMG 70; civil pensions, 1855–1935, arranged alphabetically, PMG 23; pensions, 1834–6, 1866–1932, and to widows of coastguard officers killed in service, 1830–99, 1916–18, 1921–32, ADM 23; pensions to widows and children, 1857–1935, PMG 23, 1857–1929, PMG 19/15–94, 1916–20, PMG 44/8–9, and supplementary pensions, 1916–20, PMG 43/1; grants of pensions by Royal Greenwich Hospital to orphan daughters, 1881–1911, 1951–9, and to orphan boys, 1884–1959, ADM 162; correspondence and papers, 1931–54, including awards of the Defence Medal, 1945–48, BT 106.

see *Greenwich Hospital, Royal*

Colombia Marriages of British subjects, 1824–7, RG 33/155, indexed in RG 43/7, marriages, 1846–90, FO 83, indexed in FO 802/239; Cartagena, births, 1853–1924, deaths, 1858–1927, FO 736/2–3; Santa Marta, roster of British subjects, 1845, FO 736.

Colonies, Dominions and Dependencies Charters may be located in Unbound Papers of the Privy Council, 1676–1799 (though most before 1698 were destroyed by fire), PC 1, many of which are calendared in *Acts of the Privy Council of England, Colonial Series, volume VI, Unbound Papers, 1676–1783*; registers of the Privy Council, 1540–1783, PC 2, are mostly integrally indexed from 1710, and are calendared in *Acts of the Privy Council, 1542–1631*, whilst extracts are in *Acts of the Privy Council of England, Colonial Series, I–V, 1613–1783*; Plantation Books include copies of Colonial Acts and charters, Commissions, instructions and letters to Governors, Orders in Council, warrants of appointment of colonial councillors, grants and surrenders of offices, 1678–1806, indexed, PC 5, and are included in *Acts of the Privy Council, Colonial Series, 1678–1783*. Land grants, 1714–82, CO 324/49–54; General Original Correspondence, 1689–1952, including applications for land, 1765–6, land grants, 1766, applications for colonial passports, 1796–1818, for colonial appointments, 1819–30, 1834–5, and for convict service, 1856–61, arranged chronologically by date, CO 323; various warrants of establishment and appointments, 1764–1835, AO 16; registers of applications and returns of appointments, 1744–1909, CO 325; applications may also be found in Original Correspondence, 1867–70, 1881–1919, CO 429, with a register of correspondence, 1867–70, 1887–1918, CO 430, as the key; petitions, grants and letters, 1662–1872, CO 324, names of persons naturalized in the American colonies, 1740–61, CO 324/55–56; Entry Books give details of land grants arranged alphabetically under colony, 1816–72, CO 381. American and West Indian colonies, General Series of Colonial Papers, 1574–1757, CO 1, printed in *Calendar of State Papers. Colonial, America and West Indies, 1574–1738*; America and West Indies Original Correspondence, 1606–1822, by colony, and including some land grants, CO 5;

General Registers, 1623–1849, containing Board of Trade registers and indexes to in- and out-letters, CO 326, 1850–1902, CO 336; later ones are under colony. Maps and plans, c.1617–1854, SP 112. Births, baptisms, marriages and burials of British subjects and nationals, 1831–1958, RG 32, indexed in RG 43/1–15, 18, 20–21. List of provincial Army officers in America, 1782, T 64/23; monthly and quarterly returns of pensions paid to military, Royal Naval and Marine personnel in the colonies, by the Royal Hospitals of Chelsea and Greenwich, under colony and pay-district and giving rank on retirement, regiment, date going to pension and its nature and amount, and including transfers to other districts and dates of death, 1845–80, WO 22/204, 226–44, 276–91; citations for honours, awards and decorations, to 1986, in *The London Gazette*, with annual or half-yearly subject indexes from 1848, ZJ 1. Vice-Admiralty Court proceedings, relating to maritime offences, up to 1834, with indexes of parties and of ships, HCA 1; Vice-Admiralty papers, 1740–1860, HCA 30. Returns of ships by naval officers from colonial ports, 1791–7, giving name of the master, build and tonnage, guns and men, names of owners, cargoes, when and where built and registered and the destination, HO 76; Original Correspondence relating to immigrants from the colonies, 1913–20, CO 571, registers for which are in CO 780.

see *Emigrants, Vice-Admiralty Courts*, and under individual countries

Common Pleas, Court of A court of common law, it evolved from the King's Council in the thirteenth century, and had a monopoly of civil real actions for the recovery of land, and in personal actions of debt, detinue (where goods were wrongfully detained), covenant (breach of a written obligation under seal), and account, cases of ejectment and of trespass where title to land was at stake. In 1875 it became part of the High Court of Justice as the Common Pleas Division, before being absorbed into the Queen's Bench Division in 1880. Procedure was by issue of a writ fitting the alleged facts, followed by oral and from the fifteenth century, written submissions, the case being then argued in court by serjeants at law. The records are in Latin to 1733. Plea Rolls, Placita de Banco (or De Banco Rolls), 1272–1875, CP 40, those from 1193–1272 being part of the Curia Regis Rolls, KB 26: they record the progress of civil actions, and prior to Easter 1583, they include pleas of land and enrolments of private deeds, which later were entered on the Recovery Rolls up to 1834, CP 43, and thereafter on the Plea Rolls, CP 40; affidavits, 1704–1875, CP 3; examinations of witnesses, 1831–43, and Extract Rolls, 1861–79, CP 22; posteas, 1808–74, PRO 30/44; registers of judgments, indexed by initial letter of the defendant's surname, 1836–68, CP 32.

Common Pleas Division of the High Court of Justice Formed out of the Court of Common Pleas, it was in 1880 merged with the Queen's Bench Division. Only a small sample of its archives have been preserved. Pleadings, April 1880–August 1882, listed by date of filing by quarterly division of each year, then alphabetically by plaintiff, J 54, with a card index of pleadings by case title, 1875–1880, on open access, J 55; affidavits, 1876–81, J 6; specimen judgment books, 1875 and 1880, J 89, with indexes to defendants, cause numbers and dates.

Commonwealth, British Established under the Statute of Westminster, 1931. Miscellaneous foreign returns of births, baptisms, marriages, deaths and burials of British subjects and nationals, to 1958, RG 32, with indexes in RG 43 on open access. Citations for honours, awards and decorations to 1986, in *The London Gazette*, with annual or half-yearly subject indexes, ZJ 1.
see *Colonies, Dominions and Dependencies,* and under individual countries

Commonwealth Exchequer Papers 1642–60, including work of some of the Parliamentary Committees, for example the Committee of Safety, Petitions and Arrears, of Trustees for the Sale of the King's Goods and Lands and of Fee-Farm Rents, and for the Sale of Delinquents' Estates, otherwise known as Treason Trustees, SP 28. Muster rolls kept by officers in the field or commanders of garrisons and districts, 1642–51, including powers of attorney to receive arrears of pay, 1650, SP 28/142, documents relating to assessment and collection of weekly
and monthly assessments, SP 28/148–204, arranged alphabetically by county, and including the 1642 contribution and loan for the relief of the King's distressed subjects in Ireland, SP 28/191–95, with a parish index under county on open access.

Commonwealth, Parliamentary Committee of the Some papers survive, 1649–60, SP 46.
see *Council of State*

Companies, Chartered Precursors of joint stock companies, and whose members trade with their own merchandise. Share transfer deeds, enrolled, *c*.1777–1966, J 19.

Companies, City Livery
see *London, City of*

Companies, Registration of Limited Registration began in 1844, when all companies formed from 1 November that year and with more than twenty-five members, or with freely transferable shares, were required to be registered and incorporated as joint stock companies. Each was given a number, and in 1856 a further statute created a company's limited liability. From this date, companies with seven members were to be incorporated, but could elect to be unlimited. Files of joint stock companies registered in accordance with the Companies Act of 1844, and dissolved before 1856, and those reregistered after the 1856 Act up to *c*.1860, and later dissolved, arranged in alphabetical order of title, and giving name, purpose, and address of the company, its promoters, and solicitor, a prospectus and details of capital, share issue and allocation, BT 41; representative files of companies incorporated between 1856 and 1931 and dissolved before 1932, some incorporated between 1856 and 1900, and dissolved, 1933–48, and 1% sample of public and private non-exempt companies incorporated by 1962 and dissolved between 1943 and 1963, recording memorandum and articles of association with any later amendments, a copy of the certificate of incorporation, a statement of the nominal share capital, the address of the registered office, names of directors, annual returns of share capital, and a list of shareholders, with any liquidation or dissolution documents, arranged in numerical order of company registration number, BT 31.

Companies, Winding-up or Liquidation of Announced in *The London Gazette*, to 1986, with annual or half-yearly subject indexes from 1848, ZJ 1; proceedings in the Court of Chancery and Chancery Division, 1849–1910, C 26; selected orders, petitions and examinations from winding-up proceedings under Joint Stock Company Acts 1856 and 1857, arranged alphabetically by company title, 1857–63, B 10; winding-up proceedings, 1891–1951, the files being arranged alphabetically under the company name, and including orders, petitions, judges' notes and any subsequent proceedings, and from 1949 samples only, with a card index of company titles, 1891–1951, J 13; 2% random sample from the Companies Court of the Chancery Division, 1924–58, with a list of cases, J 137; Receivers' accounts, 1859–1901, arranged in alphabetical order of company name, C 30; Liquidators' accounts, 1890–1932, under company number of those registered after 1856 and dissolved, BT 34, thereafter up to 1969, in BT 31, to which there is a printed index under company's registered legal title, 1856–1920, and of those companies still on the Companies Register at 30 June 1930 and 30 June 1937; classified index of files of dissolved exempt private companies, arranged under company number and year of incorporation, 1888–1941, BT 95; recognizances and bonds of Official Liquidators up to 1883, are enrolled on the Close Rolls, C 54, indexed annually under 'Indentures' to 1872 and then to 1882 under 'Recognizances'; thereafter to 1906 they are in C 68. Files of the *Bona Vacantia* Division of Chancery, 1824–1955, include property belonging to dissolved companies, TS 17.

Conspicuous Gallantry Medal Established in 1855 as the Naval counterpart of the Distinguished Conduct Medal, and awarded to petty officers and ratings, and

to non-commissioned officers and men of the Royal Marines, and from 1943 non-commissioned men in the Royal Air Force. Citations, 1855–1986, in *The London Gazette*, with annual subject indexes, ZJ 1; annuities, 1876–1920, PMG 16. see *Medals*

Consuls, British Out-letters from the Treasury, 1831–54, T 28.

Convict Establishments, Staff of Applications for convict service in the colonies, 1856–61, CO 323/141. Superannuations and retirement allowances, 1834–1924, PMG 28.

Convicts References in Privy Council Papers, 1481–1946, PC 1; orders of court for imprisonment and transfer papers for removal to a government prison and orders to return to gaol prisoners brought before the bar of the Court of King's Bench (Plea Side), including lists of prisoners, 1603–1877, indexed, 1792–1802, KB 125, and of the Crown Side, 1603–1889, KB 32. Warrants for arrest, jail or movement of officers and seamen for breaches of naval or criminal law, 1805–56, warrants for execution of those convicted by the High Court of Admiralty of a capital offence, 1802–56, respites of execution, 1802–20, all in HCA 55. Annual Criminal Registers, England and Wales, arranged alphabetically by county, and then chronologically by court of trial of all indicted persons, giving alleged offence, verdict and sentence, 1805–92, HO 27, London and Middlesex, 1791–1849, HO 26, and from 1850 in HO 27; quarterly returns of prison and prison hulk inmates, giving age, offence, date and place of trial, sentence, current state of health, behaviour record, 1824–76, HO 8; registers of county prisons, 1847–66, HO 23; prison registers and returns for Millbank,

Parkhurst and Pentonville, 1838–75, HO 24; registers of prisoners and gaol calendars for the Assizes and Quarter Sessions of England and Wales, Gibraltar and some hulks, 1837–60, including photographs of prisoners, listed by prison, *c*.1770–*c*.1913, PCOM 2; calendars of prisoners and other papers concerning the institution of a Criminal Registry, 1853–75, MEPO 6/90; details of penal records, 1843–71, PCOM 5, indexed, 1843–64, in PCOM 6; registered papers, including files on prisoners convicted of murder, 1901–73, PCOM 9 (some closed 50, 75 or 100 years); petitions for transportation in commutation of the death sentence, 1661–1782, correspondence and warrants, 1704–82, SP 44, described for 1760–75 in *Calendar of Home Office Papers of the reign of George III*; petitions and recommendations for pardons, 1782–1820, HO 42, 1820–61, HO 44; petitions for a free pardon, 1784–1829, HO 47, 1779–90, 1805–41, and 1854, in PRO 30/45/1, with an index in the class list; petitions for revocation or reduction of sentence, 1819–39, HO 17, with related correspondence in HO 12 and HO 13; petitions, 1839–54, HO 18, 1797–1853, HO 19, both arranged alphabetically and referring to the original petition and the outcome; names of those recommended for mercy, 1816–40, HO 6. In-letters, 1849–70, HO 14, with a nominal index giving references to original letters and petitions, 1849–71, HO 12; selected later letters up to 1878, HO 45, 1879–1919, HO 144 (some closed 100 years); Entry Book of out-letters, 1782–1871, and of pardons, 1782–1849, HO 13. Warrants for pardons, 1849–87, HO 15, 1887–1921, HO 147. Royal Prerogative of Mercy, granting a pardon for wrongful conviction, commutation of a capital sentence to life imprisonment or remission,

1887–1960, HO 188 (most closed 100 years); petitions, confirmations and remissions of sentences, medical enquiries, dates of executions, respite of capital sentences, administrations of convicts' property, 1887–98, HO 147, 1899–1921, HO 163; petitions in Scotland, 1782–1853, HO 102, out-letters, 1762–1849, mostly indexed, HO 104. Male licences to be at large, 1853–87, PCOM 3, female licences, 1853–71, 1883–7, PCOM 4, with registers and indexes of males, 1853–81, and of females, 1853–85, in PCOM 6; out-letters concerning remission, and revocation of prisoners' licences, 1899–1906, HO 169. Court of Criminal Appeal registers, 1908–9, 1914–63, giving appellant's name, when and where convicted and of what offence, sentence and nature of application or appeal, and the outcome, J 81, and these form indexes to the case files in J 82, listed chronologically, giving the name and offence, 1945–60. Criminal lunatics in Bethlem Hospital, 1823–35, HO 20. Baptisms in Westminster Penitentiary, 1816–71, PCOM 2/139, burials, 1817–53, PCOM 2/140; deaths and inquests at Millbank Prison, 1848–63, PCOM 2/165; interments at Victoria Park Cemetery, Hackney, 1853–76, RG 8/42–51.

see **Convicts, Transportation of, Criminal Appeal, Court of, Criminal Proceedings, Criminal Registers, Annual, New South Wales, Prisons, Tasmania**

Convicts, Transportation of Names and parishes of those condemned to hang but pardoned on condition of transportation, 1654–1717, C 66, 1714–27, SP 35, 1727–60, SP 36, 1760–82, SP 37, and 1661–1828, SP 44; payments to contractors arranging transportation, 1716–72, including names and counties of convicts, 1716–44, and destinations up to 1742,

T 53; transportation lists, 1747–72, T 1; contracts to transport named prisoners to New South Wales, Van Diemen's Land and Western Australia, 1842–67, TS 18/460–525, 1308–61. Convict hulk quarterly lists of crew and names of convicts, arranged alphabetically under ship, 1802–31, sickness returns, 1802–18, T 38. Lists of convicts transported for fourteen years or less, 1614–1868, PC 2; transportation registers, surgeons' reports, assignments and musters, 1787–1867, listed alphabetically by ship, and giving date and court of trial, length of sentence, health and behaviour, HO 11/1–19, list of ships, recording sailing dates, 1787–1870, HO 11/20, convicts transported, 1810–17, HO 11/2; names of prisoners on board ship, 1862–7, WO 22/226; medical journals and surgeons' reports, 1817–53, ADM 101/1–75, 1848–71, ADM 101/251–63, both listed alphabetically by vessel, and 1858–67, MT 32; lists of male convicts in New South Wales, 1788–1819, females, 1788–1819, general musters in New South Wales, 1806, 1811, 1816, 1817, 1818, 1820, 1821, 1822, 1825, 1828, 1837, November 1828 census of New South Wales, convicts embarked, 1787, convicts arrived in New South Wales, 1828–32, 1833–4, pardons granted in New South Wales, 1834–59, pardons granted in Van Diemen's Land, 1834–8, 1840–59, ledger returns, 1846, 1849, and incomplete lists of convicts in Van Diemen's Land, 1808–49, all in HO 10, and providing details of date and place of trial, sentence, settlement, religious denomination, employment in the colony, and any land and cattle acquired; convicts shipped to India, 1844–5, and to Bermuda, 1847, HO 45. America and West Indies Original Correspondence, 1606–1775, CO 5, contains references to convicts transported there; New South Wales Original Correspon-

dence, 1801–21, includes a list of convicts going to New South Wales in 1822, CO 201, with a register of correspondence, 1849–1900, CO 360, and register of out-letters, 1873–1900, CO 369; Entry Books of correspondence, 1786–1873, CO 202, and Entry Books relating to convicts in New South Wales, 1788–1868, including an alphabetical list of particulars about convicts, 1788–1842, letters from the superintendent of convicts, 1854–67, Savings Bank Books of convicts, 1824–68, CO 207; deaths of convicts in New South Wales, 1823–35, are recorded in HO 7. Petitions of wives to accompany their husbands, 1819–44, with extensive biographical information about their family background, PC 1/67–92, 1849, HO 45, 1849–71, HO 12 (with registers in HO 14 as the key); register of applications for passages to the colonies of convicts' families, 1848–73, CO 386/154. Applications for colonial convict service, 1856–61, CO 323/141.

Copyhold Land held by a tenant of the lord of the manor, evidence of the tenant's title to it being a copy of the manorial court roll on which were recorded the terms under which it was held according to the custom of that particular manor. Copyhold was abolished in 1925. Under a series of enabling statutes from 1841, it became possible to convert copyhold land to freehold, and this was made mandatory in 1925; at enfranchisement an agreement was made between the lord of the manor and his copyhold tenant on the amount of compensation he was to receive for loss of his manorial incidents, and where this was impossible, the Ministry of Agriculture could be approached to intervene and make an award. Deeds and awards of enfranchisement, arranged under county, manor, date, tenant's name, and registered number, 1841–1925, MAF 9; the deeds are for voluntary agreements, the awards for compulsory enfranchisement at the behest of either side; some evidences of title furnished by lords of the manor are included from 1900, earlier ones from 1840 being in MAF 20, and both are listed alphabetically by manor. Certificates of voluntary and compulsory compensation paid to lords of the manor, Series I, 1926–44, MAF 13, and certificates of determination of compensation, Series II, 1936–57, MAF 27, listed by county, place, owner's name and date; registered files of extinguishment of manorial incidents, 1935–54, MAF 233; registers of records of enfranchisement and extinguishment of manorial incidents, 1841–1957, indexed, MAF 76/1–12, which also forms the key to MAF 9 and gives information about the certificates in MAF 13 and MAF 27. Letters concerning compensation for enfranchisement and loss of manorial incidents, 1925–52, with a nominal list, MAF 48. Enfranchisements of Crown lands, 1851–1919, most volumes being integrally indexed, CRES 9; enrolments of memorials of enfranchisement of Crown lands, 1859–72, LRRO 37. Deeds relating to woods, 1859–90, LRRO 16, indexed in LRRO 64.

Copyright Applications and assignments, relating to paintings and drawings, photographs, literary works, dramatic and musical representations and performances, 1862–1912, COPY 1; indexes to authors of literary works and to publishers, 1907–23, and indexes of assignments of copyright, 1842–1924, indexes to entries, 1844–98, COPY 3.

Corn Rents Index Altered apportionments of Corn Rents, including copies of extracts from Enclosure Awards, setting out the apportionment of corn rents in lieu of tithes, arranged alphabetically by county, 1828–1973, IR 107; index, 1960, giving details of the originating statute, amount of rent, name of owners and apportionments, IR 103; certificates of redemption, 1886–1975, arranged alphabetically by county and parish, IR 108.

Cornwall, Duchy of Records covering the period 1299–temp. Charles II include grants of land and offices, temp. James I–Charles I, copies of grants and leases, temp. Henry VIII–Charles II, inquisitions post mortem, 1438–93, surveys of land, 1569–1627, E 306; some manorial records, PRO 30/26. Association Oath Roll, including tinners, 1696, C 213/34. Treasury out-letters, 1822–56, T 28.

Coronation Claims To certain hereditary ceremonial offices, temp. George III–George VI, C 195.

Coroners Name of coroners, c.1238–1348, JUST 1; certificates of election, 1283–1633, C 242, with a printed nominal list, and temp. Edward I–Charles I, arranged under borough, county, and regnal year, C 267; petitions for elections of coroners, listed chronologically by year, county, and name of late coroner, 1878–88, C 207; appointments, 1868–75, with a nominal and place-name index, C 202. Coroners' inquisitions, temp. Henry III (thirteenth century)–Henry VI (fifteenth century), JUST 2, temp. Edward I (thirteenth century)–1675, KB 9, 1675–1845 (London and Middlesex only), KB 10, 1675–1845 (other counties) KB 11, 1748–1808 (mostly the Western Assize Circuit), KB 13, inquests in the North and South Wales Circuit, Chester and North Wales Division, 1798–1891, ASSI 66, in

the Palatinate of Chester, temp. Edward III (fourteenth century)–Victoria, CHES 18, in the Palatinate of Lancaster, 1626–1822, PL 26, with depositions taken, 1663–1867, PL 27; inquests on the deaths of prisoners in the King's Bench Prison (Crown Side), 1747–1839, KB 14, (Plea Side) temp. Henry VIII–George IV, KB 140, inquests on prisoners dying in Millbank Prison, 1848–63, PCOM 2/165; returns of inquests on people killed on the railways, 1899–1916, HO 166.
see *Assizes*

Council of State This was the body through which the country was governed during the Commonwealth. Books and papers, including passes for English subjects to travel abroad, giving name, status or occupation, place of departure and destination, date of pass and period of validity (usually twenty days) and warrants for house searches and removal of prisoners from one place of custody to another, usually Newgate, 1650–60, with integral indexes, SP 25/111–16; Records of the Committee for the Sale of Crown Lands, and Fee-Farm Rents, 1649–60, SP 26, and SP 27; all the foregoing are listed in *Calendar of State Papers (Domestic Series) of the Commonwealth*.
see *Commonwealth Exchequer Papers*

County Courts Registers of petitions from bankrupts for protection from process, giving petitioner's name, address, occupation, court and debt, with the judgment given, 1854–1964, mainly relating to bankrupts under the Bankruptcy Act 1883, and some insolvent debtors, 1854–61, under the County Courts Act 1854, and arranged by initial letter of the petitioner's surname, LCO 28; 2% sample of interlocutory and final appeals to Court of Appeal, 1935–61, J 69.

Crenellate, Licences to Issued to allow the fortification of houses, the licences are enrolled on the Patent Rolls, C 66, with a printed descriptive list, 1256–1483 on open access.

Crimean War 1854–6. Embarkation registers, casualties, courts martial, 1854–6, WO 28; musters of the Scutari Depot, 1854–6, WO 14; Despatches, 1854–5, WO 1, and in *The London Gazette*, together with citations for gallantry awards including the Victoria Cross, and with annual or half-yearly subject indexes, ZJ 1; selected war disablement pensions, and to widows, listed under the name of the applicant, giving effective pension dates, the files including details of injury, degree of disablement and how incurred, the rank and regiment, medical record and conduct sheet, age, birthplace, parentage and current parental status, names of any siblings, present abode and occupation, annual income and marital status, signed by the pensioner, and to which any subsequent papers were attached, 1854–1977, PIN 71. Lists of Russian prisoners, WO 28/182, and ADM 102, lists of Russian prisoners in Britain, 1854–7, RG 8/180.

Criminal Appeal, Court of Created in 1907 to replace the Court for Crown Cases Reserved and abolished in 1966, when its business was brought under the aegis of the Criminal Division of the Court of Appeal. Registers, 1908–9, 1914–63, giving appellant's name, when and where convicted, for what offence, sentence, the nature of the appeal and the outcome, J 81, and these serve as indexes to the selected Case Files, 1945–60, which are organized chronologically and which give the name of the appellant and alleged offence, J 82.

Criminal Proceedings Registers of applications for advice on action made by Chief Constables, Town Clerks and other officers, giving the case name, charge, and name of applicant, and the action taken by the Director of Public Prosecutions, 1884–1933, DPP 3 (most are closed 75 years). Case papers, arranged chronologically, and made up of police and other reports, copies of depositions, exhibits, counsels' papers, and correspondence, 1889–1930, with a class list giving the first named defendant and offence charged, DPP 1 (most closed 75 years). Out-letters concerning criminal prosecutions, 1858–71, T 28; selected transcripts of proceedings, 1846–1931, DPP 4; prosecutions for coinage offences, 1586–1685, MINT 1, 1686–1884, MINT 15, 1859–69, TS 1.

Criminal Registers, Annual List all persons tried on indictment, including names of those against whom 'no true bill' was found, those acquitted and found not guilty, citing the court, date of trial, offence charged, verdict and sentence, and arranged alphabetically by English and Welsh county, then chronologically. London and Middlesex only, 1791–1849, in HO 26: from 1791–4 the lists give additionally the defendant's age, height, county of birth, and occupation, between 1795 and 1802 details of height are omitted, and occasionally birthplace is recorded, and from 1803–49 only additional information on age is cited, plus details of educational level, 1836–48; Registers for English and Welsh counties, 1805–92 (and embracing London and Middlesex from 1850, under which ages of defendants are supplied up to 1892), note additional details of age, 1834–48, and educational level, 1835–48, HO 27.

Criminals, Habitual Registers giving details of physical appearance, date of prison discharge, prison sentence and where served, and previous convictions, 1881–2, 1889–1931, 1941, MEPO 6/1–52, with a nominal index, 1896–9, MEPO 6/11; alphabetical list, relating to England and Wales, 1869–76, PCOM 2/404; *Police Gazette* Supplement A, giving names and aliases, short criminal histories, descriptions and methods employed by persons considered expert or travelling criminals, 1914–38, 1957, 1959, and *Police Gazette* or *Hue and Cry*, 1834, 1937, MEPO 6/66–76.

Crown Cases Reserved, Court for Established in 1848 for the decision of questions of law arising from criminal trials, and reserved by the presiding judge for the Court's consideration, its jurisdiction passed in 1907 to the Court of Criminal Appeal. Pleadings, concerning cases stated, and providing details of the original trial, usually at Quarter Sessions or Assize, plus some related papers, 1848–88, KB 30; Order Books, recording the results of the original trials, arranged chronologically, 1853–9, KB 31.
see *Appeal, Court of, Assizes, Criminal Appeal, Court of*

Crown Lands Surrenders of land to the Crown were normally enrolled up to 1903 on the Close Rolls and indexed under 'Rex' or 'Regina' as appropriate, C 54 (see *Close Rolls* for organization of indexes). Enrolments include surrenders of monastic lands at the Dissolution, while a separate branch of the Close Rolls, 1632–7 (Rotuli Regis Caroli), relates to conveyances made by trustees appointed by him in 1628 in return for loans made by the City of London; bargains and sales of Crown lands disposed of during the Commonwealth, including lands confiscated from delinquents (proven supporters of Charles I), to which there is a manuscript calendar and place-name index, and of fee-farm rents conveyed to trustees by Charles II in 1670–73, are also in C 54. Deeds of purchase and exchange, mainly of dissolved monastic lands, temp. Henry VIII–Edward VI, E 305 and E 315; records of the Committee for the Sale of Crown Lands, 1649–60, SP 26; particulars for the sale of the estates of Charles I, 1649–60, E 320, certificates of sale, same period, E 121, and other related papers, 1649–60, SP 28. Sales, leases, grants, and purchases, 1802–1912, and copyhold enfranchisements, 1851–1919, mostly indexed, CRES 9; estates and manors in England and Wales, sold before 1940, 1685–1940, CRES 34. Particulars for grants and leases, temp. Henry VIII–1731, E 147, temp. Henry VIII–Charles I, arranged alphabetically by grantee, temp. Henry VIII–1819, LR 10, and grants, leases, particulars for sale, books of rentals and surveys and inventories of possessions of attainted persons, temp. Henry V (fifteenth century)–1841, LR 2. Enrolment Books of grants, leases and warrants, temp. Henry VIII–1834, including surveys, inquisitions, conventual leases, exemplifications of pleadings and decrees, wills and probates, arranged under county, within eight divisions, LR 1; grants, 1547–53, SP 10, conveyances during the Commonwealth, E 304, temp. Charles II–1720, SC 4, grants, leases and surveys, 1570–1961, CRES 40. Surrenders of fee-farm rents, 1660–87, including some conveyances to and by the Crown, C 75. Deeds and evidences, including Crown grants and warrants, 1539–1947, partly indexed, later files being arranged alphabetically by county, then chronologically, TS 21; deeds and evidences, including returns of encroachments, registers of claims and rights in the Forest of Dean and New For-

est, deeds, awards and abstracts of leases, temp. Henry VIII–1917, LRRO 5; deeds and evidences, and eighteenth- and nineteenth-century transcripts, enrolments of sales of estates worth under £100, and of fee-farm rents, 1834–52, enrolments of memorials of enfranchisement, 1859–72, and presentments of offences in the New Forest, 1747–52, LRRO 37. Drafts of leases, temp. Henry VII–George I, E 380; counterpart leases made by the Court of Augmentations and the General Surveyors of Crown Lands, 1526–47, E 299; leases surrendered to the Crown, temp. Henry VIII–Philip and Mary, E 312; enrolment of leases, temp. Elizabeth–George III, E 365, abstracts and indexes of leases, temp. Elizabeth–George IV, E 381; letters patent granting leases, 1599–1696, E 403; Crown leases, temp. Charles I–William III, C 66. Constat (or Exemplification) Books, setting out consideration and lease terms as a preliminary to the formal conveyance, 1660–1851, and extracts from Enclosure Awards to 1918, CRES 6, reports on leases, 1716–86, CRES 7. Warrants for Crown leases, 1667–1727, T 54, and 1727–1818, T 55, both indexed. Entry Books of leases, 1750–1812, E 369. Card index to duplicate conveyances and leases, 1961–7, CRES 31, and to leases over fifty years, CRES 32 (but the documents themselves have been withdrawn). Indentures of wardship, and leases, temp. Henry VIII–Charles I, arranged under regnal year, WARD 6; particulars for leases by the Court of Wards and Liveries for the same time-span, WARD 12. Title deeds, temp. Edward I (thirteenth century)–1974, listed alphabetically by county, giving the date and description of each document, CRES 38. Ancient Deeds, Series E, temp. Henry III (thirteenth century)–Elizabeth I, LR 14, Series EE, c.1400–c.1700,

LR 15; Modern Deeds, Series E, seventeenth- and eighteenth-centuries, LR 16; deeds, 1668–1803, T 64. Rentals, with a descriptive list, chronologically by date, 1832–1954, LRRO 12 (most closed 100 years). Escheators' Accounts, relating to revenue derived from escheated or forfeited lands, and up to *c*.1576 providing full details about the property, its location, extent, value, and reason for seizure, temp. Henry III–James I, E 136; particulars of concealments, temp. Elizabeth I, E 302; commissions of enquiry into concealed lands, commissions to compound with purchasers of land sold during the Commonwealth, where the sales were declared void at the Restoration in 1660, E 178. Estate deeds of attainted persons after the Jacobite Rebellion of 1715, rentals and particulars of sale, 1552–1744, with a descriptive list, FEC 1; registers of claims against the forfeited estates, 1716–19, indexed, FEC 2, and undated rent rolls of forfeited estates, giving names of tenants, annual rent and acreage occupied, FEC 2/82–83; legal proceedings relating to escheats, 1584–1852, TS 11; commissions concerning escheats to the Crown for want of an heir, 1630–1887, C 205. Court rolls of Crown manors, temp. Edward I–George II, relating to fines and creating debts to the Crown, LR 11; court rolls, 1286–1837, LR 3, court rolls and other manorial documents for England and Wales, arranged alphabetically by manor and with a descriptive list, 1441–1925, CRES 5. Rentals and surveys, fourteenth century–1675, E 315, mainly temp. Henry VII, E 36, 1568–1834, LR 13, schedules of rents, under county, and lists of pensions payable out of them, with copies of related deeds, *c*.1700, 1831–57, CRES 27, with two index volumes; rentals in England, Wales, Scotland, Ireland, the Isle of Man and Alderney,

1832–1961, LRRO 12 (most closed 100 years), with indexes, 1817–1902, LRRO 65; out-letters concerning rents in Wales 1825–47, CRES 24. Surveys, 1608–1884, CRES 39, maps and plans, including Enclosure Awards, surveys and deeds, 1560–1950, LRRO 1; extents and valuations of lands and possessions of dissolved monasteries in Ireland, 1536–41, SP 65, described in *Calendar of State Papers, relating to Ireland, 1509–1647*. Correspondence and papers relating to staff of the Crown Estate Commission, 1851–1916, CRES 3, Office Establishment Books of warrants of appointment, and records concerning staff, 1851–1923, indexed, CRES 21.

see **Charter Rolls, Close Rolls, Fee-Farm Rents, Forest Proceedings, Lancaster, Duchy of, Patent Rolls, Peveril, Honour of, State Paper Office**

Cuba Baptisms of Britons, 1847–8, marriages, 1842–9, RG 33/155, indexed in RG 43/7; Havana, registers of slaves and slavers, 1819–69, FO 313.

Curaçao Births to Britons, 1897–1966, marriages, 1922–9, deaths, 1889–1925, 1930–49, 1952–65, FO 907/1–32.

Curia Regis Rolls These are the earliest court rolls in the public records, noting proceedings of the Bench (the forerunner of the Court of Common Pleas), Coram Rege (King's Bench), and of justices itinerant in eyre during the reign of Richard I. The records are in Latin: 1193–1272, KB 26, with printed transcripts, temp. Richard I (twelfth century)–1242.

see **Common Pleas, Court of, King's Bench, Court of, Placita Coram Rege**

Customs, Officers of They are responsible for the collection of customs duties on imported goods, and for the prevention of evasion by smugglers. Certificates of elections, 1303–1648, with a nominal index, C 267. Patents of 'customers' and 'searchers' to 1641, are enrolled on the Fine Rolls, C 60, 1642–1724, on the Patent Rolls, C 66, 1725–1875, in C 209; warrants for patents, 1714–84, C 208; letters patent of appointment, 1660–1895, CUST 109; admissions of Customs House officers, 1596–1875, C 216; registers of appointments, ages and capacities, listed under London and under Out Ports, various dates depending on port, and incorporating copies of correspondence between the Board of Customs in London and local collectors and vice versa, CUST 50– CUST 105; registers of ages and capacities, 1799–1823, London, and 1837 for Out Ports, CUST 39/183–87, copies of patents, 1671–1856 (indexed), register of oaths and qualification certificates, 1804– 40, CUST 39/190; declarations on taking office, 1814–1906, indexed, CUST 39/ 175–78; Board Minute Books record all officers' postings, censure or praise, and sometimes details of marriage, 1734–1885, CUST 28. Entry Books of searchers, waiters and officers of ports in England and Wales, 1565–1798, E 190. Staff lists, including salaries, and any disciplinary action taken, 1671–1912, CUST 39; Parliamentary returns, giving addresses of staff, various dates, ZHC 1 (indexes available); quarterly bills of salaries due to officers in England and Wales, 1675–1813, and including the Isle of Man from Michaelmas 1810, CUST 18, 1673–85, PRO 30/32/ 15–29, 1760–61, 1766, 1830–47, under London, and Out Ports, T 42, 1814–29,

including Scotland for the latter half of 1829, and staff of Revenue Cruisers from Michaelmas 1827, CUST 19; quarterly salary bills for Scotland, 1714–1829, T 43; registers of officers' appointments, 1761– 1823, and salary books of customs staff in Ireland, 1764–1808, with integral indexes, plus Establishment Books listing names and salaries, 1684–1826, CUST 20; Irish Establishments at Out Ports, 1840, 1860–94, CUST 39/122– 44. Applications for pensions made by staff and their dependants, 1777–1920, T 1, indexed in T 2, with subject indexes, 1830– 1920, in T 108; superannuations of staff in the United Kingdom commissioned up to 1887, 1803–1912, also containing widows' pensions, and names and dates of birth of children, indexed, CUST 39/145– 57 (later material closed 75 years); superannuations and widows' pensions for Irish staff, 1785–1898, indexed, CUST 39/ 161–62. Reports on frauds, 1681–4, reports, informations and letters, 1667– 1834, T 64, disciplinary offences, promotions, leave, and superannuation, 1818–1926, CUST 40 (closed 75 years). Out-letters from the Treasury, 1662– 1922, T 11. Musters and pay lists of boatmen recruited for part-time service as Sea Fencibles, 1798–1810, ADM 28.

Cyprus Register of deeds of Britons, 1829–39, FO 329.

Czechoslovakia Prague, files on British property in the country, and applications for British naturalization, 1948–9, FO 808/7 (some closed 50 years).

Dd

Dean, Forest of Records of the Free Miners' Court, 1668–1754, and Verderers' Court, 1846–1907, relating to rights of common, tithes, quarries, encroachments, deeds of exchange, conveyances, and court rolls, F 16; deeds and evidences, including returns of encroachments, registers of claims and rights, temp. Henry VIII–1917, LRRO 5, deeds and evidences, 1781–1891, F15.

Death Duty Legacy Duty was introduced in 1780, and, after lapsing, was again imposed in 1796 as a tax on legacies (except leases) and residues of personal estates worth £20 or more, those to offspring, spouse, parents and grandparents being at first exempt until limited in 1805 to spouse and parents, and in 1815 to the spouse only. In 1805, too, the ambit was widened to embrace sales of real estate directed to be applied to pay legacies or residues; from 1853 Succession Duty was levied on the gratuitous acquisition of real or personal estate worth £100 or more for which no Legacy Duty was payable, from 1881 Probate Duty was levied on personal property worth £100 or more left by will or administration grant, and this was absorbed into Estate Duty in 1894, and applied to all a person's property over a certain value on death. It was replaced by Capital Transfer Tax in 1975. Registers containing dates and abstracts of wills, their probate dates, and of grants of letters of administration from the Prerogative Court of Canterbury and other named ecclesiastical courts in England and Wales up to January 1858 and thereafter from the Principal Probate Registry and named District Probate Registries, with the names and addresses of executors or administrators, 1796–1903, IR 26, with annual indexes in IR 27 (there is a gap, 1864–81, for administrations). Inasmuch as the gifts attracted tax, the entries are often amplified by relationships not given in the original wills or administration grants, plus details of dates of death or marriage (and married names of daughters who were to benefit), the amount of each gift, any land sale proceeds, the date of death and occupation or status of their benefactor, and the total value of the estate (which up until 1853 excluded all property held outside Great Britain, and any debts or expenses owed by the estate), the amount of tax and when it was paid. As the registers were open for fifty years to allow contingent gifts to vest, they contain events which occurred many years after the death of the testator or intestate, and they also include reversionary registers dealing with outstanding claims for tax, usually relating to trusts, 1812–52, and Succession Duty arrears registers, 1853–78, again applying to transfers of property under trust or settlement. Specimens of Death Duty accounts, 1796–1903, IR 19, selected Death Duty accounts of famous people,

1805–1981, indexed, IR 59 (most closed 75 years); selected letters to the Estate Duty Office, 1812–36, IR 6, Scottish Papers, 1839–41, IR 7, and Treasury Letter Books, 1800–33, IR 49; reports to the Treasury on Legacy Duty cases, 1825–33, IR 50, and Case Books, 1853–66, IR 67.

see *Estate Duty, Succession Duty*

Deaths and Burials at Sea Miscellaneous returns made by British and foreign ships, of British subjects, nationals of the colonies, Commonwealth, and other countries under British jurisdiction, 1831–1958, RG 32, indexed in RG 43/4–7, 10–14, 20–21; deaths of British subjects on French vessels, 1836–71, and on Dutch ships, 1839–71, RG 35/17, indexed in RG 43/4; deaths of passengers on merchant vessels, extracted from official logs, 1854–90, BT 158, 1902–12, BT 165, 1913, BT 99, and of British nationals, reported to the Registrar General and the information passed on to the English, Scottish and Irish General Registration Offices, 1875–88, BT 159; registers of deaths of emigrants at sea, 1847–54, CO 386/169, 1854–69, CO 386/171–72; registers of reports of naval deaths, July 1900–October 1941 ADM 104 (closed 75 years), index to ships, 1893–1950, registers of reports of deaths of Royal Naval ratings, arranged alphabetically, September 1939–June 1948, and giving home town and cause of demise, indexes to killed and wounded, 1915–29, and registers, 1854–1911, 1914–29, all indexed, ADM 104.

Deaths and Burials of Britons Abroad Miscellaneous returns, being duplicates of consular registers in some of the Foreign Office (FO) classes, mainly being certificates issued by foreign registration authorities and copies of entries made by incumbents of English churches and missions, and by chaplains, and by burial authorities, and relating not only to British subjects, but to nationals of the colonies, Commonwealth or countries under British jurisdiction, 1831–1958, RG 32, indexed in RG 43/3–7, 10–14, 20–21; original registers, 1627–1958, but mainly stemming from the nineteenth- and twentieth-centuries, and encompassing African and Asian Protectorates, and deaths from enemy action in the Far East, 1941–5, RG 33, indexed in RG 43/7; miscellaneous deaths abroad, 1830–1921, including an incomplete collection of military deaths in France and Belgium, issued by the local registration authorities, 1914–21, RG 35, indexed except for the military deaths, in RG 43/4–6, 10; deaths in the African and Asian Protectorates, 1895–1950, RG 36/1–13, indexed, 1904–40, in RG 43/18. The arrangement of the indexes in RG 43 is as follows: RG 43/2, deaths, 1801–80, RG 43/3, deaths and burials, 1627–1951, RG 43/4–6, deaths, 1830–1930, RG 43/7, deaths and burials, 1627–1958, RG 43/10–14, deaths, 1921–45, RG 43/20–21, deaths, 1946–60.

see *Army, British, Merchant Seamen, Navy, Royal, Protectorates, British, World War I, World War II*, and under individual countries

Deaths, Concealed The Cestui Que Vie Act 1707 was designed to protect persons entitled in remainder or reversion to estates for life on the death of the previous life tenant and who were entitled to the rents and profits accruing from them. If they suspected the previous holder to be dead, an annual application could be made for a Chancery order obliging the trustees of such estates to produce the life tenant, on refusal of which, the tenant's death was assumed. Any life tenant overseas could be viewed by the applicant on a Chancery Order. A life tenant assumed to be dead and later proved to be alive was enabled to re-enter the land. The Act was repealed in 1888. Discoveries made under the Act, 1707–1839, C203/6.

Debtors, Insolvent Those persons unable to meet their debts in full, and until the Bankruptcy Act 1861, excluding persons defined as traders. Registers of petitions for protection from process in the County Courts, 1854–61, 1883–1964, giving name, address, occupation, court and amount of the debt, LCO 28.
see **Bankrupts, County Courts**

Debts, Extents for Writs were issued to sheriffs to recover debts due to the Crown, whereupon they made a valuation (extent) of the person's land and goods, on the oath of a jury, with a view to selling them to pay off the debt. They were abolished in 1947. Extents, 1316–1645, C131, 1529–1648, C239, 1603–1774, C228, 1685–1842, E144; commissions of enquiry into possessions of Crown debtors, temp. Elizabeth–Victoria, with a descriptive list, E178, Duchy of Lancaster, temp. Elizabeth–Charles II, DL 123.

Deeds, Ancient A massive and disparate collection, coming into Crown hands or deposited in one of the central courts of law and now organized separately. They were made between private individuals, and many relate to charitable foundations up to 1602/3: Series C, *c*.1100–1627, with a typescript descriptive list, C146, Series CC, *c*.1100 (very large deeds), C147, Series CS, temp. Edward I (thirteenth century)–Elizabeth, C148; Series A, *c*.1100–1603, catalogued for pieces

1–15910, E40, Series AA, *c*.1100–1603, E41, Series AS, *c*.1100–1603, calendared, E42; Series WS, *c*.1100–1603, calendared, E43; Series D, *c*.1150, catalogued, E210, Series DD, 1101–1645, listed, E211, Series DS, 1228, E212; Series RS, temp. Edward I, E213. Ancient deeds once belonging to religious houses, and coming into the Crown's possession at their dissolution: Series B, *c*.1200–1592, calendared and catalogued, E326, Series BX, temp. Stephen (twelfth century), E327, Series BB, *c*.1250–1569, calendared, E328, Series BS, 1148, E329, twelfth century–1730, E315. Ancient deeds filed in the Pipe Office, Series P, 1524–1608, E354, Series PP, *c*.1500–*c*.1600, E355 (most of these two last classes are also enrolled on the Close Rolls, in C54). Crown lands, Series E, temp. Henry III (thirteenth century)–Elizabeth, LR14, Series EE, *c*.1400–*c*.1700, LR15. Palatinate of Chester and Principality of Wales, Series F, temp. Edward I–Elizabeth, WALE29, Series FF, *c*.1507–1633, WALE30.
see **Deeds and Conveyances, Deeds, Modern**

Deeds and Conveyances Of transfers of land and including trust deeds, were enrolled from an early date on the back of the Close Rolls, 1205–1903, C54, later enrolments to 1987 being in J18, to which there is an annual initial index to 1948, and subsequently annual chronological listings on open access; there is a pasted-up place-name index to trust deeds, 1736–1870 and thereafter a card index on open access relating to charitable trusts up to 1905. A statute of 1381 permitted those persons who had lost their deeds in the late troubles to provide sufficient proof of their former existence and contents, and petition for a remedy, and enrolments of their details survive, along with others registered for safe-keeping, to which there is a place-name index, temp. William and Mary–George III; registration of deeds of bargain and sale from 1536–1845, of conveyances of the estates of bankrupts after 1572, and those of Papists from 1716 are also in C 54, and there are indexes to names of grantors and grantees on open access (see *Close Rolls* for fuller information on the reference system); enrolment of deeds of bargain and sale in the Palatinates was not mandatory until 1563, these and other deeds are enrolled on the Plea Rolls of the Palatinate of Chester, 1255–1831, CHES 29, 1307–1830, CHES 2, in the Palatinate of Durham, fourteenth–eighteenth century, DURH 3, 1578–1844, DURH 13, *c*.1600–*c*.1800, Series G, DURH 21, petitions and reports concerning conveyances made by infants, 1764–1801, are in DURH 8, deeds enrolled in the Palatinate of Lancaster, 1409–70, PL 2, 1354–1440, PL 37, temp. Richard II (fourteenth century)–Victoria, PL 14, and on the Plea Rolls, 1400–1847, PL 15. Plea Rolls, Placita de Banco (De Banco Rolls), 1272–1582/3, record enrolments of private deeds, CP 40, thenceforward to 1834 on CP 43, which include some deeds of Papists enrolled after 1716. Enrolments of deeds in the Exchequer relate to the thirteenth- and fourteenth-centuries, E159, with catalogues of deeds, between the fourteenth- and sixteenth-centuries, in E36/137–43. Some private deeds are enrolled on the Coram Rege Rolls, 1272–1701, KB 27, 1702–1875, KB 122, indexed by regnal year, temp. Edward I and Edward II, 1595–1647, with a manuscript calendar arranged by county and place, and then chronologically, 1656–1805, on open access. Deeds enrolled in the Duchy of Lancaster,

c.1100–*c*.1700, Series L, DL 25, Series LL, DL 26, Series LS, DL 27, while original deeds may be found, temp. Henry I (twelfth century)–James I, DL 36, and evidences of title to land, temp. Henry III–Victoria, DL 41. Deeds relating to Queen Anne's Bounty to benefit clergy with incomes less than £50 a year, up to 1839, QAB 1. Deeds relating to land in East and West New Jersey, Pennsylvania and New England, 1658–1921, TS 12; deeds concerning land in Cumberland, Northumberland and Kent, forming part of the Greenwich Hospital Estates, 1340–1931, with two index volumes, ADM 75; deeds and evidences relating to the Forest of Dean, 1781–1891, F 16. Deeds, produced as Masters' exhibits in the Court of Chancery, listed alphabetically by county, place, and then chronologically, 1294–1808, C 116; Duchess of Norfolk's deeds, arranged similarly, *c*.1150–*c*.1850, C 115; 1597–1648, listed by document, name of case, and date, C 171. Specimen certificates of acknowledgement of deeds by married women, 1838, 1875, 1899, 1900, with a nominal list, J 89/1/1–7.

see *Charter Rolls, Close Rolls, Court Rolls, Crown Lands, Deaths, Concealed, Deeds, Ancient, Deeds, Modern, Manorial Courts and Records, Patent Rolls, Roman Catholics*

Deeds, Modern These are a continuation of Ancient deeds, commencing in the reign of James I. Temp. James I, C 149, *c*.1600–*c*.1700, E 44, 1672–1851, which is listed and indexed, E 214; former monastic archives, Series B, temp. James I, E 330; deeds relating to Crown lands, Series E, seventeenth- and eighteenth-centuries, LR 16; Rolls Estate, *c*.1700–*c*.1900, SC 3; Welsh deeds, including the Palatinate of Chester, temp.

James II–nineteenth century WALE 31; the Palatinate of Lancaster, Series H, c.1550–c.1850, PL 29.

see **Deeds, Ancient**

Degrees, Lambeth Degrees in Divinity, Arts, Law, Medicine, and Music, conferred since 1535 by the Archbishop of Canterbury as a mark of favour. Enrolments of confirmations, 1595–1747, C 58; Church Warrant Books, 1828–1969, with integral indexes, HO 115.

Delegates, High Court of This was the Court of Appeal from the Prerogative Courts of Canterbury and York, of the Court of Chivalry, and the High Court of Admiralty, to 1834, when it was succeeded by the Judicial Committee of the Privy Council. Processes in the Courts of First Instance in ecclesiastical and maritime causes, 1609–1834, DEL 1, indexed in DEL 11; Cause Papers, arranged alphabetically under name of appellant, 1533–1832, DEL 2, with indexes in DEL 11; Repertory Books, listing cases and their nature, 1619–1789, DEL 8; examinations, depositions and answers, 1557–1735, DEL 3; Muniment Books, containing documents exhibited to the Court, 1652–1834, DEL 9, indexed in DEL 11; wills, affidavits, 1636–1834, filed with appeals against judgments in ecclesiastical courts, DEL 10, indexed in DEL 11; sentences, decrees and orders, 1585–1802, DEL 5; notes of proceedings in Court (Acts), 1538–44, 1601–92, DEL 4, continued from 1650–1838 (Assignation Books), in DEL 6, which is mostly indexed; Case Books, being printed proceedings, annotated with judgments on Appeal, 1796–1834, DEL 7.

see **Canterbury, Prerogative Court of, Privy Council, Judicial Committee of the**

Delinquents, Committee for Compounding with This Parliamentary Committee dealt with the fines or compositions paid by self-confessed or reported Royalists (called delinquents), based on a percentage of the value of their estates and goods. The records are also known as Royalist Composition Papers, and are divided into two series, the first being the correspondence and orders of the Commissioners for the sequestration and sale of the estates of Royalist nobility and gentry, and the second being the original particulars given under oath about their estates and property, on whose valuations, if accepted as accurate, the fines were based. Any concealments brought severe financial penalties. 1643–60, SP 23, with a printed *Calendar of Proceedings of the Committee for Compounding*, 5 volumes, including an index volume.

Delinquents' Estates Certificates of land sequestrated from the late King's supporters by the Committee or Commissioners for Sequestrations, 1649, and 1656, arranged alphabetically by county, and including the City of London, giving name, status, abode and date of sequestration, C 203/2–3. Bargains and sales effected during the Commonwealth of lands sequestrated from Royalists are enrolled on the Close Rolls, C 54, with a place-name index on open access. Other records of the Committee for the Sale of Delinquents' Estates, including sequestration accounts and papers, 1642–60, SP 28/205–18. At the Restoration of the monarchy in 1660, the sales were declared void, and a Commission was set up to compound with their purchasers: records of the enquiries, with a descriptive list, are in E 178.

see **Crown Lands, Delinquents, Committee for Compounding with, Seques-**

tration of Delinquents' Estates, Committee for the, State Paper Office

Denization Letters patent under the Crown granted aliens status as British subjects under whatever terms the Crown designated; usually they remained liable for taxation and customs and excise duties at the higher alien rate. Publication of grants, 1665–1986, in *The London Gazette*, with subject indexes occasionally from 1790, and invariably from 1848, ZJ 1; enrolments to 1844 may be found on the Patent Rolls, C 66, and sporadically thereafter, but between August 1844 and August 1873 they are on the Close Rolls, C 54, 1872–8, HO 45, 1879–1949, HO 144 (closed 100 years); there are indexes to denizations, 1509–1935, in HO 1, on open access, and this class also contains denization application papers, 1801–40, certificates issued to denizens, 1844–71, and general correspondence, 1789–1837; some enrolments, 1540–44, and 1562, are in C 67, and there are fifteen original letters patent, temp. George II and George III, in C 97; other original patents, 1804–43, may be located in HO 4. Applications for denization, 1688–1784, SP 44, and denizations, 1678–88, SP 44/67, applications 1794–1921, HO 5, 1872–8, HO 45; warrants for letters patent, 1852–76, indexed, HO 141. Fees for grants to 1641 are enrolled on the Fine Rolls, with printed *Calendars* to 1509, C 60; fees paid between 1869 and 1877, HO 143.
see *Aliens, Naturalization*

Denmark Marriages of Britons, 1846–90, FO 83, indexed in FO 802/239, marriage affidavits, 1853–70, FO 211; deaths in Denmark and its colonies, 1842–72, RG 35/4–7, indexed in RG 43; records of the Commission set up in 1834 to investi-gate claims by British subjects for confiscation of their property, 1807, and containing supporting documents, plus eventual awards, 1834–55, T 78; Copenhagen, marriages, 1853–70, FO 211/236, 1853–74, RG 33/35, indexed in RG 43/7, baptisms, 1866–70, marriages and burials, 1869 onwards, RG 32, indexed in RG 43.

Derby House Committee
see *Both Kingdoms, Committee for*

Designs Representations under Designs Copyright Act 1839, affording twelve months' protection after the date of registration of textiles, and for three years on most other non-metal manufactures, 1839–42, BT 42, with indexes of proprietors, BT 44; representations under the Ornamental Design Act 1842, 1842–84, BT 43; with an index in BT 44; representations made under the Non-Ornamental (Useful) Designs Act 1843, conferring three years' protection, 1843–84, BT 45, with registers in BT 46. In all the foregoing, details are given of registration date, the name and address of each proprietor, and the subject or class of design, and any subsequent transfers or extension of protection. Provisional registrations for twelve months, with provision for a further six months, and including people exhibiting new inventions certified by the Attorney General, and designs for the Great Exhibition, 1851, 1851–83, BT 48; representations made under Patents, Designs and Trade Marks Act 1883, bestowing five years' protection after registration, 1884–1908, BT 50, with registers for the same period, plus an index to firms and individuals, 1884–94, in BT 51.

Devotion Money
see *Subsidy, Lay*

Disentailing Deeds Introduced in 1834 these are assurances by which a tenant in tail bars an entail of land in order to convert it to a freehold estate in fee simple, or to bar it only for his own direct line, so creating a base fee; until 1925 they were required to be enrolled in a central court of record, since which date it has not been necessary. Enrolments to 1903 were effected on the Close Rolls, C 54, thereafter until 1925 in the Enrolment Books, J 18, to both of which are annual initial indexes.

Dissenters, Protestant Authenticated registers of births, baptisms (and marriages to 1754), and burials, 1567–1858, listed alphabetically under county, and then by place, and including under Middlesex the Presbyterian, Independent and Baptist Registry of births, 1742–1837, at Dr Williams' Library, and the Wesleyan Methodist Metropolitan Registry, 1818–38 (see entries), and giving denomination, date of foundation of each chapel, and the dates covered by deposited registers, RG 4; unauthenticated registers, not qualified to be used as evidence in a court of law, 1646–1951, RG 8. Licences to individuals to hold meetings, April–June 1672, by county, SP 44/38B, registers of places of worship, 1689–1852, arranged chronologically by registration date, RG 31; registers of persons authorized to perform marriages in certified places of worship, 1899–1931, RG 42. Returns of dissenters, 1547–53, SP 10, with a printed *Calendar*, index of nonconformists, 1663, SP 9; Association Oath Roll of London dissenters, 1696, C 214/9, and of Baptist ministers, C 213/170. Recusant Rolls, recording in Latin, under each county, and for Wales, the names and residences of non-attenders at Anglican churches and the subsequent fines or further action taken against them, 1591–1691, E376 and E377.

see *Bethnal Green Protestant Dissenters' Burying Ground, Bunhill Fields Burial Ground, Dr Williams' Library, Friends, Society of, Marriages and Baptisms, Clandestine, Non-Parochial Registers, Recusant Rolls, Wesleyan Methodist Metropolitan Registry*

Distinguished Conduct Medal Instituted in 1845 for Army sergeants, extended in 1854 to include non-commissioned officers and men, it replaced the Meritorious Service Medal for gallantry in action. In January 1943 it was widened to include non-commissioned Airmen, and also includes the non-commissioned men of the Royal Navy involved in ground operations. Commander in Chief's correspondence on medals, 1854–7, WO 3; submissions and recommendations made to the Sovereign, 1855–1909, with a nominal list giving name, rank and regiment, WO 146, and for World War I, ADM 171/61; registered papers, 1859–1951, WO 32 Code 50 S. see *Medals*

Divorce Until the enactment of Matrimonial Causes Act in 1857, divorce was by Private Act of Parliament, or a marriage was formally ended in one of the ecclesiastical courts. Private Acts of Parliament, temp. Henry VIII–1800, C 89, and temp. James I–1764, C 204. Divorce files, including papers relating to petitions, judicial separations, and declarations of legitimacy, heard by the Court for Divorce and Matrimonial Causes, 1858–74, and by its successor, the Probate, Divorce and Admiralty Division of the High Court, 1875–1937, are in J 77 (the files are mostly closed for 75 years, but permission to inspect them may be sought from the Principal Registrar of the Family Division), with indexes to matrimonial causes, 1858–1958, in J78; registers of divorces, containing examples of cases where a decree nisi was not made absolute, or where the Procurator General intervened or assisted the Divorce Court, 1875–1924, TS 29 (closed 75 years); petitions for divorce under Poor Persons Rules, 1913, where payment of legal fees was voluntary, 1918–19, LCO 32/8.

see *Delegates, High Court of, Matrimonial Causes*

Dockyards, Royal Naval Warrants of appointment as yard officers, 1695–1815, ADM 6/3–32, 1803–15, ADM 11/18, 1804–17, ADM 11/17, applications, 1842–58, ADM 6/1; Civil Branch index, 1873–1934, ADM 23; yard paybooks at home and abroad, 1660–1857, ADM 42, pay lists, musters and pension lists of various yards, registers of labourers and description books, 1703–1857, ADM 113, 1808–23, ADM 7/859, 1822–32, ADM 7/861; certificates of service of artificers, 1817–45, ADM 29/8; Description Books of artificers at various yards, 1748–1830, ADM 106; registers of protections from impressment into the Royal Navy, 1794–1815, ADM 7/377–80; registers of baptisms at the Dockyard Church, Sheerness, 1813–81, 1885–1960, ADM 6/429–33, 438, and births, baptisms, marriages and burials in the church at Bermuda, 1826–1946, ADM 6; indexes to reports of deaths of dockyard employees, 1893–1950, ADM 104/102–08; retirement pensions of artificers, 1884–1926, and civil salaried officers, 1884–1910, arranged alphabetically, ADM 23, and of labourers' pensions, 1836–1928, pensions and civil superannuation allowances to salaried staff at home and overseas, and to widows and orphans, 1836–1918, PMG 24, superannuation and retirement pensions of yard officers, 1666–1781, ADM 18/39–119, 1781–1826,

ADM 22, 1832–5, ADM 6/222, 1834–6, 1857–84, ADM 23; pensions to widows of employees of dockyards and victualling yards killed in service, 1836–9, 1867–80, 1885–91, 1899–1932, ADM 23; outpensions from the Royal Hospital, Greenwich, 1814–46, ADM 22/254–443, and payments out of the Chatham Chest to widows and orphans, 1831–7, ADM 22/52–55.

see *Chatham Chest*

Doctors' Commons The building in which ecclesiastical and Admiralty courts sat from 1568, presided over by doctors in civil law, it also served until January 1858 as the probate registry for the Prerogative Court of Canterbury, and then as the Principal Probate Registry until 1874. Association Oath Roll, 1696, C 213/164; Treasurers' Books, 1567–1828, PRO 30/26/8–9; cases and opinions, 1796–1834, and Admiralty Bill Books, 1816–57, PRO 30/28.

see *Admiralty, High Court of, Canterbury, Prerogative Court of, Clements Inn, Proctors*

Dr Williams' Library Situated in Red Cross Street, Cripplegate, London, it was founded in 1742 as a birth registry principally for Presbyterians, Independents and Baptists, issuing numbered birth certificates in exchange for a small fee. Parents often registered their own births as well as those of their offspring, perhaps several at a time, and the certificates were signed by the parents and at least two witnesses of the birth. After central registration began on 1 July 1837, the registry was closed at the end of that year. Authenticated registers of births, arranged chronologically by initial letter, giving children's names, dates and places of birth, parentage and names of maternal grandparents, with dates of registration and registration numbers, 1742–1837, with photocopies on open access, RG 4/4666–76; parchment certificates, 1742–1840, arranged under registration number, RG 5.

Dog Tax 1796–1882.
see *Land Tax and Assessed Taxes*

Domesday Book A survey of the kingdom, undertaken in 1086–7 at the behest of William I, E 31.

Dominican Republic Proclaimed in 1844. Santo Domingo, registers of birth to Britons, 1868–1932, marriages, 1921–8, deaths, 1874–89, and burials in the British Cemetery, 1849–1910, registers of British subjects, 1811–1932, FO 683/2–6.
see *Haiti, Santo Domingo*

Dormant Funds Being unclaimed moneys held by the Chancery Division of the Supreme Court, for upwards of five years, where no next of kin can be located or where entitled legatees are untraceable in spite of advertisements. Printed lists, 1890–1974, on open access, relating to funds held since 1876. The records themselves are in the custody of the Supreme Court, Strand, London, where further information can be given concerning the sums on written request (including copies of supporting evidence) from any person believed to be an interested beneficiary.

Dower A portion of land set aside for a wife's lifetime use and maintenance of her children after her husband's death, or where the land was inheritable, a third of it was for her lifetime. Dower was abolished in 1925. Partitions of land for dower are contained in Miscellaneous Inquisitions, 1218–1484, C 145, calendared up to 1389; pleadings on writs of partition of lands for dower in the common law Court of Chancery, temp. Edward I (thirteenth century)–Richard III, C 44, temp. Henry VII–James I, C 43, temp. Elizabeth–Commonwealth, C 206; assignments of dower, temp. Henry III–1660, are included in inquisitions post mortem, C 132–C 142.
see *Inquisitions post mortem*

Drunkards, Habitual Lists circulated to licensees and club secretaries, and including portraits and descriptions, 1903–14, MEPO 6/77–88.

Durham, Palatinate of Cursitor's records, 1311–1865, including abstracts and registers of inquisitions post mortem, 1318–1567, originals, 1438–1637, inquisitions *ad quod damnum*, fourteenth- and fifteenth-centuries, Halmote Court Books, 1348–1619, leases and enrolments of deeds, court rolls, 1381–1494, and coroners' inquisitions, temp. James I, DURH 3; concords of fines, 1661–1834, DURH 11, feet of fines, 1535–1834, DURH 12; deeds, Series G, *c.*1600–*c.*1800, DURH 21; some rentals and surveys, temp. Henry III (thirteenth century)–William IV, SC 11 and SC 12; Enclosure Awards, 1632–1834, DURH 26. Judicial records (1) *Equity* Chancery records of bills, answers and other pleadings, 1576–1840, DURH 2, interrogatories and depositions, 1557–1804, DURH 7, affidavits, 1657–1812, DURH 1, Entry Books of decrees and orders, 1633–42, 1661–1818, 1847–50, 1879–1958, and including some Enclosure Awards integrally indexed from 1879, DURH 4, original decrees and orders, 1613–1775, DURH 5.
(2) *Common Law* Judgment Rolls, 1344–1844, include pleas, recoveries, and deeds enrolled in the Court of Pleas, 1578–

1844, DURH 13, jury panels, temp. James I–Victoria, DURH 14; Minute Books of the Assizes and Gaol Delivery Sessions, 1770–1876, DURH 15, Crown Books, 1753–1876, DURH 16, jury panels at the Assizes, 1702–38, DURH 19, Assize proceedings, 1662–1775, DURH 19, indictments, 1582–1877, DURH 17, depositions, 1843–76, DURH 18, estreats from Halmote Courts, Quarter Sessions and Assizes, 1576–1774, DURH 20. Returns of Members of Parliament, 1722–1865, DURH 3. Affidavits of attorneys' clerks, 1750–1834, indexed, 1785–1842, and giving dates and places of residence, DURH 9; admissions of attorneys, 1660–1723, DURH 3/218, Oath Roll, 1730–1837, DURH 3/217. Alehouse recognizances, 1583–4, convictions and informations against Quakers, 1671–85, and petitions and reports for conveyances by infants, 1764–1801, DURH 8.
see *Assizes*

Dutch East Indies
see *Indonesia*

E*e*

East Florida Claims Commission Enquiry into losses suffered on secession to Spain. Claims and reports, title deed lists and papers concerning the management of estates, 1740–89, with an index of claimants in the class list, T 77.

Ecclesiastical Causes Enrolments of writs *de excommunicato capiendo*, 1330–1813, and of *de contumace capiendo*, 1813–43, are on the Controlment Rolls of the Court of King's Bench, KB 29, continued up to 1880 in KB 5. These writs were directed towards the arrest by sheriffs of obstinate excommunicated individuals in contempt of the ecclesiastical courts so that their authority could be upheld and satisfaction made. The enrolments are in Latin to 1733, arranged by legal term, and contain numerical references to the indictments. Proceedings, 1272–1701, KB 27, 1702–1911, KB 28, under legal term and regnal year. Appeals from the ecclesiastical courts went from 1535 to the High Court of Delegates, from 1834 to the Judicial Committee of the Privy Council.
see *Delegates, High Court of, Divorce, Ecclesiastical Causes, Court of High Commission for, Excommunication, King's Bench, Court of, Privy Council, Judicial Committee of the, Testamentary Causes*

Ecclesiastical Causes, Court of High Commission for The Court was set up in 1583 to investigate alleged offences including those against the Acts of Supremacy and Uniformity 1559; it served as the ecclesiastical counterpart of the Star Chamber, but was inferior to the High Court of Delegates, and was abolished in 1641. Minute Books, 1634–40, SP 16, printed in *Calendar of State Papers (Domestic Series) of the reign of Charles I*.
see *Delegates, High Court of*

Ecclesiastical Returns Made and signed by incumbents of total attendances at church or chapel in England and Wales, on 30 March 1851, with average attendance during the previous year, and setting out the type of accommodation provided for worship, number of services, and occasionally additional comments, arranged by county, census registration district and sub-district, HO 129.

Ecuador Guayaquil, births, marriages and deaths of Britons, 1879–96, FO 521/2, registers of British subjects, 1915–21, of deeds, 1850–99, and passports issued, 1915–34, FO 521.

Embassies and Legations, British Letter Books and correspondence, 1568–1796, SP 105, other archives of the seventeenth- and eighteenth-centuries are in SP 110. Letters to British Consuls, 1831–54, T 28.
see *Foreign Office*, and under individual countries, *Offices, Royal and Public*

Emigrants Licences to pass beyond the seas, including to St Kitts, 1633–4, 5 June 1634, 1634–5; Barbados, 1634–5, 1677; New England, 24 April 1634, 1634–5, March–September 1637; Virginia and Maryland, 1677, in E 157; all printed. Weekly emigration returns under English and Welsh ports, and recording names, ages, occupations, place of abode, intended destination and purpose of journey, with the name and type of vessel in which passengers sailed, 1773–6 (gaps, 13–18 April, 27 April–9 May 1774, and 7–12 November 1775), with a nominal card index, and of Scottish emigrants to America, 1774–5, T 47/9–12. Both series are published. Medical journals of emigrant ships, listed alphabetically by ship, 1825–53, ADM 101/76–79. Registers of births and deaths of emigrants at sea, 1847–54, CO 386/169, deaths at sea, 1854–69, CO 386/171–72; ships' passenger lists, arranged chronologically under port of departure, 1890–1960, BT 27, registers of passenger lists, by month and port, 1906–51, on open access, BT 32. Poor Law Union papers, arranged alphabetically by county and Union, and then chronologically by date, include references to intending emigrants supported by the local Boards of Guardians, 1834–1909, MH 12, with subject indexes, 1836–1920, in MH 15; other correspondence from Urban and Rural District Councils to the Poor Law Board in London, 1847–71, MH 13, and on emigration, 1853–4, MH 13/252; correspondence from the Board concerning emigration, 1836–76, MH 19/22; official sanctions for expenditure on assisted emigration of the poor, 1916–32, MH 64. Original correspondence, America and West Indies, 1606–1822, CO 5, Colonial papers, 1574–1757, CO 1, both printed up to 1738 in *Calendar of State Papers, Colonial, America*

and West Indies; Barbados, original correspondence, 1681–1951, CO 28, Entry Books of correspondence, 1627–1872, CO 29. Plantation books, including charters, Commissions and warrants of appointment, 1678–1806, PC 5, Privy Council Registers, 1613–1783, PC 2, both classes being calendared in *Acts of the Privy Council of England, Colonial Series, 1613–1783*, five volumes, and volume VI includes Unbound Papers for the period 1676–1783, in PC 1. Original Correspondence relating to emigration to the colonies, 1817–96, including lists of settlers in Australia, North America and the West Indies, 1819, 1820–25, CO 384, list of North American settlers, 1837–8, CO 384/51; registers of correspondence 1850–96, CO 428; Entry Books of correspondence, 1814–71, including letters concerning bounties and loans to emigrants to Australia, 1831–2, CO 385, and a list of Scottish settlers in Canada, 1815, CO 385/2; list of settlers intending to go to Canada, enrolled at Edinburgh, 1815, AO 3/144; original correspondence relating to British North America and Canada, 1700–1922, CO 42, and 1816–68, CO 6, register of correspondence on emigration there, 1850–63, CO 327/1–2, emigration registers, 1864–8, CO 328; Original Correspondence and Entry Books of the Agent General for Emigration, the Land and Emigration Commissioners, and South Australian Commissioners, 1833–94, including embarkation registers of land purchasers and labourers, 1835–41, a register of emigrant labourers' applications for free passages to South Australia, 1836–41 (partially indexed), registers of applications from convicts' families for assisted passages to the colonies, 1848–73, CO 386; correspondence relating to Overseas Settlement, 1918–25, CO 721, 1925–36, DO 57, and correspondence and papers concerning migration to the Dominions, 1943–51, DO 114/107; applications for assisted passages to Australia of those born there and now resident in the United Kingdom, 1947–8, DO 35/3368, appointments of escorts for boys aged between fifteen and seventeen emigrating under the Big Brother Scheme, 1947–52, DO 35/3383; New South Wales Original Correspondence, 1784–1903, CO 201, Entry Books of correspondence, 1786–1873, CO 202; New Zealand Company records, 1837–61, including a register of cabin passengers, 1839–50, their applications, 1839, register of passage allowance certificates, 1842–3, list of maintained emigrants, 1839–42, register of emigrant labourers applying for free passages, their original applications and lists of emigrants, 1839–50 (indexed), lists of candidates for employment, 1839–50, receipts for remittance payments to emigrant labourers' families, 1841–4, register of land orders, 1839–43, and a list of German emigrants, 1840, all in CO 208; Cape of Good Hope, original correspondence, 1808–1910, CO 48, including lists of settlers, 1819, CO 48/41–46, 1820, CO 48/52–53, and in 1827, CO 48/57; Entry Books of correspondence, 1795–1872, CO 49; correspondence relating to Natal, 1849–1910, CO 357; leases of land and licences to work the coal mines in Labuan, 1848–69, CO 386.

see *Births at Sea, Colonies, Dominions and Dependencies, Convicts, Transportation of, Deaths and Burials at Sea, Evacuees, Marriages at Sea, Ships' Passenger Lists*, and under individual countries

Enclosures Of lands for grazing, or to consolidate an existing holding, enclosures were a common feature of the Tudor period, and gathered pace again in the eighteenth- and nineteenth-centuries. It was supposedly done by agreement between the lord of the manor and his tenants, though could be effected by Private Act of Parliament, or by General Act after 1801. Enrolments of awards and agreements, 1756–7, 1853, C 54, 1762–1849, CP 40 and CP 43, 1771–1832, E 13, 1817–51, E 159, 1760–1842, KB 122, all listed by county, place and giving reference number, in *Deputy Keeper's Report XXVII*, Appendix, pp 1–26. Enclosure awards, 1847–1936, MAF 1, various awards and orders, including Boundary Awards amended by them, 1845–1963, MAF 2; schedules of claims delivered to valuers by landowners and persons claiming rights of common, with valuers' awards, 1846–1913, MAF 24; Orders of Exchange made under Enclosure Acts 1845–1964, arranged by county, place, date, interested persons, and number, MAF 11; details of tithe extinguishment by Enclosure Act and Award, awards and apportionments, arranged alphabetically by county and place, 1836–*c*.1870, IR 18; extracts of awards relating to Crown lands, 1660–1918, CRES 6, correspondence, 1740–1867, arranged under county, then alphabetically by place, and dated, CRES 2, other extracts relating to enclosures of Crown lands by award, 1560–1953, LRRO 1; extracts of awards in the Duchy of Lancaster to temp. Victoria, DL 41, awards, 1775–1872, DL 45, listed 1760–1834 in the above *Report*, Appendix, pp 27–9, enquiries prior to making an award, 1558–1853, DL 44; awards in the Palatinate of Chester before 1830, CHES 38, and in the Palatinate of Durham, 1632–1836, listed alphabetically by county, and then by place, DURH 4, 1632–1834, DURH 26.

see *Tithes*

Error, Writs of In relation to a defect on the record of a criminal trial, these transferred proceedings from an inferior to a superior court (of King's Bench) for review. They were abolished in 1907. Petitions, giving full details of the case, the grounds on which the writ was based, and signed by the petitioner, 1661–1782, SP 44, described in *Calendar of State Papers (Domestic Series)* to 1704, and *Calendar of Home Office Papers of the reign of George III*, for 1760–75; petitions, 1784–1898, HO56.

see *King's Bench (Crown Side), Court of, State Paper Office*

Escheators Officers appointed by the Crown to enquire into its financial interests derived from feudal incidents, for instance on the deaths of tenants-in-chief of the Crown and before livery of seisin to the next heir, or prior to the granting of a licence to alienate land, and with a right to escheat (take into possession) lands on reversion to the King on failure of heirs, or because of felony, treason, or judgment of outlawry against their owner. The post was abolished in 1660. Certificates of election, arranged under county, and regnal year, with a nominal index, temp. Edward I (thirteenth century)–Charles I, C267, 1570–temp. Charles II, with a nominal and place-name index, C202; writs of appointment, enrolled on the Fine Rolls to 1641, C60, with printed *Calendars*, 1272–1509; letters patent of appointment in the Palatinate of Durham, 1618–43, DURH 3/153–54. Escheators' files, temp. Henry III (thirteenth century)–Richard III, including inquisitions into goods and chattels of felons and outlaws, and lands alienated without a licence, and writs of livery of seisin, E153; accounts relating to revenues arising from escheated or forfeited lands, temp. Henry III–James I, E136.

see *Alienation, Inquisitions* ad quod damnum, *Inquisitions post mortem*

Estate Duty Imposed from 1894 on the value of a deceased's real and personal estate, at the prevailing rate, and including that under a settlement passing on death from 1 August the same year, it was abolished for deaths on or after 13 March 1975, and replaced by Capital Transfer Tax. Registers of estates on which duty was imposed, arranged chronologically, and giving details of the probate registry where a will was proved or letters of administration were granted, the date of death, of the will, probate or administration grant, names and addresses of executors or administrators, names of beneficiaries with their relationship to the deceased, their subsequent marriages or deaths before duty was due, and their share of the estate, with duty payable and when paid, 1894–1903, IR 26, to which there are annual indexes in IR 27; cases of delayed payments because of special circumstances such as bequests to the nation, IR 62; petitions concerning assessment, with orders, answers, evidence and other papers, 1888–1917, E 188.

see *Death Duty, Probate Duty, Succession Duty*

Estates, Administration of
see *Administration, Letters of, Bona Vacantia Division, Intestacy, Procurator General, Her Majesty's, Treasury Solicitor*

Estonia Pernau, births to Britons, 1894–1930, deaths, 1894–1933, FO 399/11–12; Tallinn (Reval), births to Britons, 1866–1940, marriages, 1921–39, deaths, 1875–1940, FO 514/1–9.

Evacuees In 1940 the Children's Overseas Reception Board was set up for the care of children, including orphans, going accompanied or otherwise from the European War Zone: registers of child applicants to go to Australia, Canada, New Zealand and South Africa, 1940, selected case files, 1940–46, escorts files, listed by name, 1940–46, casualties and survivors of the sinking of *SS City of Benares*, 1940, DO 131/106–12; casualties among children going to New Zealand, 1941–5, DO 131/17–18; lists of mothers and children evacuated to America and now in the United Kingdom, 1942–4, DO 131/31.

see *World War II*

Exchequer Chamber, Court of A title used by four appellate courts: as a court of error from the Exchequer from 1357, and from the fourteenth century to decide on difficult points of law, from 1585 as a court of Equity for the Exchequer and a court of error from the Court of King's Bench, and from 1830 as a Court of Appeal from the Courts of King's Bench, Common Pleas, and Exchequer. In 1875 its business was transferred to the Court of Appeal. Minute Books, setting out decrees and orders made by the Court in Equity cases, 1584–1841, E 162, and in revenue cases, 1616–1888, E 161. Appeals from the Court of King's Bench (Plea Side), 1702–1875, KB 122, Entry Books of Causes, 1675–1876, KB 139.

see *Appeal, Court of*

Exchequer (Equity Side), Court of Evolved in the late fifteenth century, it covered a wide variety of suits, mainly relating to debts, wills, land, mineral rights, and tithe disputes, until absorbed into the Court of Chancery in 1842. The records are in English. Bills, answers and depositions, temp. Henry VII–Philip and Mary, with a descriptive list, E 111, bills and answers, temp. Henry VIII–1841, listed, E 112 (with access to the class via the Bill Books, 1558–1841, giving suit numbers, and arranged under county, IND 1/16820–53); replications and rejoinders, 1558–1841, partially indexed from 1700, E 193; Appearance Books, under the name of defendant, 1558–1841, E 107; depositions made before the Barons of the Exchequer, and listed alphabetically by plaintiff and by defendant, temp. Elizabeth–1841, E 133, depositions by Commission, taken in the provinces, listed chronologically, for the same period, E 134, with a typescript index of deponents, 1559–1695; affidavits, temp. Elizabeth–1774, E 207, 1695–1822, E 218, 1774–1841, E 103; exhibits, *c*.1650–*c*.1850, E 140, and seventeenth–nineteenth century, with a descriptive list, and card index of known plaintiffs, E 219; reports and certificates, 1648–1841, indexed by plaintiff, E 194; miscellaneous reports, temp. Charles II–1841, E 195; original decrees and orders, 1580–1663, E 128, with a supplementary series, to *c*.1840, E 129, original decrees, 1663–1841, E 130, original orders, 1663–1842, listed, E 131; Entry Books of decrees and orders, Series I, 1558–1606, E 123, Series II, 1603–25, E 124, Series III, 1625–62, E 125, Series IV (decrees only), 1604–1841, E 126, Series V (orders only), 1661–1841, E 127, all of these being listed; decrees and orders, sixteenth century–1841, E 159; Minute Books, containing decrees and orders enrolled in Exchequer Chamber, 1584–1841, E 162. Petitions, including those relating to funds paid in and out of the Court, 1800–41, listed by party, E 185, Account Books of funds of Court, 1675–1841, E 217.

Exchequer Division of the High Court of Justice Set up in 1875 to replace the

Exchequer of Pleas, and abolished in March 1880, its common law cases then going to the Queen's Bench Division, and the revenue suits to the Chancery Division. Specimens of Judgment Books, 1875, 1876, 1880, with indexes giving the names of defendants, cause number, and date, J 89; pleadings, 1875–80, with a card index to case titles on open access, J 55; common law depositions, 1875–80, J 16, indexed in IND 1/6631; affidavits, 1876–80, J 7 and J 5; some appeals from inferior courts to this Division, giving details of the Court's decision and arranged chronologically, 1875–80, are in KB 25. see *Chancery Division of the High Court of Justice, King's Bench Division of the High Court of Justice*

Exchequer of Pleas A common law court, it originally had jurisdiction over revenue matters where the Crown had an interest, but was widened to encompass disputes between subjects, which rendered the plaintiff less able (*quo minus*) to pay his own debts to the Crown. In 1875 it became part of the Exchequer Division of the High Court, and in 1880 its business passed to the Queen's Bench Division. The records are in Latin until 1733. Plea Rolls, 1235–1875, including tithe suits, temp. Edward IV (fifteenth century)– George III, E 13, with a printed *Calendar*; posteas recording an account of the proceedings, dating from the nineteenth century, PRO 30/44.

Excise, Officers of Minute Books, containing details of appointments, postings, praise or censure, and retirement, 1695– 1867, integrally indexed, CUST 47; Entry Papers, being letters of recommendation, giving age, birthplace, marital status and character reference for each applicant, and from the Excise officer

having trained him, setting out standard of proficiency in writing, spelling and arithmetic, 1820–70, with an alphabetical index, CUST 116; miscellaneous records, including letters patent of appointment, 1660–1895, CUST 109; Irish Excise Board Establishment, 1824–9, minutes and appointments, February 1824–May 1830, English officers in Ireland, 1826–9, appointments, 1827–33, Irish Excise Surveying Establishment, 1825, CUST 110; Establishment Book of the Irish Board of Customs, 1684–1820, includes excisemen, CUST 20/33–153; Establishment lists and appointments of Irish Revenue Police, embodied to combat illicit making of malt and spirits, 1830–57, CUST 111. Quarterly salary lists of English officers, 1705– 1835, T 44, and in Scotland, 1708–1832, with Establishment lists for the collection of Excise and duties on salt, malt and tobacco, T 45; registers of Scottish maltsters' bonds, 1848–73, CUST 120. Pension records, containing also widows' pensions in which names and dates of children's births may be found, 1856– 1922, CUST 39/157–59 (closed 75 years). Correspondence with the Treasury, 1668–1839, indexed, CUST 48; outletters from the Treasury, 1667–71, 1801–50, T 11. see *Inland Revenue Life Assurance and Benevolent Fund Society*

Excommunication Significations of excommunication, written in Latin to 1733, and in which details of residence, occupation, paternity and offence giving rise to excommunication might be given, 1220– 1611, C 85, temp. Elizabeth–Victoria, with a card index by diocese, C 207; Palatinate of Chester, 1378–96, 1551, 1663–8, 1671–90, CHES 38. Enrolments of writs to enforce excommunications are on the

Controlment Rolls, 1330–1843, KB 29, and 1844–80, KB 5; subsequent proceedings are recorded on the Coram Rege Rolls, 1272–1701, KB 27, and Plea Rolls, 1702–1911, KB 28.

see *Canterbury, Prerogative Court of, Ecclesiastical Causes, King's Bench (Crown Side), Court of*

Exhumation of Bodies Warrants, 1871–87, HO 15, thereafter to 1921, HO 85.

Existence, Certificates of Relating to persons entitled to salaries, annuities or pensions from the Crown and produced by them to the appropriate pay office to prove their survival, 1578–1724, E 403/2417 (1), temp. Elizabeth, E 407/72–6, and of military personnel, 1770–1820, WO 18.

see *Annuities, Deaths, Concealed, Offices, Royal and Public, Tontines*

Exploration Africa: correspondence, 1794–1843, CO 2, with indexes, 1794–1870, under colony, CO 714; General Correspondence concerning Africa, 1825–1905, FO 2, registers of correspondence, 1817–1911, FO 566, with indexes to correspondence, 1810–90, arranged by subject and personal name, FO 605. Ships' logs, arranged under 'Explorations', 1669–1852, ADM 51, and supplementary Series II, Explorations 1766–1861, ADM 55, both listed alphabetically by ship.

Extents, Ancient Surveys and valuations made by sheriffs and escheators relating to forfeited lands, mainly of the Knights Templar and attainted nobility, temp. John (thirteenth century)–Henry VI (fifteenth century), E 142.

see *Crown Lands, Felons and Fugitives, Forfeitures and Escheats, Manorial Courts and Records*

Extradition Confidential out-letters, 1798–1864, HO 79, 1871–1905, HO 151; correspondence and papers of the New York Consulate concerning extradition, 1893–1901, FO 285.

Eyre, General Justices in eyre were regularly established in 1176, with delegated authority from the King to go on circuit throughout the kingdom once every seven years to try causes and review local administration, which was suspended during their sessions. By Magna Carta 1215, the circuits became annual, but as the power of the justices in Assize increased, theirs fell away, and the eyres effectively ended by 1294. The records are in Latin. Eyre Rolls, temp. Richard I (twelfth century), KB 26, 1201–1348, JUST 1, files of writs, 1248–c.1450, JUST 4; pleas in the Palatinate of Chester, 1306–1523, CHES 17.

F*f*

Falkland Islands Births and baptisms, 1853–1951, RG 32, marriages, 1854–1951, RG 34, burials, 1854–1951, RG 35/20–44, all indexed in RG 43; land orders, 1859–74, CO 386/144.

Falklands War 1982, Despatches, casualties, dead, missing and wounded, awards and decorations, published in *The London Gazette*, with subject index, ZJ 1.

Fee-Farm Rents Perpetual dues arising out of land held in fee simple and payable by the freeholder. Records of the sale of fee-farm rents, 1649–60, SP 26, listed in *Calendar of State Papers (Domestic Series) of the Commonwealth*, other sales, 1649–60, in SP 28, particulars of sales during the same period, E 308 and E 367, plus counterparts of deeds of sale, E 307; surrenders of fee-farm rents, 1660–87, C 75; deeds of bargain and sale of lands conveyed by Charles II to trustees, 1670–73, are enrolled on the Close Rolls, C 54, with abstracts in IND 1/17347; other sales, arranged alphabetically by county, 1670–1833, LR 1, 1834–52, LRRO 37, 1852–90, LRRO 16 (indexed in LRRO 64); out-letters concerning sales, 1789–1891, CRES 24. Warrants for grants in fee-farm of the Duchy of Lancaster, temp. Henry VII–George IV, DL 12.

Felons and Fugitives Conviction of a felony brought with it forfeiture of goods and lands, plus the death penalty, unless found guilty of the lesser offence of petty larceny. Forfeiture was abolished in 1870. Fugitives were persons fleeing to escape trial for felony. The records are in Latin to 1733. Extents of lands and goods of felons and fugitives from justice, 1554–8, E 387. Commissions of enquiry into lands forfeited to the Crown, 1636–1854, C 205; enquiries into goods and chattels in the Duchy of Lancaster, 1558–1853, DL 44, with a published list. Escheators' accounts, temp. Henry III (thirteenth century)–James I, relating to revenues arising from forfeited property, which to 1576 give details of the property, where situated, its extent and value, under headings including 'goods of outlaws, felons and fugitives', while from 1577 this information is no longer forthcoming, E 136; escheators' files include inquisitions as to goods and chattels of felons, temp. Henry III–Richard III, E 153. Blood money certificates upon conviction of felons, detailing rewards paid to informers, 1649–1800, E 407/27–30. Warrants for arrest, jail or movement of officers and seamen for breaches of naval or criminal law, 1805–56, warrants for execution of those convicted by the High Court of Admiralty, 1802–56, respites of execution, 1802–20, HCA 55. *Hue and Cry*, and *Police Gazette*, 1828–45, giving descriptions of fugitives, HO 75, and fortnightly Supplement A of *The Police*

Gazette, 1914–38, 1957, 1959, and *Police Gazette* or *Hue and Cry*, 1834, 1937, MEPO 6/66–76.
see *Assizes, Convicts, Outlaws, Prisons*

Female Servants, Tax on 1785–92.
see *Land Tax and Assessed Taxes*

Fencibles Local auxiliary forces under the control of county lords lieutenant, training for a few weeks each year. Musters of Fencible Infantry, 1799–1802, Fencible Cavalry, 1794–1800, listed alphabetically by county, WO 13.
see *Volunteers*

Feudal Aids
see *Aids*

Field Books
see *Valuation Office*

Fine Rolls Enrolments recording moneys or payments in kind to the King for passing or renewing charters, licences to alienate or for pardons, for grants of privileges, liberties, offices, lands, wardships, and exemptions from tolls and other dues, pardons for exoneration from knighthood, letters of safe conduct, naturalization or denization, and other marks of royal favour. The entries are in Latin. Temp. John (thirteenth century)–1641, C 60, with printed *Calendars*, 1272–1509, and a Latin transcript of those dating from John's reign, described as *Oblata Rolls*; Palmer's index of places and an alphabetical calendar of persons run up to 1641.

Fines, Feet of The chirograph (court copy) of the agreement (concord) to settle a fictitious dispute between a purchaser (the querient) and the vendor (deforciant), whereby the latter recognized that the former held the land by his gift, and in return for a specified sum quit any future claim which he or his heirs might have to it for the duration of an agreed period, or forever. The earliest surviving chirograph dates from 1189, and the records are in Latin until 1733. Fines were abolished in 1834. Writs of covenant, calling on the deforciant to keep to the terms of the agreement, and including approximate valuations of the land involved, with a note of the pre-fine of a tenth of the value payable to the King, 1576–1661, A 7, and Nil Books, where the land's value was too low to attract a pre-fine, 1668–1800, A 8; post-fines (King's Silver), payable once leave was given to agree, 1560–1834, CP 34, 1595/6–1837, E 374, in the Palatinate of Lancaster, 1400–1585, PL 15, 1586–1834, PL 18; concords, temp. Edward II (fourteenth century)–William IV, arranged alphabetically, CP 24, for the Palatinate of Durham, 1661–1834, DURH 11, Palatinate of Lancaster, 1362–1834, PL 17; notes of fines, temp. Henry III (thirteenth century)–William IV, arranged chronologically by regnal year and legal term, CP 26; feet of fines, temp. Henry II (twelfth century)–1838, arranged alphabetically by county, by regnal year and term, CP 25, with manuscript indexes and calendars, 1509–1798, on open access, arranged by regnal year, then alphabetically by county, giving name of querient, deforciant, and place; feet of fines in the Palatinate of Chester, 1307–1830, CHES 2, also enrolled on the Plea Rolls, 1255–1831, CHES 29, and 1280–1831, including original writs and concords, CHES 31, and 1585–temp. Anne, CHES 32, Palatinate of Durham, 1535–1834, DURH 12, Palatinate of Lancaster, 1362–1834, original feet and including writs and concords, PL 17, enrolments of fines, 1400–1585, PL 15, 1585–1834, PL 18; proclamations of the fines in court, 1620–1841, CP 27.

Finland Helsinki (Helsingfors), births to Britons, 1914–24, deaths, 1924, FO 753/19, FO 768/5; Kristinestad, deaths, 1928, FO 756/1; Raahe (Brahestad), deaths, 1930, FO 755/1; Tampere, births, 1906–23, deaths 1909–34, FO 769/1–2; Turku (Abo), births and deaths, 1928–9, FO 754/1–2; Vibora (Viipuri), births, 1924–31, deaths, 1929–37, FO 757/1–3.

First Fruits and Tenths were the first year's income from a benefice (annates), and a tenth of the annual value of its spiritual and temporal possessions payable to the Pope and from 1535 diverted to the King. They were extinguished or redeemed in 1926.

see *Clergy*

Fishermen Register of apprentice fishermen at Colchester, 1639–44, HCA 30/897; registers of apprenticeship indentures, 1704–57, 1804–44, BT 167/103; five-yearly samples of apprenticeship indentures, 1895–1935, BT 152. Registers of certificates of service for skippers and mates etc of fishing boats, arranged by certificate number and giving details of date and place of birth, 1880–98, BT 129, certificates issued between 1883 and 1908 for service 1883–92, also under certificate number, BT 130, both records being indexed in BT 138/1–3 (which also give dates and places of birth). 10% sample of agreements and crew lists of vessels under eighty tons, 1884–1919, BT 144, and 1920–38, BT 99, the class lists recording addresses of other repositories in which the other agreements have been dispersed. Registers of protections against impressment into the Royal Navy, 1755–8, 1770–81, 1787–1815, for the Southern Whale Fishery, 1777–1811, and Greenland Whale Fishery, 1793–1811, ADM 7.

Selected returns of five-year engagements as Royal Naval Reserve, recruited, 1860–1913, arranged by deck, and giving personal details, training, service record and retainers paid, BT 164; any subsequent five-year engagement is often noted on the back of the entry. Musters and pay lists of fishermen recruited as part-time Sea Fencibles, 1798–1810, ADM 28. Census returns, 4–20 April 1861, RG 9, 25 March–14 April 1871, RG 10, 26 March–15 April 1881, RG 11, and 4 April–3 May 1891, RG 12, record crews in port or arriving there during set intervals before and after enumeration night.

see *Fishing Vessels, Merchant Seamen*

Fishing Vessels 10% sample of agreements and crew lists of boats under eighty tons, 1884–1919, BT 144, 1920–38, BT 99, the class list showing the disposition of the rest. Census returns of those boats in port or arriving, 4–20 April 1861, RG 9, 25 March–14 April 1871, RG 10, 26 March–15 April 1881, RG 11, and 4 April–3 May 1891, RG 12.

Fleet Prison Housed debtors and those persons in contempt of the common law courts of Chancery, Common Pleas, and Exchequer. It was closed in 1842 and replaced by Queen's Prison. Commitment Books, giving date of admission, on whose authority, with notes of subsequent action taken and if discharged, 1685–1842, PRIS 1, indexed from 1725; orders for commitment, 1758–1842, PRIS 2, the numbered entries corresponding with those in PRIS 1; discharges, recording the original warrants for discharge, 1775–1842, PRIS 3; Commitment Books, entry books of discharges, habeas corpus books, and lists of prisoners, 1696–1842, PRIS 10. Unauthenticated registers of marriages, and some baptisms, performed

outside Fleet Prison, 1667–*c*.1777, RG 7.
see *Queen's Prison*

Flying Corps, Royal Formed in 1912 out of the British Army, and amalgamated on 1 April 1918 with the Royal Naval Air Service to create the Royal Air Force. Medals from World War I, 1917–26, WO 329; Despatches, casualties, awards and decorations announced in *The London Gazette*, with subject indexes, ZJ 1. Disablement pensions and gratuities, 1916–20, PMG 42, pensions paid to relatives of deceased officers, 1916–20, PMG 44. Representative medical sheets, giving age, rank and treatment, 1916–17, MH 106/2202–6.
see *Air Force, Royal, Medals, Naval Air Service, Royal*

Foreign Churches in England Authenticated registers of births, baptisms, marriages and some burials, of Walloon, French, Huguenot, Dutch, German, and Swiss congregations, 1567–1840, are to be found in RG 4, unauthenticated registers (including a series from the Greek and Russian Orthodox congregations in London), 1646–1921, RG 8; both classes are listed alphabetically by county and then by place.
see *Aliens, Refugees*

Foreign Merchants Passes allowing them to travel in safety within the kingdom during a prescribed period, usually twenty days, to specified ports or places giving name, country or place of abode, and destination, 1697–1784, SP 44/386–413.
see *Aliens*

Foreign Office General correspondence, 1745–1905, FO 83, to which there are nominal and place-name indexes, 1814–93, FO 802, including France, 1761–8, and United States of America from 1793;

General Correspondence, 1817–1919, FO 566, indexed, 1761–1893, FO 605; card index to correspondence, 1906–19, subject indexes to General Correspondence, 1920–51, FO 409. The correspondence itself is arranged in classes by country.

Foreign Service Sign manual warrants for foreign service, 1777–1863, HO 37; licences to enter foreign service, 1782–1877, indexed, HO 38.

Foreign Troops
see *Army, British*

Forest Proceedings Taken in connection with offences committed in the Royal Forests against animals, game, and for land encroachment. The records are in Latin to 1733. Temp. John (thirteenth century)–Charles II, E 32, temp. Henry III (thirteenth century)–Charles II, E 101, temp. Henry III–1653, including rolls of fines and amercements for forest offences, inquisitions, and rolls of local forest courts, the latest containing claims of rights during the Commonwealth, E 146, temp. Henry VIII–Charles I, including claims and their enrolments before the Justices in Eyre of the Forest, and some grants of land, the material mainly relating to Charles I's attempt to reinforce the ancient Forest Laws, C 99; Duchy of Lancaster, temp. Henry III–Victoria, DL 39. Informations on intrusions into the Royal Forests and Wastes, 1217/18 onwards, E 159; commissions of enquiry into encroachments and intrusions, temp. Elizabeth–Victoria, E 178, Duchy of Lancaster, 1558–1853, DL 44. Encroachments in the Forest of Dean, 1781–1891, F 16, deeds and evidences, returns of encroachments, registers of claims and rights in this Forest and the New Forest, with deeds and awards, abstracts of leases, temp. Henry

VIII–1917, LRRO 5, presentments of offences in the New Forest, 1747–52, LRRO 37.

see *Crown Lands*

Forests, Royal Sales of encroached lands, 1852–90, LRRO 16, indexed in LRRO 64.

Forfeited Estates, Commissioners of see *Roman Catholics*

Forfeitures and Escheats Until 1870 the goods and chattels of a person convicted of a felony or under a judgment of outlawry were forfeit and his lands escheated to the Crown. Ancient extents of forfeited lands, temp. John (thirteenth century)–Henry VI (fifteenth century), E 142, listed by name and place; miscellaneous inquisitions, 1218–1484, C 145, with a printed *Calendar*; escheators' accounts, temp. Henry III (thirteenth century)–1578, E 136; special Commissions of enquiry concerning estates forfeited to the Crown, arranged by cause, 1607–1889, C 205; contained in the records of the Committee for Compounding with Delinquents, 1643–60, SP 23, with a printed *Calendar*. Reports and surveys of forfeited estates in Scotland, 1745–56, T 64.

see *Felons and Fugitives, Jacobite Rebellions, Roman Catholics*

Foundling Hospital, Coram's Fields, London Births, baptisms, deaths and burials, 1741–1838, and a marriage, 1754, RG 4/4328, 4396; many of the children were given the names of famous people or benefactors of the Hospital.

France and its Colonies Incomplete registers of deaths of British military personnel, 1914–21, RG 35/45–57; deaths of Britons in France, 1831–71, RG 35/

8–13, and its colonies, 1836–71, RG 35/14–16, index in RG 43; Boulogne, baptisms, 1815–96, marriages, 1829–95, burials, 1815–96, RG 33/37–48, indexed in RG 33/161; Brest, births, 1842, RG 33/155, indexed in RG 43/1; Calais, baptisms, 1817–78, marriages, 1818–72, burials, 1819–78, RG 33/50–55, indexed in RG 33/49; Damascus, births, 1934–5, marriages, 1935, FO 684/16–17; Diego Suarez, births, 1907–21, FO 711/1; Dieppe, births, 1872–92, deaths, 1871–94, FO 712/1–3; Le Havre, baptisms, marriages and burials, 1817–63, RG 33/56–57, indexed in RG 43/1, 7 and 3 respectively; Le Treport, births, 1917–26, deaths, 1899–1929, FO 713/1–2; Nantes, marriages, 1851–67, FO 384/1; Papeete, births, 1818–1941, marriages, 1845–1941, and deaths, 1845–1936, FO 687/23–32, indexed in FO 687/33, registers of British subjects, 1887–1921, FO 687/44–45, estates, wills, and deeds, 1840–1903, FO 687/8; Paris, baptisms, 1784–9, 1801–9, 1815–69, marriages, 1784–9, 1801–90, burials, 1784–9, 1801–69, RG 33/58–77, deaths, 1846–52, RG 35/11, indexed in RG 43, marriages, 1852–90, FO 83, indexed in FO 802/239, 1935–7, FO 630/1; Raiatea, births, marriages and deaths, 1853–64, FO 687/34, 1856–90, FO 687/36–38; Reunion, marriages, 1864–1921, FO 322/1–2, deaths, 1836–71, RG 35/14–16; Rouen, baptisms, 1843–4, RG 33/78, indexed in RG 43/1; St Omer, baptisms, 1817–47, RG 33/50, indexed in RG 33/49; Tamatave, deaths, 1935–40, FO 714/1; Tananarive (Antananarivo), births, 1865–68, FO 710/1. Certificates of passes from Exeter to France, 1634–5, E 157; accounts and claims, letters and vouchers for expenses during the war in Germany, 1765, SP 9/222–38; registers of payments made by the French government to British claimants under the Treaty of Paris 1815, 1835–53, PMG 64, and for violations of the Treaty of Commerce 1786, 1833–6, arranged alphabetically and including supporting documents and details of awards, T 78.

Freehold Estates Case files of applications for orders discharging or modifying restrictions on freehold or leasehold land arising out of covenants or otherwise, with the resultant orders made by the Official Arbitrator or Lands Tribunal, 1926–71, arranged by file number, LT 3, with indexes under names of applicants, giving a brief résumé of each case and outcome, its number and date of application, 1926–66, LT 4.

Friends, Society of Authenticated registers of Minutes of Meetings, recording births, marriages, deaths and burials in England and Wales, 1613–1841, listed alphabetically by county or county grouping, and then by Quarterly or Monthly Meeting, RG 6. Recusant Rolls, recording in Latin the names of people fined or imprisoned for non-attendance at church, giving abode and status, but not religious persuasion, and arranged by county, and for Wales, 1591–1691, E 376 and E 377; informations against Quakers, and convictions, in the Palatinate of Durham, 1671–85, DURH 8; Association Oath Roll, Colchester, 1696, C 213/473; Quakers' Affirmations, 30 October–27 November 1723, E 169; Oath rolls of Quaker attorneys, in the Exchequer of Pleas, 1831–85, E 3, in the Court of Common Pleas, 1835–42, CP 10.
see *Recusants*

Fugitives
see *Felons and Fugitives*

Gg

Gallantry, Awards for
see under respective Armed Services,
Medals, and under individual award

Garter, Most Noble Order of the The
country's most senior chivalric Order,
founded in 1348, and whose Companions
are limited in number to twenty-five.
Petitions, orders, precedent books, and
programmes of investitures, *c.*1520–
1920, LC 5; announced in *The London
Gazette*, 1665–1986, with sporadic subject indexes from 1790, and invariably
from 1848, ZJ 1.

**General Surveyors of Crown Lands,
Court of The**
see *Augmentations, Court of*

Gentlemen Pensioners, Band of Introduced by the Tudors, it was composed of
heavy cavalry, which with the Yeomen,
formed the royal guard. Wages paid quarterly or yearly to the Captain and other
named officers and men, 1557–1809,
E 407/1–2.

George Cross Instituted in 1940 as a
mark of gallantry and primarily designed
for civilians, or for fighting services where
no other purely military honour was
granted. Recommendations for civilian
awards, 1940–49, HO 250, and military
awards, 1941–6. AIR 2 Code B 30; Medals, 1940–48, MINT 16; citations up to

1986, in *The London Gazette* with subject
indexes, ZJ 1.

Germany Deaths of Britons, *c.*1831–
1920, RG 35/20–44, indexed in RG 43;
Aachen (Aix la Chapelle), deaths, 1925,
FO 604/7; Bavaria, baptisms, marriages
and deaths, 1860–61, FO 151/3, marriages, 1884–97. FO 149/99; Berlin,
births and deaths, 1944–5, births to
British subjects, 1947–53, and to citizens
of the United Kingdom and Colonies,
1949–54, FO 601/2–6, marriages, 1846–
90, FO 83, indexed in FO 802/239;
Bremen, births, 1872–1914, marriages,
1893–1908, declarations of intended marriage, 1903–14, 1921–33, FO 585/1–5;
Bremerhaven, births, 1872–93, FO 585/
1, declarations of marriage, 1903–14, FO
586/1; Breslau, births, 1929–38, deaths,
1932–38, FO 715/1–2; Cologne, births
and marriages 1850–66, deaths, 1850–66,
1879–81, FO 155/5–11, 17, births,
1880, marriages, 1920–34, FO 604/8–
10; Danzig (Grünberg), births, 1891–
1900, FO 634/16; Danzig, births, 1851–
1910, marriages, 1893, deaths,
1850–1914, FO 634/16–18; Darmstadt,
births, 1869–98, deaths, 1871–1905, FO
716/1–2, marriages, 1870–90, FO 83, indexed in FO 802/239; Dresden, births,
baptisms and burials, 1817–36, RG 33/
79, indexed in RG 43/1 and 3 respectively,
births and deaths, 1859–66, RG 33/80,
indexed in RG 43/1 and 3, births,

1901–7, marriages, 1899–1900, FO 292/2, 4–5, marriages, 1846–90, FO 83, indexed in FO 802/239; Düsseldorf, births, 1873–84, baptisms, 1903–7, marriages, 1873–8, deaths, 1876–84, FO 604/1–6, 8; Essen, births 1922–27, FO 604/11; Frankfurt, marriages, 1836–65, FO 208/90, 1846–69, FO 83, indexed in FO 802/239; Hanover, baptisms, marriages, deaths and burials, 1839–59, RG 33/81, indexed in RG 43/1, 7 and 3 respectively, births, 1861–6, FO 717/1, marriages, 1846–69, FO 83, indexed in FO 802/239; Karlsrühe, births, 1860–64, deaths, 1859–64, FO 718/1–2; Königsberg, marriages, 1857–1933, FO 509/1–4; Leipzig, marriages, 1850–65, deaths, 1850–69, FO 299/22; Munich, marriages, 1846–90, FO 83, indexed in FO 802/239; Saxony, marriages, 1850–65, deaths, 1850–69, FO 218/3; Stettin, births, 1864–1939, deaths, 1857–1933, FO 719/1–2; Stuttgart, marriages, 1847–90, FO 83, indexed in FO 802/239. Claims arising out of losses due to military operations during the War of Austrian Succession, 1748–50, and the Seven Years' War, 1762–72, SP 81, and in 1765, SP 9/222–38.

Gibraltar Applications for passports to, 1810–11, CO 323; register of wills at the Naval Hospital, 1809–15, ADM 105/40.

Gibraltar Burying Ground
see *Bethnal Green Protestant Dissenters' Burying Ground*

Graves and Tombstones, Removal of Copies of records of local authorities and Church Commissioners, and including some plans of plots, 1923–88, with inscriptions, 1601–1980, bearing lists of names, sometimes the full dedication and details of place of re-interment, RG 37 (some are closed).

Greece Athens, marriages at British embassies and legations, 1846–90, FO 83, indexed in FO 802/239; Ionian Islands, baptisms, marriages and burials, 1849–59, RG 33/82, indexed in RG 43/1, 7 and 3 respectively (indexes to births, baptisms and marriages, 1818–48, deaths and burials, 1836–48, are in the same indexes, but the registers are housed at the General Register Office, London).

Green Cloth, Board of The countinghouse of the Royal Household, made up of the Lord Steward, Treasurer, Comptroller and Master of the Household, with their assistants, it was replaced by the Lord Steward's Department in 1782. Draft Minutes, 1719–24, PRO 30/23.
see *Lord Steward's Department*

Greenwich Hospital, Royal Established in 1694 as a Royal Naval Hospital for infirm seamen and marines, it housed in-pensioners until 1869. Register of candidates for admission, 1737–1905, register of ratings' widows applying to work there as nurses, 1817–31, 1819–42, ADM 6; in-letters, including those relating to admissions of pensioners, 1702–1869, ADM 65; applications by warrant officers, ratings and marines for admission as in-pensioners, arranged alphabetically, with physical descriptions, record of disability and service details, 1791–1846, ADM 73/1–35, registers of in-pensioners, 1704–1812, ADM 73/36–39, rough entry books of pensioners, 1775–1869, ADM 73/51–64, general registers of pensioners and their families, 1825–66, ADM 73/42–50; out-pension paybooks, with signatures of recipients, 1781–1809, ADM 73/95–131, list of pensioners receiving medals, 1848–9, burial registers, 1844–1936, ADM 73/460–62, register of graves at the Royal Hospital Cemetery, 1857–1966, indexed, and registers, 1888–1966, 1857–1981, ADM 73/463–65; out-pensions paid to commissioned officers on top of half-pay at the discretion of the Admiralty, 1846–65, PMG 71; pensions paid to naval and marine officers, 1871–1931, 1951–61, ADM 165; special pensions paid to warrant officers unable to contribute to their own support, at the discretion of the Admiralty, depending on grade of disability and other circumstances, 1874–80, PMG 69; pensions paid to commissioned and warrant officers of the Coastguard, captains of the Royal Marines, 1866–1928, and Travers pension payments to retired naval officers, 1892–1928, PMG 70; registers of pensions and allowances to widows and children of seamen and marines, 1882–1917, and registers of their initial applications, 1892–1933, indexed, ADM 166. Registers of baptisms, 1720–1855, marriages, 1724–54, and burials, 1705–58, 1773–1857, at the Wesleyan Chapel attached to the Hospital, RG 4/1669–79, which also includes baptisms at the Royal Naval Asylum, 1822–56, and burials at the Royal Hospital School, 1807–56; baptisms at the Hospital and School, and burials, 1848–64, RG 8/16–18. Applications of children for admission to the School attached to the Hospital, arranged alphabetically, and almost all containing certificates of fathers' services, 1728–1870, ADM 73/154–389, children admitted, 1803–83, including school registers of both the Lower School, 1845–65, and Upper School, 1767–1865, entry and binding out of boys, 1728–1870, disposal of boy apprentices into the Navy from the Lower School, 1818–23, and receipts, 1846–54, with many of the entries recording details of birth or baptism, parents' marriage and father's service record, indexed, ADM 73/390–449; registers of claims by children, 1803–1930, including those of boys aged thirteen, 1867–1930, claims of children of deceased or distressed commissioned officers for places at schools at the expense of Hospital funds, 1883–1916, indexed, ADM 161; registers of claims by orphaned daughters of warrant officers, ratings, marines and Coastguard for maintenance, 1881–1911, 1951–9, with integral indexes, and for admission of orphan boys to orphanages, at the Hospital's expense, 1884–1959, indexed, ADM 162; registers of claims by children of commissioned officers, 1883–1922, ADM 163, with grants made for their education and maintenance, 1907–33, ADM 164. Entry and discharges of officers of the Hospital, 1695–1865, ADM 80/169, salaries paid, 1865–1957, indexed, ADM 80/170–1, 177–9; lists and registers of staff at the Hospital, 1736–1869, ADM 73/70–88, including a book of warrants for appointments of staff, 1800–65, register of appointments, 1851–64, Establishment Book, 1830–63, muster book of servants, 1865–9, register of nurses and servants, 1847–65, ADM 73; general entry book of nurses, 1704–1864, ADM 73/83–88, muster book of nurses, house labourers and servants, 1766–1863, ADM 73/84; register of nurses, 1783–1863, artificers' muster and wage books, 1845–66, ADM 73/132–53; salary lists and pensions, 1807–15, T 47; civil pensions to staff, 1871–1931, 1951–61, ADM 165; civil superannuation and allowances to staff at the School, 1867–75, PMG 24, and 1875–1928, PMG 70.

Greenwich Hospital Estates, Royal
These include lands coming to the

Hospital on the forfeiture of the Earl of Derwentwater, after the failed Jacobite Rebellion of 1715. Court rolls relating to manors held in Cumberland, Northumberland and Kent, 1473–1930 (in Latin to 1733, except for the Commonwealth period), ADM 74, deeds, 1340–1931, ADM 75, surveys and rentals, 1547–1928, including an undated list of tenants of the Derwentwater Estate, ADM 79.

Guernsey Births, marriages and deaths, 1831–1958, RG 32, indexed in RG 43. Census returns, 6 June 1841, HO 107, 30 March 1851, HO 107, 7 April 1861, RG 9, 2 April 1871, RG 10, 3 April 1881, RG 11, and 5 April 1891, RG 12. Association Oath Roll, 1696, C 213/463. Pensions paid to naval and military personnel, their widows or orphaned children, 1842–52, giving details of former rank and regiment at retirement, nature and amount of pension, and any transfer elsewhere, plus the date of death, WO 22/205. Calendars of prisoners, giving age, occupation, charge, verdict and sentence, 1868–1958, HO 140 (some closed 75 years). Correspondence, 1771–82, SP 47, included up to 1775 in *Calendar of Home Office Papers of the reign of George III*.
see *Channel Islands*

H*h*

Hair-Powder Tax 1795–98.
see *Land Tax and Assessed Taxes*

Haiti Births to Britons, 1833–50, marriages, 1833–93, deaths, 1833–50, FO 866/14, 21–22, births, 1870–1907, FO 376/1–2, deaths, 1836–71, RG 35/16.
see *Dominican Republic, Santo Domingo*

Hawaii Honolulu, births to Britons, 1848–93, FO 331/59, marriages, 1850–53, RG 33/155, indexed in RG 43/7. Registers of British subjects, 1895–1944, FO 331/60–61.

Hawkers and Pedlars Registers of licences, 24 June 1697–24 June 1699, arranged in numerical order, and giving the date, residence, name, number of horses traded with, the date surety was offered and in what sum, and when received by the Audit Office, AO 3/370–71; appointments of Stamp Distributors and others to issue and inspect licences, under county and town, 1832–60, IR 51.

Health, Medical Officers of Applications for appointment, accompanying testimonials, curriculum vitae and names of successful candidates for posts, with salaries offered and terms of appointment to Union workhouses, arranged alphabetically by county, then Union, 1834–

1909, MH 12, with subject indexes, 1836–1920, MH 15; appointments, giving the date of commencement, pay rate and date and cause of resignation or dismissal, 1837–1921, MH 9; appointments, arranged alphabetically under local authority, 1868–1935, MH 48; correspondence with the Local Government Board on public health matters, 1872–1904, arranged alphabetically by county, MH 30, with registers of correspondence, 1867–1920, MH 31.

Health, Ministry of Personal files, concerning appointments to outside Committees and bodies, retirement pensions and superannuation of senior officers in Established posts on the Local Government Board, and including some obituaries, 1875–1969, with a nominal list, MH 107.

Hearth Tax Levied 1662–89, it was farmed out to contractors for collection between 1666 and 1668, and from 1674. It was paid in two equal half-yearly instalments on all non-industrial hearths, with exemption given to the poor. Parish returns of payers, and total hearths attracting tax, plus exemption certificates, Michaelmas 1662–Lady Day 1666, and Michaelmas 1669–Lady Day 1674, listed by county, chronologically by date, and then by hundred, City or Borough, E 179; arrears schedules, arranged alpha-

betically by county, then by parish, 1665–76, E 178.
see *Subsidy, Lay*

Heirs
see *Age, Proofs of, Homage, Certificates of, Inquisitions post mortem*

Heraldic Funeral Certificates Heraldic funerals probably commenced in the fifteenth century, and gave an opportunity for the display of coats of arms in ways conforming to the rank or status of the deceased; they were originally presided over by the heralds, and from 1568 certification was taken by them from relatives or executors of the deceased, about date of death and burial, residence, marriage and progeny, plus a description of the arms; the practice declined after the Restoration in 1660. Certificates, temp. Charles I, mainly relating to Derbyshire, Nottinghamshire and Wales, SP 17 Case G.
see *Arms, Coats of Arms, College of,*

Hidage
see *Carucage*

High Seas, Crimes on the
see *Admiralty, High Court of, Central Criminal Court*

Highway Boards Correspondence with district auditors, district surveyors and clerks of the Boards, 1879–1900, arranged alphabetically by Board, MH 21, registers of correspondence, 1879–1900, MH 22.

Highwaymen Blood money certificates issued on conviction of highwaymen, detailing rewards to informers, 1649–1800, E 407/27–30.

Holland
see *Netherlands*

Homage, Certificates of Warrants addressed to the Keeper of the Privy Seal to prepare warrants for writs of livery of seisin to an heir of lands held as tenant-in-chief of the Crown, that he might be presented and do homage to the King, temp. Richard II (fourteenth century)–Henry VII, PS 01.
see *Inquisitions post mortem*

Hong Kong Deaths of Britons from enemy action, 1941–45, RG 33/11, indexed in RG 43/14.

Honours and Awards Out-letters, 1806–1922, indexed, HO 117; Honours Lists and papers, 1915–41, PREM 2; lists up to 1986 in *The London Gazette*, with subject indexes, ZJ 1; recommendations for Birthday Honours Lists, 1919–45, AIR 2 Code B 30, 1938–9, ADM 116/4016, and 1939–45, ADM 116 Code 85. Returns of recipients of foreign honours and awards and of foreigners receiving British ones, 1745–1905, FO 83, with selected files, 1906–60, FO 371, to which there is a card index, 1906–19, and printed index, 1920–51, in FO 409.
see *Medals* and under individual honours and awards

Honours, Colonial Original Correspondence, including Despatches, 1858–1940, 1947–52, CO 448, (closed 50 years), register of correspondence, 1859–1926, CO 728, register of out-letters, 1872–1934, CO 729. Honours Lists and papers, 1915–41, PREM 2; citations in *The London Gazette* to 1986, with subject indexes, ZJ 1.

Horse Guards and Park Gates Entry Books Out-letters giving authority to named persons to ride in and out of St James's Park, London, 1809–1921, HO 120.

Horse Tax 1784–1874.
see *Land Tax and Assessed Taxes*

Hospitals Establishment Books of Royal Naval hospitals, 1807–19, and lists of clerks and storekeepers etc in Royal Naval hospitals, 1874–90, ADM 104; returns of Income Tax on salaries of employees of the Sick and Hurt Board, and hospital staff, 1807–9, ADM 102/841; general entry book of patients in overseas hospitals, 1806–29, ADM 102/843, death certificates from Admiralty hospitals, 1809–15, ADM 102/842; hospital musters of patients at home and abroad, including those on hospital ships in harbour and sea-going vessels, 1688–1842, ADM 36–ADM 37, monthly musters, including details of staff pay, and deaths of patients, listed alphabetically by ship or port or station, 1740–1860, ADM 102, patients in the Military Hospital at Malta, 1802–4, ADM 102/555, in New York Military Hospital, 1777, ADM 102/583; deaths of seamen in Haslar Hospital, 1755–65, ADM 102/374, deaths of Russians in Haslar Hospital, 1808–12, ADM 102/349, deaths in London hospitals, 1788–1816, ADM 102/491–500, including Guy's Hospital, 1809–16, ADM 102/498, St Bartholomew's Hospital, 1809–15, ADM 102/499, St Thomas's Hospital, 1807–16, ADM102/500; register of wills at the Naval Hospital,

Gibraltar, 1809–15, ADM105/40; letters from surgeons and medical officers of hospitals and hospital ships, 1702–1862, ADM 97, with a nominal index of correspondents, 1832–62, giving registered number, ADM 133, and weeded registers of letters, giving date of receipt, 1832–62, ADM 132; accounts of surgeons of London hospitals, 1810–22, ADM 100, and reports of medical officers and inspectors of hospitals, 1803–63, ADM 105; case book of the Royal Naval Hospital, Bermuda, 1832–6, 1840–44, 1850–62, 1870–83, ADM 104.
see *Medical Officers, Royal Naval, Surgeons*

Huguenots
see *Aliens, Denization, Foreign Churches in England, Naturalization, Refugees*

Hundred Rolls Mainly being the returns (in Latin) of county by county fiscal enquiries during the reigns of Henry III and his son Edward I, 1255, 1274–5 and 1280, SC 5, mostly printed in *Rotuli Hundredorum*; action taken on presentments made from the Hundred Courts to the justices itinerant in eyre, 1278–89, JUST 1.

Hungary Budapest, marriages, 1872–99, FO 114/1–5.

I*i*

Idiots and Lunatics Supervision over them and their estates rested with the Lord Chancellor until the Court of Wards and Liveries was established in 1541; when this Court was abolished in 1660, the Lord Chancellor again assumed responsibility. In 1842 two permanent Commissioners in Lunacy were appointed (later called Masters in Lunacy) to establish the circumstances of lunacy and the whereabouts of the patient's estate. They came to form the Management and Administration Department of the Lunacy Office in 1890, and since 1959, the Court of Protection. If lucidity was restored the land and property was returned. All grants relating to their custody and estates were enrolled on the Patent Rolls, C 66, with printed *Calendars*, 1216–1582, and 1584–7; indentures of wardship and leases, 1540–*c*.1641, arranged under regnal year, WARD 6; inquisitions post mortem held on lands of deceased lunatics or idiots, temp. Henry III (thirteenth century)–Charles II, C 132–C 142, with Exchequer copies, temp. Henry III–James I, in E 149–E 150, and duplicates filed in the Court of Wards and Liveries, temp. Henry VIII–Charles I, WARD 7; there are printed *Calendars* up to 1405, and for the reign of Henry VII, while later ones are listed under reign and alphabetically by surname; inquisitions held on estates held in the Palatinate of Chester, temp. Edward I (thirteenth century)–Charles I, CHES 3,

to which there is a nominal index. County registers of private asylums and of patients admitted, with copies of removal orders of pauper lunatics to other asylums, 1798–1812, MH 51; registers of admissions kept by the Lunacy Commission, 1846–1913, and its successor Board of Control, 1913–60, giving patient's name, sex, hospital, asylum or licensed house where placed, date of admission and of discharge or death, and including diaries recording medical and legal information about them, plus any action taken and other remarks, MH 94; returns of inmates of workhouses and asylums, arranged alphabetically by county and Poor Law Union, then chronologically, and giving name, age, type of disability, and whether considered dangerous, 1834–1909, MH 12, with subject indexes, 1836–1920, MH 15; names of criminal lunatics in Bethlem Hospital, London, 1823–35, HO 20; warrants for removal from jail to asylums, 1882–1921, with out-letters, 1899–1921, HO 145; papers and exhibits in lunacy proceedings, 1774–1830, C 217; letters in cases where the Treasury Solicitor became involved, arranged chronologically, 1813–61, and with integral indexes, TS 3; register of Lunacy Bonds issued at the Lunacy Office by the Management and Administration Department, to Committees of Estate who entered into a bond with the Crown, offering at least two sureties, 1817–1904,

J 103. Lord Chancellor's Visitors' reports on Chancery lunatics, giving date of request for a visit by the Masters in Chancery, the patient's name, address, age, income and allowance, and date of the report, 1879–1967, LCO 10 (most closed 75 years); selected case papers on mental patients, 1849–1960, MH 85 (most closed 75 years). Commissions and inquisitions to establish lucidity, 1627–1932, arranged alphabetically to 1852 (indexed in IND 1/17612), and then chronologically, C 211; the commissions were directed to local men holding the inquisition before a jury. The inquisitions discovered when and how the person had become a lunatic, and if any land had been alienated by him while in that condition, and if so, what, when and to whom, and what property still remained to him, plus the name of his next heir; from 1853, the records consist of abstracts of petitions from the next of kin or orders for an inquisition and a report by a Master in Lunacy, indicating if at the time of the inquisition the person was of unsound mind; lunacy inquisitions in the Palatinate of Lancaster, temp. Charles II–William IV, PL 5. An indication of whether a person was an idiot, imbecile or lunatic was recorded in the census returns from 1871.

see *Census, Protection, Court of, Wards and Liveries, Court of*

Immigrants
see *Aliens, Denization, Naturalization, Refugees, Ships' Passenger Lists*

Imperial Service Order Instituted in 1902 for colonial civil servants. Out-letters, 1902–21, HO 180; nominal lists, in *The London Gazette* to 1986, with annual or half-yearly subject indexes, ZJ 1.

Income Tax 1799–1802, 1803–16, 1842–. Receipts for payments, and for salaries paid to local tax surveyors, names of defaulters and persons in arrears, arranged in yearly county bundles, 1799–1802, 1803–16, E 182; assessments of members of the Royal Household and others in the Lord Chamberlain's Department, giving annual salary, allowances, deductions and amounts falling due at the current rate under Schedule E, 1854–69, LC 3; returns for staff at the Royal Mint for years ending 5 April 1863, 1872, 1876, 1877, 1879, 1880 and 1881, MINT 3; 'property tax' assessments on persons in the Treasury Department, 1803–16, T 95; returns on salaries of employees of the Sick and Hurt Office and Hospital, 1807–9, ADM 102/841; returns of persons confined in jail for non-payment of taxes, 1848–53, IR 84/6, 1853–56, IR 83/17; Schedule D assessment books, samples from ten tax offices at twenty-year intervals, giving name, address, partnership or company, trade, profession or vocation, amount of assessed profits or income, and tax charged, 1887–1918, IR 88 (closed 75 years).

see *Land Tax and Assessed Taxes*

Indemnity, Committee and Commissioners for A Parliamentary Committee, whose dated cases, arranged alphabetically, give the name, estate, informer and indemnity imposed on Royalists, 1647–56, SP 24.

India Births and deaths of Britons in Indian Native States, 1894–1947, RG 33/90–113, indexed for births, 1915–47, and deaths, 1923–40, in RG 43/15; Jammu and Kashmir, births, 1917–47, RG 33/157; Kolhapur and Deccan States, births, 1930–46, RG 33/158; Srinagar, deaths, 1926–47, RG 33/159; Udaipur, births,

1938–47, RG 33/160, indexed in RG 43/15; deaths in French India, 1836–71, RG 35/16; deaths in the Sub–Continent, c.1831–1920, RG 35/20–44. Returns of pensions paid by the Royal Hospitals of Chelsea and Greenwich to retired military, naval and marine personnel, arranged under pay-district and giving rank at retirement, regiment, amount and nature of annual or quarterly pension, any transfers elsewhere, and ultimately the date of death, those for the Presidency of Bengal, 1845–80, WO 22/228–30, and of Bombay, 1855–80, WO 22/237–38, and of black persons, 1845–80, WO 22/231–36. Treasury out-letters to the Board of Control, East India Company, and India Office, 1849–56, 1859–85, T 28.

Indonesia (Dutch East Indies) Deaths of Britons, 1839–1920, RG 35/17, 20–44; Borneo: Balik and Papan, births, 1907, deaths, 1897–1907, FO 221/2–3; Borneo and Sarawak, deaths from enemy action, 1941–5, RG 33/132; Java: Semarang, births, 1869–1941, baptisms, 1906, deaths, 1874–98, 1912–40, FO 803/1–3, deaths, 1839–71, RG 35/20–40; Sumatra: Oleh Leh, births and deaths, 1883–4, FO 220/12.

Infants Cases concerning wardship of infants and the care of infants' estates, brought before the Chancery Division of the High Court, 1875–1953, TS 18 (some closed 75 or 100 years), with a descriptive list arranged under subject, and a nominal card index to TS 33, which gives cross-references to related material in this class; petitions and reports for conveyances by infants in the Palatinate of Durham, 1764–1801, DURH 8.
see *Age, Proofs of, Inquisitions post mortem, Wards and Liveries, Court of*

Inhabited House Duty 1692–1924, replacing the Window Tax in 1851.
see *Land Tax and Assessed Taxes*

Inland Revenue Life Assurance and Benevolent Fund Society Set up in 1845 as the Excise Benevolent Fund Society, to grant annuities and allowances to the widows and orphans of Excise officers, and to help superannuated staff effecting policies with the Atlas Assurance Company, it was widened to include all staff on the Board of Inland Revenue from 1849, and was wound up in 1972. Membership registers, 1843–1966, assignments of bonuses and assurance policies to the Fund, 1908–66, new and cancelled policies, 1902–39, annuities, 1897–1972, IR 92.

Inns of Court Association Oath Roll, 1696, C 213/165–67.
see under individual Inns, and *Barristers*

Inquisitions ad quod damnum Were taken by county escheators on behalf of the Crown after an application by a tenant-in-chief for a licence to alienate his land, or for a grant of a market, fair, or other privilege such as the right of free warren, in order to ensure that the King's approval would not prejudice his or others' financial interests. The records are in Latin. Inquisitions, temp. Henry III (thirteenth century)–Richard III, C 143, temp. Henry VII–Charles I, C 142, and temp. Henry III–Henry VI, E 151, temp. Henry VII–James I, E 150, to which there are printed *Calendars* up to the reign of Richard III; inquisitions in the Palatinate of Chester, temp. Edward I (thirteenth century)–Charles I, indexed, CHES 3, in the Palatinate of Durham, 1438–1637, indexed, DURH 2.
see *Alienation*

Inquisitions post mortem On the death of a tenant-in-chief of the Crown, the King's escheators took possession of his lands, and held an enquiry in every county where they lay on the oaths of sworn local jurors to determine the type of tenure under which they were held, their annual value, the owner's date of death, and the name, age and relationship of the next heir, before the heir did homage and fealty to the King and took livery of seisin of them. If the heir was under age the lands and its profits were retained by the Crown with the right of wardship and marriage over the heir until he attained his majority, upon which a proof of age was filed. Where there were daughters as co-heiresses, the land was shared equally between them. If the heir was an idiot or lunatic, the lands and wardship again vested in the Crown. The inquisition was returned to Chancery and the escheator sent another copy to the Exchequer in accounting for the profits of the lands. Inquisitions ceased on the abolition of feudal tenure in 1660. The records are in Latin. Writs for inquisitions, 1272–c.1641, on the Fine Rolls, C 60, with printed *Calendars* to 1509; county inquisitions, temp. Henry II (1236–1272), C 132, temp. Edward I (1272–1307), C 133, temp. Edward II (1307–27), C 134, temp. Edward III (1327–77), C 135, temp. Richard II (1377–99), C 136, temp. Henry IV (1399–1412/3), C 137, temp. Henry V (1412/3–1422), C 138, temp. Henry VI (1422–61, 1470–71), C 139, temp. Edward IV (1461–83), C 140, temp. Richard III (1483–5), C 141, temp. Henry VII–Charles II (1485–c.1660), C 142; Exchequer series, temp. Henry III–Richard III, E 149, temp. Henry VII–James I, E 150; Court of Wards and Liveries, 1541–c.1641, WARD 7; printed *Calendars* run up to 1405, and for the reign of Henry VII,

during the intervening years there is a descriptive list in Latin, including a nominal and topographical index of Chancery inquisitions, and a manuscript index of names, giving county of inquisition, and regnal year, for Exchequer inquisitions, while the means of reference to inquisitions from the reign of Henry VIII onwards is by a printed union index of all three sets, arranged under reign, and then alphabetically by name, giving county and regnal year. Inquisitions taken in the Duchy of Lancaster, temp. Henry III–Charles I, indexed, DL 7; Duchy of Cornwall, 1438–93, E 306; Palatinate of Chester, temp. Edward I–Charles I, indexed, CHES 3; Palatinate of Durham, original inquisitions, 1438–1637, abstracts and registers, 1318–1567, indexed, DURH 3; Palatinate of Lancaster, temp. Henry IV–Henry VII, calendared, PL 4.

see *Age, Proofs of, Wards and Liveries, Court of*

Insolvents
see *Bankrupts, Companies, Winding up or Liquidation of, Debtors, Insolvent*

International Genealogical Index Microfiche indexes of births, baptisms and marriages principally drawn from parish registers, but including non-parochial registers of dissenters deposited in the Public Record Office in class RG 4, and other sources, such as the registers of the British Lying–In Hospital, in London, also deposited in the Office. They are arranged by English and Scottish county, under Wales, Ireland and the Isle of Man, being indexed by surname and then by forename, with a second set of indexes for Wales recording entries by forename. The Index is frequently updated as more entries are fed into it, the latest dated entry currently falls in 1912. The Index is on open access, and recourse should be had to the Vital and Parish Listings Index to discover exactly what places and periods are covered for a particular county on the current edition. The Index is not fully comprehensive, does not include deaths and burials, and should under no circumstances be solely relied on for the reconstruction of a family's history, but it is extremely useful for identifying stray entries of individuals, and the distribution of a surname over time and place.

see *British Lying-In Hospital, Endell Street, Holborn, London, Non-Parochial Registers*

Internees German internees, 1915–16, WO 900/45–46, particulars and effects of German dead, 1914–15, 1918, WO 900/43–44. Selected personal files, listed by name and date, 1940, HO 214 (later files are closed for 50 years).
see *Prisoners of War*

Intestacy When a person dies without leaving a will, or where part of his property is left undisposed of by will, he is said to be intestate. Legal proceedings concerning intestacy, 1584–1852, TS 11; selected cases, 1818–1940, including some pedigrees filed as evidence, 1698–1955, and grants of letters of administration, 1808–57, with a nominal list giving date, and amount estate sworn under, TS 17, and 1517–1953, TS 18 (some files closed 75 or 100 years), to which there is a descriptive list, and a card index for TS 33 cites references to related material in TS 18; memorials relating to cases referred by the Treasury to the King's Proctor (Procurator General), 1804–15, indexed, TS 8, 1815–44, TS 9; letters from the Treasury to the King's Proctor, 1857–76, and to the Treasury Solicitor and others, 1876–

1913, concerning intestates' estates, T 16; other correspondence between 1813 and 1924, TS 3. Royal warrants and authorizations for ex gratia payments and release of estates to lawful claimants, 1807–1936, listed alphabetically, TS 30. Pedigrees relating to administration of wills and intestacy cases before the Chancery Division, 1852–1974, listed under the name of the earliest forebear, date of death, and under title of each suit, giving cause number, J 68.

Inventions Petitions for patents, protecting inventions within the kingdom for periods of up to fourteen years, 1661–1782, SP 44, 1782–1852, indexed from 1792, HO 43; correspondence relating to petitions, 1782–1820, HO 42, 1820–52, HO 44; warrants to law officers to prepare a bill leading to a grant of letters patent, 1783–1834, HO 89, law officers' bills, 1661–1851, SO 7; particulars for inventions, caveats against the issue of letters patent, proceedings, disclaimers and oppositions, 1839–85, LO 1. Warrants to extend monopoly rights over inventions, 1852–76, indexed, HO 141. Warrants for letters patent in Ireland, 1627–1876, SO 1 (indexed in SO 2), and 1776–1915, HO 101. Warrants for patents in Scotland, 1774–1847, indexed, HO 106, and 1840–55, HO 105. Specifications of inventions, including drawings or plans, are enrolled on the Close Rolls, 1712–1853, and disclaimers of patents, 1854–67, C 54, with a printed *Calendar* and index of specifications, 1826–53; other enrolments of specifications, 1712–1848, with a calendar (Rolls Chapel Series), C 73, and 1709–1848, with a calendar and index of specifications (Petty Bag Series), C 210: *Alphabetical Index of Patentees of Invention*, and *Reference Index of Patents of Invention*, indicate the appropriate enrolment.

Letters patent for invention are enrolled on the Patent Rolls to 1853, C 66, with printed abstracts, 1617–1745. Claimants for awards to inventors, under Royal Commission, 1919–37, listed in alphabetical order, giving the date and nature of invention, T 173, and later ones, under Royal Commission, 1946, indexed, T 166.

Inventories of goods of attainted persons and others, temp. John (thirteenth century)–1721, listed, E 154.
see *Canterbury, Prerogative Court of* for probate inventories

Iran (Persia) Title deeds relating to Britons, 1808–1944, FO 251; Birjand, Hagnadan, Qazvin, Kerman, Kermanshah, Meshed, Resht, Sistan, and Kain, consular registers of births to Britons, 1903–50, marriages, 1895–1950, deaths 1889–1950, FO 923/1–25; Bushire, births, baptisms, marriages and deaths, 1849–95, births, 1881–1947, and register of British subjects, 1917–46, FO 560/1–3; Isfahan, births, 1892–1950, marriages, 1893–1951, deaths, 1892–1943, and lists of British subjects, 1926–7, FO 799/34–38 (some closed 50 years); Tabriz, births, 1851–74, 1879–1932, 1940–42, 1949–51, marriages, 1850–1903, foreign marriages registered at the British Consulate, 1909–50, deaths, 1882–1931, 1939–44, certificates of baptism and marriage, deeds of property transfer, powers of attorney etc, 1856–1923, FO 451/1–9; British claims for damaged property and other losses, 1892–1930, FO 251/78–80.

Iraq (Mesopotamia) Births, 1915–31, and baptisms of British children, 1919–24, marriages, 1917–31, and deaths, 1920–31, RG 36, indexed in RG 43/16, and also in RG 33/133–37, with indexes to marriages only, 1917–31, RG 33/138–39.

Ireland Registers of people leaving the ports of Chester and Liverpool for Ireland, 1632–3, and from St Ives, 1632–3, E 157; Association Oath Roll of nobility and gentry of Ireland now in England, 1696, C 213/402. Irish pedigrees compiled by Lord Burghley and Sir Joseph Williamson in the sixteenth- and seventeenth-centuries, SP 63/213, notes on Ireland and Irish genealogy, SP 63/278–79, with an alphabetical index, SP 63/280. Peerage claims, 1828–31, HO 100, warrants for letters patent creating peerages, 1776–1915, indexed, HO 101. Entry Books of letters, 1681–1783, including warrants, 1713–76, indexed, 1713–45, 1761–76, SP 67 (also included in *Calendar of State Papers (Domestic Series)* up to 1704, and *Calendar of Home Office Papers of the reign of George III, 1760–1775*), and continued, 1776–1955, in HO 101. Irish letter books, 1627–1872, SO 1, calendared to 1670 in *State Papers relating to Ireland*, and to 1704, as above, and indexed, 1643–1872, in SO 2; Entry Book of letters, 1800–06, indexed, SO 5. State Papers, 1509–47, SP 60, with printed transcripts, 1547–53, in SP 61, 1553–8, SP 62, 1558–1782, SP 63, described in *Calendar of State Papers relating to Ireland, 1509–1670*, thereafter to 1704 in *Calendar of State Papers (Domestic Series)* and *Calendar of Home Office Papers of the reign of George III, 1760–1775*. Order and Warrant Books, Entry Books of in- and out-letters of the Committee on Irish Affairs, 1644–50, SP 21, printed in *Calendar of State Papers (Domestic Series) of the reign of Charles I*. Extents and valuations of lands and possessions of dissolved monasteries, 1536–41, and proceedings of the Commissioners for Claims in Munster, 1588, SP 65, described in *State Papers relating to Ireland*; rentals of Crown lands, 1832–1954, with a descriptive list arranged chronologically,

LRRO 12 (most closed 100 years). Maps, temp. Elizabeth–James I, SP 64, listed in *State Papers relating to Ireland*, maps and plans, *c*.1617–1854, SP 112. Records in error from the Court of King's Bench (Crown Side) in Dublin brought to the Westminster Bench on a writ of error, reciting the original hearing and later proceedings, 1737–1836, KB 7, and from other Courts to the Court of King's Bench (Plea Side), temp. Henry VIII–William IV, KB 140. Military commissions and appointments, 1768–1877, HO 123; admission books relating to infirm military personnel examined at the Royal Hospital at Kilmainham (founded in 1679), recording name, rank, regiment, brief service details, age, birthplace, date of examination and nature of disability, and physical description of out-pensioners, 1704–1922, WO 118, and the discharge numbers given in these are the key to the discharge documents, providing service details, 1783–1822, WO 119; selected out-pensions, 1798–1817, listed by name and regiment, WO 900; from 1822 pensions were paid out by the Royal Hospital at Chelsea, returns for which, 1842–62, 1882–83, are in WO 22/141–203, 209–25, and including name, rank and regiment at retirement, date of commencement, nature and amount of pension, arranged under pay-district, and recording any transfers elsewhere, and the date of death; Militia musters, 1793–1876, arranged alphabetically by county, and musters of Volunteers, 1797–1814, 1873–8, listing alphabetically within each the men's names, ages and parishes, WO 13. Letter books of correspondence sent to Irish officers of the Board of Stamps, 1807–19, IR 43, 1819–27, IR 45, 1827–33, IR 47. Nominations for appointments in the Irish Coastguard, 1821–49, ADM 175/99–100. Salary books of Customs revenue staff in Ireland, 1764–1808, indexed, Establishment Books, 1684–1826 (including Excise officers), registers of officers' appointments, 1761–1823, CUST 20; Irish Establishments at Out Ports, 1840, 1860–94, CUST 39/122–44; superannuations and widows' pensions of Customs staff, including details about children's births, 1785–1898, indexed, CUST 39/161–62, and superannuations, to Customs staff commissioned up to 1887, *c*.1856–1912, indexed, CUST 39/157 (others closed 75 years); appointments of Irish Commissioners of Excise, and Establishment list, 1824–33, CUST 110; nominations and appointments of Irish Revenue Police, 1830–42, minutes of appointments, June 1830–November 1857, Establishments in the Northern and Western Districts, 1830–31, CUST 111. Warrants for bills for patents for inventions, 1627–1876, SO 1 (indexed in SO 2), 1776–1915, HO 101. Irish State Tontines, 1773, 1775, 1777, listing names of subscribers, and nominees, and including payment books of annuities, certificates of marriages and deaths and declarations of identity, 1773–1870, NDO 3; contributors to, and recipients of relief of distressed English subjects in Ireland, 1642, arranged by county, hundred and parish (and with a parish index, under county, on open access), SP 28/191–95, and E 179, with the class list organized alphabetically by county, then by regnal year, and giving the name of the hundred, city or borough concerned; list of borrowers and defaulters, arranged by county and local association, for the Irish Reproductive Loan Fund, set up to relieve the poor during the famine of 1822, whereby money was lent at interest to certain counties in Munster and Connaught for the industrious poor, 1822–74, T 91; letters relating to poor relief, 1847, T 64. War diaries, 1920–22, General Establishment records relating to administration of the Army in Ireland, and the Easter Rising, 1916, raid and search reports, claims for damage allegedly caused by military personnel while undertaking raids and searches, 1920–21, proceedings of military and civil courts in lieu of inquests on civilians, 1920–22, biographical details about prominent Irish nationalists, WO 35; claimants for compensation under the Compensation (Ireland) Commission, for damage and personal injury sustained between 21 January 1919 and 11 July 1921, CO 905/1–15, with an alphabetical nominal card index, 1922–30, and numerical indexes, CO 905/19–22; criminal injuries claims under the Irish Distress Committee (to March 1923) and the Irish Grants Committee, giving details of loans made to valid claimants against either government, 1922–30, CO 762/3–206; loans to loyalists in Southern Ireland who had suffered hardship or loss, 11 July 1921–12 May 1923, CO 905; awards made by the Irish Deportees (Compensation) Tribunal, 1923–4, T 80/10. Births, marriages and deaths of British passengers at sea, 1854–90, BT 158, births at sea, 1875–91, BT 160, and deaths at sea, 1875–88, BT 159.

Ireland, Adventurers for Lands in Receipts for subscriptions in support of the Parliamentary cause, in return for promises of land in Ireland, and papers of claims and assignments, arranged by initial index, and including names, abodes, occupations or status of contributors, the sum pledged, dates of quarterly subscriptions, and assignments to relatives or others on their deaths, giving relationship, name and abode of the heir or assign, 1642–59, SP 63/288–302.

Irish Affairs, Committee on
see *Both Kingdoms, Committee for*

Irish Constabulary, Royal Local constables were embodied as the Irish Constabulary in 1836, which from 1867 until its disbandment in 1922 was known as the Royal Irish Constabulary. Constabulary lists, 1836, 1839–1921, HO 184/81–105, 238–42; records of service, arranged numerically, 1816–1922, HO 184/1–44; returns of personnel, arranged by county, 1910–21, HO 184/55–61; officers' registers, arranged by service number, giving age, height, religious denomination, native county and that of any wife, trade, date of appointment and counties where served, with date of retirement or death, 1817–1921, HO 184/45–48, Auxiliary Force, 1881–2, HO 184/49, Auxiliary Division, 1920–22, HO 184/50–53, clerical staff service records and salaries, 1897–1920, and indexes of recruits, 1920–22, HO 184/75–80, British and Irish recruits at disbandment, arranged by county, 1922, HO 184/129–209, specimen attestation forms, 1902–21, with names given in the class list, HO 184/237; pensions and gratuities, 1873–1948, HO 184/213–16, new pensioners, 1888–1900, HO 184/217; completed application forms for injury pensions, 1921–2, HO 184/218; widows' and orphans' gratuities, 1821–1946, HO 184/219–221; pensions and allowances paid to officers, men and staff, and to their widows and offspring, 1875–1925, including registers of deceased pensioners, 1877–1918, and rolls of awards of pensions on disbandment on 31 August 1922, PMG 48; selected pensions and allowances paid to members and their dependants, 1951–70, HO 340; list of superannuations, 1832, ZHC 1/1045.

Irish Revenue Police
see *Ireland*

Italy Deaths of Britons, 1871–1920, RG 35/20–44, indexed in RG 43; Agrigento (Grigenti), births and deaths, 1857– 75, births, 1877–1904, deaths, 1879–85, FO 653/2–4; Catania, births and deaths, 1878–1904, births, 1907–39, deaths, 1919–40, FO 653/5–7; Florence, marriages, 1840–55, 1865–71, RG 33/114–15, indexed in RG 43/7, marriages, 1856, FO 352/43, marriages, 1846–90, FO 83, indexed in FO 802/239; Gela (Terranova), births, 1904–30, FO 653/8; Leghorn, baptisms, marriages and burials, 1707–1824, RG 33/116–17, indexed in RG 43/1, 7 and 3 respectively; Licata, births and deaths, 1871–1900, FO 720/1; Marsala, births and deaths, 1847–1904, births, 1905–22, deaths, 1908–19, FO 653/9–11; Mazzara, births, 1810–1904, 1906–11, FO 653/12–13; Messina, births, 1854–1929, 1931–57, deaths, 1854–1957, FO 653/14–17; Milazzo, deaths, 1887–1903, FO 653/18; Naples, baptisms, marriages and burials, 1817–22, RG 33/118, 1835–6, RG 33/155, both indexed in RG 43/1, 7 and 3 respectively; Palermo, births, 1837–91, 1932–40, deaths, 1850–1919, FO 653/19–21; Porto Empedocle, births, 1906, FO 653/22; Rome and Tuscany, baptisms and marriages, 1816–52, FO 170/6, marriages, 1872–89, RG 33/119, indexed in RG 43/7, marriages, 1870–90, FO 83, indexed in FO 802/239; Sicily, births, 1810–1957, deaths, 1847–1957, FO 653/2–28, and FO 720/1, baptisms, 1838, RG 33/155, indexed in RG 43/1, registers of passports, 1811–60, FO 166; Syracuse, births, 1909–18, deaths, 1912–19, 1953–7, FO 653/23–25; Taormina, deaths, 1909–22, FO 653/26; Trapani, births, 1871–1906, 1924–27, FO 653/27–28; Turin, marriages, 1847–69, FO 83, indexed in FO 802/239, marriages, 1858–64, RG 33/120, indexed in RG 43/7; Venice, marriages, 1874–1947, RG 33/121, indexed in RG 43/7.

Jj

Jacobite Rebellions Minute Books of proceedings after the 1715 Rebellion, held at Preston, Essex House, the Inner Temple and Westminster, 1716–26, FEC 2; King's Bench material is in Latin to 1733: indictments, exhibits, and convictions filed in the Baga de Secretis of the Court of King's Bench (Crown Side), 1716–60, KB 8; records of the trials are in KB 8/66, with a printed nominal index, giving address, occupation, offence, sentence and names of informers. Prosecutions brought in England and Scotland after the 1745 Rebellion, 1745–53, including lists of rebels, and of prisoners, and details of proceedings, evidence of witnesses and special Commissions and actions taken against Scottish peers, TS 20 and TS 11; draft indictments, trial transcripts and lists of prisoners, KB 33, trials recorded in KB 8; other details relating to the trials may be found in Assize records of the North–Eastern Circuit, ASSI 41–47, the Palatinate of Chester Crown Books, CHES 21, gaol files, CHES 24, the Palatinate of Durham indictments, DURH 17, and in Miscellanea, DURH 19, the Palatinate of Lancaster Assize Rolls, PL 25, indictments, PL 26, depositions, PL 27, and miscellanea, PL 28. Lists of prisoners and information on their trials after both Rebellions may be located in State Papers, Scotland, 1688–1783, SP 54, State Papers, Domestic, 1714–27, SP 35, and State Papers, Domestic, 1727–60, SP 36. Estate deeds of persons attainted during the 1715 Rebellion, claims, proceedings and returns of names and estates of Papist recusants in England and Wales, arranged by county, with a nominal index, FEC 1; registers of claims against the estates, 1716–19, and decree books, 1716–21, both indexed, appeals against the decrees and an indexed register of claims for losses at Preston, FEC 2; reports and surveys of forfeited estates in Scotland, 1745–56, T 64; miscellaneous papers concerning Jacobites, PRO 30/26.
see *Assizes, Greenwich Hospital Estates, Royal, Roman Catholics, State Trials*

Jamaica Minute Book of the British and Portuguese Court relating to slaves, 1843–51, FO 314.
see *Slaves, West Indies*

Japan Marriage declarations of British subjects and certificates, 1870–87, papers relating to foreign settlements and house taxation, 1855–1941, FO 345, correspondence concerning marriages, 1873–89, FO 97/503; Kobe, baptisms, 1874–1941, marriages, 1874–1940, burials, 1902–41, RG 33/122–26, indexed in RG 43/1–3, 6–8, 10–14; Nagasaki, register of British subjects, 1906–21, certificates of title, bills of sale, births, 1864–1940, marriages, 1922–40, deaths, 1859–

1944, FO 796/236–38; Osaka, marriages, 1892–1904, RG 33/127–40, indexed in RG 43; Shimonoseki, register of British subjects, 1906–21, births, 1903–21, marriages, 1906–22, deaths, 1903–21, FO 797/48–50; Taiwan (Formosa), deaths, 1873–1901, FO 721/1; Tokyo, marriages, 1870–90, FO 83, indexed in FO 802/239, marriages, 1875–87, FO 345/34; Yokohama, marriages, 1847–90, FO 83, indexed in FO 802/239, marriages, 1870–74, FO 345/34.

Java
see *Indonesia*

Jersey Births, marriages and deaths, 1831–1958, RG 32, indexed in RG 43; census returns, 6 June 1841, HO 107, 30 March 1851, HO 107, 7 April 1861, RG 9, 2 April 1871, RG 10, 3 April 1881, RG 11, 5 April 1891, RG 12; Association Oath Roll, 1696, C 213/462; register of French refugees, 1793–6, FO 95/602–03; pensions paid by Royal Hospitals of Chelsea and Greenwich to military, naval and marine personnel, giving date, nature and amount of pension, rank, any regiment and number, arranged by pay-district, and recording any transfers elsewhere and date of death, 1842–62, WO 22/205–06, and paid to merchant marines, 1852–3, WO 22/208; calendars of prisoners, 1868–1958, noting age, occupation, charge, verdict and sentence, HO 140 (some closed 75 years); correspondence, 1771–82, SP 47, included up to 1775 in *Calendar of Home Office Papers of the reign of George III*.
see *Bouillon Papers, Channel Islands*

Jews Some baptism certificates, 1693–1826, marriages, 1744–1829, and burials, 1721–1831, from London parishes, listed, KB 101/26. Jews' Rolls, 1212–94, recording receipts from tallages, fines and amercements, E 401/1564–1610; tallage receipts, conversions to Christianity, extents and inquisitions on possessions, enrolments of loan bonds and charters, temp. Henry II (twelfth century)–James I, E 101; inquisitions on former property of Jews, temp. Henry III (thirteenth century)–Edward I, E 143; Plea Rolls relating to civil and criminal matters, affairs between Jews and the Crown, or Christians, and including counterparts of deeds recording loans, 1218–87, E 9, with a printed *Calendar*. Enquiries made by the Jewish Tribunal under the Shops Acts 1936 and 1950, relating to Sunday trading by persons claiming closure on the Jewish Sabbath because of their conscience, to establish whether they were practising Jews, listed by name, premises and trade, 1938–63, HO 239.
see *Aliens, Denization, Naturalization*

Jordan
see *Trans–Jordan*

Judges Oaths, 1946–87, indexed, 1910–87, KB 24.
see *Serjeants at Law*

Judicature, Supreme Court of Set up in 1875, and comprising the High Court of Justice (five Divisions, of Chancery, Common Pleas, Exchequer, Queen's Bench, and Probate, Divorce and Admiralty to 1880, and thereafter Chancery, Queen's Bench and Probate, Divorce and Admiralty, the last re-formed as the Family Division in 1970), and the Court of Appeal, and from 1971, the Crown Courts. Enrolment Books of change of name by deed poll, deeds of relinquishment of Holy Orders, conveyances relating to Queen Anne's Bounty for the augmentation of curacies, of charitable trusts, and of disentailing deeds to 1925, 1903–87, J 18, with annual initial indexes to 1948, and thereafter listed chronologically by date, on open access; Enrolment Office deeds, c.1777–1966, including memorials of charities, and transfers of shares in chartered companies, J 19.

see under the appropriate Divisions

Juries Gaol Delivery Rolls and files include jury panels, 1271–1476, JUST 3; original Oath Rolls, including signatures and occasionally addresses and qualities, 1709–1868, E 169; jury panels in the Court of Pleas of the Palatinate of Durham, temp. James I–Victoria, DURH 14/39–44, and Assizes, 1702–38, DURH 19; Palatinate of Lancaster, 1811–48, PL 19.

Justice, High Court of
see *Judicature, Supreme Court of*

Justices of the Peace Appointed under Commission from the Crown, and published in *The London Gazette*, 1665–1986, with subject indexes sporadically from 1790, invariably from 1848, ZJ 1. Commissions up to 1564, and 1595–c.1665, are enrolled on the Patent Rolls, C 66, with printed *Calendars* to 1582, and 1584–7; Entry Books of Commissions of the Peace in boroughs and liberties, 1601–73, C 181; lists of borough and shire justices, temp. Henry VIII, 1622–57, 1663, 1679–80, temp. James II, and registers of Commissions of borough justices, 1837–75, 1897–1911, 1938–66, 1938–74, appointments, 1938–67, removals,

1938–66, Entry Books of English and Welsh borough magistrates, 1851–1937, and in the Duchy of Lancaster, 1938–74, arranged alphabetically by borough, C 193; fiats for appointment of justices of English and Welsh boroughs, 1837–1973, and Scottish burghs, 1823–1929, C 234; list of names of borough magistrates, giving occupations and dates of appointment, 1841, arranged alphabetically by borough, HO 90. Appointments of borough and shire justices, 1571–1921, C 202, with a nominal and place-name index on open access; appointments, 1929–69, LCO 34 (most closed 50 years); lists of shire justices, 1547–53, SP 10, described in printed *Calendar of State Papers (Domestic Series)*; lists, c.1819–39, HO 94; registers of Commissions of shire justices, 1836–77, Entry Book of justices in England and Wales, 1937–66, appointments to counties, 1938–67, removals, 1938–66, arranged alphabetically by county, Entry Book of justices of English counties, 1830–1937, first list of justices in Scotland, 1708, Commissions of Scottish justices, 1838–75, Entry Book of Scottish justices, 1879–1975, C 193; fiats for appointment and removal of justices, 1705–1929, arranged alphabetically under county, and for Scottish counties, and Wales, 1930–73, C 234; returns of magistrates, temp. George IV, HO 94; magistrates' Oath Rolls, 1945–87, indexed, 1910–87, KB 24. Commissions in the Palatinate of Chester, 1797–1825, CHES 38, Palatinate of Lancaster, 1675–1875, DL 20.

K*k*

Kashmir Births to Britons, 1917–47, RG 33/157, indexed in RG 43.

Kendal Corn Rents In 1834 tithes and dues payable to the incumbent were commuted to a corn rent, the levy, an aggregate sum, being apportioned among the twenty-seven townships; in 1932 a statute made provision for redemption. Certificates of redemption, 1931–61, arranged by date, place and address, MAF 28.

Kenya Births to Britons, 1905–24, RG 36, partially indexed in RG 43/18.

Kilmainham Hospital, Royal Founded near Dublin in 1679, like the Royal Hospital at Chelsea it catered for both military in- and out-pensioners. Payments to out-pensioners were transferred to Chelsea in 1822, and the in-pensioners were moved to Chelsea in 1929. Admission books, arranged chronologically, giving discharge number, rank and regiment, date and details of the medical examination, disability, physical description, age and birthplace of soldiers on the Irish Establishment discharged in Ireland, 1704–1922, WO 118, discharge documents, arranged by discharge number (found in WO 118), 1783–1822, providing brief service summaries, WO 119; selected pensions, 1798–1817, with a nominal list, giving rank and regiment, WO 900.

King's African Rifles Original Correspondence, including recommendations for awards and medals, 1905–26, CO 534, with a register of correspondence, 1905–26, CO 623; correspondence, 1927–40, CO 820.

King's Bench (Crown Side), Court of This Court stemmed from the King's Council and criminal cases ranging from trespasses and breaches of the King's peace to treason were heard before the King in person even as late as the eighteenth century; enrolments of results of trials held nisi prius at Assizes were enrolled among its records. Appeals from lower courts were brought here, and it was used to reinforce judgments made in ecclesiastical courts. In 1875 it became part of the High Court of Justice as the Queen's Bench Division. The records are in Latin to 1733. Ancient indictments, temp. Edward I (thirteenth century)–1675, KB 9, and some are in JUST 1; indictments for London and Middlesex, 1675–1845, KB 10, and other counties, 1675–1845, KB 11, thereafter to 1875 for all counties, KB 12, and most of which relate to cases commenced in the inferior courts but called to the King's Bench on writs of certiorari or of error for determination, indexed; the indictments from 1675 are arranged under legal term. Indictments, exhibits and convictions, Baga de Secretis, 1477–1813, including State Trials, KB 8, with a printed *Calendar*. Pleadings, 1820–56, 1860–75, KB 19; the Coram Rege Rolls record proceedings on 'Rex Rolls', 1272–1701, KB 27, 1702–1875, on the Crown Rolls, KB 28, to which the Controlment Rolls, 1329–1843, are the key, as they contain details of the course of proceedings, with outcome, and marginal references to the Coram Rege and Crown Rolls, KB 29; they are arranged in three sections: the Bag Roll refers to the indictments found in KB 10–KB 12, the second (the Roll of Entries) to entries of appearance and pleas within each term found in KB 27 and KB 28, and the last (Special Writ Roll) notes special writs including mandamus and writs of error from the Court to the House of Lords, giving details of the original hearing and proceedings, enrolments of writs *de excommunicato capiendo* and *de contumace capiendo* to uphold the authority of ecclesiastical courts and ordering the arrest of an individual in contempt of a court order until satisfaction was given; by the seventeenth century the Controlment Rolls are organized in rough geographical order, corresponding to the Assize circuits; KB 27–KB 29 are arranged by legal term by regnal year until the Interregnum, and thereafter by calendar year, from 1660–1726 by regnal year, 1727–1819 by legal year, commencing with Michaelmas Term, and from 1820 by calendar year; later enrolments of writs, 1844–75, KB 5; Posteas, noting nisi prius trial results at Assizes, 1664–1839, KB 20, 1702–1875, KB 28; depositions taken mainly before justices of the peace, and including informations, exhibits and recognizances, and relating to cases before inferior courts transferred to this Court, 1836–75, KB 6; affidavits, 1683–1875, KB 1, with indexes, 1738–1875 (gap for 1755–60) in KB 39; supplementary series of affidavits, 1689–1737,

KB 2. Collection of precedents in cases of treason, riot, libel, murders abroad, insults against foreign rulers, seventeenth–nineteenth centuries, KB 33. Records in error on writs, mostly from the Court sitting in Dublin, 1737–1836, KB 7.

see **Assizes, Lords, House of**

King's Bench (Plea Side), Court of
This common law court dealt with civil cases, and had special jurisdiction over inferior courts using the prerogative writs of mandamus, certiorari and prohibition, and held *quo warranto* and habeas corpus proceedings. By the fictitious Bill of Middlesex it widened its business over civil disputes between subjects by directing a bill to the Sheriff of Middlesex ordering the arrest of a named person for an imaginary trespass so that he might be brought to court: once there the trespass was dropped and the real cause of action dealt with; if the defendant could not be located a further writ of *latitat* was issued to the county Sheriff where the person 'lurked about', citing the Bill of Middlesex, and ordering his arrest; it was abolished in 1832. The Court was absorbed into the High Court of Justice in 1875 to form part of the Queen's Bench Division. The records are in Latin to 1733. Writs, 1629–1837, including *latitats*, 1689–1778, KB 137; Coram Rege Rolls, recording proceedings, 1272–1701, KB 27, Plea Rolls or Judgment Rolls record those 1702–1875, KB 122; Posteas, nineteenth century, PRO 30/44; Rule Books include many entries of orders to return to gaol prisoners brought to the bar of the Court and often include long lists of inmates, 1603–1877, with indexes, 1792–1802, KB 125, this class together with lists of causes, 1668–87, depositions by commission, 1827–37, dockets of commitments, 1730–1822, informations, presentments, pleas, and

Posteas temp. Henry VIII–George IV, in KB 140, forms the main means of reference to KB 122; other material in KB 140 are writs of error and certiorari, with transcripts of proceedings in local and inferior courts, temp. Henry VIII–William IV, outlawry extents, temp. George III–Victoria, and enrolments of writs of habeas corpus, 1617–1818, and returns from Queen's Prison, 1849–52; Rules, Entry Books of final judgments on Posteas and inquiries, 1675–1837, and lists of prisoners, 1729–34, 1782–1838, KB 139; depositions, 1802–1875, KB 144, indexed in IND 1/6630; affidavits, 1734–1875, KB 101. Declarations for ejectment, to try the title to freeholds, alleging a lease to 'John Doe' by the claimant and Doe's eviction by 'Richard Roe', the nominal defendant, were served on the actual tenant in possession with a letter from Roe advising him to defend the title; the tenant might 'Consent to rule', making him the defendant in Roe's place: Rules in ejectment, Series I, 1720–28, then at ten-yearly intervals, 1730–1840, and 1842, Series II, 1728, 1730, and ten-yearly intervals to 1830, 1834–36, give the outcome, J 89, to which there are nominal indexes, though to 1790 the lessors' names are not included. Warrants of attorney to confess judgment in actions for debt, 1802–22, KB 128, 1825–52, KB 133, both arranged alphabetically by defendant; copy warrants of attorney and cognovits, 1822–5, KB 134, and a supplementary series, 1821–4, KB 135 (the originals of which are in CP 48 and E 17), with indexes.

King's/Queen's Bench Division of the High Court of Justice Established from the Court of King's Bench in 1875, it absorbed the Common Pleas Division and common law side of the Exchequer Division in 1880 and the Admiralty Division in 1970. Indexes on open access to Cause Books, recording details of actions entered for trial, giving the names of parties, number and nature of the suit, solicitors acting, and from 1909 the outcome, 1879–1906, 1921–37, J 87; specimens of Judgment Books, 1875, and at ten-yearly intervals from 1880–1930, arranged chronologically in alphabetical groupings, by plaintiff's name, indexed, 1875 and 1880, J 89, the later entries located via J 87; (Crown Side) enrolments of writs *de contumace capiendo*, 1875–80, KB 5; indictments, mostly on writs of certiorari from lesser courts, 1875–1926, indexed, KB 12; pleadings, 1875–1906, KB 19, with a card index of plaintiffs, 1875–80, on open access, J 55, pleadings, 1880–1942, arranged by date of filing, under quarterly divisions of each year, and then alphabetically by plaintiff, J 54; proceedings, 1876–1911, KB 28; affidavits, 1876–1963, arranged by year and legal term, KB 1 (some closed 75 years), indexed 1876–1984 (gap 1922–4) by name of party on behalf of whom they were drawn up, the name of the party or organization filing them, and the date of filing, KB 39; depositions relating to cases referred on from inferior courts, 1875–86, KB 6; (Plea Side) warrants of attorney to confess judgment, 1875–85, indexes only, J 58; depositions, 1875–80, J 16, 1880–1919, J 17, indexed in IND 1/6630; affidavits, 1876–82, J 5; exhibits, c.1700–1918, with a descriptive list giving the title of the cause and date, to which there are indexes on open access, J 90. Appeals from inferior courts, 1876–1963, including copies of judgments and judges' notes, indexed, KB 3 (some closed 75 years); Rule or Order Books of orders made on appeal from inferior courts and tribunals, arranged by date of judgment order, 1875, 1877, 1880, 1882–1920, J 74, Divisional Court Orders, 1920–72, J 95 (some closed 75 years); Rule Books of Appeals to the Court of Appeal, arranged in chronological order with brief details of cases, and the Court's decision, 1875–1906, most with integral indexes, KB 25, Final and Interlocutory Appeals to the Court of Appeal, Motions, 1918–26 (2% sample of Interlocutory Appeals, 1921–6), and 2% sample, 1927–61 (including County Courts from 1935), J 69 (some closed 75 years).

see *Appeal, Court of*

King's Bench Prison Used as a place of custody for debtors and those under sentence for contempt of court, and renamed the Queen's Prison in 1842, when the Fleet and Marshalsea Prisons were closed. Commitment and Discharge Books, Habeas Corpus Books, lists of prisoners, 1696–1842, PRIS 10; Commitment Books, giving the date, authority for detention, subsequent action and date of discharge, 1719–1842, indexed, PRIS 4; Abstract Book of Commitments, giving date of imprisonment, amount of the debt, prosecutor's name and date of discharge, 1780–1815, indexed, PRIS 5; original warrants of discharge, 1776–1842, PRIS 7; Execution Books, arranged alphabetically by inmate, giving prosecutors' names, attorneys, and damages, 1758–1842, PRIS 8; coroners' inquisitions on prisoners (Crown Side), temp. Edward I (thirteenth century)–1675, KB 9, 1675–1845, KB 11, 1747–1839, KB 14; unauthenticated registers of marriages, and some baptisms performed outside the Prison, 1667–c.1777, RG 7.

see *Queen's Prison*

King's Bills Up to 1851 these signified royal authority for certain appointments or actions. Warrants for bills, containing brief instructions for drafting, Series I, 1661–1800, SO 8, Series II, 1800–51, SO 6; bills, arranged in monthly files, 1609–42, SP 39, 1661–1851, SO 7, with monthly docket books giving short summaries of their contents, 1549–1761, SP 38, and 1584–1851, SO 3, indexed 1584–1851, in SO 4.

see *State Paper Office*

Kirkby's Quest
see *Knights' Fees*

Knighthood Returns of persons holding twenty or forty librates of land and called on to accept knighthood, plus compositions paid by those men not doing so, temp. Henry II (twelfth century)–Charles I, E 198; names, abodes, status and fines paid by those failing to appear at the Coronation of Charles I and take up knighthood, arranged alphabetically by county, 1630–32, E 407/35; original inquisitions of defaulters, by county, 1631–2, E 178, with a calendar of depositions and Commissions on open access; writs for receiving knighthood, c.1642, are enrolled on the Close Rolls, C 54; exonerations of men in distraint of knighthood up to c.1641, are enrolled on the Fine Rolls, C 60. Warrants for a King's Bill of creation, 1783–1851, and for letters patent, 1852–9, integrally indexed, HO 116; creations, 1665–1986, in *The London Gazette*, with subject indexes sporadically from 1790, and invariably from 1848, ZJ 1.

Knights' Fees Hereditary lands held in return for feudal services, abolished in 1660. Transcripts of Fees, 1285 (Kirkby's Quest), E 179/240/251, and PRO 31/16, printed in *Feudal Aids, 1284–1431*; transcripts of Fees, temp. Edward I (thirteenth century)–Elizabeth I, E 36/37–74; returns, including wardships and escheats to the Crown (the Ladies Roll, 1185), recording names of persons holding twenty or forty librates of land and called on to accept knighthood, and accounts of fines paid for failing to do so, temp. Henry II (twelfth century)–Charles I, E 198; returns in the Duchy of Lancaster, temp. Henry II–Charles I, DL 40; compositions for Fees in Cumberland and Yorkshire, 1629–30, E 407.

see **Subsidy, Lay**

Korean War 1950–53. Despatches, casualties dead, missing or wounded, citations and recommendations for awards and decorations, in *The London Gazette*, with subject indexes, ZJ 1; lists of British and Commonwealth prisoners in Korean hands, 1951–3, WO 208/3999, Commonwealth prisoners, 1954, WO 308/54.

see **Medals**

L*l*

Labuan Leases of land and licences to work the coal mines, 1848–69, CO 386/ 147.

Ladies Roll
see *Knights' Fees*

Lancaster, Duchy of Pleadings in the Equity Court, temp. Henry VII–1835, DL 1, papers in law suits, 1502–1853, DL 49, depositions and examinations, temp. Henry VII–Philip and Mary, DL 3, temp. Elizabeth–1818, DL 4, sealed depositions, 1695–1739, DL 48, affidavits, orders and petitions, 1560–1857, DL 9, Entry Books of decrees and orders, 1472–1872, DL 5, draft decrees, temp. Henry VIII–1810, DL 6, draft injunctions, 1614–1794, DL 8. Forest Proceedings, temp. Henry III (thirteenth century)–Victoria, DL 39. Coroners' inquisitions and returns, 1804–96, DL 46. Estreats of fines and amercements, mainly taken from Quarter Sessions and Assizes, temp. Henry V (fifteenth century), temp. Elizabeth–Victoria, DL 50. Inquisitions post mortem, temp. Henry III–Charles I, DL 7; returns of Knights' Fees, temp. Henry II (twelfth century)–Charles I, DL 40; letters patent, indentures, leases, homages of heirs, 1440–78, presentations to benefices, abstracts of leases, grants of offices and annuities, temp. Henry VII, DL 37; drafts and particulars for patents, especially for offices, temp. Henry VIII–

George III, DL 13; warrants for grants in fee-farm, patents of offices, temp. Henry VII–George IV, DL 12; draft presentations to benefices, temp. Elizabeth–George I, DL 16; manorial court rolls, temp. Edward I (thirteenth century)–1925, DL 30, *c*.1200–*c*.1900, SC 2; cartularies, registers of grants and leases, temp. John (thirteenth century)–1835, DL 42; original deeds and charters, temp. Henry I (twelfth century)–James I, DL 36; deeds, *c*.1100–*c*.1700, Series L, DL 25; Series LL, DL 26, Series LS, DL 27; feet of fines, temp. Henry II–1839, CP 25; drafts and particulars for leases, temp. Henry VIII–George III, DL 14, counterparts of leases, temp. Edward VI–1875, DL 15; maps and plans showing manorial boundaries, temp. Henry VIII–Victoria, DL 31; rentals and surveys, temp. Henry III (thirteenth century)–George III, DL 43, manorial surveys, enquiries into concealed lands, encroachments and enclosures, extents of goods and chattels of felons and outlaws, oaths of officials, temp. Elizabeth–1853, DL 44; extents for debt, temp. Elizabeth–Charles II, DL 23; Parliamentary surveys during the Commonwealth, DL 32; writs and various manorial records, PRO 30/ 26; extracts from Enclosure Awards, evidences of title, inventories, petitions and inquisitions, temp. Henry III–Victoria, DL 41, Enclosure Awards, 1775–1872, DL 45; Chantry and College certificates, temp. Henry VIII and Edward VI, DL 38; lists of borough magistrates, 1938–74, C 193/160.

Lancaster, Palatinate of

(1) *Common law jurisdiction* (the records are in Latin to 1733) Plea Rolls, including deeds of bargain and sale, feet of fines, King's Silver payments, and common recoveries, and judgments in actions for recovery of land, 1400–1845, PL 15, dockets, 1362–1848, PL 16, sessional papers, including pleadings, temp. Henry VIII–1848, PL 21; jury panels and verdicts of suits, 1811–48, PL 19; writs returned at sessions, 1438–1846, PL 20; declarations in ejectment, 1788–1849, PL 22. Assize Rolls, 1422–1843, PL 25, indictments, 1424–1868, coroners' inquisitions, 1626–1822, PL 26, depositions, 1663–1867, PL 27; outlawry rolls, temp. Richard II (fourteenth century)–Edward VI, Order Books and pardons, temp. Richard II–Victoria, PL 28. Articles of clerkship and admissions of attorneys, 1730–1875, PL 23; Commissions of justices of the peace, 1675–1875, DL 20; inquisitions post mortem, temp. Henry IV (fifteenth century)–Henry VIII, PL 4, lunacy inquisitions, temp. Charles II–William IV, PL 5; Patent Rolls, 1380–1506, PL 1, Close Rolls, 1409–70, PL 2, and 1354–1440, DL 37. Feet of fines and concords of fines, 1362–1834, PL 17, enrolments of fines and payment of King's Silver, 1586–1834, PL 18; deeds, *c*.1550–*c*.1850, Series H, PL 29.

(2) *Equity Court* Bills, 1485–1853, PL 6, answers, 1474–1858, PL 7, replications, rejoinders etc, 1601–1856, PL 8; depositions, 1581–1854, PL 10, affidavits, 1610–1836, PL 9, exhibits, 1795–1860, PL 12, decrees and orders, 1524–1848, PL 11, miscellanea, including enrolments of deeds and decrees, warrants and writs, temp. Richard II (fourteenth century)–Victoria, PL 14; Causes, 1853–1922, PL 38, decrees and orders, 1857–1922, both in the Manchester District Registry of the Chancery Court, PL 34, with an index of Causes to *c*.1920, PL 31; Liverpool District Registry decrees and orders, 1853–1944, PL 35, and Cause Books, 1867–1954, PL 39; Preston District Registry decrees and orders, 1862–1971, and Blackburn Office, 1893–1947, PL 36, Cause Books, 1851–1956, and Blackburn Office, 1893–1947, PL 37. Accounts ledgers concerning administered funds, especially for infants, wills and legacies and sales of testators' businesses, 1873–1970, PL 40, Reports and certificates, 1813–49, PL 30.

Land Grants, Colonial Petitions for grants, 1688–1782, SP 44, warrants for grants, 1688–1801, CO 324/22–46, 1714–80, CO 324/49–50, 1766, CO 323/22, 1816–72, CO 381, leases of land in Labuan, 1848–69, land orders and land certificates, 1840–74, land orders in the Falkland Islands, and Natal, 1859–74, land order book for South Australia, 1839, all in CO 386, grants of land from the New Zealand Company, 1839–50, CO 208.

see *Colonies, Dominions and Dependencies* and under individual countries

Land Revenue, Exchequer Office of the Auditors of Took over the work of the Court of Augmentations when it was abolished in 1554.

see *Augmentations of the Revenues of the King's Crown, Court of, Crown Lands*

Lands, Concealed Crown lands disposed of during the Interregnum often to *bona fide* purchasers, and which the Crown attempted to recover after the Restoration in 1660.

see **Crown Lands**

Lands Tribunal Established in 1949 to determine questions concerning compensation for compulsory acquisition of land and other matters, and appeals from local valuation courts. Specimen case files, 1951–74, LT 8 (some closed), with registers to them, 1921–69, LT 9.

Land Tax and Assessed Taxes Land Tax was payable on the beneficial ownership of land, and was originally levied in 1692, and made redeemable from 1798 on payment of a lump sum representing so many years' value of the tax; redemption was made compulsory in 1949, and the Tax was abolished in 1963. Assessments for England and Wales, arranged alphabetically by county, then by hundred and parish, listing owners and occupiers, amounts assessed, redemption contract number if applicable, 1798, with a few, 1799–1801, plus appeals by Roman Catholics under a statute of 1794 against double liability for the Land Tax, arranged under county, 1828 onwards, IR 23; some certificates of returns of double assessments on Papists, temp. George I, E 174; assessments on offices in the Liberty of the Rolls, under a statute of 1692, 1756, 1810–96, and default schedules, 1848–78, 1893–7, arranged by street, J 151; parish books of redemptions, alphabetically listed by English and Welsh county, then Land Tax parishes, giving redemptioner's name, that of the occupier, the amount of tax redeemed and contract registration number, 1799–1953, IR 22, registers of redemption contracts, 1799–1963, arranged by number (between 1905 and 1950 plans of affected property are included), IR 24; enrolment books of deeds, 1799–1885, and assignments, 1799–1803, of Land Tax and its redemption by public and corporate bodies, and by charities, arranged by number, and indexed, IR 20; exonerations of ecclesiastical benefices and charitable institutions with annual incomes lower than £150, 1806–69, IR 21; Inland Revenue cases concerning Land Tax, 1823–58, IR 12/1–3, indexed in IR 12/4; returns of names of persons jailed for non-payment of taxes, 1848–53, IR 84/6, and 1853–6, IR 83/17. A variety of certificates of receipts of Income Tax, 1799–1802, 1803–16, of arrears and surcharges on Land Tax, 1692–1830, imposts between 1689 and 1830, including aids and grants, on hair powder, 1795–8, armorial bearings, 1793–1830, inhabited houses, 1692–1830, houses and windows, 1696–1830, male servants, 1777–1830, female servants, 1785–92, carriages, 1747–82, horses for riding or used in husbandry, 1784–1830, and on dogs, 1796–1830, arranged in yearly county bundles, and then by parish, some with names of payers, of Papists assessed to pay double, and others naming defaulters, or persons against whom no distraint was possible to recover the tax, because they were dead or gone away, E 182; Receivers' accounts record in yearly county bundles the basis of assessment, amounts, collectors, and names and addresses of payers, Papists, defaulters, and exemptions, 1689–1830, E 181 (both these classes do not have uniformly full returns for every county, but those of London and Middlesex parishes are particularly good, as might be expected); duplicate assessments of various counties, 1689–97, SP 33 Cases B–D.

Latvia Libau, births to Britons, 1883–1932, deaths, 1920–32, FO 661/4–5, deaths, 1871–1915, FO 440/10, certified copies of births and deaths, 1887–96, 1920–40, FO 440/9; Riga, births, 1850–1910, deaths, 1850–1915, FO 377/3–4, births, 1921–40, marriages, 1920–40, deaths, 1921–40, FO 516/1–9, and a card index of British subjects; Windau, births, 1906–9, FO 399/19.

League of Mercy Established in 1899 to reward personal service, or the promotion of welfare of hospitals, especially King Edward's Hospital in London, and dissolved in 1947. Roll, 1902–47, MH 11/1–2.

Leases Leases surrendered to the Crown, temp. Henry VIII–Philip and Mary, E 312, temp. Mary–James I, E 311, temp. Charles II–James II, C 203; leases of Crown lands, temp. Elizabeth–George III, E 365, particulars of leases and warrants, temp. Elizabeth–George IV, E 367, abstracts and indexes to leases, same period, E 381, drafts of leases, temp. Henry VII–George I, E 380; letters patent granting Crown leases, 1599–1696, E 403; warrants for Crown leases, 1667–1727, indexed, T 54, 1727–1818, indexed, T 55; Entry Books of leases, 1750–1812, E 369; Constat Books, giving details of lease terms and value of consideration prior to formal conveyances, 1660–1851, CRES 6; Crown leases, 1570–1961, CRES 40, reports on leases of Crown lands, 1716–86, CRES 7, 1802–1919, integrally indexed, CRES 9; card index to duplicate leases, 1961–7, CRES 31 (documents destroyed), and to those over fifty years, 1961–7, CRES 32 (documents destroyed); counterparts and transcripts of conventual leases made by dissolved monasteries, 1357–1545, E 118, 1330–1552, E 303, with an index of names and places for the reigns of Henry VII and Henry VIII; counterparts of leases made by the Court of Augmentations and the General Surveyors of Crown Lands, 1526–47, E 299, and warrants for the leases, temp. Henry VIII–Edward VI, E 300; enrolments in the Augmentation Office, 1560–1601, E 309, particulars for leases, counterparts and transcripts, c.1501–c.1700, E 310. Leases made by the Court of Wards and Liveries, c.1541–Charles I, WARD 6, particulars for leases, temp. Henry VIII–Charles I, WARD 12. Leases in the Duchy of Cornwall, temp. Henry VIII–Charles II, E 306, enrolments in the Palatinate of Durham, fourteenth–eighteenth centuries, DURH 3; leases in the Duchy of Lancaster, 1440–78, and abstracts, temp. Henry VII, DL 37, registers of leases, temp. John (thirteenth century)–1835, DL 42, drafts and particulars for leases, temp. Henry VIII–George III, DL 14, counterparts of leases, temp. Edward VI–1875, DL 15. Leases used as evidence in or enforced by order of the Court of Chancery, 1691–1816, C 45. Case files of applications for orders modifying covenants or other restrictions on leasehold land, with the resultant orders made by the Official Arbitrator or Lands Tribunal, 1926–61, arranged by file number, LT 3, with an index to the file numbers under applicant's name, giving case summary, date of application, property concerned and its nature, and the date and nature of any order, 1926–66, LT 4. Chancery miscellanea, concerning specific performance of contracts about real estate, including leases, 1517–1953, with a descriptive list arranged under subject, TS 18 (some closed 75 or 100 years).

Leases and Releases A written indenture of lease of land for a year was followed a day later by another indenture of release of the reversion of the freehold of the same land at the end of the term of the lease, to the same person, and used after 1536 as a

device avoiding enrolment as a deed of bargain and sale, because it did not convey a freehold estate within the terms of the statute. After 1841 the release was effective without the lease, and from 1845 a deed of grant was held to be sufficient. Deeds of lease and release enrolled on the Close Rolls to 1845, C 54, and some original indentures, 1691–1816, C 45.
see *Close Rolls*

Lebanon Beirut, marriages of Britons, *c.*1859–1939, FO 616/5.

Legacy Duty see *Death Duty*

Legations, British
see *Embassies and Legations, British*

Lenten Certificates Under a proclamation of 1561 enquiries were made about who had killed, dressed, or eaten meat or sold unlicensed drink during Lent. Returns for the City of London, 1593–1641, C 265; licences and presentments relating to the selling of meat in taverns and cookshops in the City of London, temp. James I–Charles I, C 203; bonds made by victuallers concerning the slaughter, dressing and eating of flesh in Lent, temp. Elizabeth–Charles II, E 180.

Levant Company (Turkey Company) Founded in 1581 and originally open only to freemen of the City of London until 1753, its monopoly over trade with the Levant was brought to an end in 1825. Books and papers, 1606–1866, SP 105, described to 1670 in *Calendar of State Papers (Domestic Series)*; other Company archives, of the Factory at Aleppo, 1616–1825, SP 110.

Libya (Tripoli) Certificates of British nationality, notices, certificates and dec-larations of marriage, wills and death certificates, *c.*1742–1951, FO 161, marriages, 1916, 1931–40, deaths, 1938–9, FO 161/4–7.

Licences, Royal For change of name and arms. Out-letters, 1806–1922, indexed, HO 117; correspondence, 1841–1950, HO 45; fees paid for licences, 1782–1880, HO 88.
see *Arms, Coats of, Name, Change of*

Licences to pass beyond the Seas Granted to persons going to the Continent or elsewhere, 1573–8, 1621, 1624, 1628–9, 1631–2, 1638–9, from Chester and Liverpool to Ireland, 1632–3, Plymouth to St Christopher, 1633–4, Dartmouth to St Christopher and Barbados, 1634–5, London to New England, 1634–5, Holland and New England, 1637, to New England, 1634, persons transported from St Ives to Ireland, 1632–3, Penrhyn to St Christopher, 1634, to Holland, 1621, 1624, passes from Exeter to France, Gravesend to Barbados, Virginia, Maryland, Holland and Scotland, 1677, soldiers taking the Oath of Allegiance, 1632–3, and before going to the Low Countries in 1613–14, 1616–21, 1623–5, 1631–5, and to Vienna, Utrecht and elsewhere, 1632–3, E 157 (of which the American and West Indian entries have been printed in J.C. Hotten's *Original Lists of Persons Emigrating to America, 1600–1700*, 1874).
see *Emigrants, Merchants, Passes and Passports*

Lieutenants, Deputy Warrants for appointment, 1679–1782, SP 44, described between 1760–75, in *Calendar of Home Office Papers of the reign of George III*; appointments published in *The London Gazette*, 1665–1986, with subject indexes sporadically from 1790, invariably from 1848, ZJ 1.

Lieutenant, Lords Commissions of appointment are enrolled on the Patent Rolls, 1551–1962, for which there are printed *Calendars* to 1582, and 1584–7, C 66, and announced in *The London Gazette*, 1665–1986, with subject indexes sporadically from 1790, and invariably from 1848, ZJ 1.

Lincoln's Inn Black Books, including admissions and appointments of officials, investigation and punishment for offences of members, and from 1518 lists of those called to the Bench and Bar, 1422–1971, PRO 30/77.

Lithuania Kovno and Memel, births to Britons, 1924–40, deaths, 1922–40, FO 722/1–4.

Livery, Writs of These entitled an heir to inherited land held in-chief of the Crown to obtain livery of seisin (take possession) of it, having attained his majority, for which he paid half a year's profit. The records are in Latin. Escheators' files, temp. Henry III (thirteenth century)–Richard III, E 153, and writs in the Court of Wards and Liveries, *c*.1541–1652, WARD 9.

Loans Orders for a loan made in 1590, arranged under English counties (except Cumberland and Northumberland) and dioceses, and recording names and qualities of subscribers, sometimes their parish of residence, and contributions, and names of collectors, SP 12/236; assignment books of a loan made by City of London goldsmiths, 1677, indexed, E 406/1–26, deeds, wills, and administration grants effecting share transfers in the loan interest, 1677–1704, indexed, E 406/27–44;

assignments of orders on bankers' annuities from loans, 1704–17, E 407/16–17; registers of subscribers to loans, 1696–1847, E 401/2591–98.
see *Annuities, Subsidy, Lay*

Local Government Board Personal files on careers of senior officials and others in Established posts, including some obituaries, 1911–69, MH 107.

London, City of Names of freemen of City Livery Companies, arranged by Company temp. Henry VIII, E 36/93; Poll Tax of Companies, listing officers, liverymen and freemen, 1641, E 179/251/22; Land Tax and other assessed taxes, including Aids and grants, arranged under ward and then by parish, in yearly bundles, and including payers, with abodes and status, defaulters, those gone away or dead, and Papists paying double charges, 1689–1830, E 182, and E 181; Association Oath Roll of City Companies, 1696, C 213/171, of London dissenters, C 214/9. Returns of new buildings erected between 1580 and 1597, with names of owners, 1597, E 163/15/14; redemption certificates of the tithe, arranged by parish, and address, and providing details of agreements for commutation or apportionment, orders and awards, and declarations of merger, 1886–1947, MAF 8. Registers of murders and deaths by violence in the Metropolitan Police Area, giving in chronological order the name, address and occupation of the victim, the date and place of death, and details of any subsequent charge and conviction, 1891–1909, 1912–17, 1919–66, the later ones record also deaths of women in abortion, MEPO 20.

London, Commissary Court of Registers of wills, with estate valuations for probate, details of bequests, and legatees' relationship to the deceased, 1792–4, T 64/293.

London, Consistory Court of Registers of wills, with estate valuations at probate, details of bequests and the legatees' relationship to the deceased, 1792–4, T 64/292.

London Court of Hustings
see *Outlaws*

The London Gazette The official twice-weekly newspaper of the government, first published from Oxford in 1665 and thenceforward in London, it contains Acts of State, Proclamations, appointments and Commissions under the Crown, ecclesiastical preferments and resignations, Service senior appointments and resignations, Despatches, Honours Lists, awards and decorations, citations for gallantry medals, dissolutions of partnerships, proceedings in bankruptcy and insolvency, winding-up and liquidations of companies, enrolments of change of name by deed poll or royal licence, names of Royal Warrant holders and awards for exports, denizations and naturalizations, and any other information directed for publication, including special editions, 1665–1986, with sporadic annual or half-yearly subject indexes from 1790, invariably from 1848, ZJ 1. There is an index from 1830–83 available.

Lord Chamberlain's Department Embraces the Royal Chambers, Wardrobes, Office of Robes and Ceremonies, Revels, Musicians, Chapels, Housekeepers, Messengers, Yeomen of the Guard, Heralds, Watermen, Physicians, Artists, Craftsmen, the Poet Laureate, and others 'above stairs'. Association Oath Roll of the Royal Household, 1696, C 213/365–72.

Appointments of officers, servants and tradesmen, 1660–1851, LC 3/61–71, 1851–1901, LC 5/237–41, incomplete appointment books, 1685–1838, LC 3/56–60; Established servants, 1641–1849, LC 3/1–23, list of officers and servants, 1864–97, LC 5/247; salary, livery and pension books, 1667–1875, LC 3/37–52, arrears of salaries and wages, 1667–85, LC 3/37, claims for arrears of wages and salaries, temp. Charles II, LC 9/377–90; servants of the Office of Robes, 1830–1901, LC 13/1–5; Warrant Books, including names of servants such as rat killers, necessary women, herb strewers, and choirboys, 1628–1900, LC 5; Entry Books of wills and letters of attorney, 1547–1791, LC 5; Wardrobe Bill Books, 1667–1768, of the Great Wardrobe, 1749–82, and Lord Chamberlain's Bill Books, 1782–93, LC 9, 1784–1894, LC 10, and 1784–1900, LC 11, all including bills of messengers and tradesmen; payments, 1516–1782, partially indexed, LC 5/11–83, and to suppliers of goods, 1628–1810, LC 5/132–63; persons assessed for taxes, 1759–98, 1854–69, giving name, office, salary, deductions and allowances, and amount of tax, LC 3/35–36; in-letters, 1710–1858 (indexed, 1812–57), out-letters, 1783–1853 (indexed from 1804), semi-official out-letters, 1851–7 (indexed), general in-letters and drafts of out-letters concerning appointments, Court affairs, theatres etc, 1719–1902, LC 1; correspondence, 1858–1902, LC 3; registers of people present, invitations and presentation lists for Royal Levées and Drawing Rooms, 1773–1924, LC 6.
see *Offices, Royal and Public, Royal Warrant Holders, Theatres*

Lord Chancellor's Department Selected personal files of officers employed, listed alphabetically by category (disciplinary offences, career, and judicial), 1917–81, LCO 33 (closed 50 or 75 years).

Lords, House of Records in error on writs from the Court of King's Bench (Crown Side), giving details of the original hearing and proceedings, 1737–1836, KB 7; judgments on appeal from the Court of Appeal, and filed with the petitions, 1855–1906, KB 34, listed. Some judgments in Chancery actions, 1876–1955, indexed in the annual 'A' and 'B' Books to 1955, under date of filing, within each term, and initial index of plaintiffs' names, and citing folio reference, J 15.

see *King's Bench (Crown Side), Court of, King's Bench Division of the High Court of Justice, Peers*

Lord Steward's Department This replaced the Board of Green Cloth in 1782, and until the Master of the Royal Household was appointed in 1854 it was responsible for employees and tradesmen 'below stairs' in the kitchens, gardens and stables. Association Oath Roll of the Royal Household, 1696, C 213/365–72. Warrants of appointment as servants and officers, 1660–1820, LS 13/246–67, Entry Book of appointments, 1627–41, LS 13/251; Cheque Rolls giving names and dates of being sworn in and authorization of appointment, temp. James I–George II, contracts, 1669–1812, Establishment Books recording board wages, 1627–1812, and orders placed with tradesmen and others, 1763–1851, LS13/6–13; original warrants to purveyors of goods to the Royal kitchens, cellars, stables and gardens, 1627–1820, LS 13/251–67, and 1761–82, LS 13/246–50; receipt books for wages and allowances, 1761–1816, Entry Books of assigned board wages in the Office of the Clerk of the Kitchen, with copies of grants of letters of administration

and probates of wills, 1712–26, salaries showing tax deductions, 1790–1827, LS 13/154–67; lists of servants, recording dates of admission and those on special duty, 1672–1820, LS 13/197–204; salary and wage lists of stable, chamber and chapel staff, 1761–81, LS 13/210–30; taxpayers, 1715–1825, LS 13/196, 232–33, and a Poll Tax assessment book, 30 July 1689, naming Royal servants and their relations, LS 13/231; Bounty payments, with signed receipts, 1758–1813, LS 13; monthly accounts of creditors not paid by salary, 1641–1854, divided from 1761–1815 into Household, Kitchen and Incidental, LS 8; kitchen ledgers, noting payment of board wages and for ales, wines and fish, 1660–1729, LS9/60–77; labourers in the Royal Gardens at Kew, Windsor and Hampton Court, 1834–5, LS 11/19–20; ledgers and bills paid at the Royal Residences, 1821–51, LS 3, bills at Royal Residences, with names of tradesmen and the nature of the account, 1825–49, LS 7.

see *Green Cloth, Board of, Marshalsea, Court of the*

Lotteries Registers of beneficiaries in the Adventure of Two Million, 1711, E 401/2600, and the Classis Lottery of £1,800,000, 1712, E 401/2599, arranged under five classes according to the date of purchase of a lottery ticket, and giving ticket number, name and address of the owner, the sum invested and the annuity granted from it, plus a list of unclaimed premiums entered into the lottery as prizes; annuities payable from lotteries, 1706–9, 1805, 1807, 1810, E 351/53–56.

see *Annuities, Million Bank, Tontines*

Lunatics
see *Idiots and Lunatics, Protection, Court of*

M*m*

Madagascar (Malagasay Republic) Diego Suarez, births to Britons, 1907–21, FO 711/1; Tamatave, deaths, 1935–40, FO 714/1; Tananarive (Antananarivo), births, 1865–68, FO 710/1.

Malawi
see *Nyasaland*

Malta Muster of patients in the Military Hospital, 1802–4, ADM 102/555; applications for passports, 1810–11, CO 323; marriages of Britons, 1904–36, FO 161/7.

Malta, Knights of St John of
see *Refugees*

Malaysia Births, marriages and deaths of Britons, 1915–*c.*1946, RG 36, indexed in RG 43/18, births, 1920–48, RG 33/131, indexed in RG 43/1, deaths, 1941–5, RG 33/132, indexed in RG 43/14; Borneo, births, 1907, deaths, 1897–1907, FO 221/2–3; Borneo and Sarawak, deaths from enemy action, 1941–5, RG 33/132; Johore, births, 1924–31, RG 36, indexed in RG 43; Sarawak, births, 1910–48, marriages, 1921–35, deaths, 1910–48, RG 36, indexed in RG 43.

Male Servants, Tax on 1777–1852. List of persons paying duty, arranged alphabetically by county, and then by initial letter of surname, and giving address and number of servants, 1780, T 47/8; people in arrears and defaulters, arranged

in annual county bundles, and then under parish, 1777–1830, E 182.

Maltsters Registers of bonds, giving names, addresses and those of two sureties, 1848–73, CUST 120; licence books for maltsters in the Palatinate of Chester, 1723–34, CHES 38/12.

Management and Administration Department of the Lunacy Office
see *Idiots and Lunatics, Protection, Court of*

Man, Isle of Census returns, 6 June 1841, HO 107, 30 March 1851, HO 107, 7 April 1861, RG 9, 2 April 1871, RG 10, 3 April 1881, RG 11, and 5 April 1891, RG 12; ecclesiastical census of church and chapel attendances on 30 March 1851, and average attendance over the previous year, sent in by ministers, HO 129; payment of pensions to military, naval and marine personnel by the Royal Hospitals at Chelsea and Greenwich, recording under pay-district, rank, regiment and number, date, nature and amount of pension, and any transfer elsewhere, plus date of death, 1852–62, WO 22/207; staff lists of Customs officers, 1671–1922, CUST 39 (closed 75 years), quarterly bills of salaries due to officers, 1810–13, CUST 18, 1814–29, CUST 19, superannuation registers, including widows' pensions, and recording the names and dates of children's births, 1803–1922,

CUST 39 (closed 75 years); calendars of prisoners, giving age, occupation, offence charged, verdict and sentence, 1868–1958, HO 140 (some closed 75 years); rentals of Crown lands, 1832–1954, with a descriptive list arranged chronologically, LRRO 12 (most closed 100 years); State Papers, 1761–83, SP 48, included to 1775 in *Calendar of Home Office Papers of the reign of George III*.

Manorial Courts and Records The records of the courts enshrine surrenders of copyhold tenants' lands back to the lord of the manor and admissions of new tenants in their place, plus judicial and administrative business. The other records are half-yearly or annual rentals, and surveys, maps and plans drawn up at infrequent intervals, in which tenants will be named. They are generally written in Latin until 1733, though are in English during the Commonwealth period. Court rolls, mainly of manors, Honours and other local jurisdictions in the Duchy of Lancaster, the Augmentation Office, Exchequer, Palatinate of Chester, and Wales, *c*.1200–*c*.1900, SC 2, to which there is a topographical index; court rolls of Crown lands, 1286–1837, LR 3; court rolls and other documents of English and Welsh manors, listed alphabetically by manor, 1441–1950, CRES 5; court rolls of the Duchy of Lancaster, temp. Edward I (thirteenth century)–1925, DL 30; various manorial records relating to the Duchies of Lancaster and Cornwall, PRO 30/26; Halmote Court books of the Palatinate of Durham, 1348–1619, DURH 2; court rolls of some Gloucestershire manors, 1684–1917, F 14, and of the Forest of Dean, 1781–1891, F 16; deeds and evidences relating to the Forest of Dean, 1781–1891, F 15; court rolls, rentals and other documents of manors in Paglesham,

Essex, 1386–1926, MAF 5, and deeds and evidences, 1720–1863, MAF 6; records of manors in Surrey, Westmorland and Wiltshire, 1483–1936, TS 19; rentals and surveys, temp. Henry III–William III, including terriers, extents and surveys or valuations of monastic and other possessions formerly in the Exchequer and Augmentation Office, some from the Principality of Wales, and the Palatinates of Chester and Durham, SC 11 and SC 12; surveys of manors in the Duchy of Lancaster, 1558–1853, DL 44, Parliamentary surveys during the Commonwealth of Duchy of Lancaster manors, DL 32, maps and plans, manorial boundaries, extents and valuations of manors in the Duchy of Lancaster, temp. Henry VIII–Victoria, DL 31, and rentals and surveys, temp. Henry III (thirteenth century)–George III, DL 43; court rolls relating to Greenwich Hospital estates in Cumberland, Northumberland and Kent, 1473–1930, ADM 74; Chancery Master's exhibits, containing court rolls, rentals and surveys, 1294–1808, listed alphabetically by county, then chronologically, and with a place-name index, C 116; Duchess of Norfolk's deeds, *c*.1150–*c*.1850, listed alphabetically by county and manor and then by date, C 115.

see *Augmentations of the Revenues of the King's Crown, Court of, Crown Lands, Land Revenue, Exchequer Office of the Auditors of*

Manors Manor files, arranged alphabetically, giving county, being evidences of title furnished by lords of the manor on voluntary enfranchisement of copyhold into freehold tenure from 1841, 1840–1900, MAF 20; lists of manors at the time of compulsory enfranchisement, commencing in 1925, 1925–52, MAF 48/609.
see *Copyhold*

Maps and Plans Of Crown lands, 1560–1953, LRRO 1; temp. Elizabeth I, SP 46; of Ireland, temp. Elizabeth–James I, SP 64, listed in *Calendar of State Papers, relating to Ireland*; Duchy of Lancaster, manorial boundaries, temp. Henry VIII–Victoria, DL 31; West New Jersey Society, 1658–1921, TS 12.

see **Census, Manorial Courts and Records, Ordnance Survey, Registrars, Superintendent and District, Tithes, Valuation Office**

Marines, Royal A Corps of Marines was set up in 1755, under Admiralty control, to replace the former Marine Regiments raised from the mid-seventeenth century onwards for wartime purposes only. It was organized in numbered companies, distributed among Divisions, with depots at Plymouth, Chatham and Portsmouth, joined between 1805 and 1869 by Woolwich. Association Oath Roll of the First and Second Marine Regiments, 1696, C 213/290–91. Attestation forms, giving age, birthplace, trade, physical description at recruitment, details of enlistment and attestation, summary of service, date and place of discharge, arranged by Division (Chatham, 1790–1883, Plymouth, 1804–38, 1842–83, Portsmouth, 1804–83, Woolwich, 1839–69), by year of attestation or discharge, and then alphabetically, plus attestations of those serving only days or months, 1869–83, attestations between 1884 and 1901, and ranks sequestrated from Portsmouth to the Royal Marine Artillery, 1834–5 (indexed), ADM 157; duplicate information may be found in Description Books, *c.*1750–1940, which include signatures of medical officers passing recruits fit for service, and full discharge details, arranged initial-alphabetically by date of attestation, under Division, including the Deal depot, 1881–

1940, ADM 158; births, marriages and deaths of the Chatham Division, 1755–1941, ADM 183, the Plymouth Division, 1760–1941, ADM 184, Portsmouth Division, 1763–1941, ADM 185, and Woolwich Division baptism and marriage registers, discharge and embarkation books, 1805–69, ADM 81; registers of baptisms, marriages and burials at the Dockyard and Royal Marine churches on the Isle of Sheppey, 1688–1960, and Bermuda, 1826–1946, ADM 6; registers of service, 1842–1905, arranged under regimental number (located in ADM 157 and ADM 158), ADM 159; service records, 1900–23, ADM 175. Registers of marines, 1688–1837, effective and subsistence lists, musters, Commission and Establishment Books, widows' pensions and wills of marines, 1688–1862, and an address book of officers, 1816, ADM 96; seniority lists of officers, 1757–1850, ADM 118; commissions and appointments, registers of officers on half-pay, 1703–1833, ADM 6; lists of officers, including date commissioned, pay rate, company number, details of Establishment of Corps, 1760–1886, ADM 192; officers' certificates of service, giving dates of entry and discharge, date of birth, rank, seniority, orders and commissions, 1756–1922, including warrant officers, executive officers, and civil branches, and of officers in the Royal Marine Artillery, 1798–1855, mostly indexed, ADM 196. Ships' musters, arranged bi-monthly or yearly, 1688–1808, ADM 36, 1792–1842, ADM 37, 1793–1878, ADM 38, 1667–1798, ADM 39, and of hired armed vessels, 1794–1815, ADM 41, each listed alphabetically by ship. Half-pay, retired and unattached pay of officers, 1836–1920, PMG 15; half-pay to officers, 1867–71, and listed alphabetically, 1881–1900, ADM 23; hospital musters, arranged monthly, 1740–1860, ADM 102; service records of surgeons, 1756–1954, most indexed, ADM 196 (some closed 50 or 75 years); card index of officer casualties, 1914–20, giving rank, age, birthplace, date, place and cause of death, and the name and address of the next of kin, ADM 242/1–5, and an alphabetical War Graves Roll, 1914–19, ADM 242/7–10; repayments of half-pay and retired pay when no longer on the effective list, or when widows or children were in receipt of a pension or allowance, 1837–40, PMG 22; addresses of officers on unattached, retired full and reserved half-pay, 1837, PMG 73; pensions paid to officers, 1871–1931, 1951–61, ADM 165; pensions and allowances paid by the Royal Hospital at Greenwich to field officers and captains, 1866–1928, PMG 70; reports of deaths, arranged alphabetically giving name and rank, date, place and cause of death, and home town, 1939–48, ADM 104/127–39, indexes to reports of death, 1893–1950, ADM 104/102–08; registers of powers of attorney, 1825–99, PMG 51, seamen's wills, 1786–1882, ADM 48, indexed 1786–1909, in ADM 142; probate registers, 1836–1915, PMG 50; Bounty papers, 1675–1822, ADM 106; seamen's effects and papers, 1800–60, ADM 44, the registers in ADM 141 forming an index to the records, 1802–61; pensions and allowances paid to widows and children of marines, 1882–1917, which from 1901 relate to those dying in warlike operations, excluding World War I, registers of applications for pensions and gratuities made by widows and relatives, 1892–1933 (up to 1911 because of death through warlike operations, and the later applications for other causes), ADM 166, and 1921–26, PMG 72; pensions and gratuities to marines, including those paid overseas, 1879–1921, PMG 71; disability pensions, retired pay and gratuities, 1917–19, PMG 42/1–12; additional pension books of officers, 1834–3, 1866–84, old and disabled officers' pensions, 1875–85, 1891–5, pensions paid to widows of officers, 1866–85, 1899–1927, and a register of widows' pensions, c.1830–60, pensions paid to widows, children and dependent relatives of marines killed in warlike operations, 1922–6, compassionate list, 1867–70, and payment of compassionate allowances, 1873–1926, ADM 23; pensions and allowances to widows of late officers, 1876–1920, PMG 16; compassionate allowances paid out to children and dependent relatives of late officers, 1837–1921, PMG 18; widows' pensions and allowances to relatives of officers killed in service, 1870–1919, PMG 20. War diaries, 1939–57, ADM 202; marine prisoners in German hands, 1939–45, ADM 201/111; Medal Rolls, 1793–1972, ADM 171; Despatches, casualties, citations for awards and decorations published in *The London Gazette*, to 1986, with subject indexes sporadically from 1790 and invariably from 1848, ZJ 1; courts martial, 1812–1916, indexed, ADM 194 (most closed 75 years); records of courts martial, 1890–1957, ADM 156 (most closed 75 or 100 years).

see **Falklands War, Greenwich Hospital, Royal, Korean War, Medals, Prisoners of War, War Pensions, World War I, World War II**

Maritime Causes
see **Delegates, High Court of, Privy Council, Judicial Committee of the**

Marriages and Baptisms, Clandestine
Performed outside the rites of the Anglican church, and without the usual formalities, they were proscribed from 25 March 1754. Registers of marriages and

baptisms at the Fleet and King's Bench Prisons, the Mint, Mayfair Chapel and other places, 1667–c.1777, RG 7.

Marriages at Sea On board Royal Naval ships, 1842–79, RG 33/156, indexed in RG 43/7; entries taken from the official logs, of passengers on board merchant vessels, 1854–83, BT 158, 1902–12, BT 165, and 1913, BT 99; of British subjects on British and foreign ships, 1831–1958, RG 32, indexed in RG 43/8–14, 20–21.

Marriages of Britons Abroad Registers from miscellaneous foreign countries, kept by local authorities or churches, and copies of entries made by British embassies and ministers of churches and chapels, including marriages of servicemen, 1826–1921, RG 34, indexed 1826–1921, in RG 43/8–10; miscellaneous returns, 1831–1958, including nationals of colonies, RG 32, indexed to 1945 in RG 43/8–14; foreign registers and returns, 1627–1958, including marriages registered by British Consuls before 1859 and some records of the African and Asian Protectorates, 1895–1957, RG 33, indexed to 1960 in RG 43/7–14, 20–21; marriages in the African and Asian Protectorates, 1895–1950, RG 36/1–13, indexed, 1904–40, in RG 43/18; returns of marriages at British embassies and legations, 1846–90, FO 83/1136–47, and correspondence concerning marriages, 1814–1905, FO 83, returns of marriages, 1873–89, FO 97, both classes indexed, 1814–93, in FO 802/239.

Marshalsea, Court of the Dealt with litigation between the King's domestic servants, presided over by the Lord Steward and Marshal of the Royal Household; in 1611 it was established as the Court of the Verge, hearing personal actions and trespass cases arising within twelve miles of the King's residence, and where at least one of the parties was a member of his Household. A statute of 1623 allowed cases to be transferred by writ of habeas corpus to a higher court if the damages were more than £5, and the Court was finally superseded by the Palace Court in 1630. Plea Rolls, 1316–99, and 1613–23, E 37.
see **Palace Court**

Marshalsea Prison Housed debtors, and those confined under sentence or charged with contempt of the Court of the Marshalsea, Palace Court or High Court of the Admiralty, and Admiralty prisoners detained under sentence of court martial. It was abolished in 1842, and its inmates moved to Queen's Prison. Commitment books and registers of Admiralty prisoners, 1773–1842, PRIS 11.
see **Queen's Prison**

Marylebone, Middlesex Register of lodging-house keepers, Division of Marylebone, 1890–1923, IR 83/60.

Matrimonial Causes Papers, 1609–1834, DEL 1, indexed in DEL 11/7, 1834–58, in PCAP 1; cases on appeal, c.1600–1834, DEL 2, 1796–1834, DEL 7, appeals, 1834–70, PCAP 3, arranged chronologically; some found their way from the ecclesiastical courts to the Court of King's Bench (Crown Side), enrolments of memoranda recording progress and results, plus marginal references to the Coram Rege Rolls, are on the Controlment Rolls, 1536–1843, KB 29, while the pleas setting out the background to the case, are on the Coram Rege Rolls, 1536–1701, KB 27, and thereafter to 1857 on the Crown Rolls, KB 28 (the records of this Court are in Latin to 1733, and are arranged by legal term).

see *Divorce, King's Bench (Crown Side), Court of, Probate, Divorce and Admiralty Division of the High Court of Justice, Procurator General, Her Majesty's, Treasury Solicitor*

Mayors Certificates of election, listed by town and county, by regnal year, 1303–1648, C 267.

Mechanical Engineers, Institution of Membership lists, 1902–36, ZLIB 22.

Medals
(1) Army campaign and war medals, arranged alphabetically under title of campaign or war, and giving regiment, rank, number and name of recipient, with a note of any bars to which entitled, 1793–1935, WO 100; Waterloo Medal Book, 1815, MINT 16/112; World War I medals, 1917–26, WO 329, indexed by name, giving unit and service number and reference on the Medal Roll, WO 329/1 gives the old reference, and the class list the new. Gallantry medals, recommendations 1854–1983, WO 32 Code 50; for the Boer War, 1899–1902, WO 108; rewards and pensions awarded for Distinguished Services, including the Victoria Cross, 1873–1941, PMG 35; Meritorious Service Medal, 1846–1919, WO 101, Long Service and Good Conduct Awards, 1831–1953, WO 102, annuities, 1846–79, WO 23/84; medals and discharges, out-letters, 1854–7, WO 3; card indexes to entitlement to Meritorious Service Medal, Distinguished Conduct Medal, and Military Medal, arranged alphabetically, giving initials or forename, unit, rank and number, and date of issue recording citation, in *The London Gazette*, 1919,

ZJ 1. Commemorative medals for coronations and other occasions, WO 100 and WO 330.

(2) Royal Navy and Royal Marine campaign medal rolls, 1793–1972, indexed under ship to 1914, ADM 171, for World War I, ADM 171/89–134; list of men in Royal Greenwich Hospital who received medals, 1848–9, ADM 73/94. Gallantry medal recommendations, 1939–45, ADM 1 Code 85, and ADM 116 Code 85; awards to naval officers in World War I, indexed, ADM 171/78–88; miscellaneous Medal Roll, 1866–1966, including Conspicuous Gallantry Medal, Distinguished Conduct Medal and Military Medal for World War I, and Commemorative Medals, 1866–1966, to which there is a nominal index, ADM 171/61; index to entries in *The London Gazette*, 1919 and 1942, ZJ 1.

(3) Royal Air Force campaign medals of the Royal Flying Corps, 1917–26, WO 329, with an index to old references in WO 329/1, matched up with new ones in the class list; campaign medals of the Royal Naval Air Service, ADM 171. Before the Royal Air Force was established in 1918, the Royal Flying Corps received Army Gallantry awards, and the Royal Naval Air Service those of the Navy; recommendations for World War I Gallantry medals are in AIR 1, and from 1918 in AIR 2 Code B 30, including military awards of the George Cross, George Medal and British Empire Medal, 1941–6; submission papers, excluding World War II, 1918–55, giving citations, AIR 30.

(4) Civilian awards, including those to merchant seamen, 1841–1950, HO 45, 1916–41, PREM 2; medals for gallantry in the Merchant Navy, 1854–1959, MT 9 Code 6, and 1856–1981 (with alphabetical registers for 1941–9, and 1968–79),

BT 261; British medals for saving life at sea, 1839–82, FO 83/769; recommendations for the civilian George Cross, George Medal and British Empire Medal, 1940–49, HO 250 (some closed 75 or 100 years).

(5) Foreign awards to Britons and British awards to foreigners, correspondence, 1745–1905, FO 83, and a selection, 1906–51, FO 371, to which there is a card index, 1906–19, and printed index, 1920–51 in FO 409, on open access.

(6) Correspondence on the striking of medals, and containing some references to recipients, 1657–1948, MINT 16.
see *Albert Medal, Conspicuous Gallantry Medal, Distinguished Conduct Medal, George Cross, Victoria Cross*

Medical Officers, Royal Naval Medical Officers' Lists, 1805–86, medical officers serving on ships and at shore establishments of the Royal Navy, 1870–1924, submissions for promotion, and records of service, 1854–1926, services, 1827–93, and of Temporary Consultants and Physicians, 1914–16, medical officers on the retired list, 1805–75, ADM 104; reports on qualifications of Royal Naval Medical Officers, 1822–32, and reports of medical officers and inspectors of Naval hospitals, 1803–63, ADM 105; letters from medical officers of hospitals and hospital ships, 1702–1862, ADM 97, indexed, 1832–62, giving registered number, ADM 133, and weeded registers of letters recording date of receipt, 1832–62, ADM 132.
see *Health, Medical Officers of, Hospitals, Surgeons*

Merchants Petitions concerning foreign trade, 1654–95, CO 338; Association Oath Roll of English merchants in Geneva, 1696, C 213/461, and the English Factory in Malaga, C 213/460; passes issued to go abroad, giving name, port of departure and destination, cargo, ship, burden, master, and valid period of travel, 1697–1784, SP 44/386–413. References are frequently made to and petitions received from them among State Papers.
see *Licences to pass beyond the Seas, State Paper Office*

Merchant Seamen Muster rolls of merchant ships, giving names of crew, usual abode, date of joining and leaving ship, name of previous vessel, 1747–1851, agreements and crew lists of vessels embarked on foreign voyages, and British registered ships of eighty tons or more in the coastal or fishing trade, 1835–60, arranged to 1854 by port and ship's registry number, and thereafter by its official number (located in BT 111), giving name, wage rate, capacity and nature of the voyage, BT 98; 10% sample of agreements, 1861–1938, including all casualty and dead lists, 1914–18, listed under ship's official number, BT 99 (the class list notes other repositories holding the remainder of the agreements); agreements for famous ships, 1835–1954, BT 100; 10% sample of agreement for fishing vessels under eighty tons, 1884–1919, BT 144, and 1920–38, BT 99. Census returns, including crew and passengers, a few of which survive for 1851, of ships in port or arriving, 15–30 March, and of those in the home trade arriving, 31 March–30 April, HO 107, of foreign- and home-going ships, arriving 25 March–7 April 1861, and arriving in port after home or coastal trade up to 7 May, RG 9, British and foreign ships arriving between 25 March and 2 April 1871, and those on coastal trade arriving in port, 3 April–2 May, RG 10, vessels arriving in port, 26 March–3 May 1881, RG 11, and all vessels in port on 30 March 1891, or arriving up to

5 April, thereafter British and foreign ships on the coastal trade arriving 6 April–30 June, RG 12. Registers of seamen, arranged alphabetically, 1835–6, BT 120, 1835–44, BT 112 (indexed in BT 119), give details of age, birthplace, date of entry into the merchant service, capacity, date and port where registered; Register Tickets, 1845–54, BT 113 (indexed in BT 114), giving name, date and port of issue, date and place of birth, physical description, writing ability, year and capacity when first going to sea, subsequent capacities, any service in the Royal Navy or foreign service, present capacity, age at ticketing, and home address, while columns alongside indicate by coded numbers the port from which the seaman had sailed, the registered number of the ship, and date of sailing, and the date and port of return; registers of seamen, 1854–7, arranged alphabetically and giving similar information, BT 116. Alphabetical register of Tickets of Masters, 1845–53, BT 115, registers of certificates of competency of masters and mates of British merchant ships engaged in foreign trade, 1845–1900, which was voluntary until 1850, and then mandatory, the registers recording date and place of birth, Register Ticket number, rank examined for or serving in, ships sailed in, date and place of certificate issue, and details of death, injury or retirement, BT 122 (indexed in BT 127); registers of certificates of competency and service, relating to men passing the voluntary examinations for masters and mates, 1845–9, BT 143; registers of certificates of service of masters, 1850–84, and mates, 1850–75, both in the foreign trade, BT 124 (indexed in BT 127); registers of certificates of competency of masters and mates of steamships engaged in foreign trade, 1881–95, BT 123 (indexed in BT 127); registers of certificates

of competency of masters and mates in the home trade, 1854–88, BT 125, and certificates of service, 1854–88, BT 126 (both indexed in BT 127); registers of certificates of competency of masters and mates in colonial ports, 1876–1921, entered under colony and port of certification, and numbered, BT 128 (indexed in BT 127); registers of certificates of competency, skippers and mates of fishing boats, 1880–98, BT 129, and certificates of service, 1883–1917, BT 130 (both indexed in BT 138); registers of certificates of competency of engineers, 1861–1907, BT 139, and registers of certificates of service, 1862–1921, BT 142 (both indexed in BT 141); registers of certificates of competence of engineers, colonial, 1870–1921, entered under colony, port of certification and number, BT 140 (indexed in BT 141). Black Books, recording disciplinary action against holders of certificates of competency and service, 1851–93, BT 167; registers of protections against impressment into the Royal Navy, of merchant seamen in the coastal trade, 1755–8, 1770–81, 1787–1815, ADM 7. Indexes to apprenticeship indentures, 1824–1953, BT 150, and five-yearly specimens of indentures, 1845–1950, BT 151; register of apprentice seamen at Colchester, 1704–57, 1804–44, BT 167/103. Cases of gallantry at sea and rewards, giving accounts of the actions, 1935–46, gallantry at sea awards, 1856–1981, including government awards, 1876–1981 (gap 1881–6) and colonial and foreign awards, 1909–73, with alphabetical registers, 1941–9, 1968–79, BT 261; register of Albert Medal recipients for saving life at sea, 1866–1913, and photographs, 1866–79, BT 97, and recommendations, 1866–1902, MT 9 Code 6; other medals for saving life at sea, 1839–82, FO 83/769, 1903–53, MT 9 Code 6; recommendations for George Cross, George Medal and British Empire Medal, 1940–49, HO 250. Pension returns, England, Scotland, Wales and Jersey, giving addresses, and arranged under pay-district, 1852–3, WO 22/208; service gratuities and compensation, 1933–42, ADM 116/4534. Selected lists of five-year engagements as Royal Naval Reserve, recruited from seamen, arranged by deck, giving personal details, information on training, service, and retainers, and any subsequent five-year engagement endorsed on the back, 1860–1913, BT 164. Monthly lists of deaths of seamen giving age, rating, nationality or birthplace, last address, date and cause of death, 1886–90, BT 156; half-yearly lists, arranged under cause of demise, 1882–8, BT 157; registers of wages and effects of deceased seamen, recording date and place of engagement and death, its cause, the ship's name, and from 1854 the official ship's number, port, master and date and place of payment of wages, 1852–89, BT 153, with a nominal index, 1853–89, in BT 154, and of ships' names, 1855–89, in BT 155. Deaths at sea of British nationals, 1875–88, BT 159.

see *Albert Medal, Fishermen, Medals, Naval Reserve, Royal*

Merchant Ships Register of merchant ships in England, 1572, SP 15; Trinity House certificates of requests to arm ships in the Thames, giving ship's name, builder, owner and master, and destination, 1630–38, SP 16/17. Returns from colonial ports by naval officers, giving names of masters, build and tonnage, guns and men, owners, cargoes and destinations, 1697–1850, BT 6, 1791–97, HO 76; passes to go to specified continental or overseas ports, giving names of merchants, ships, masters, cargoes, and duration of pass, 1697–1784, SP 44/386–

413. Certificates of registration of British ships with a deck and fifteen tons' burden, 1786–1854, including from 1825 names of the sixty-four requisite shareholders and their assignees, and of masters, recording port registry number, date and place of registration, names, occupations and addresses of owners, ship's construction and nationality, name and employment of surveying officer, BT 107, with indexes to registrations, 1786–1854, in BT 111; official numbering, arranged annually by port, 1855–89, including colonial transcripts, 1869–89, for the East Indies, 1855–68, and Nova Scotia, 1855–68, BT 108, and transactions, 1855–92, for the United Kingdom, 1856–82, colonies, BT 109, whose numbers can be found on the dorse of the transcripts in BT 108, both indexed in BT 111. A few census returns relate to 1851, giving name, registration number, and date, tonnage, whether employed in home trade, fishing or conveying passengers, the name of the master, his ticket number, and date and port where it was received, and the position of the ship at midnight on 30 March, plus the name of the port to which the completed census schedule was delivered, HO 107, returns for British ships in foreign and home trade, and coastal vessels in port, 25 March–7 April, and home trade and coastal vessels arriving in port, 8 April–7 May 1861, RG 9, British and foreign ships in port between 25 March and 2 April, and those in the home and coastal trade, 3 April–2 May 1871, RG 10, 26 March–3 May 1881, RG 11, and 30 March–5 April, and ships in the coastal trade, 6 April–30 June 1891, RG 12. Official logs, 1902–19, including births, marriages and deaths on board, 1901–12, BT 165, and in 1913, BT 99.

see *Fishing Vessels, Ships' Passenger Lists, Shipwrecks*

Mesopotamia
see *Iraq*

Mexico Marriages of Britons, 1850–1921, RG 34, deaths, *c*.1850–1921, RG 35/16, 20–44; passports and certificates of nationality, 1816–1927, FO 207; Mexico City, births and deaths, 1854–67, FO 723/1–2, marriages, 1846–69, FO 83, indexed in FO 802/239, burials, 1827–1926, FO 207/58; Vera Cruz, births, deaths and burials, 1858–67, RG 33/140, indexed in RG 43/1, 3; claims for losses under the 1866 Convention, FO 318, and under the 1884 Convention, FO 319.

Militia Indentures of military service, 1297–1527, including returns for the Agincourt Expedition, 1415, E 101/68–74, indentures, 1399–1485, with a nominal and topographical index, E 404. Musters of able-bodied men, aged between sixteen and sixty, armed according to their income, temp. Henry VIII, mostly for 1539 and 1542, E 36/16–55a, and for 1522, E 101/58–59, 61–62, 64–65, 549, arranged under English and Welsh county, hundred and parish; certificates for Cornwall, 1522, E 315/77, and 1525, E 315/78, Berkshire and Norfolk, 1522, E 315/464, 466; musters temp. Henry VIII, especially 1539, SP 1 and SP 2 Case S; 1548, SP 10/3–4; 1569, 1573, 1577, 1580, SP 12; for Cheshire, 1588, 1596, SP 46/52/138–40, and temp. James I, SP 14, temp. Charles I, especially 1638–40, SP 16 and SP 17; muster rolls for districts set up by Parliament, 1642–51, SP 28/120–25. From 1757–1831 the militia was mustered by ballot of fixed quotas from parish lists of conscripts aged between eighteen and fifty, the upper limit of which was reduced to forty-five in 1762. From 1832 recruitment was voluntary. A supplementary militia was recruited by ballot, 1796–1816, and a local militia of able-bodied men, aged between eighteen and thirty, from 1808–13. In 1881 militia regiments were regrouped as part of the regular Army, and in 1906 was renamed the Special Reserve. Surviving musters, *c*.1780–1878, for Great Britain and Ireland, are listed by regiment, and there are some for Canada, 1837–50, for supplementary militia, 1798–1816, and for local militia, 1808–16, arranged under county, giving name, age and parish, WO 13; some eighteenth-century American militia musters, T 64; attestation papers include details of date and place of birth, trade, physical description, conduct and service record, arranged alphabetically by the regular Army regiments to which they were attached from 1881, 1806–1915, WO 96, while others may be found *c*.1760–1854, in WO 97, under regiment, and then alphabetically by surname; Enrolment Books, Description Books, pay lists and other nominal rolls, casualty books, records of courts martial, and some registers of birth, baptism and marriage, 1759–1925, WO 68. Lists of commissions, warrants, and returns, 1758–1855, HO 51, 1782–1840, HO 50, and fees paid for commissions and appointments, 1782–1880, HO 88; pay books of officers, 1816–24, WO 25; births, baptisms, marriages and deaths of officers, 1777–1892, WO 32/8903–19; names of wives paid allowances of 8*d* a week derived from parochial Land Tax receipts, while their husbands were absent on service in Ireland, or at war, 1689–1830, arranged in yearly county bundles, E 182; allowances paid to disbanded militia, 1793–1927, PMG 13; registers of pensions paid to militiamen from the Royal Chelsea Hospital, 1821–9, giving age, length of service, how invalided out, and death details, WO 23/25, and

1868–92, WO 23/89–92; admissions as out-pensioners, 1757–1882, arranged chronologically, giving age, birthplace, service record and details of disability causing discharge, with the date of medical examination, WO 116, and a similar series of registers relating to militiamen discharged in Ireland, as out-pensioners of the Royal Hospital at Kilmainham, 1759–1863, WO 118.

Million Bank Founded by subscribers to King William III's Million Lottery in 1694, and dissolved in 1796 when the unclaimed balance after division among surviving proprietors was transferred to the Accountant General of Chancery. Indenture of assignment, 1695, and 1702 schedule of tallies and orders for annuities and reversionary annuities payable out of Excise and of the numbers and names of nominees and the sums subscribed, C 46/1. The ledgers, 1696–1798, include notifications of death and by whom reported, and daily dividend payments, C 114/9–12, 153; receipt book, 1695–1798, C 114/13, signed list of original subscribers, 1695–1700, C 114/16, dividend books, 1701–96, C 114/17–21, details of transferred stock, arranged chronologically, 1734–96, giving names of proprietors between 1732 and 1734, annuities remaining in 1732, setting out the number, name of contributor, proprietor and nominee, the tally and annuity, C 114/22, miscellaneous papers, including affidavits by Directors, a printed list of names and addresses of proprietors on 25 June 1793, with an initial index, and on 25 June 1795, plus an account of the final division of stock in 1796, giving names, addresses, amount of stock, and allotment of annuities, C 114/23. Minute Books of Directors, 1700–98, C 114/15, Minute Books of sub-committees, 1718–97, and orders of general meetings, 1695–1796,

C 114/14, rough journal, 1786–98, and journal, 1796–8, C 114/13.

Mint, Royal Appointments and petitions, 1587–1910, mostly indexed, MINT 1; letters patent of officers, 1680–1725, Income Tax returns of officers for years ending 5 April 1863, 1872, 1876, 1877, 1879, 1880 and 1881, list (by grade) of artificers, workmen and boys, 1823, messengers, assistants, tellers, packers, labourers and their wages, 1826, officers, 1823, 1829, and staff lists 1823–1900 (gaps), salary and wage books 1898–1923, 1932–5, MINT 3, staff list index, 1774–1851, MINT 3/177.

Monks Files of warrants for pensions, 1536–9, and some commissions and returns, 1552–3, under monastic establishment, giving names and amounts, E 101; pensions assigned on the dissolution of the monasteries, giving detailed statements of immorality charges, SP 5, described in *Calendar of Letters and Papers (Foreign and Domestic) of the reign of Henry VIII, 1509–47*.

Montserrat Baptisms of British children, 1721–9, 1739–45, marriages, 1721–9, burials, 1721–9, 1739–45, CO 152/18, 25. Registers of slaves, 1817–34, T 71.
see *Chancery (Equity), Court of, Chancery Division of the High Court of Justice*

Morocco Casablanca, files on nationality, and property belonging to British subjects, 1915–51, FO 835; Rabat, registers of British subjects, 1847–1927, FO 442.

Mortgages Indentures, used in evidence or enforced by Court order, 1691–1816, C 45/1; Chancery miscellanea, including cases from the Equity Court of Chancery and Chancery Division, relating to redemption or foreclosure of mortgages, 1517–1953, TS 18, for which there is a descriptive list (some closed 75 or 100 years).

Mortmain Alienation of land to corporations (usually perpetual religious bodies) whereby incidents of tenure were lost by the Crown, required a licence between 1279 until abolished in 1960. Gifts in mortmain made by will were forbidden after 1736, and any unauthorized grants rendered the land forfeit to the Crown. Grants enrolled on the Patent Rolls, 1279–1960, C 66, with printed *Calendars* to 1582, and 1584–7, on the Close Rolls, 1279–1903, C 54, with printed *Calendars* to 1509, and 1903–60, in J 18, with annual initial indexes to 1948 and then listed chronologically; fees for licences are recorded on the Fine Rolls, 1279–1641, C 60, with printed *Calendars* to 1509; enquiries about whether the grant of a licence would prejudice the Crown's financial interests or those of others, sur-

vive in the inquisitions *ad quod damnum*, 1279–1485, C 143, and later ones to temp. Charles I, C 142; licences, 1852–76, are also found in HO 141, indexed, and fees, 1869–77, in HO 143.

Munster, Commission for Claims in Proceedings, 1588, SP 65, described in *Calendar of State Papers relating to Ireland*.

Murders Commissions into lands forfeited to the Crown by persons found guilty of murder, 1636–1854, C 205; registered papers, including files on prisoners convicted of murder, 1901–73, PCOM 9 (some closed 50, 75 or 100 years); London Metropolitan Police Area murders and deaths by violence, giving name, address, and victim's occupation, date and place of death, any subsequent charge and conviction, 1891–1909, 1912–17, 1919–66, and later ones including deaths of women in abortion, MEPO 20; precedents concerning murders abroad, seventeenth–nineteenth centuries, KB 33.

N*n*

Name, Change of Enrolments of changes effected by deed poll are on the Close Rolls, 1851–1903, C 54, 1903–87 in J 18, both with annual initial indexes (from 1948 listing is chronological), though to 1904 the entry is usually under the name used by the person at the time of making the declaration, thereafter under each name with cross-references; petitions for changes of name and arms by Royal licence, 1661–1782, SP 44, 1783–1837, including reports from the College of Arms, HO 54, 1841–1950, HO 45, warrants for change of name, 1782–February 1868, indexed, HO 38, March 1868–1969 (gaps 1922–30, 1957–61), indexed, HO 142, and 1879–1919, HO 144; fees paid for a licence, 1782–1880, HO 88, and 1869–77, HO 143; announcements of change of name in *The London Gazette*, 1665–1986, with subject indexes sporadically from 1790 and invariably from 1848, ZJ 1.

Natal Correspondence relating to emigration, 1849–1910, CO 357; land orders, 1859–74, CO 386/144.

National Assistance Board Correspondence about appointments of some officers and staff, 1920–66, MH 52. Selected case papers, 1935 onwards, AST 1 (closed 75 years, but access granted by permit to material over 30 years old).

Naturalization Granting status as a British subject to an alien, according to prevailing legislation. Indexes to Acts of Parliament granting naturalization, and from 1844 to certificates granted by the Home Secretary, giving reference number, name, abode, country of origin and date, 1509–1935, HO 1, on open access; Private Acts of Parliament, *c*.1400–1900, on the Parliament Rolls, C 65, with payments to 1641 on the Fine Rolls, C 60; naturalizations, temp. Henry VIII–1800, C 89, with a descriptive list; Oath Roll of Naturalization for Protestant refugees under a statute of 1708, 1709–11, E 169/86, and accompanying sacrament certificates, E 196/10, and another set of Oath Rolls, 1708–12, KB 24; names of persons naturalized in the American colonies, 1740–61, CO 324/55–56. Correspondence, 1789–1837, memorials and petitions, 1802–March 1871, HO 1, April 1871–8, HO 45, 1868–1914, HO 144 (closed 100 years); certificates of naturalization, August 1844–August 1873, C 54; duplicates, 1870–1949, giving name, address, trade or occupation, country of origin and name of spouse and of issue, relating to the United Kingdom, and 1915–49 for Imperial certificates of naturalization in British Possessions overseas, plus certificates issued under the British Nationality and Status of Aliens Act 1914, 1915–49, and Declarations of British Nationality, 1870–72, by which foreign nationality was renounced, and Declarations of Alienage, 1871–1914, renouncing British nationality, Declarations of British nationality under the Burma Independence Act 1947, 1948–50, indexed, HO 334. Announcements of naturalization appear in *The London Gazette*, 1782–1986, with subject indexes sporadically from 1790, and invariably from 1848, ZJ 1.

Naval Air Service, Royal Formed in 1914 and combined with the Royal Flying Corps on 1 April 1918 as the Royal Air Force. Registers of officers' services, August 1914–April 1918, indexed, ADM 273 (closed 75 years); war casualties, 1915–18, AIR 1/2395–96; disablement pensions and gratuities, 1916–18, PMG 42, pensions to relatives of deceased officers, 1916–20, PMG 44. Campaign medals, 1914–18, ADM 171/78–88, recommendations for World War I gallantry medals, AIR 1, and awards, 1917–26, ADM 171/78–88, indexes to entitlement to Distinguished Conduct Medal, 1919, announced in *The London Gazette*, ZJ 1. Muster of Royal Air Force personnel, 1 April 1918, AIR 1/819 and AIR 10/232–37.
see *Air Force, Royal, Flying Corps, Royal, Medals*

Naval Colleges, Royal Lists of officers, masters, and cadets at the Royal Naval College, Dartmouth, 1931–January 1942, September 1946–May 1968, and at the Royal Naval College, Eaton Chester, February 1943–January 1946, and Royal Naval College, Greenwich printed results of Final Examinations, 1880–1906, Intermediate and Final Examination results, 1876–80, 1907–11, 1918–57, (indexed), applications for appointments, 1872–6, ADM 203; in-letters, Royal Naval College, Portsmouth, 1808–36, including lists of names of candidates and their parents, with an index on open access, ADM 1/3506–21.

Naval Reserve, Royal Established in 1859 from the Merchant Navy. Service records, by date of entry, of officers, from midshipmen to commanders, assistant engineers to chief engineers, assistant paymasters to paymasters, some volumes being indexed, 1862–1909, ADM 240; representative records of service by deck, 1860–96, of firemen, 1888–94, and ratings, 1860–1913, giving personal details, training, service and retainers, of five-year engagements, and where another five-year engagement was agreed this is endorsed on the back, BT 164; service gratuities and compensation, 1933–42, ADM 116/4534; card index of casualties among officers, 1914–20, giving rank, date and place and cause of death, and the name and address of the next of kin, ADM 242/1–5, and an alphabetical War Graves Roll, 1914–19, ADM 242/7–10, both on open access; Despatches, citations for awards and decorations, and casualty lists, announced in *The London Gazette*, to 1986, with annual or half-yearly subject indexes, ZJ 1; pensions paid to widows and children of ratings killed in warlike operations, 1922–6, ADM 23.
see *Merchant Seamen*

Naval Ships, Royal Census returns of ships in port or in home and foreign waters, giving names and details of all on board, 7 April 1861, RG 9, 2 April 1871, RG 10, 3 April 1881, RG 11, and 5 April 1891, RG 12; lists of ships and their officers, 1673–88, 1699–1756, ADM 6; returns of ships and stations, 1651–1855, ADM 7; list books of monthly returns, showing disposition of ships and names of officers, 1673–1909, ADM 8; bi-monthly and yearly musters, 1688–1808, ADM 36, 1792–1842, ADM 37, 1793–1878, ADM 38, 1667–1798, ADM 39, and of hired armed vessels and cutters, 1794–1815, ADM 41, giving dates of entry, rank or rate of crew, whether left ship, when and for what reason, indicating charges on wages for victuals, etc, and from 1764 usually containing age at entry and place or country of birth, listed alphabetically by ship; quarterly musters of Revenue Cruisers, 1834–57, ADM 119. Medical journals of selected ships, c.1796–1880, ADM 101/80–250, up to 1856 listed by ship, and thereafter by station, and 1856–1943, listed by station, ADM 101/264–618 (some closed 75 years): there is an index in the class list to ADM 101/128–293; hospital musters, including ships and sick quarters, and staff pay lists, 1740–1860, ADM 102; sick quarters musters, 1757–8, ADM 30/51–52. Controller's monthly pay books, arranged under ship's name, 1693–1710, ADM 31, 1692–1856, ADM 32, 1669–1778, ADM 33, 1766–85, ADM 34, 1777–1832, ADM 35, for which there are alphabets of crew on board from c.1765 in ADM 33 and ADM 34, and all these classes contain similar information to the musters, with additional details in ADM 33–ADM 35 on payments made to executors and administrators of deceased seamen. Admirals' journals, 1702–1916, ADM 50, and selected log books and letter books, 1648–1740, ADM 7; Captains' logs, 1669–1852, ADM 51, Masters' logs, 1672–1840, ADM 52, 1808–71, ADM 54, Ships' logs, 1799–1963, ADM 53 (some closed 50 or 75 years), logs of 'Explorations', 1669–1852, ADM 51, and Supplementary Series II, Explorations 1766–1861, ADM 55; these classes are listed alphabetically by vessel and their

contents record daily navigation, position, weather, orders, signals, manoeuvres, events, encounters with the enemy, loss, damage and casualties, starting at noon each day until c.October 1805, and thereafter at midnight. Bounty lists, 1695–1708, 1741–2, ADM 30/6. Ships lost, 1914–19, listed alphabetically, some giving the date, and number of casualties, others the class and cause and place of loss, ADM 242/6, statistical casualty books, giving ship's name, reason for casualties, numbers killed, and missing and wounded, or prisoners of war, 1914–19, ADM 242/11–12. Marriages on board ship, 1842–89, RG 33/156, indexed in RG 43/7; registers of reports of death, under ship, 1893–1909, ADM 104/109 (later registers are closed 75 years), and an index to the registers, 1893–1950, ADM 104/102–08.

Navy, Royal

(1) *Commissioned Officers* (Admirals, Commodores, Captains, Commanders, Lieutenants, Mates/Sub-Lieutenants, Masters from 1808, from 1843 Pursers, Chaplains, Surgeons and Naval Instructors or Schoolmasters, and from 1847 Engineers) Oaths of Allegiance sworn in 1660, C 215/6; Association Oath Roll, 1696, C 213/385–89. *Confidential Navy Lists*, 1914–18, 1939–45, ADM 177; alphabetical lists down to the rank of lieutenant, 1660–85, ADM 10/15, 1660–88, and 1688–1746 by order of seniority, ADM 10/10, 1688–1737, excluding lieutenants, ADM 7/549; seniority lists, including officers on half-pay, 1717–1848, ADM 118; address books of officers on retired and half-pay, 1837, PMG 73/2. Warrants and commissions, 1649–60, SP 18, 1660–85, SP 29, 1685–8, SP 31, 1689–1782, SP 44, some containing integral indexes; Commission Books, 1695–1849, ADM 6; lists of commissions of captains and lieutenants regis-

tered with the Navy Board, 1730–1818, ADM 10, registers of commissions, arranged under ship and with nominal indexes, 1780–1849, ADM 11. Lieutenants' passing certificates, at the Navy Board, bearing details of length of previous service and at what rate in named vessels, and from the mid-eighteenth century including baptism certificates, 1691–1832, integrally indexed, 1691–1794, ADM 107/1–63, examination records, 1795–1832, ADM 107/64–70, and certificates of service, 1802–48, ADM 107/71–75, both series being indexed; lieutenants' passing certificates, at the Admiralty, 1744–1819, and from overseas, 1788–1818, ADM 6/86–116, survey of midshipmen and other candidates for lieutenant with notes on age, service and character, 1814–16, and masters' passing certificates, c.1800–50, the certificates yielding similar information to ADM 107, ADM 6; lieutenants' passing certificates and those of masters and paymasters from the Admiralty Board, 1851–1902, ADM 13; original application papers and certificates of captains and masters, 1660–1830, Establishment Books of the Navy Board, 1785–1824, ADM 24; returns of services and of appointments, 1741–1869, ADM 11, registers of officers appointed to ships, 1733–1826, ADM 106. List Books of monthly returns of the disposition of ships and names of officers on board, 1673–1909, ADM 8. Officers' services, including dates of entry and discharge, birth, seniority, dates of appointments, orders and commissions, the later returns giving parentage, name of spouse and date of death, mostly indexed, 1756–1954, ADM 196 (some closed 50 or 75 years); returns of officers' ages, 1744–7, 1816–17, 1 April 1822, and each giving seniority dates, whether in receipt of any other office than for Navy rank, ADM 6;

signed surveys of officers' services, 1817–22, and 1846, ADM 9; service papers of officers at the Cape of Good Hope, 1815–30, ADM 7. Marriage certificates of officers, 1806–1902, ADM 13/70–71, 186–92; births, marriages and deaths, 1813–35, of candidates for the Navy, ADM 7/1. Leave Books, 1783–1847, ADM 6/200–11, Black Books, recording names of those whose misconduct meant they were not to be re-employed, 1759–1815, ADM 12/27B–27E. Admirals' journals, 1702–1916, ADM 50, Captains' logs, 1669–1852, ADM 51, Masters' logs, 1672–1840, ADM 52, and 1808–71, ADM 54, listed alphabetically by ship, and the contents recording daily navigation, weather, manoeuvres and events on board. In-letters to the Admiralty from Naval commanders, 1689–1782, SP 42, from captains, 1698–1839 (indexed up to 1792 in ADM 10/8, and thereafter there is a nominal index on open access to 1815 up to surnames beginning with 'P'), from lieutenants, 1791–1839, ADM 1, indexed by personal and ship's name, in ADM 12; letters from the Royal College of Surgeons, 1718–1816, ADM 1/4280–81, to which there is a nominal index on open access; petitions, 1793–1839, ADM 1/5125–37; out-letters from the Admiralty to admirals, and captains, 1746–1815, and to lieutenants, 1809–15, ADM 2, and from 1869 copies of out-letters are in ADM 1, to which there are nominal indexes and digests of subject-matter, 1793–1938, in ADM 12; in-letters to the Navy Board from officers, 1790–1832, masters, 1808–32 (arranged alphabetically), out-letters to captains, 1795–1832, various officers, 1806–32, and officers at foreign stations, 1770–1832, indexed 1822–32, ADM 106; surgeons' reports on wounded officers, 1816–55, deaths, 1823–32, and lunacy, 1822–32, ADM 105/28–32, officers invalided from overseas, 1847–63, ADM 105/33–35. Salary and pension books, 1694–1914, ADM 7, salaries and pensions, 1734–1851, ADM 22; full pay registers, 1795–1905, arranged by rank to 1830 and thereafter in indexed general registers, ADM 24; half-pay registers organized by seniority, 1693–1836, ADM 25, 1774–1845, ADM 6, 1867–1900, ADM 23, 1836–1920, PMG 15; superannuation lists, 1809–32, ADM 106; Greenwich Hospital pensions, 1871–1931, 1951–61, ADM 165, pensions and allowances from the Hospital to officers, 1866–1928, and Travers pensions paid to retired officers, 1892–1928, PMG 70, pensions paid to retired officers at the discretion of the Admiralty on top of half-pay and known as 'Greenwich out-pensions' to 1865, and then as Naval pensions, 1814–46, ADM 22, 1846–1921, PMG 71; disability, retired pay and gratuities, 1917–19, arranged alphabetically, PMG 42/1–12, pensions to old and disabled officers, 1878–85, 1891–5, ADM 23; repayments to Receivers General of Customs and Excise of half-pay and retired pay of officers where no longer effective, or when widows and offspring were in receipt of pensions and allowances, 1837–40, PMG 22; officers' effects, papers and wills, 1830–60, ADM 45, indexed in ADM 141. Naval Establishment pensions to engineers, 1874–1924, arranged alphabetically, PMG 69; pensions for good or meritorious service, to Flag Officers retired from 1837, allowances paid to lieutenants of Naval Hospitals, and compassionate allowances to widows, children and dependent relatives of those killed in action, 1810–36, ADM 22, 1837–1921, PMG 18, 1834–6, 1867–80, 1885–91, 1916–18, and 1921–32, to widows, 1891–1932, and to relatives, 1899–1927, some arranged alphabetically, ADM 23. Dates of death of those on half-pay are recorded in the salary and pension books of the Admiralty, plus details of pensions paid to widows of admirals, captains and commanders, 1694–1832, ADM 7/809–22, indexed under name, office, yard and department in ADM 7/823, and other payments, 1766–81, ADM 18/39–119; widows' pensions, 1836–1929, arranged alphabetically, PMG 19; pensions and allowances to relatives of officers killed or dying in service, 1836–70, PMG 16, 1870–1919, PMG 20. Bounty papers, 1675–1822, ADM 106/3017–35; charity papers for the relief of poor widows with annual incomes lower than £50, giving date of officer's death, the vessel, his rank, details of marriage, age at decease and widow's name, 1732–1829, ADM 6/332–402, 1734–1835, ADM 22/56–237, 1830–1932, ADM 23; registers and papers of officers, widows and dependants receiving or claiming allowances, 1759–1846, ADM 6; a Compassionate Fund was instituted in 1809, and there is an indexed register of orphans and other dependent relatives of officers killed in action, 1809–36, ADM 6, plus a Compassionate List, 1873–1926, and resultant allowances paid out, 1867–85, ADM 23. Index cards of casualties, giving rank, date, place and cause of death, and the name and address of the next of kin, 1914–20, ADM 242/1–5, and an alphabetical War Graves Roll, 1914–19, ADM 242/7–10.

(2) *Warrant Officers* (Boatswains, Gunners, Carpenters, Pursers, Cooks, Armourers, Masters at Arms, Sailmakers, Artificers, Chaplains, Surgeons, Naval Instructors or Schoolmasters, and Engineers) Seniority lists, 1780–1844, ADM 118; address book of those on retired and half-pay, 1837, PMG 73/2; Warrant

Books, 1695–1849, appointments, 1673–1918, ADM 6; officers appointed to ships, 1733–1826, ADM 106; appointments and registers of warrants, 1780–1849, arranged by ship, with nominal indexes, ADM 11; List Books of monthly returns showing the disposition of ships and names of officers, 1673–1909, ADM 8; applications for promotion, transfer or appointment, 1770–1820, ADM 6; Oaths of Allegiance, 1660, C 215/6. Passing certificates of pursers, 1816–20, of boatswains, 1810–13, and gunners, 1731–1812, arranged alphabetically by year, and masters' passing certificates and statements of service, c.1800–50, ADM 6; passing certificates of boatswains and gunners, 1851–1902, ADM 13, indexes to engineers' passing certificates, 1863–1902, ADM 13/200–05; returns of officers' services, 1741–1869, ADM 11, certificates of servitude, and records of service, 1802–1919, indexed, ADM 29; registers of chaplains' services, 1812–80, indexed under year of entry, ADM 6/440; indexes of pursers' services, 1834, ADM 6/193–96, certificates of service of boatswains, pursers, carpenters and gunners, 1803–04, ADM 6; description books of artificers at various yards, 1748–1830, ADM 106. Officers on leave of absence, 1783–1847, ADM 6/200–11; letters from the Royal College of Surgeons, 1718–1816, ADM 1/4280–81, with a nominal index of officers on open access. Black Books of those whose misconduct meant they were not to be re-employed, 1741–1814, ADM 11/39. Masters' logs, 1672–1840, recording daily navigation, weather, and events on board ship, ADM 52. Index cards of casualties, recording rank, date and place and cause of demise, and name and address of next of kin, 1914–20, ADM 242/1–5, and an alphabetical War Graves Roll, 1914–19,

ADM 242/7–10. Effects papers, 1830–60, including wills, ADM 45, indexed in ADM 141. Registers of salaries and pensions, 1734–1851, ADM 22; full pay registers, 1795–1905, including chaplains and surgeons, with a separate register for each rank up to 1830, indexed, ADM 24; half-pay registers, 1693–1924, ADM 25, 1774–1845, ADM 6, 1836–1920, including those on unattached pay, indexed, PMG 15; pay arrears, 1739–42, ADM 30; superannuation lists, 1809–32, ADM 106. Pensions, 1694–1785, ADM 7/809–44, indexed in ADM 7/823, 1874–1924, including special pensions from Greenwich Hospital, 1874–80, arranged alphabetically, PMG 69; Naval out-pensions, 1814–46, ADM 22; pensions to half-pay officers, 1867–1900, and additional pensions to engineers and warrant officers, 1880–1931, ADM 23; repayments to Receivers General of Customs and Excise where the officer was no longer effective or widow and offspring were in receipt of a pension or allowance, 1837–40, PMG 22; Bounty papers for widows or dependent mothers of officers, recording details of death, proof of marriage or parentage, and giving abode, 1675–1822, ADM 106/3017–35; Bounty paid to chaplains, 1689–1836, ADM 30; papers relating to the Charity for the Relief of Poor Widows, 1732–1830, giving details of rank, circumstances and date of death, and accompanied by proof of marriage, ADM 6; Chatham Chest pensions to widows of officers killed in service, 1653–1799, ADM 82, 1831–37, ADM 22/52–55; pensions and compassionate allowances paid to widows and dependent relatives, 1830–1932, and after casualty in warlike operations, 1922–6, ADM 23; pay books of pensions to widows, 1734–1835, ADM 22; widows' pensions, 1836–1929, PMG 19; register of officers' widows and orphans applying to the Compassionate Fund, 1809–36, ADM 6; pensions and allowances paid to them from Greenwich Hospital, 1866–1928, PMG 70; pensions and allowances to widows, children and dependent relatives of officers killed or drowned, and pensions for meritorious and good service, 1836–1920, PMG 16, 1870–1919, PMG 20; compassionate allowances to children and relatives of deceased officers, 1837–1921, PMG 18.

(3) *Petty Officers and Ratings* (Mates, Midshipmen, Cadets, Able and Ordinary Seamen) Oaths of Allegiance sworn by all serving men, 1660, C 215/6. Bi-monthly and yearly ships' musters, 1688–1808, ADM 36, 1792–1842, ADM 37, 1793–1878, ADM 38, 1667–1798, ADM 39, indexed under ship, and the contents giving date of entry to ship, rate, whether and when left ship and for what reason, and any deductions from wages, plus from 1764 age and place or country of birth. Pay books, 1691–1710, ADM 31, 1692–1856, ADM 32, 1669–1778, ADM 33, 1766–85, ADM 34, 1774–1832, ADM 35, containing similar information to the musters, and from *c*.1765, alphabets of men on board are included in ADM 33 and ADM 34. Continuous Engagement Books, recording date and place of birth, physical description on entry, date of entry to named vessel, a service summary, and present rank, and arranged under number with a nominal index, 1853–72, ADM 139; Record and Establishment Books give details of continuous service number, date and place of birth, draftings and desertions, by ship, 1857–73, ADM 115, followed from 1872–8 by quarterly ledgers, noting full pay and allowances of all on board, ADM 117. Certificates of servitude or service records, 1802–1919, ADM 29, with an index

volume; register of seamen's services, giving date of birth, ship or Shore Establishment and service details, 1873–95, ADM 188, and which acts as an index to continuous service numbers; service records, 1900–23, ADM 75; registers and returns of service, 1799–1854, ADM 6; survey of midshipmen and other candidates for lieutenant, giving age, service and character assessment, 1814–16, ADM 6; letters concerning midshipmen and clerks, 1815–54, ADM 2. Examination marks of cadets on HMS *Britannia*, Dartmouth, 1877–1902, ADM 6. Bounty paid to volunteers, 1695–1708, 1714–42, pay arrears, 1739–42, miscellaneous pay lists and registers of letters of attorney, 1689–1836, ADM 30; powers of attorney registers, *c*.1800–39, PMG 51; registers of remittances to relatives against wages and prize money, 1795–1851, home remittances, 1795–1824, foreign remittances, 1838–51, and lists of checks and remittances, 1795–1839, ADM 26; allotments of pay to wives and relatives, arranged under ship, 1795–1812, and declaration lists of allotments, 1830–52, ADM 27. Monthly hospital musters, 1740–1860, ADM 102. Monthly and quarterly Royal Greenwich Hospital out-pensions, paid to retired personnel at home and overseas, arranged by pay-district and recording rank, date of commencement of pension, rate and type, plus details of any transfer elsewhere and date of death, 1842–80, WO 22; pensions and gratuities to seamen abroad, 1879–1921, PMG 71; registers of pensions to widows and seamen, 1882–1949, ADM 166; selected pensions paid to disabled seamen and to widows of men killed before 1914, listed alphabetically by applicant, and giving effective dates of payment, the signed contents of the records including age, birthplace, marital status, parentage, parental status, names of siblings, physical description of the seaman, cause of injury or death, a conduct sheet and details of religious denomination, employment record and annual income, 1854–1977, PIN 71. Registers of reports of death of ratings, September 1939–June 1948, arranged alphabetically and giving cause of death and home town, ADM 104/ 127–39. Seamen's effects, 1800–60, ADM 44, indexed 1802–61, and including names of next of kin, ADM 141; registers of discharged dead cases, including some marriage certificates and giving names of legal representatives applying for back-pay, 1859–78, ADM 154 (partly duplicating ADM 141); seamen's wills, 1786–1882, ADM 48, indexed 1786–1909, giving date of death, and the earlier entries details of the name, address and relationship of the executor or administrator to the deceased, ADM 142; certificates sent by the Navy Pay Office to the High Court of Admiralty enabling the next of kin of seamen dying intestate to obtain a grant of letters of administration, 1795–1807, HCA 30; pay books, including payments of arrears to executors and administrators, 1669–1778, ADM 33, 1766–85, ADM 34, 1777–1832, ADM 35; registers of dead men's wages, 1639–1919, ADM 80; names of widows or dependent mothers entitled to Royal Bounty, giving details of marriage or parentage, 1675–1822, ADM 106/3017–35; Chatham Chest pensions to widows of men killed in service, 1653–1799, ADM 82, 1831–7, ADM 22/52–55, pensions and allowances to widows, children and other dependants of seamen dying of causes other than war, 1882–1917, ADM 166, 1921–6, PMG 72; pensions to widows and relatives of seamen killed in warlike operations, 1922–6, ADM 23; registers of ratings' widows applying for admission to the Royal Hospital at Greenwich as nurses, 1817–31, 1819–42, ADM 6; pension grants made by the Hospital to orphan daughters, 1881–1911, 1951–9, and orphan sons, 1884–1959, ADM 162; children apprenticed to the sea by Christ's Hospital, 1766, T 64/ 311; receipts for apprentices from the Lower School at Greenwich Hospital sent into the Navy, 1846–54, ADM 73.

(4) *Civilians* Establishment Books of the Navy Office, 1785–1824, ADM 106; pay lists, musters and pensions paid at various ports, including registers of labourers and description books, 1703–1857, ADM 113; appointments, salaries, pay and allowances of staff and resident agents of the Transport Department, 1795–1814, to which there is a place-name index, MT 23; Sheerness Dockyard Church baptisms, 1813–81, 1885–1960, ADM 6; pay books of employees of the Transport Office at Deal, 1796–1816, ADM 108; repayment to Receivers General of Customs and Excise of pay of civil salaried officers, artificers and labourers in receipt of pensions and allowances, 1837–40, PMG 22; pensions, 1834–6, 1866–84, to civil artificers, 1884–1926 (indexed from 1902), to civil salaried officers, 1884–1910, with a Civil Branch Index, 1873–1934, ADM 23; salary and pensions books of the Civil Establishment of the Admiralty, 1694–1832, ADM 7/809–22, with a nominal index, under office, yard and department, ADM 7/823; pensions and superannuation allowances to salaried staff at home and overseas, 1836–1918, and special pensions paid to high-ranking officers, 1890–1918, PMG 24; service gratuities and compensation, 1933–42, ADM 116/ 4534; effects papers, 1830–60, ADM 45, indexed in ADM 141.

(5) *Miscellaneous* Paylists of part-time Sea

Fencibles, drawn from fishermen and boatmen for coastal defence, arranged under district, 1798–1810, ADM 28. Register of protections from being pressed into the Royal Navy, 1702–03, 1711–12, 1740–1815, and for persons over and under age, 1803–15, apprentices, 1740–59, 1761–2, 1795–1806, foreigners and others, 1761–2, 1795–1806, and miscellaneous, 1781–2, yards, 1794–1815, firemen, 1780–1828, fishermen and coasting trade, 1755–8, 1770–81, 1787–1815, Southern Whale Fishery, 1777–93, Southern and Greenland Whale Fishery, 1793–1811, ADM 7/363–400, 650. Census returns of ships in port or in home and foreign waters, listing all those on board, 7 April 1861, RG 9, 2 April 1871, RG 10, 3 April 1881, RG 11, and 5 April 1891, RG 12. Campaign medal rolls, 1793–1972, indexed under ship to 1914, ADM 171; list of men in Greenwich Hospital who received medals, 1848–9, ADM 73/94; awards to Naval officers in World War I, indexed, ADM 171/78–88, and Conspicuous Gallantry Medal, Distinguished Conduct Medal and Meritorious Service Medals in the same War, indexed, ADM 171/61; Honour Sheets, 1914–19, ADM 171/56, with a card index; index to entries of citations in *The London Gazette*, 1919, and in 1942, ZJ 1; recommendations for gallantry awards, 1939–45, ADM 1 Code 85, and ADM 116 Code 85; allowances for meritorious service, 1830–1902, and the Victoria Cross, 1857–1902, ADM 23. Commemorative medals, 1793–1972, ADM 171. Registers of killed or wounded, indexed, 1854–1911, 1914–29, ADM 104/144–49; index to registers of reports of deaths: ships, 1893–1950, ADM 104/102–08, and registers, 1893–1909, ADM 104/109 (later registers are closed 75 years); registers of reports of deaths, 1900–14, ADM 104/122 (closed 75 years), and indexes to registers of killed and wounded, 1915–29, ADM 104/140–43. Alphabetical index of Naval men charged and sentenced by courts martial, 1803–56, and a chronological register, 1812–55, ADM 13, 1812–1916, indexed, ADM 194; courts martial records, 1890–1957, ADM 156 (most closed 75 or 100 years); courts martial reports and returns from Nore Station, 1848–63, ADM 153; letters concerning courts martial, 1781–1816, ADM 2; prisoners under sentence of court martial held in the Marshalsea Prison, 1773–1842, PRIS 11; warrants for arrest, jail or movement for breaches of naval or criminal law, 1805–56, warrants for execution of those convicted of a capital offence by the High Court of Admiralty, 1802–56, respites of execution, 1802–20, HCA 55.

see **Dockyards, Royal Naval, Greenwich Hospital, Royal, Hospitals, Medals, Medical Officers, Royal Naval, Naval Colleges, Royal, Prisoners of War, Surgeons, War Pensions, World War I, World War II**

Netherlands Names of gentlemen serving in the Low Countries, 1585, SP 84/63B; licences to pass to Holland, 1621, 1624, 1631, 1632, 1637, Oaths of Allegiance taken by soldiers going to the Low Countries, 1613–14, 1616–17, 1617–18, 1619–20, 1620, 1621, 1623, 1624, 1625, 1634–5, E 157; Association Oath Roll of the King's subjects in Holland, 1696, C 213/459; claims for compensation during the campaign in Holland and Cleves, 1796–7, T 64. Letters and papers, 1584–1780, SP 84, with a descriptive list, 1590–1603. Births and deaths of Britons, 1897–1909, FO 221/1–3, deaths, 1839–71, RG 35/17; consular returns from Aruba, births, 1930–62, deaths, 1926–46, 1949, 1954–64; Curaçao, births, 1897–1966,

marriages, 1922–9, deaths, 1889–1925, 1930–49, 1952–65; Paramaribo, births, 1941–51, deaths, 1943; and Surinam, births, marriages and deaths, 1889–1966, all in FO 907/1–32; The Hague, births, 1837–9, 1859–94, baptisms, 1627–1821, marriages, 1627–1889, deaths, 1859–1907, RG 33/83–88, indexed in RG 43/1, 7 and 3, marriages, 1846–90, FO 83, indexed in FO 802/239; Rotterdam, baptisms and marriages, 1708–94, RG 33/89, indexed in RG 43/1 and 7; Samerang, births, baptisms and deaths, 1869–1941, FO 803/1–3.
see *Indonesia*

Nevis Baptisms and burials, 1726–7, 1733–4, 1740–45, CO 152/16, 21, and 25; register of letters of attorney for debentures, 1707–45, E 407/26. Registers of slaves, 1815–34, T 71.
see *West Indies*

New England Licences to pass beyond the seas, and registers of passengers from England, 1634–9, and 1677, E 157 (printed in J.C. Hotten's *Original Lists of Persons Emigrating to America, 1600–1700*, 1874).

New Forest Deeds and evidences, including returns of encroachments, registers of claims and rights, temp. Henry VIII–1917, LRRO 5; presentments of offences, 1747–52, LRRO 37.

New South Wales Lists of male convicts, 1788–1819, female convicts, 1788–1819, general musters of convicts, 1806, 1811, 1816, 1818, 1820–22, 1825, 1828, 1837, names of convicts embarked, 1787, convicts arrived, 1828–32, 1833–4, November 1828 census returns (arranged alphabetically and giving details of age, residence and employment and whether came free, born in the colony or transported and for how long, on what ship and when), pardons granted, 1834–59, all giving details of age, place and date of trial, ship and date of arrival, HO 10; alphabetical list of convicts, with personal details, 1788–1825, 1823–5, 1840–42, Savings Bank Book ledgers, 1824–49, 1830–68, and letters from the superintendent of convicts, 1854–66, all in CO 207; convicts going to New South Wales, 1822, CO 201/118–20. Lists of emigrants and convicts, included in Original Correspondence, 1801–21, CO 201, with an index 1823–33, on open access; names of settlers, 1824, CO 201/159; Entry Books of correspondence, 1801–73, CO 202; register of correspondence, 1849–1900, CO 360; register of out-letters, 1873–1900, CO 369. Births, marriages and deaths, 1822, CO 201/138, deaths of convicts, 1823–35, and reports on prison conditions, HO 7. Public Service Lists, 1895–1916, CO 580.
see *Convicts, Transportation of, Emigrants*

Newspaper Proprietors Some London proprietors are named in Stamp Duty Accounts, 1712–1848, AO 3, and 1816–44, including also printers and publishers of newspapers, IR 72.

New Zealand List of agents of New Zealand Company, 1839–50, land surveyors, 1839–50, address book of land- and shareholders in the Company, register of certificates and shares, 1840–53, deeds of transfer and declarations of identity in order to receive dividends, register of dividend receipts, 1840–43, cancelled debentures, 1843–50, numerical registers of land orders, 1839–43, notices of transfers, 1839–50, registers of certificates of payments for land, 1840–50, supplementary land orders, 1850–51, applications for and grants of land, 1839–50, lists of land-owners, 1839–53; applications for land in the settlement at Nelson, 1841–2, register of delivery of land orders, 1841–3, transfer papers, 1841–50; application registers for land in New Plymouth, 1847–9; applications for land in Cook's Strait, 1849; list of landholders and register of choice of land at Wellington, 1841, CO 208; candidates for employment in New Zealand, 1839–50, CO 208/279, and original signed receipts for remittance payments to wives or dependants of emigrant labourers, arranged under settlement, 1841–4, CO 208/240, correspondence concerning emigrants, 1841–58, CO 208; registers of cabin passengers, 1839–50, indexed by ship, and giving name, age, occupation, destination, and number and sex of those in the party, CO 208/269–70, applications for cabins, 1839, CO 208/268, applications of emigrant labourers for free passages, 1839–50, giving names, residence, age, occupation, wife's name and age, and number and ages of children by sex, CO 208/272–73, indexed in CO 208/275, original applications, including names and addresses of referees, religious denomination, employment record and present state of health, and lists of emigrants, 1839–50, CO 208/274, lists of maintained emigrants, 1839–42, arranged under ship, giving date and port of sailing, name of head of each family party and the number of adults and ages of children, and amount of maintenance, CO 208/278, register of passage allowance certificates, 1842–3, CO 208/271, list of German emigrants, 1840, CO 208/277. Monthly and quarterly pensions paid by the Royal Hospitals of Chelsea and Greenwich to retired military, naval and marine personnel, arranged under pay-district and recording rank, regiment and number, date of commencement, amount and nature of pension, and any transfer elsewhere, with some signed receipts and death certificates, 1845–78, WO 22/276–91.

see *Emigrants, Ships' Passenger Lists*

Non-Parochial Registers In 1840 and 1857, the Registrar General ordered the deposit of registers of birth, baptism, marriage and burial from all non-Anglican churches, so that they might be examined and authenticated for future use as evidence of parentage and proof of age in a court of law. Not all chapels responded. Authenticated English and Welsh registers, 1567–1858, are in RG 4, listed alphabetically under county and place, and include registers of foreign congregations, Dr Williams' Library registers of births of Presbyterians, Independents and Baptists, 1742–1837, and registers of births from the Wesleyan Methodist Metropolitan Registry, 1818–38; other authenticated registers, 1646–1970, including some from Anglican chapels, royal, military, naval and charitable hospitals, admissions and births at the British Lying-In Hospital at Holborn, and records of the Russian Orthodox Church in London, RG 8, to which there are descriptive lists; authenticated registers of the Meetings of the Society of Friends in England and Wales, 1613–1841, RG 6; unauthenticated registers, including marriages and baptisms at Mayfair Chapel, the Mint, Fleet and King's Bench Prisons, 1667–1777, RG 7. Registers of persons authorized to perform weddings in certified places of worship, 1899–1931, RG 42.

see *Bethnal Green Protestant Dissenters' Burying Ground, British Lying-In Hospital, Bunhill Fields Burial Ground, Dr Williams' Library, Fleet Prison, Foreign Churches in England,*

Foundling Hospital, Friends, Society of, King's Bench Prison, Wesleyan Metropolitan Registry

Norfolk List of persons holding stores of corn, 1527, E 163/16/10.

Norway Bodo, births to British subjects, 1888–90, deaths, 1895, FO 724/1–2; Drammen, deaths, 1906, FO 532/2; Kragero, deaths, 1895, FO 725/1; Lofoten Islands, births, 1883–91, FO 726/1; Oslo (Christiania), births, 1850–1932, marriages, 1853–1936, deaths, 1850–1930, FO 529/1–14; Porsgrund, births, 1885–91, and including Skien, FO 531/2.

Notaries Public Names and addresses of notaries public on the Notarial Faculty Register, 1873–1924, C 193/94–96, 1927–52, C 193/152.

Nova Scotia Pensions paid by the Royal Hospitals of Chelsea and Greenwich to retired military, naval and marine personnel, arranged by pay-district, and recording rank, regiment and number, date of commencement, amount and nature of pension, any transfer elsewhere, and date of death, 1858–80, WO 22/294–96.

Nuisances, Inspectors of Some appointments made by local authorities, c.1896–c.1921, MH 48.

Nurses General Entry Books of nurses at the Royal Greenwich Hospital, 1704–1864, arranged alphabetically, ADM 73/87–88; registers of service, 1704–1865, ADM 73/83–86, 1783–1863, ADM 73/85, both giving name, birthplace, age at entry, date of entry, husband's name, and date of death or whether hurt or wounded, in which Service, amount of pension, number of children and ages at time of entry; registers of ratings' widows applying for admission as nurses at the Hospital, 1817–31, ADM 6/329, 1819–42, ADM 6/331. Returns of services of naval nursing sisters, giving rank, date of birth, date of entry and discharge, 1884–1909, indexed, ADM 104/43; annual reports on nursing sisters, arranged by seniority, giving age, hospital where stationed, dates of service, and including character and work reports, 1890–1908, ADM 104/95; Establishment Book of nursing sisters and wardmasters of hospitals and barracks, arranged chronologically, giving rank, date of appointment, and date and reason for discharge, 1921–39, ADM 104/96. Testimonials relating to women applying to serve as military nurses in the Crimea, 1854–5, arranged alphabetically, WO 25/264; professional qualifications and recommendations for appointment as staff nurses in Queen Alexandra's Military Nursing Service, 1903–26, WO 25/3956; service records of those nurses appointed, 1857–1905, at the Royal Chelsea Hospital, arranged chronologically and giving age, date of appointment and of resignation or retirement, and later returns giving date of birth, January 1878–December 1910, WO 23/181; pension records, detailing age at retirement, former place of work, length of service, amount of pension, and date of death, 1820–90, WO 23/93–95; pensions to nurses in Queen Alexandra's Imperial Military Nursing Service, 1909–28, PMG 34/1–5; temporary retired pay and gratuities for disabilities of nurses in all three Services, 1917–20, PMG 42/1–12; representative medical sheets of nurses and for other women's Services in World War I, giving age, rank and treatment, 1916–17, MH 106/2207–11. Queen's Africa Medal Roll for nurses, 1899–1902, WO 100/229; King's South Africa Medal Roll for nurses, 1899–1902, WO 100/353; Royal Red Cross Medal Roll for military nurses, 1883–1918, annotated to 1952 with dates of death of recipients, WO 145/1; medal rolls for World War I, 1917–26, with a nominal index for military nurses, WO 329, and for naval nurses, ADM 171; Royal Air Force nurses held as prisoners of war, 1943–51, AIR 49/383. Appointments of nurses and matrons in Poor Law institutions, 1837–1921, arranged alphabetically by county and Union, MH 9; correspondence relating to appointments in district schools, 1848–1910, MH 27, and in Poor Law Unions, 1834–1909, MH 12, both containing details of previous experience of applicants, age, address, testimonials, reason for vacancy, and salary (with subject indexes, 1836–1920, to MH 12 in MH 15); names of nurses on the Register and Roll, from the opening of the Register on 30 September 1921, to the closure of the General Council of Nursing on 30 June 1983, indexed, DT 12; Register of nurses, 1921–73, DT 10; Roll of male and female assistant nurses, 1944–60, State Enrolled Nurses, 1961–73, and mental nurses, 1962–73, each recording qualifications, training, home address, subsequent marriage and change of address, removal from the Register or Roll, or date of death, indexed, DT 11; index of student nurses, 28 September 1982, DT 12/26; Combined Register and Roll of nurses, 1977 and 28 September 1982, DT 12/24–25; staff lists, 1929–34, DT 39/34; deceased State Enrolled Nurses, 1946–November 1975, DT 13/68–70; deceased State Registered Nurses, 1962–April 1974, DT 13/72–75; names removed by order of the Disciplinary Committee, 1969–November 1975, DT 13/71; lists of nurses trained overseas and registered by reciprocity, 1973–4, DT 13/44–57, or holding a certificate of the Royal Medico-Psychological Association, 1943–82, DT 13/79–80; lists of pupil nurses assessed for educational attainment prior to enrolment, 1949–73, DT 24 (closed 30 years); pupil nurses' examination pass lists, 1949–83, DT 25 (closed 30 years); preliminary and intermediate examination pass and failure lists for State Registered Nurses, 1924–72, DT 27 (closed 30 years), and pass and fail lists for final examinations, 1925–83, DT 28 (closed 30 years).

Nyasaland Births, 1904–c.1950, RG 36, indexed to 1940 in RG 43/18.

O*o*

Oath Rolls A series of statutes, commencing in 1559, ordered the taking of oaths by military, naval and civil office-holders under Commissions from the Crown, swearing loyalty to the monarch and the Protestant Succession; they were to be taken at one of the central courts of record in London, or at county Quarter Sessions. Surviving central enrolments in the Courts of Chancery, Common Pleas, Exchequer of Pleas and King's Bench are outlined below, plus some from the Palatinates and Duchy of Lancaster: Oaths of Allegiance and Supremacy, under a statute of 1605/6, taken by soldiers before going to the Low Countries, 1614–24, and by others going abroad, 1624–32, E 157, of officers holding commissions under the Crown, 1639–1701, C 193/9, of Crown and court officers, 1701–1906, indexed 1701–60, and later volumes integrally indexed, C 184, sworn by naval officers and men, 1660, C 215/6; Oaths of Allegiance and Supremacy, under the Corporation Act 1661, taken by military and civil office holders, certifying that the Anglican sacraments had been taken within the previous year, Test Oaths after the Test Act 1673, declarations against transubstantiation, plus certification by a priest, a churchwarden and two credible witnesses of having taken the Anglican sacraments within the previous six months, 1661–Victoria, C 214: Oaths of Allegiance and Test Oaths, 1685, C 214/1, enrolment of persons taking the Test Oath, 1673–84, C 215/7; sacrament certificates, 1673–1778, C 224, and 1676–1828, KB 22; Association Oath Rolls, containing signatures of those sworn to defend the King and the Protestant Succession against the Pretender and the Pope, 1696, C 213 and C 214; Abjuration Oath Roll, 1702, C 214/14, original Oath Rolls of Abjuration, Allegiance and Assurance, taken by jurors, 1715–19, 1728–57, 1769, and of Allegiance, Supremacy and Abjuration, 1723–1866, 1868, declarations against Transubstantiation, 1722–1824, Papists' Oaths, 1778–86, 1791–1822, 1839–57, giving names, addresses and qualities, E 169; Oaths of Allegiance taken by clergymen, 1789–1836, and by Papists, 1778–1829, CP 37; Roman Catholic Oath Rolls, 1830, 1837–8, C 214/21; Quakers' Affirmations, October–November 1723, E 169; certificates of recusants and non-jurors refusing to swear the Oath prescribed under the Security of the Sovereign Act 1714, C 203/6; Scottish peers' Oath Roll, 1837, C 214/21; Oath Roll of Commissioners for Affairs of Taxes, 1815, E 169; Judges' Oaths, 1946–87 (indexed 1910–87), and Recorders' Oaths, 1947–64 (indexed), KB 24; Oath Rolls of barristers, on call, 1673–1868, Swearing or Oath Rolls of barristers, 1673–1906, 1910–44 (with index volumes for 1910–85), KB 24; attorneys' Oath Rolls, 1779–1847, CP 10, 1750–

1874 (gap 1841–60), KB 113, 1830–72, including Catholic attorneys, 1831–7, and Quaker attorneys' Affirmations, 1831–35, E 3; attorneys' Oath Rolls in the Palatinate of Chester, 1729, 1754, 1787–1800, CHES 36/3, in the Palatinate of Durham, 1730–1837, DURH 3/217; solicitors' Oath Rolls, temp. George III, George IV and Victoria, C 214/30, Oath Rolls of solicitors, 1730–1841, E 200; Oath Rolls of solicitors in Chancery, 1778–1836, C 217/180/1–3, of Roman Catholic solicitors in Chancery, 1791–1813, C 217/180/5; Oaths of Supremacy taken before admission to Clement's Inn, c.1815–c.1866, PRO 30/26; Magistrates' Oaths, 1945–87 (indexed 1910–87), KB 24; Oaths taken by officers in the Duchy of Lancaster, 1558–1853, DL 44; Oath Roll of Naturalization for Protestant refugees under a statute of 1708, 1709–11, E 169/86, plus sacrament certificates, E 196/10, and other Oath Rolls under the same statute, 1708–12, KB 24.

see *Association Oath Rolls, Sacrament Certificates*

Oaths, Commissioners for Register of applications for appointment, 1895–1905, C 193; Oath Rolls, 1730–1841, E 200; register of London Commissioners to issue Oaths in Chancery, 1853–76, and County Commissioners, 1867–91, with a general register, 1876–1941, C 193/114–23, and 1930–60, C 193/153–54.

Offices, Royal and Public Writs of appointments, enrolled on the Fine Rolls, 1272–1641, C 60, with printed *Calendars* to 1509; enrolments of grants of offices and pensions, on the Patent Rolls, 1201–1962, C 66, with printed *Calendars*, 1216–1582 and 1584–7; some original letters patent, listed, C 248. Appointments made under Commission from the Crown, announced 1665–1986 in *The London Gazette*, with sporadic subject indexes from 1790, and invariably from 1848, ZJ 1. Enrolment books of letters patent of appointment and warrants for patents, 1510–1834, including details of pensions from 1538, payment of salaries, pensions and annuities, 1527–33, E 403/2444 with indexes to patents, 1838–53, and of appointments, 1559–1831 (incomplete); registers of fees, annuities, and pensions, 1558–74, 1600–28, 1697–8, E 403/2362–70; ledgers of salaries and pensions, 1600–25, 1709, 1782–1834, registers of warrants for pensions, 1821–34, registers of deductions from salaries for taxes, 1738–90, of debentures for salaries and pensions, 1700–08, 1820–34, registers of certificates of existence proving the pensioner was still alive, 1578–1724, and reports relating to salaries and pensions, 1637–67, 1698–1704, E 403/2390–2417 (1); certificates of existence, temp. Elizabeth I, E 407/72–76; warrants and letters patent for payment of salaries and pensions, 1667–1857, T 52, and 1671–9, PRO 30/32/41–44; accounts of receipts and issues of fees and pensions, temp. Henry VII–1714, E 405/477–561, and temp. Henry VII–1717, E 36/123–36; assignments of pensions and annuities, including abstracts of wills and letters of administration, 1622–1834, E 406/45–80, with letters granting powers of attorney, 1791–1834, E 406/68–75; registers of powers of attorney, 1706–68, E 407/18–25. Registers of Establishments in the Lord Chamberlain's Department, 1626–1849, admissions to offices, 1660–1850, people assessed for taxes, 1759–1869, salary, livery and pension books, 1667–1875, sign manual warrants for appointments, 1689–1853, appointment books, Series I, 1685–1838, Series II, 1660–1851, LC 3; in- and out-letters relating to appointments in the Lord Chamberlain's Department, 1710–1901, the in-letters (1710–1858) being indexed from 1812, and out-letters (1783–1858) from 1804, and thereafter being filed together, LC 1; salaries paid in the Lord Steward's Department, 1761–1854, LS 2, ledgers of salaries paid out, 1775–82, LS 3, Cheque Rolls, giving names of officers, dates sworn and authority by which they were appointed, with Household salaries and tax deductions, 1790–1827, temp. James I–George IV, LS 13; warrant books for payment of arrears of salaries to servants of Charles II, indexed, E 403. Civil Lists, 1673–1854, including Establishments and lists of pensions and Royal Household salaries, 1710–1820, T 38; Civil List, 1829–33, and appointments of Ambassadors, 1832–34, E 403. Treasury warrants of appointment, 1667–1849, T 54. Public appointments, 1782–1877, indexed, HO 38, 1852–76, indexed, HO 141, and appointments of Secretaries of State, etc, 1792–1862, HO 68. Correspondence concerning applications and grants of appointments, 1661–1782, in State Papers (see entry), and petitions and appointment warrants, 1679–1782, in SP 44, 1782–1820, HO 42, 1820–61, HO 44; applications for appointments, 1846–52, T 64/361; out-letters concerning appointments, 1782–1898, indexed from 1792, HO 43; prime ministerial patronage appointments, 1907–67, PREM 5 (some closed 50, 75 or 100 years). Admissions of officers in the Court of Chancery, 1596–1875, C 216, and surrenders of offices, 1709–1848, indexed, C 210; appointments of Exchequer officers, sixteenth century–1926, E 159. Manuscript indexes of appointments, nominally and by office, royal, public and legal, 1543–1828, from E 407/174–75, on open access; lists of public officers, 1547–53, SP 10; roll of names of prominent persons, by town, county or borough, to whom commissions were to be issued, temp. James I, E 163/18/10; Posting Books, recording salaries and pensions paid to judges and law officers, 1718–1834, indexed, E 403; lists of warrants to pay half-yearly wages to judges, attorneys, serjeants at law and others holding office by letters patent, thirteenth–nineteenth centuries, with nominal and topographical indexes, E 404; salaries paid by the Paymaster General's Office, 1785–93, T 47, by the Ministry of Works, 1727–1832, WORK 5; salary lists, 1794–1856, T 41; special claims for work done and services rendered, 1834–47, PMG 54. Public service pensions and gratuities, 1871–98, HO 15; superannuation and retired allowances to staff of public departments, convict establishments and commissions, and including some civil service salaries, expenses of ministers abroad, and compensation paid for abolished offices in the Courts of Justice, arranged in alphabetical order of department from 1870, and with integral indexes, 1834–1924, PMG 28, letters from the Treasury relating to pensions and compensation allowances, 1857–1907, indexed, T 21. Letters from the Treasury to British Consuls and Ministers abroad, 1831–54, T 28; in-letters, 1680–1777, T 4, 1777–1920, T 2. Surrenders of offices, 1660–87, C 75, temp. Charles II–James II, C 203, 1712–1848, C 73, 1709–1848, C 210, 1849–75, C 212. Commissions held concerning forfeitures of offices, 1629–1833, C 205. Drafts and particulars of letters patent for offices in the Duchy of Lancaster, temp. Henry VIII–George III, DL 13, and warrants for patents for offices, temp. Henry VII–George IV, DL 12, grants of offices in the Duchy, temp. Henry VII, DL 37.

see *Annuities, Civil Servants, Lord Chamberlain's Department, Lord Steward's Department, Marshalsea, Court of the, Oath Rolls, Palace Court, State Paper Office*

Old Bailey Sessions Had jurisdiction over indictable offences in the Metropolitan and adjacent area, meeting twelve times a year, until superseded in November 1834 by the Central Criminal Court. It also heard criminal cases of the Instance Court of the High Court of Admiralty. Annual Criminal Registers set out chronologically the date and session of trial, the charge, verdict and any sentence on indicted persons, 1791–1834, HO 26. Returns of committals for trial, noting the charge and trial outcome, 1815–34, HO 16. Sessions papers, 1801–34, and of the High Court of Admiralty, 1807–8, indexed, PCOM 1.
see *Admiralty, High Court of, Central Criminal Court, Criminal Registers, Annual*

Orders and Decorations, British and Foreign Correspondence, 1841–1950, with subject indexes, HO 45; correspondence relating to conferment on foreigners and foreign conferments on British subjects, 1745–1905, in FO 83, and selected correspondence, 1906–60, FO 371, to which there is a card index, 1906–19, and printed index, 1920–51, in FO 409; sign manual warrants, 1777–1863, HO 37, and warrants to wear foreign Orders, 1782–1877, indexed, HO 38; announcements are published in *The London Gazette*, to 1986, with subject indexes sporadically from 1790, and invariably from 1848, ZJ 1.
see also under individual orders and decorations

Orders in Council Made by the monarch with the advice of the Privy Council, by virtue of the Royal Prerogative, or under statutory authority. They may be found among Unbound Papers of the Privy Council, 1481–1946, PC 1, and Privy Council Registers, 1540–1941 (gap 1602–13), PC 2 (closed 50 years), and in the Minutes, 1670–1928, indexed from 1795, PC 4; Entry Books, 1660–1900, PC 6, supplement PC 2; other Entries of Orders, 1782–1840, HO 31, 1816–38, HO 72, and 1841–1950, HO 45, 1793–1830, T 9; Orders relating to the colonies, 1678–1806, PC 5, are printed in *Acts of the Privy Council, Colonial Series, 1678–1783*; they are published in *The London Gazette*, 1665–1986, with subject indexes sporadically from 1790 and invariably from 1848, ZJ 1.
see *Privy Council*

Ordnance Survey Originating between 1747 and 1755 to fulfil a need for a military map of the Scottish Highlands, the first official map was produced in 1801. It became a separate organization from the Board of Ordnance in 1841. Unindexed list of Royal Engineer officers, 1791–1927, OS 1/1/1; register of deceased soldiers in 13 Survey Company, giving cause of death and disposal of their effects, 1829–92, OS 3/3000; list of Royal Engineers and civil assistants serving with the Survey on 1 July 1890, OS 1/1/4; register of marriages of men in 16 Survey Company, 1901–29, and dates of birth of their offspring, OS 3/341; seniority lists of the Survey Battalion, 1935–42, OS 3/275–77; list of civil staff in England, 31 March 1863, ZHC 1/2817, in Scotland, 1854–8, ZHC 1/2451; register of civil assistants to the Survey Battalion, 1935–42, giving dates of entry, OS 3/285; selected personal files of employees, 1919–

74, OS 10 (one closed 75 years). Maps of one inch to the mile, 1805–97, IR 105, and six inches to the mile, mainly used to establish parochial boundaries, where no tithe map had been prepared or where only those lands subject to tithe had been mapped, 1846–1915, IR 93; later maps, using a variety of scales, but usually of 1:2500, and bigger for urban areas, marking boundaries and assessment numbers of valued properties for the Valuation Office, 1910–c.1914: London Region, IR 121, South East Region, IR 124, Wessex, IR 125, Central, IR 126, East Anglia, IR 127, Western, IR 128, West Midland, IR 129, East Midland, IR 130, Wales, IR 131, Liverpool, IR 132, Manchester, IR 133, Yorkshire, IR 134, and Northern Region, IR 135.

see *Valuation Office*

Outlaws Persons placed outside the protection of the law, by judgment of outlawry, where an indictment was found and the defendant was summoned and failed to appear; by the fifteenth century it also extended to civil proceedings, in order to secure the appearance of defendants in the courts of common law, and from the sixteenth century was used against persons failing to pay damages in cases of debt. It was tantamount to a conviction as the punishment was attainder, forfeiture of goods and escheat of land to the Crown; it was abolished in 1938. The records are in Latin to 1733. Names of outlaws occur on the Coroners' Rolls, temp. Henry III (thir-teenth century)–Henry VI (fifteenth century), JUST 2; writs of certiorari filed in order to obtain a pardon, 1277–1628, C 88; outlawry rolls of the Court of King's Bench, 1397/8–1412, and Court of Common Pleas, 1398–1416, E 370; outlawry proceedings, 1217–1926, E 159, 1821–69, CP 38; reversals of outlawry, 1736–1859, and proceedings in the London Court Hustings, 1821–38, CP 39; lists of outlaws (Crown Side of the Court of King's Bench), temp. Henry VI–Henry VIII, and temp. Elizabeth, KB 9, outlawry books (Plea Side), 1684–1840, KB 139; proceedings in the Crown Side, 1739–1834, KB 17; outlawry rolls of the Palatinate of Chester, temp. Edward IV–Edward V (fifteenth century), CHES 27; in the Palatinate of Lancaster, temp. Richard II (fourteenth century)–Edward VI, PL 28. Escheators' accounts, including up to c.1577 details of forfeited property, temp. Henry III–James I, E 136; escheators' files, including requisitions of goods and chattels, temp. Henry III–Richard III, E 153; extents of lands and goods, 1554–8, E 387, enrolments of extents of lands and goods, 1602–Victoria, E 172, 1639–1884, E 173; extents and inquisitions, temp. George III–Victoria, KB 140; inquisitions into goods held in the Duchy of Lancaster, 1558–1853, DL 44; pardons to outlaws are usually enrolled on the Patent Rolls, 1201–1938, C 66, with printed *Calendars*, 1216–1582, and 1584–7; lists of persons outlawed and pardoned, 1534, E 163/10/24.

P*p*

Palace Court Replacing the Court of the Marshalsea and Court of the Verge in 1630 to try personal pleas and actions arising within twelve miles of the Palace of Westminster, and outside the jurisdiction of the City or other liberties, it came to deal mainly with the recovery of small debts under £5. It was abolished in 1849. Docket Books, arranged by Court sitting and naming parties, verdict and reference number to the original plea, 1802–49, indexed by plaintiff, PALA 3, forming the key to the Plea Rolls, 1630–1849, PALA 6; Plaint Books, reporting all actions brought to the Court and whether determined there or transferred by writ of habeas corpus to a superior court, 1686–1849, PALA 5; Habeas Corpus Books, indexed by defendant, and naming the superior court to which the cause was removed, 1700–1849, PALA 4; proceedings, including warrants and recognizances, informations, petitions and commitments, 1673–1762, petitions and orders (mainly for debt), 1684–1800, LS 13; Bail Books, naming parties, names and addresses of special bail, and with integral indexes from 1799, 1692–1836, PALA 1; Custody Books, listing prisoners imprisoned for debt defaults, with date of admission, name of prosecutor and date of discharge, 1754–1842, indexed, PALA 2. see *Marshalsea, Court of the*

Palestine Births and deaths of British subjects, 1920–35, RG 33/141, indexed for births, 1919–35, and deaths, 1923–35, in RG 43/17, births, 1923–48, and deaths, 1941–5, RG 36, indexed, 1936–40, in RG 43/18; baptisms, 1939–47, and banns of marriage of military personnel, 1944–7, WO 156/6–8; Jaffa, births, 1900–14, FO 734/1; Jerusalem, births, 1850–1914, 1920–21, deaths, 1851–1914, FO 617/3–5, baptisms of children of military personnel, 1939–47, WO 156/6; Sarafond, baptisms, 1940–46, and marriage banns of military personnel, 1944–7, WO 156/7–8.

Papists
see *Roman Catholics*

Paraguay Births to British subjects, 1863–1958, RG 32, deaths, 1831–1920, RG 35/20–44.

Pardons
see *Alienation, Convicts, Convicts, Transportation of, Outlaws*

Parliament, Acts of Public and Private Acts are enrolled on the Parliament Rolls, 1327–1986, though from 1533 some of the Private Acts are omitted, and from 1593 only their titles appear, disappearing altogether from 1758, C 65. Statutes between 1278 and 1714 are printed in *Statutes of the Realm*, and *Acts and Ordinances of the Interregnum, 1642–60*, and there is a printed *Chronological Table of the Statutes,*

1235–1975, 1976, all being on open access. Private Acts, temp. James I–George III, including some relating to divorce, may be found in C 204; petitions to Parliament, temp. Henry III (thirteenth century)–James I, SC 8, and included in House of Commons Sessional Papers, 1693–1978, ZHC 1.

Parliament, Members of Writs and returns, by constituency, 1275–1983, C 219, with a printed list and nominal index to England, 1213–1705, Great Britain, 1705–1800, and the United Kingdom, 1801–85, for Scotland, 1357–1707, and Ireland, 1559–1800, on open access; draft lists, 1553–1695, returns, 1689–1841, return books of General Elections, 1837–1929, C 193, returns, 1814–26, T 28; writs and returns for the Palatinate of Durham, 1722–1865, DURH 3. Certificates of property qualifications under the Parliament Act 1710, temp. George I–George III, C 203/8; signed receipts for allowances to MPs, 1645, E 404/517; Association Oath Roll, 1696, C 213/1.
see **Lords, House of, Peers**

Partnerships, Dissolution of
see **Bankrupts, Chancery (Equity), Court of, Chancery Division of the High Court of Justice, Lancaster, Palatinate of**

Passes and Passports Passes were issued to allow safe passage within the kingdom to aliens, and to request safe conduct abroad for British subjects, providing details of date of issue, name, abode, status or occupation, port of departure and destination, and period within which the pass was valid. Passports are issued to British subjects for travel abroad, again requesting safe conduct, and for a determinate period. Passes issued by the Council of State and in-

cluding post-warrants allowing travel to destinations within the realm, 1650–60, SP 25/111–16, listed in *Calendar of State Papers (Domestic Series) of the Commonwealth*; dated passes issued to prevent the return from the Continent of persons under attainder for the plot against William III in 1696 and which were to be shown to port officers by his subjects entering the country, setting out name, rank, regiment, date of discharge, or occupation, name of husband in the case of women, abode, and port of departure and destination, the prescribed period, those issued to aliens going abroad, and for merchants to do trade overseas, giving name of ship, its burden, ship's master, cargo, and ports of departure and destination, and period of validity, 1697–1784, indexed to 1722, SP 44/386–413, and described in *Calendar of Home Office Papers of the reign of George III, 1760–75*; passes issued to aliens, giving name, nationality, religious denomination, occupation, port of entry, place of residence within the previous six months, and specified destination, 1793–1836, HO 1. Entry Books of passes and passports, 1748–94, and correspondence, 1834–1903, FO 366/544–45; Entry Book of passport issues, giving intended destination, arranged chronologically, 1795–1948, FO 610, with indexes to passport holders, 1851–62, 1874–1916, FO 611; selected British and foreign passports, 1802–1961, FO 655, and representative case papers, 1916–83, including United Kingdom passports, 1955–60, 1961, 1963, collective passports, 1964–72, renewals, 1950–66, and visa applications, 1961–72, FO 737; selected original passports, 1880–1903, FO 96, March–May 1915, FO 613/2; correspondence, 1815–1905, 1920–74, FO 612 (some closed 75 years), 1868–93, 1898–1905, FO 613; colonial applications for passports, 1796–1818, CO 323/97–116, thereafter found among Original Correspondence of the country of issue; passports to Peking, China, 1874–1926, FO 563 and FO 564; to Germany, 1850–81, FO 155; to Hanover, 1857–66, FO 159/28, 56, to Saxony and Saxon Duchies, 1819–75, FO 218; to Sicily and Naples, Italy, 1811–60, FO 166; to Mexico, 1816–1927, FO 207; to Warsaw, Poland, 1830–1914, FO 394; to Barcelona, Spain, 1775–1922, FO 639.

see **Licences to pass beyond the Seas, Safe Conduct, Letters of** and individual countries

Patent Rolls Letters patent, addressed to 'all to whom these presents shall come', and announcing royal grants and confirmations of Crown grants and leases of land, liberties, privileges, wardships, appointments to offices, commissions of all kinds, licences and pardons for alienation of land to 1660, patents for invention to 1853, denizations, letters of protection and safe conduct, creations of peerages and baronetcies, presentations to church livings and to dioceses, are enrolled on the Patent Rolls from 1201–1962, C 66; from 1516 grants previously made by Charter were effected by letters patent, and when the Civil List was established in 1701, the Crown's ability to dispose of its land revenues was limited to leases of up to thirty-one years or three lives, so ensuing enrolments are almost all of grants of offices and pensions, of creation, and for invention and denization. The enrolments are in Latin to 1733, to which there are printed *Calendars*, 1216–1582, and 1584–7, and for the reign of Henry VIII they are included in *Letters and Papers (Foreign and Domestic) of the reign of Henry VIII, 1509–47*; for 1583 and from 1588, access is by manuscript initial alphabet of grantees, listed by divisions or parts

of each regnal year, on open access; there is an alphabetical list of grants, temp. Anne–George II, IND 1/17408, and a card index to Rolls, temp. George V, on open access. Some original letters patent, temp. Henry III (thirteenth century)–Charles I, indexed, E 313; temp. James I–George IV, E 407/181–84, and in the Williamson Collection, 1463–nineteenth century, SP 9; entries of letters patent, 1761–1856, indexed, T 64; letters patent enrolled in the Duchy of Lancaster, 1440–78, DL 37, and temp. John (thirteenth century)–1439, DL 42, drafts of patents for offices in the Duchy, temp. Henry VIII–George III, DL 13; letters patent issued in the Palatinate of Chester, 1327–1830, CHES 2, and in the Palatinate of Lancaster, 1354–1440, DL 37, 1380–1506, PL 1, and 1409–70, PL 2.

Patronage
see **Clergy, Offices, Royal and Public**

Paymaster General's Office Salaries, 1785–93, T 47. Registers of probates, letters of administration etc, 1836–1915, PMG 50.

Pedigrees On the Curia Regis Rolls, 1193–1272, KB 26, Coram Rege Rolls, 1273–1702, KB 27, and de Banco Rolls, 1272–1875, CP 40, all being Plea Rolls and written in Latin, and produced in court to the mid-fourteenth century to establish status as a free man, as well as established property rights by descent; many have been extracted and published in *Pedigrees from the Plea Rolls, 1200–1500*, ed. G. Wrottesley, *c*.1906. Found amongst Chancery Masters' records, mid-nineteenth century–1974, listed by name of the earliest progenitor, giving date of death, and title of case, with an index on open access, J 46, J 63, J 64, J 66, J 67 and J 68 (closed 30 years), those in J 68 mainly relating to administration grants, wills and intestacy cases, and to which there is a second index to suits, giving cause number, and date of filing since 1946; pedigrees for peerage claims and cases, 1795–1949, listed alphabetically by case title and giving date and name of claimant, TS 16 (closed 50 years); selected pedigrees of intestates after their estates became *bona vacantia* because they were undisposed of as residue under will or where there was no lawful heir, 1698– 1955, removed from case files, TS 17, and 1517–1953, TS 18 (some closed 75 or 100 years); pedigrees showing descendants of a named progenitor and prepared for claims in matters handled by the Treasury Solicitor (mostly *bona vacantia*), arranged under date of compilation, and the class list noting the first ancestor, occupation, abode and date of birth, marriage or death, making reference to any related material in TS 18, 1794–1944, TS 33, and to which there is a nominal card index on open access citing both TS 33 and TS 18 where appropriate; pedigrees drafted by Sir Joseph Williamson, covering the period *c*.1463–1702, SP 9.

Pedlars
see *Hawkers and Pedlars*

Peers Letters patent of creation are enrolled on the Patent Rolls, 1201–1962, C 66, with printed *Calendars*, 1216–1582, and 1584–7; warrants for King's Bill of creation, 1783–1851, and for letters patent, 1852–9, and writs of summons to Parliament, 1783–1921, indexed, HO 116; writs of summons to Parliament to 1541 are enrolled on the Close Rolls, C 54, to which there are printed *Calendars* to 1509; fees for letters patent and for

writs of summons, 1869–77, HO 143; creations published in *The London Gazette*, 1665–1986, with subject indexes sporadically from 1790 and invariably from 1848, ZJ 1. Letters from proxies substituted for peers unable to attend Parliament, temp. Henry VIII, SC 10. Peerage claims and creations, 1661–1782, SP 44, petitions and reports from the College of Arms about claims, 1783–1837, HO 54, pedigrees, cases, petitions and papers concerning claims, submitted to the House of Lords Committee for Privileges, 1795– 1949, TS 16; claims and creations, 1841– 1919, with a descriptive list arranged under subject, HO 45; petitions, 1784– 1898, mostly indexed, HO 56, petitions, reports and letters, 1820–40, 1860–84, and claims concerning Scottish peerages, 1822–38, HO 80; Scottish peers' Oath Roll, 1837, C 214/21; proceedings taken against Scottish peers after the Jacobite Rebellion, 1745–53, TS 20; Irish peerage claims, 1828–31, HO 100, and warrants for patents of creation, 1776–1955 (Northern Ireland only from 1924), indexed, HO 101.
see *Association Oath Rolls, Lords, House of, Oath Rolls*

Persia
see *Iran*

Peru Births to Britons, 1837–41, marriages, 1827, 1836, and deaths, 1837–41, RG 33/155, indexed in RG 43/1, 7 and 3 respectively.

Petitions, Ancient Addressed to the King, to his Council and to Parliament, to the Lord Chancellor and other Officers of State, and asking for favours, liberties, patronage, and rectification of grievances, temp. Henry III (thirteenth century)–James I, SC 8. Many of the petitions to Parliament have been printed, temp. Edward I (thirteenth century)–Henry VII, in *Rotuli Parliamentorum*, 1783–1832, to which there is an index.

Peveril, Court of the Honour of Administered for the Crown from the fourteenth century, it was abolished in 1850. The records are in Latin to 1733. Action Books, containing names of parties and their attorneys and details of the cases and proceedings, 1682–1790, to which there are some integral indexes of plaintiffs, pleadings, 1682–1761, pleas, 1847–9, PEV 1.

Physicians Association Oath Roll of the College of Physicians, 1696, C 213/168. see *Medical Officers, Royal Naval*

Placita Coram Rege Pleas before the King, enrolled on the Curia Regis Rolls, 1193–1272, KB 26, which have been transcribed and printed to 1242; Coram Rege Rolls, recording all later proceedings in the Court of King's Bench, the first part the civil pleas and the final part (the 'Rex Roll') the pleas on the Crown Side, 1272–1701, KB 27; the entries are in Latin. see *King's Bench, Court of*

Plundered Ministers, Committee for One of the Parliamentary Committees, whose orders and papers survive, 1645–7, and original orders, 1644–50, in SP 22, recording yearly sums to be paid out of tithes and revenues of benefices sequestrated from named delinquent Impropriators towards the maintenance of named ministers and incumbencies.

Poland Breslau (Wroclaw), births to Britons, 1929–38, deaths, 1932–8, FO 715/1–2; Danzig (Gdansk), births, 1851–1910, marriages, 1893, deaths,

1850–1914, FO 634/9, 16–18; Grünberg, births, 1891–1900, FO 634/16; Lodz, births, 1925–39, FO 869/1; Stettin, births, 1864–1939, deaths, 1857–1933, FO 719/1–2. Some lists of foreign nationals in the Polish Land Forces, and Poles in the British Army, and Polish Palestine Group, 1945–7, WO 315/23; Polish Resettlement Corps officers, appointments and nominal rolls, 1946–8, WO 315/28 (the Corps was embodied in 1946 to help Poles fighting in units attached to the Allied Armies to settle into civilian life in Britain and abroad and most of the records in this class are not open to inspection).

Police Force, Metropolitan Formed in 1829, the area covered extends to a radius of about seven miles from Charing Cross, London; maps and plans of divisions, 1894–6, Northern Areas, 1915–16, and of Metropolitan Police Districts, 1914, 1965, 1972 and 1973, are in MEPO 15. Pensions of men employed in the old Admiralty Dockyard Service, 1830–66, ADM 23, 1867–94, arranged from 1870 in alphabetical order of department and with nominal indexes, PMG 25. Registers of officers' warrant numbers, 1–3147, September 1829–March 1830, MEPO 4/31–32; alphabetical list of members of the Force, 1829–36, HO 65/26; alphabetical register of joiners, September 1830–April 1857, July 1878–1933, MEPO 4/333–38; attestation ledgers, containing signatures and those of attesting witnesses, December 1869–May 1958, MEPO 4/352–60; alphabetical index of joiners, 1880–89, giving date of warrant and of joining, and date of leaving the Force, MEPO 7/42–51, on open access; certificates of service, containing a physical description, date and place of birth, previous trade, marital status, abode, number of children, name and address of late employer, any previous public service, a surgeon's certificate, details of postings to divisions, dates of promotion and demotion or removal and the reason, January 1887–November 1909, MEPO 4/361–477; register of leavers, giving class, number of certificate if not dismissed, and when sent to the division, March 1889–January 1947, MEPO 4/339–51; returns of deaths whilst in service, stating the cause of demise, 1829–89, MEPO 4/2, indexed in MEPO 4/448; correspondence relating to pensions for twenty-five years' service, and gratuities, 1829–1907, indexed by subject, MEPO 5/1–90; general alphabetical index giving details of promotion, transfers, demotion, awards, retirement, and dismissals, and other personnel matters, 1829–1968, MEPO 7 (most closed 50 years), with personal name indexes, 1835–52 (MEPO 7/156–64), and a printed subject index, 1829–66 (MEPO 7/28); pensions of those retiring or resigning, 1852–1932, granted or from 1890 qualified for a police pension, MEPO 21; joining papers and particulars of service of senior officers and selected women officers, 1858–1933, MEPO 3/2883–922 (some closed 75 years); issues of *Hue and Cry* and *Police Gazette*, 1828–45, including lists of deserters, HO 75; King's Police Medal, established in 1909; lists of awards, 1909–12, MEPO 2/1300, out-letters concerning the Medal, 1920–21, HO 178, and files, 1909–50, HO 45. see *Medals*

Poll Tax Initially imposed at a flat rate for all aged fourteen and over, in 1377, in 1379 it became a graded tax according to a person's wealth and status, and was levied on all of sixteen and over, except beggars; the last medieval imposition was in 1381, on those aged fifteen and above, returns

for all of which are in E 179, listed alphabetically by county, then chronologically by hundred and township or vill; further mulcts were made in 1640, 1667/8, 1678/9, 1689/90 and 1698, those up to 1678/9 being in E 179, and the last two in E 182, arranged in county bundles, by year, and with uneven coverage of nominal listings under parish; further lists may be found for the last two years in E 181, and both the latter classes include names of Papists and aliens assessed to pay double, people who were in default, or had died or gone away, and persons exonerated from payment; aliens were subjected to a Poll Tax if not found liable for the lay subsidies from 1523, a practice extended to denizens in 1571, but limited to those aged fourteen and over, and lowered to seven in 1576; Popish recusants convict, aged seventeen, and non-communicants within the previous year, aged twenty-one and upwards, also attracted a Poll Tax at the time of collection of lay subsidies, to which were added indicted Roman Catholics between 1640 and 1660: lists of their names may be incorporated in the lay subsidy assessments, or separately, E 179; Poll Tax assessment on royal servants below stairs and their relatives, 30 July 1689, LS 13/231.

Poor Law Unions Set up in 1834 to make provision for indoor and outdoor relief of paupers where they were legally settled. Plans of land and buildings, listed alphabetically, 1861–1918, MH 14; registers of paid officers, appointed by English and Welsh local Boards of Guardians, giving date of appointment, remuneration, date and cause of resignation or dismissal, listed alphabetically by county and then by Union, or London Districts, and finally by category, c.1837–c.1921, MH 9; appointments of staff, 1834–50,

MH 19; correspondence from the Boards and local authorities with the Poor Law Commission to 1847, and its successor, the Poor Law Board, and papers including applications for posts as Relieving Officer, schoolteacher, chaplain, medical officer, master and matron of the workhouse, embracing curriculum vitae, testimonials from previous employers or friends, letters of appointment, resignation and dismissal, vaccination records, details of lunatic inmates, examinations of paupers seeking help, provision for emigration, and information on outbreaks of infectious diseases, listed alphabetically by county, then by Union and the records arranged chronologically, 1834–1909, MH 12, with subject indexes, 1836–1920, in MH 15. Correspondence with Government Offices concerning emigration of the poor, 1836–76, MH 19/22; official sanctions permitting expenditure on assisted emigration of the poor, and for casual vacancies on the Boards of Guardians, 1916–32, MH 64; correspondence of Assistant Poor Law Commissioners and Inspectors, arranged alphabetically by name and reporting on workhouse conditions, 1834–1904, MH 32, registers of the correspondence, 1834–46, being in MH 33; correspondence between Poor Law Boards and Poor Law School Districts for administration and control of schools, appointment of managers, teaching and nursing staff, 1848–1910, MH 27; Visiting Officers' diaries concerning Metropolitan Casual Wards of vagrants, some containing dates of death of officers, and applications for vacant posts, 1874–8, 1881, MH 18. Census returns of staff and inmates of Union workhouses, 6 June 1841, HO 107, 30 March 1851, HO 107, 7 April 1861, RG 9, 2 April 1871, KG 10, 3 April 1881, RG 11, and 5 April 1891, RG 12.

Port Books Kept by English and Welsh Customs officers, including the names of vessels, their masters, merchants, cargoes, destinations and duty paid, 1565–1798, E 190; after 1600 few omit ports of departure and destination, but none survive for the Port of London, 1696–1795. Some passenger lists are located here for people travelling to the Continent or America, the latter of which have been printed in J.C. Hotten's *Original Lists of Persons Emigrating to America, 1600–1700*, 1874.
see *Coast Bonds*

Port of London Compensation Commission Memorials of claims by persons whose property had been taken or suffered loss before London Dock Act 1799, or East India Dock Acts 1803 and 1806, 1799–1824, indexed, T 76.

Portugal Deaths of Britons, 1831–1920, RG 35/20–44; Azores, Ponta Delgada, births, baptisms, marriages, deaths and burials, 1807–66, FO 559–1, baptisms, marriages and burials, 1835–7, RG 33/155, indexed in RG 43/1, 7 and 3 respectively, baptisms, 1850–57, RG 32, burials, 1850–57, RG 35/20; Funchal, register of charters and petitions relating to British privileges dating from the fifteenth century, c.1750–1931, FO 811; Lisbon, index to marriages, 1822–59, RG 43/7 (the registers are at the General Register Office, London), marriages, 1846–90, FO 83, indexed in FO 802/239, marriage notices, 1859–76, FO 173/8, Minute Book of the British Factory in Lisbon, 1811–24, including correspondence concerning the Relief of Distressed Portuguese subjects, FO 180; Oporto, baptisms, marriages and burials, 1814–74, RG 33/142, baptisms, marriages and burials, 1833, RG 33/155, indexed in RG 43/1, 7 and 3, baptisms, 1835–1958, RG 32, marriages, 1835–1921, burials, 1835–44, RG 35/

20; St Vincent (Cape Verde), marriage notices, 1894–1922, marriage oath book, 1905–10, FO 767/6–7; British officers in the Portuguese Service, 1809–14, AO 11; claims and awards by the Slave Trade Commission, under the 1817 Convention against illicit trade trafficking, 1819–24, FO 308; claims of British subjects serving in the Portuguese Army and Navy during the War of Liberation, 1840–49, indexed, FO 309.

Post Office Entry Book of commissions and agreements, 1687–1703, AO 3/871/1; salary lists, arranged by grade under quarter of the year, 1765, 1824–5, AO 3/871/2.

Principal Probate Registry 7% sample of contentious probate cases, 1858–1960, listed alphabetically by year under the name of the testator and case title, J 121 (closed 30 years).

Prisoners of War, British, Commonwealth and Dominion Lists of prisoners in Spain, Portugal and France, 1698–1703, 1793–6, AO 3; British prisoners in France, 1779–81, 1794–1815, at Verdun, Tours and Tangiers, 1806, deaths of British prisoners in France, 1794–1815, and in America, 1814–15, exchanges for French prisoners, 1780–97, and prisoners released from Spain, 1798–1807, ADM 103; enquiries concerning British prisoners in enemy hands, and responses, 1799–1810, ADM 105/57, 1810–24, ADM 105/47–54, enquiries about applications for prisoners, 1799–1801, ADM 105/55–56; liberated British prisoners in America, 1783, T 64/24; list of British and Dominion prisoners in German hands, 1915, ADM 1/8420/124, correspondence relating to prisoners taken in Austro–Hungary, the Balkans, Belgium, Egypt, France, Germany and Turkey, 1915–19, including British civilians in Germany, 1916–19, FO 383; British prisoners in Turkey, 1917, CO 537/1123; lists of British and Dominion subjects held in Germany, March–April 1916, in Turkey, February 1916, and Switzerland, June 1916, AIR 1/892/204/5/696–98; miscellaneous foreign deaths, 1830–1921, RG 35; British and Commonwealth prisoners of war and internees in Germany, 1939–45, lists of missing servicemen circulated to Camps, 1941, British subjects in Italy and prisoners of war there and in Greece, 1941, lists of British subjects in enemy territory on whose behalf remittances were made here, 1941, lists of prisoners of war in Germany, 1942, all in FO 916; lists of Naval prisoners in German hands, 1939–45, ADM 116 Code 79; Royal Marines held by Germany, 1939–45, ADM 201/111; alphabetical list of British and Dominion Air Force prisoners in German hands, 1944–5, AIR 20/2336; lists of Royal Air Force nursing service prisoners in Camps, January 1943–September 1951, Royal Air Force prisoners in Horoshima Camp, November 1942–September 1945, and November 1944–6, AIR 49/383–85; some notifications of death, including internees, 1939–45, RG 32, indexed in RG 43; British and Commonwealth prisoners in Korean hands, 1951–3, WO 208/3999; Commonwealth prisoners of the Koreans, 1954, WO 308/54.

Prisoners of War, Enemy French prisoners of war, 1793–5, AO 11; deaths of French prisoners in England, 1794–1815, with a general index to all prisons and prison ships in Britain, distinguishing between officers on parole and inmates, by depot or ship, and including French, Spanish, dutch, Danish, Russian and Prussian prisoners, 1780–97, Americans at the Cape of Good Hope, 1813–14, and an undated alphabetical list of American prisoners in Dartmoor, ADM 103; register of sick taken from French vessels, recording age, birthplace, ailment, rank, date of entry and discharge, 1812–13, ADM 7/848; list of American prisoners in Britain, 1813, ADM 6/417; petitions from prisoners, 1750–1810, ADM 1/ 3977–81, prisoners' applications, 1810– 16, ADM 105; names of escaped prisoners, 1810–13, ADM 105/45. Letters from surgeons and medical officers of hospitals and hospital ships, 1702– 1862, ADM 97, hospital musters, 1740– 1860, ADM 102, including a roster of Russians in Haslar Hospital, 1808–12, ADM 102/349; wages and salary lists of persons employed in the care of prisoners of war, 1803–15, ADM 104. Lists of Russian prisoners in Britain, 1854–7, RG 8/180. Registers of Boer prisoners, 1899–1902, WO 108/305–05, and correspondence relating to Boer prisoners, 1899–1902, CO 537/403–09, 453, and FO 2/824–26. Representative medical records of German sick and wounded, arranged by field ambulance, casualty clearing station, hospital and including an ambulance train and hospital ship, 1914– 21, MH 106; papers concerning prisoners of war, 1914–19, with a descriptive list, HO 144; German prisoners held in Germany, 1918, FO 383; specimen documents, 1914–18, and 1939–45, including German internees, 1915–16, WO 900; lists of temporary internees in the Tower of London, 1939–45, WO 94/105; internees, 1940–49, including some British subjects, HO 214 (some closed 50 years); prisoners of war and internees, 1939–48, FO 916 (some closed 50 or 75 years); prisoners of war at RAF Cosford, August 1944–August 1945, AIR 49/386–87;

personal files on German prisoners in the Allied National Prison, Werl, 1945–57, listed by name, FO 1024; War Crimes papers, listed by case or camp, and giving name and date of trial, with a nominal index, 1939–45, WO 235.

see under respective Wars, and *Internees*

Prisons References to prisoners may be found in Unbound Papers of the Privy Council, 1481–1946, to which there is a descriptive list, arranged chronologically by date, PC 1. Warrants for the removal of named prisoners from one place to another, usually to Newgate, 1650–60, integrally indexed, SP 25/111–16. Returns of prisoners committed by the Court of Chancery and Chancery Division, 1860–81, and committal warrants of the Chancery Division, 1904–61, J 93; entries of orders to return to gaol prisoners brought before the Court of King's Bench (Plea Side), including lists of prisoners, 1603–1877, indexed 1792– 1802, KB 125; registers of prisoners, Assize and Quarter Sessions gaol calendars relating to England and Wales, with lists for Gibraltar and prison hulks, 1770– c.1913, arranged alphabetically by gaol, PCOM 2; calendars of prisoners after trial by Assizes or Quarter Sessions, giving name, number, age, occupation, degree of education, date of warrant and custody, charge, date and place of trial, verdict and sentence, listed alphabetically by county, and including Jersey, Guernsey and the Isle of Man, 1868–1915, HO 140 (closed 75 years); registers of convicts on hulks, 1802–49, HO 9; quarterly lists of crews and convicts on hulks, 1802–31, and sickness returns, 1802–18, T 38; sworn and attested quarterly returns of inmates of hulks and prisons, recording age, conviction, sentence, state of health and behaviour, 1824–76, HO 8; registers of county prisons, 1847–66, indexed, HO 23; prison registers and returns for Millbank, Parkhurst and Pentonville, 1838–75, HO 24; Newgate Prison Calendar, including trial results from July 1822, 1782–1853, HO 77; calendar of prisoners at Winchester at the Special Commission of Assize after the 1830 agricultural riots, HO 130. Warrants for removal to asylums, 1882–1921, HO 145. Census returns of prisons, recording personal details about staff, but initials for inmates, 6 June 1841, HO 107, 30 March 1851, HO 107, 7 April 1861, RG 9, 2 April 1871, RG 10, 3 April 1881, RG 11, and 5 April 1891, RG 12; appointments of staff, 1887–98, HO 160. Baptisms at Westminster Penitentiary, 1816–71, burials, 1817–53, PCOM 2/139–40; deaths and inquests at Millbank, 1848–63, PCOM 2/165; interments in Victoria Park Cemetery, Hackney, 1853–76, RG 8/42–51.

see **Assizes, Convicts, Convicts, Transportation of, Criminal Registers, Annual, Fleet Prison, King's Bench Prison, Marshalsea Prison, Queen's Prison**

Privy Council The principal council of The Crown, composed of members chosen from distinguished persons. Petitions and letters, reports, memorials, law officers' opinions, papers in appeal cases, orders and minutes, and proclamations covering a variety of topics such as charters, convicts, sheriffs, schools and universities, and Papists, and with a separate series for the colonies, 1677–1799, in Unbound Papers, to which there is a descriptive list arranged chronologically, 1481–1946, PC 1 (though many before 1698 were consumed by fire): many of the colonial papers have been included in *Acts of the Privy Council of England, Colonial Series*, volume VI, 1676–1783; Privy Council Registers, including orders and proclamations, 1540–1941 (with a gap 1602–13), and fully indexed from 1710, PC 2 (closed 50 years), included in *Proceedings and Ordinances of the Privy Council, 1540–42*, and *Acts of the Privy Council of England, 1542–1631*, and colonial entries being extracted and included in *Acts of the Privy Council of England, Colonial Series*, volumes I–V, 1613–1783; Minutes of the Privy Council, being mainly abstracts of Orders in Council from the mid-nineteenth century, 1670–1928, indexed from 1795, PC 4, supplementing PC 2; Entry Books of Orders in Council, 1660–1900 and daily registers of correspondence, 1834–60, containing brief summaries of petitions and letters, PC 6; selected original correspondence, 1860–1955, PC 8 (some closed 50 years), and registers of correspondence, 1860–1964, with subject indexes, PC 9.

see **Orders in Council**

Privy Council, Judicial Committee of the This replaced the High Court of Delegates in 1834, and is made up of a permanent committee drawn from Privy Councillors, to hear all appeals concerning ecclesiastical and maritime causes, and from the Dominions or Dependencies of the Crown unless specifically excluded by the country; it also deals with appeals in connection with professional bodies with power to strike off a member from the register. In 1876 Admiralty causes excluding prizes and matters referred from colonial courts were removed to the Court of Appeal. Appeals Assignation Books, 1833–78, PCAP 2; Appeals Case Books, 1834–70, PCAP 3; exhibits produced in ecclesiastical causes, 1833–59, DEL 9; processes, giving the outcome to proceed-

ings in ecclesiastical and maritime cases, 1834–79, PCAP 1.
see *Appeal, Court of, Delegates, High Court of*

Probate, Court of Set up in 1858 to deal with probate matters formerly under the jurisdiction of ecclesiastical courts, and merged into the Probate, Divorce and Admiralty Division of the High Court of Justice in 1875. Probate cases referred to the Procurator General, 1858–75, indexed, TS 15.

Probate, Divorce and Admiralty Division of the High Court of Justice Established in 1875 on the merger of the High Court of Admiralty, the Probate Court and Court of Divorce and Matrimonial Causes, it was renamed the Family Division in 1970 when Admiralty cases were removed to the Queen's Bench Division, and probate matters passed to the Chancery Division. Only a small selection of its records have been preserved: Minute Books of the Instance Court, 1875–1965, HCA 27, indexed to 1918 in HCA 56; index cards to the Cause Books, giving year, cause title and number, names of the parties, date of filing of pleadings and entries of appearance, date of any judgment and judgment number, 1879–1906, 1921–37, on open access (the documents themselves being destroyed), plus judgment books, 1875, 1880, and at ten-yearly intervals to 1930, arranged under judgment number, indexed 1876–80, with access also via the index cards, J 89.

Probate Duty A Stamp Duty on personal property worth £100 or more left by deceased persons in this country, for whom probate or letters of administration should be granted, 1881–93. It was absorbed into Estate Duty in 1894.
see *Death Duty, Estate Duty*

Proclamations, Royal To prevent offences and admonish subjects to keep the laws; offences against them were tried before the Court of Star Chamber to 1640. Up to 1896 they were endorsed on the back of Patent Rolls, and thereafter on the last Roll for each regnal year, 1201–1962, C 66; some appear on the Close Rolls to 1903, C 54; proclamations may also be found in Privy Council Unbound Papers, 1481–1946, PC 1, to which there is a descriptive list, and Privy Council Registers, 1540–1941, (gap 1602–13), fully indexed from 1710, PC 2; proclamations, 1625–1805, SP 45; original proclamations, 1620–76, SP 46. They are also published in *The London Gazette*, 1665–1986, with subject indexes sporadically from 1790, and invariably from 1848, ZJ 1.
see *Privy Council, Star Chamber, Court of, State Paper Office*

Proctor, King's/Queen's
see *Procurator General, Her Majesty's*

Proctors Lawyers acting in ecclesiastical and Admiralty courts, they were renamed solicitors in 1875. Appointments and admissions, 1727–1841, HCA 30; letters appointing them as proxies for spiritual peers unable to attend Parliament, temp. Henry III (thirteenth century)–Henry VIII, SC 10; appointed as proxies in the Prerogative Court of Canterbury in probate litigation in the sixteenth century, PROB 55, and 1674–1718, PROB 19; select index of proctors, seventeenth–nineteenth centuries, on open access.
see *Clements Inn, Doctors' Commons*

Procurator General, Her Majesty's Originally this officer dealt with Admiralty and ecclesiastical matters and prerogative law, but since 1876 the office has been combined with that of the Treasury Solicitor, specializing after the Matrimonial Causes Act 1950 with interventions in divorce or nullity proceedings when asked by the Court, or where information suggests collusion. He has the power to recover the property of intestates, and to act for the Crown in ecclesiastical matters, and prize matters in wartime and subsequently. Memorials in intestacy cases, and wills referred on by the Treasury, 1804–15, indexed by subject and name of memorialist, TS 8, 1815–44, TS 9; legal proceedings of State Trials, escheats, and administration cases, 1584–1852, TS 11, 1517–1953, TS 18 (some closed 75 or 100 years), to which there is a descriptive list arranged under subject, and a card index to pedigrees and papers in TS 33 contains references to related material in this class; selected administration of estates case papers, including letters of administration to 1857, and pedigrees in *bona vacantia* cases (where the testator failed to dispose of residuary estate, or died without a lawful heir), 1698–1955, TS 17; registers of divorce cases, where the decree nisi was not made absolute, or where the officer intervened or assisted the court, 1875–1977, TS 29 (most closed 75 years); Assignation Books, of notes of proceedings in appeals from the Admiralty Instance, Prize and Vice-Admiralty Courts, 1827–62, indexed, and including some probate cases from the Prerogative Court of Canterbury, Court of Probate, and Probate, Divorce and Admiralty Division, 1845–78, TS 15.

see *Treasury Solicitor*

Protection, Court of Instituted as the Management and Administration Department of the Lunacy Office under the Lunacy Act 1890, it was renamed in 1959, and has jurisdiction over persons of unsound mind and their estates. 2% sample of administrations of patients' estates and their medical histories, 1900–83, J 91 (most closed 75 years); Commissions to Lords Chancellor to act, 1852–1956, J 80.

see *Idiots and Lunatics*

Protectorates, British Births, marriages and deaths, including British nationals, in Asian Protectorates, 1895–1957, arranged under country, RG 33, indexed in RG 43/1–3, 5–14, 20–21; and in African and Asian Protectorates, 1895–1950, RG 36/1–13, indexed, 1904–40, in RG 43/18.

see under individual countries.

Public Houses Petitions for compensation for non-renewal of licences under the Licensing Act 1904, 1905–31, E 205. Papers from the London Office and Local State Management Districts, concerning the Central Control Board (Liquor Traffic) set up in 1915 for Carlisle and 320 square miles around it to try and reduce the incidence of drunkenness by the erection of new public houses with pleasant surroundings, 1915–51, HO 185.

Qq

Quarter Sessions Annual Criminal Registers for England and Wales, arranged alphabetically by county, listing chronologically names of indicted persons, date and place of trial, the charge, verdict and sentence, and including between 1834 and 1848, ages, and from 1835–48, educational level, 1805–92, HO27. Calendars of prisoners, 1770–c.1913, arranged by English and Welsh house of correction or prison, PCOM 2; calendars of prisoners after trial, giving number, age, occupation, degree of education, charge, verdict and sentence, the name and address of the committing magistrate, and date of warrant and of custody, listed alphabetically by county, 1868–1915, HO 140 (closed 75 years).

Queen Anne's Bounty A perpetual fund set up in 1704 to apply sums collected from larger benefices to make up the deficiencies of those with incomes less than £50 a year. Records, including bonds for payment and for excess of First Fruits, commissions to collect arrears, returns of promotions and admissions, and deeds of conveyance of land put in trust for the fund, Exchequer processes and returns, 1704–1839, QAB 1; conveyances of land to augment curacies with annual incomes lower than £50, are enrolled on the Close Rolls to 1903, C 54, with a pasted-up topographical index, 1736–1870, and a card index of places to 1903, on open access; later conveyances are enrolled in J 18 to 1987, to which there is a topographical card index to 1905 on open access, and later entries being located by annual initial indexes, to 1948, and thereafter by chronological listing.
see *Clergy*

Queen's Bench Division
see *King's Bench Division*

Queen's Prison From 1842–62 this served as the only prison for debtors and bankrupts, and was formerly called the Queen's (King's) Bench Prison. Inmates of the Fleet and Marshalsea Prisons were transferred here on their closure in 1842. Commitment Books, giving date, by whose authority, and any subsequent action taken, plus date of discharge or death, 1842–1862, indexed, PRIS 4; Commitment Books, Entry Books of discharges, Habeas Corpus Books and lists of prisoners, 1842–62, PRIS 10; writs of habeas corpus and returns of names of prisoners, 1849–52, KB 140; Execution Books, arranged alphabetically by prisoner, citing the name of the prosecutor, attorney, and amount of damages, 1842–51, PRIS 8; original warrants of discharge, 1842–62, PRIS 7.
see *Fleet Prison*, *King's Bench Prison*, *Marshalsea Prison*

Rr

Railways Lives of early railway pioneers, 1838–1980, ZLIB 1; *Universal Directory of Railway Officials, 1898–1932*, and *Railway Year Book*, 1933–84, ZPER 47. Reports of Railway Inspectors, 1840–1958, indexed by company, or region after nationalisation, MT 29; indexes to works locations, 1871–1949, MT 30. Returns of inquests on people killed on the railways, 1899–1909, HO 166. Staff records of the following companies: Barry Railway Company, 1886–1922, registers of accidents including those to passengers, 1898–1922, workmen's compensation for injuries sustained at work, 1898–1922, RAIL 23/46–60, 64–65; Brecon and Merthyr Tydfil Junction Railway Company, 1880–88, accidents 1912–22, RAIL 65/31–35; Cambrian Railways Company, 1898–1922, accidents, 1898–1906, 1919–22, RAIL 92/142–48; Cardiff Railway Company, 1869–1922, accidents, 1908–23, RAIL 97/32–36; Chester and Holyhead Railway Company, list of crew and their grade, *SS Hibernia*, 1854, RAIL 113/53; Cleator and Workington Junction Railway Company, 1879–1923, RAIL 119/13; East Lincolnshire Railway Company, paylist including Railway Police, 1848–50, RAIL 177/21; Furness Railway Company, 1852–1922, RAIL 214/97–104; Great Central Railway Company, 1857–1949, RAIL 226/193–235; Great Eastern Railway Company, including staff histories, 1855–1930, RAIL 227/445–90; Great Northern Railway Company, 1848–1943, RAIL 236/727–45; Great Western and Midland Railway Companies Joint Committee, 1865–1915, RAIL 241/28; Great Western Railway Company, 1835–1954, including some indexes, RAIL 264/1–463; Hull and Barnsley Railway Company, 1885–1927, RAIL 312/77–81; Hull and Selby Railway Company, 1845–75, RAIL 315/30; Isle of Wight Central Railway Company, 1860–1923, RAIL 328/16–18; Lancashire and Yorkshire Railway Company, 1853–1941, RAIL 343/827–45; Lancashire, Derbyshire and East Coast Railway Company, appointment of a General Manager, 1904–06, RAIL 334/56; Liverpool and Manchester Railway Company, 1833–47, RAIL 384/284–89, indexed in RAIL 384/291; London and North Eastern Railway Company, c.1920–42, RAIL 397/1–3, 6, 8, 11 (closed 50 years), passed firemen, awards and cautions, RAIL 397/12, staff histories, 1914–63, RAIL 397/13 (closed 30 years); London and North Western and Great Western Railway Companies Joint Committee, 1871–97, RAIL 404/177–80; London and North Western and Midland Railway Companies Joint Committee, 1861–1911, RAIL 406/16, staff register of coaching and Police departments at New Street and Derby, 1861–1911, RAIL 406/16; London and North

Western Railway Company, 1853–73, RAIL 410/1217–18, 1831–1927, RAIL 410/1797–1986, some with indexes, and including cautions and disciplinary action taken; London and South Western Railway Company, including cautions, 1838–1944, and some with indexes, RAIL 411/483–537; London Brighton and South Coast Railway Company, 1837–1925, including workmen's compensation awards, 1892–1904, and some volumes indexed, RAIL 414/750–96; London Midland and Scottish and London and North Eastern Railway Companies Joint Committee, 1891–1938, RAIL 417/16; London Midland and Scottish Railway Company, 1923–44, RAIL 426/1–15; London, Tilbury and Southend Railway Company, 1888–1923, RAIL 437/44–57; Manchester, Sheffield and Lincolnshire Railway Company, 1845–1926, RAIL 463/210–45, 1870–94, RAIL 463/177; Midland and Great Northern Railways Joint Committee, 1879–93, RAIL 487/115; Midland and South Western Junction Railway Company, 1891–1921, RAIL 489/21; Midland Railway Company, 1859–1924, including accidents, 1875–1921, RAIL 491/969–1081, settled cases of workmen's compensation claims, 1908–15, RAIL 491/1042–57; Neath and Brecon Railway Company, 1903–20, RAIL 505/13; Newcastle upon Tyne and Carlisle Railway Company, 1845–8, RAIL 509/96; North and South Western Junction Railway Company, 1883–1916, RAIL 521/19; North Eastern Railway Company, 1843–1957, including fines, staff histories and some with indexes, RAIL 527/1895–97, 1909–13, 1917, 1925–6, 1929–33, 1938–62, 1964–5; North London Railway Company, 1854–1920, RAIL 529/130–38; North Staffordshire Railway Company, 1847–1923, RAIL 532/

58–67; North Sunderland Railway Company, 1931–48, RAIL 533/76, application for the post of auditor, 1893, RAIL 533/75; Otley and Ilkley Joint Line Committee (Midland and North Eastern Railway Companies), 1865–1901, RAIL 554/24–25; Port Talbot Railway and Docks Company, 1883–1918, RAIL 574/13; Rhondda and Swansea Bay Railway Company, 1882–1922, RAIL 581/36–37; Rhymney Railway Company, 1860–1922, including accidents, 1896–1922, RAIL 583/41–65; Sheffield District Railway Company, three staff appointments, 1897, 1904–16, RAIL 611/25–26; Shropshire Union Railways and Canal Company, 1844–97, RAIL 623/66–68; Somerset and Dorset Joint Line Company, 1844–97, indexed, RAIL 626/44–53; Somerset and Dorset Railway Company, 1863–77, RAIL 627/6; South Eastern and Chatham Railway Companies Managing Committee, including punishments and awards, and superannuations, 1850–1944, RAIL 633/343–82; South Eastern Railway Company, including punishments and awards, 1845–1944, RAIL 635/302–10; South Wales Railway Company, 1844–60, RAIL 640/55–56, 1864, RAIL 640/45, fines, 1846–56, RAIL 640/47; Cockett Tunnel expenses, 1847–8, RAIL 640/52; Southern Railway Company, 1923–57, including cautions and workmen's compensation awards, 1927–57, RAIL 651/1–8, 11; Stockton and Darlington Railway Company, 1835–56, including fines, RAIL 667/1283–91; Stratford-upon-Avon and Midland Junction Railway Company, 1873–1923, RAIL 674/11; Taff Vale Railway Company 1840–1924, including accidents, 1897–1922, RAIL 684/94–120, workmen's compensation awards, 1905–22, RAIL 684/123–25, list of policemen, 1858, RAIL 684/55; Trent Valley Railway Company, 1845–6, RAIL 699/5; Wirral Railway Company, 1884–1926, RAIL 756/10–11; York and North Midland Railway Company, 1848, RAIL 770/77–80, 1843–50, RAIL 770/81; York, Newcastle and Berwick Railway Company, 1845, RAIL 772/106, 1847–8, RAIL 772/121, 1845–60, RAIL 772/123–25.

Rates Rating appeal registers of local Valuation Courts, giving name, date of entry, case reference number, name and address of appellant and respondent, and the outcome, 1950–70, indexed, LT 11; a selection of appeals is in LT 10.

Recorders Oaths, 1947–64, indexed, KB 24.

Recoveries, Common Fictitious disputes allowing for the barring of entailed land to convert it to fee simple which was freely disposable, rather than passing in a pre-determined line under fee tail, and replaced in 1834 by disentailing assurances. The collaborating demandant alleged that the tenant in tail's title was defective, for he himself had previously been wrongly ejected from the land, and now demanded restitution, and evidence of the defendant's good title. The defendant called on a vouchee (the court crier) to warrant the title, the vouchee asked leave to imparl with the defendant, and defaulted, so that judgment was given to the demandant, who afterwards granted the land free of existing restrictions to the defendant tenant in tail. Sometimes a double voucher was used, the defendant having given a life interest in the land to a third party, who then became the defendant, citing the tenant in tail, who again cited the vouchee

with a similar outcome, and this judgment in default also exterminated any latent rights over the land, and was therefore more effective. In the fifteenth century these disputes were grafted onto already existing procedures for restitution of land through writs of *praecipe* in the Court of Common Pleas, and the records are in Latin to 1733. Fifteenth century–1582/3, listed alphabetically by county, then by regnal year and legal term, CP 40, Easter 1583–1834, CP 43; writs of entry, giving extracts of land conveyance, names of parties, an outline of the property, its valuation and fine, 1595–1858, A 9; common recoveries effected in the Palatinate of Chester, fifteenth century–1831, CHES 29, and Docket Books, covering the same period, giving chronologically names of most parties and the places involved, 1509–15, 1547–1830, CHES 31, and enrolments, 1585–1714, CHES 32; in the Palatinate of Durham, 1578–1834, DURH 13; the Palatinate of Lancaster, fifteenth century–1834, PL 15; and the Principality of Wales, Anglesey, 1509–16, WALE 16/1, and Carnarvon, 1386–99, 1530–33, WALE 20/1–3.

Recusants Persons suspected, indicted or convicted for non-attendance at the Anglican church services may be found in a variety of sources: from 1625–60 convicted Roman Catholics of seventeen and above, and non-communicants within the past year aged twenty-one or more, were liable to pay double assessed amounts of tax, or a Poll Tax (extended to indicted Catholic recusants, 1640–60), surviving assessments and returns for which are arranged alphabetically by county, then by hundred, township or vill, E 179; the Recusant Rolls, recording in Latin the names of persons within each county, and in Wales, who were from 1581 fined £20 a month on a penalty of imprisonment for non-payment, and from 1586 subjected to seizure of their goods, and two-thirds of their land until they conformed, in lieu of fine, 1591–1691, E 376 and E 377: what they do not often provide is any indication of denomination; some summonses for collection of recusancy fines, temp. Elizabeth–Charles I, and 1655, E 370/106, 117–24, 169–70; certificates relating to land sequestrated from recusants during the Commonwealth, 1656, SP 23/261, and C 203/4; lists of recusants refusing to take the oath of loyalty to the Crown under the Security of the Sovereign Act 1714, and furnished by county clerks of the peace, giving name, address, occupation and date of conviction by Quarter Sessions, 1715–16, C 203/6; lists of Welsh recusants, temp. Henry VIII–William IV, CHES 21.

see *Dissenters, Protestant, Non–Parochial Registers, Poll Tax, Roman Catholics, Subsidy, Lay*

Refugees Hostel lists relating to war refugees, 1917, MH 8/10. Alphabetical list of distressed American refugees, 1781, 1782, allowances, 1832–5, T 50; compensation paid to American Loyalists and other refugees, 1788–1837, AO 3/276; history cards, arranged alphabetically, for Belgian refugees, giving name, age, relationship within the family, wife's former name, allowances and address to which paid, 1914–18, MH 8/39–92; payments to Breton refugees, 1797, 1811, to Corsican refugees, and reports on their applications and allowances, 1834–40, allowances made to Dutch refugees, 1832–5, and other relevant papers, 1829–41, T 50; specimen personal files on Czechoslovakian refugee families, 1939–60, HO 294/328–98, 423–66, and case

papers, 1950–72, arranged by number, HO 294/592–611 (other files are closed 50 or 75 years); Anglo–Egyptian Resettlement files, 1957, HO 240; Minute Books, memorials, pension lists and records of the committees of subscribers to relieve the laity and clerical refugees from the French Revolution, 1792–1828, T 93; expenses paid to French refugees, 1798–1817, T 50; Entry Book of Channel Island authorities responsible for the relief of French emigrés, 1793–1812, FO 95; register of French refugees in Jersey, 1793–6, FO 95/602–03; payments made to refugees from Normandy, 1793–1831, and from Toulon, 1834–40, arranged alphabetically, T 50; applications and allowances relating to Knights of Malta, 1834–40, T 50; allowances paid to Polish refugees, 1855–1909, PMG 53, and pay lists, 1841–56, T 50; Oath Roll of naturalization of foreign Protestants under a statute of 1708, 1709–11, E 169/86, and attendant sacrament certificates, E 196/10, and similar Oath Rolls, 1708–12, KB 24; alphabetical list of allowances paid to refugees from Santo Domingo, 1832–5, T 50; pay lists of Spanish refugees, 1828–9, T 50, and 1855–1909, PMG 53.

see *Aliens, American Loyalists' Claims, Bouillon Papers, Denization, Foreign Churches in England, Naturalization*

Registrars, Superintendent and District Appointed since 1837 for the registration of births, marriages and deaths in England and Wales. Reference maps, 1861–1921, indicating their districts and sub-districts, marked out in different coloured inks and used as the basis for census enumeration under their supervision: two complete sets for London, 1891, and three incomplete sets for 1861,

1891 and 1921, with two maps of municipal wards and ecclesiastical parishes in the City of London, c.1911, two complete sets of maps for England and Wales, 1891, and two incomplete sets, 1870, and 1921, RG 18. Applications, appointments, resignations and dismissals may be found in the papers of the Poor Law Unions, 1836–1909, arranged alphabetically by county, then by Union, chronologically, MH 12, with subject indexes, 1836–1920, MH 15; 1836–71, MH 19, and c.1896–c.1921, in MH 48; correspondence concerning appointments, 1836–50, HO 39, and 1836–1963, including provision of accommodation, RG 21 (some closed 50 or 75 years); correspondence with the Registrar General in London, 1836–1978, RG 20 (some closed 50 years), and 1874–1985, RG 48 (some closed 50 or 75 years).

Relieving Officers Responsible for the provision of poor relief under the Poor Law Amendment Act 1834, 1834–1930. Applications, appointments, resignations and dismissals, and including curriculum vitae, testimonials, details of remuneration and performance record, 1834–1909, arranged alphabetically by county, then by Union and chronologically, MH 12, with subject indexes, 1836–1920, in MH 15 appointments, resignations and dismissals, 1837–1921, MH 9; other applications and appointments may be located c.1896–c.1921 in MH 48.

Rentals and Surveys
see *Crown Lands, Manorial Courts and Records*

Requests, Court of An Equity court, established by Henry VII to determine poor men's causes and those of the King's

servants, its proceedings, similar to those in the Court of Chancery, are in English. It was abolished in 1642. Proceedings, containing the originating bill, answers and subsequent pleadings and depositions of witnesses, temp. Henry VII–Charles I, REQ 2, to which there are nominal indexes of suitors and topographical indexes to 1625, on open access, arranged by reign; miscellaneous proceedings, including some exhibits, temp. Henry VII–Charles I, REQ 3; affidavits, Witness Books, Process Books and Order Books, temp. Elizabeth–Charles I, and Order and Decree Books, temp. Henry VII–Charles I, REQ 1; documents of Shakespearean interest, REQ 4.

Residence, Certificates of Local Tax Commissioners attested that a named person had already been assessed for a stated amount of tax at one specified place of residence, thereby rendering him immune from any further liability at residences elsewhere. Introduced with the lay subsidy in 1523, any surviving certificates for the reign of Henry VIII are filed with the assessment lists in E 179, listed alphabetically by county, then by hundred, township or vill, under regnal year; those temp. Edward VI–Charles II are in E 115, with an alphabetical list of persons, giving county, and regnal year when issued, on open access.
see *Subsidy, Lay*

Riots and Civil Disturbances Correspondence, 1812–55, HO 40; Cato Street Conspiracy, 1820, in HO 44; calendar of prisoners at Winchester at the Special Commission of Assize after the agricultural riots of 1830, HO 130; papers, 1879–1919, including material on the suffragettes, 1908–14, HO 144, to which there is a descriptive list, arranged under subject and then chronologically; there are selected files in the same class for a later period (subject to closure for 30 years), including reports on Fascist disturbances in the 1930s.

see *Assizes, Criminal Registers, Annual, Star Chamber, Court of, Suffragettes*

Rolls Chapel Baptisms, 1837, 1860–92, marriages, 1736–49, marriage licences, 1744–6, and burials, 1738–1826, PRO 30/21/3/1.

Roman Catholics Authenticated registers of births, baptisms and burials, deposited with the Registrar General and which could henceforward be produced in a court of law and used as evidence of parentage and proof of age, seventeenth century–1858, mostly relating to Yorkshire, Durham and Northumberland, listed alphabetically by county and then by place, RG 4; registers of places of worship drawn up by clerks of counties and borough sessions, diocesan registrars and archdeacons, listed chronologically by registration date, 1791–1852, RG 31. Recusant Rolls of persons penalized for non-attendance at Anglican church services, arranged by county, and for Wales, by regnal year, and detailing name, residence, status, any fine imposed, sequestration of lands or goods, or imprisonment, but not indicating denomination, 1591–1691, E 376 and E 377 (the entries on both sets of Rolls are in Latin). Inventories of Catholics' possessions, 1642–60, SP 28; index of nonconformists, indicating denomination, 1663, SP 9. Returns of Papists' estates, registered temp. George I, under statutes of 1714 and 1722, and made by county clerks of the peace, with a few certificates of double assessments for the Land Tax, E 174, to which there is a list of names, abodes and qualities, arranged alphabetically by English and Welsh county on open access; Papists' Oaths of Allegiance, 1778–86, 1791–7, 1798–1822, 1839–57, giving names and addresses, and qualities, E 169/79–83, and 1778–1829, CP 37, 1830, 1837–8, C 214/21; returns by clerks of the peace to the Commissioners of Forfeited Estates, of the names and estates of Papists in England and Wales, after the 1715 Jacobite Rebellion, arranged under county, FEC 1, and 1715–26, FEC 2, both classes having descriptive lists; certificates of names of those refusing to swear the oath under the Security of the Sovereign Act of 1714, returned by county clerks of the peace, and recording addresses and occupations and date of conviction by Quarter Sessions, 1715–16, C 203/6; returns of names of Papists in Lancaster, refusing to take the oaths of loyalty to the King and deemed convicted recusants and possible supporters of the Jacobites still at large, 1715, and giving names and occupations, KB 18; deeds and wills of Papists, 1716–1836, enrolled on the Close Rolls, C 54, and Recovery Rolls, CP 43. Oath Rolls of Catholic attorneys, 1790–1836, CP 10, and 1831–7, E 3, and of solicitors, 1791–1813, C 217/180/5. From 1625 Roman Catholics convict, aged seventeen and over, were assessed to pay double rates of the lay subsidy, extended between 1640 and 1660 to those who had been indicted; Catholics whose wealth did not attract this mulct were charged a Poll Tax, nominal returns of which are listed alphabetically by county, by hundred, and arranged by township or vill, by regnal year, E 179; the Land Tax and other assessed taxes from the reign of William III and Mary II imposed a double liability on Catholics, though in 1794 relief was afforded: lists of

Papists are usually kept separately from the parish assessments, and often survive where the regular returns do not, being found, 1689–1830, in E 182, and E 181, both classes being arranged in annual county bundles, and therein by parish; because relief from double-rating was unevenly applied, a further Act of 1831 allowed Catholics to appeal, an examination to be made of their complaints and a certificate issued showing any amount of overcharge, while any future double liability was discharged; papers relating to these appeals, often containing genealogical information on descent of land over several generations since the onset of the tax in 1692, plus the final outcome, are located in IR 23, arranged alphabetically by county, and dating from 1828.

see *Delinquents, Committee for Compounding with, Jacobite Rebellions, Poll Tax, Recusants, Subsidy, Lay*

Romania Braila, births to Britons, 1922–30, deaths, 1921–9, FO 727/1–2; Bucharest, births, 1851–1931, baptisms, 1858–1948, deaths, 1854–1929, FO 625/2–4, 6, marriages, 1870–90, FO 83, indexed in FO 802/239; Constanta (Kustendje), births and deaths, 1862–73, FO 887/1–2; Galatz, marriages, 1891–1939, FO 517/1–2; Jassy consular district, Moldavia, British subjects, 1844–59, FO 786/119, and 1851–1948, FO 625/2–4; Lower Danube, baptisms, 1869–1907, FO 625/5, marriages, 1868–1914, RG 33/143, indexed in RG 43/7, burials, 1869–70, FO 786/120; Sulina, births, 1861–1932, deaths, 1860–1931, FO 728/1–2, births, 1870–77, deaths, 1866–77, FO 886/1–2.

Royal Household
see *Chapels Royal, Green Cloth, Board of, Lord Chamberlain's Department,*

Lord Steward's Department, Offices, Royal and Public

Royalist Composition Papers
see *Delinquents, Committee for Compounding with*

Royal Warrant Holders Since 1830, the Lord Chamberlain has granted warrants allowing tradesmen supplying the Royal Household to display the royal coat of arms. Warrants, 1830–1901, LC 13/1–5, 1837–1901, with integral indexes, LC 5/243–46; original bills presented by tradesmen, 1830–1900, LC 11.

see *Lord Chamberlain's Department, Lord Steward's Department*

Russia Births, marriages and deaths of Britons, 1835–70, RG 35/18–19, deaths, 1871–1920, RG 35/20–44, undated index to baptisms and marriages, RG 43/4, births, 1849–1909, marriages, 1849–61, deaths, 1849–1915, FO 267/44–46; Archangel, births, 1849–1909, marriages, 1849–61, deaths, 1849–1915, FO 267/44–46; Batum, births, 1884–1921, marriages, 1891–1920, deaths, 1884–1920, FO 397/1–6; Berdiansk (Osipenko), marriages, 1901, FO 399/1; Ekaterinburg (Sverdlovsk), deaths, 1918–19, FO 399/5; Helsingfors (Helsinki), births, 1914–24, FO 768/5, deaths, 1924, FO 753/19; Konigsberg (Kaliningrad), births, 1869–1933, marriages, 1864–1904, deaths, 1857–1932, FO 509/1–4; Moscow, births, 1882–1918, marriages, 1894–1924, deaths, 1881–1918, FO 518/1–4; Nicolayev, births, 1872–1917, deaths, 1874–1915, FO 399/7–8; Novorossisk, births, 1911–20, deaths, 1896–1920, FO 399/9–10; Odessa, births and deaths, 1852–1919, baptisms, 1893, marriages, 1851–1916, FO 359/3–12; Poti, births, 1871–1906, deaths, 1871–1920, FO 399/13–14; Rostov on Don, births, 1891–1914, marriages, 1904–18, deaths, 1906–16, deeds, 1891–1918, FO 398/1–9; St Petersburg (Petrograd, Leningrad), English Church of the Independents, baptisms, 1818–40, burials, 1821–40, RG 4/4605, indexed in RG 43/1 and 3, other records of British births, baptisms, marriages, deaths and burials, 1840–1918, RG 33/144–52, indexed in RG 43/1, 7 and 3, index to births, baptisms, marriages, deaths and burials, 1886–1917, RG 33/162, births, 1856–1938, marriages, 1892–1917, deaths, 1897–1927, FO 378/3–9, births, 1882–1918, marriages, 1894–1924, deaths, 1881–1918, FO 518/1–4; index to marriages, 1826–58, RG 43/7 (the registers are held at the General Register Office, London), marriages, 1870–90, FO 83, indexed in FO 802/239; Sebas-topol, births, 1886–98, marriages, 1910, deaths, 1893–1908, FO 399/3, 15–16; Tammenfors (Tampere), births, 1906–23, deaths, 1909–34, FO 769/1–2; Theodosia (Feodosiya), births, 1904–06, deaths, 1907–18, FO 399/17–18; Vladivostock, births, 1911–27, marriages, 1916–23, deaths, 1908–24, registers of British subjects, 1908–27, FO 510/1–10; Vyborg, births, 1924–31, deaths, 1929–37, FO 757/1–3.

Russian Orthodox Church, London
Births, baptisms, marriages and deaths, and a variety of material relating to the congregation, 1721–1927, including Greeks, in unauthenticated registers, RG 8/111–304.

Ruthin, Lordship of
see *Wales, Principality of*

Ss

Sacrament Certificates Were produced to one of the central courts of record or to county Quarter Sessions by persons holding civil, military, or naval office, or Commissions from the Crown at the time of swearing the Oath of Allegiance, or within a prescribed period afterwards, in accordance with the Test Acts of 1672 and 1673; the certificates were signed by the minister and a churchwarden of the parish where the Anglican sacraments had recently been taken, and by two credible witnesses. Surviving certificates filed in the Westminster courts, 1673–4, 1677–8, 1681–5, 1691, 1700–11, 1719–78, C 224; 1700–1827, E 196, 1676–1828, KB 22; for the Palatinate of Chester, 1673–1768, CHES 4. Protestant refugees taking the Oath of Allegiance and producing sacrament certificates were granted naturalization under a statute of 1708, certificates, 1709–11, are in E 196/10.

see *Naturalization Oath Rolls*

Safe Conduct, Letters of Enrolled on the Patent Rolls, 1216–c.1641, C 66, to which there are printed *Calendars* to 1582, and 1584–7; payments for the letters are recorded on the Fine Rolls, 1272–c.1641, C 60, to which there are printed *Calendars* to 1509.

see *Passes and Passports*

St Christopher (St Kitts) Baptisms, 1721–30, 1733–4, 1738–45, marriages, 1733–4, 1738–45, burials, 1721–30, 1733–4, 1738–45, CO 152/18, 21, 25; passengers arriving from Plymouth, Devon, 1633–4, and Dartmouth, 1634–5, transported from Penrhyn, Cornwall, 5 June 1634, E 157, published in J.C. Hotten's *Original Lists of Persons Emigrating to America, 1600–1700*, 1874; register of letters of attorney for debentures, 1707–45, E 407/26. Registers of slaves, 1817–34, T 71.

see *West Indies*

St Michael and St George, Most Distinguished Order of Created in 1818 for the benefit of Maltese natives and those of the Ionian Islands, and British subjects holding high office there or in Royal Naval service in the Mediterranean, it was extended in 1868 to all colonies. In 1879 distinguished persons connected with the conduct of foreign affairs were admitted. Awards and recommendations, 1818–36, CO 136, and CO 537 for the Ionian Islands, and CO 158, CO 159 and CO 162 for Malta, thereafter, 1836–1932, in CO 447, 1838–1934, CO 734, 1852–99, CO 844, 1869–1930, CO 845, and 1818–1940, CO 745; announcements of conferments are in *The London Gazette*, 1818–1986, with sporadic subject indexes up to 1847, and thereafter either annually or half-yearly, ZJ 1; correspondence may also be found to 1905 in FO 83, and a selection of letters, 1906–60 in FO 371, to which there is a card index, 1906–19, and index, 1920–51, in FO 409.

Santo Domingo Absentees' estates, administered by the government which occupied the French portion (now Haiti) between 1793 and 1798, 1794–1803, T 64: after the evacuation, a committee was set up to deal with claims for compensation made by ruined proprietors, the proceedings of which, including Council Minutes and decisions, 1794–1812, are in T 81; papers relating to refugees, 1832–5, T 50.
see *Haiti, Dominican Republic*

Schools Names and assessments of pupils at elementary schools (established from 1870), included in examination schedules, listed alphabetically by county, then place, 1872–1904, in which there are also reports and recommendations made by Inspectors on returns made by local authorities in 1870 about population size, school accommodation, enlargements, closures, and elections of School Boards in towns and villages in their areas, but excluding boroughs and the Metropolis, ED 2.
see *Poor Law Unions*

Schoolteachers Applications, curricula vitae (giving age, birthplace, career to date, marital status, and current address), testimonials, appointments, remuneration, resignations and dismissals, in schools attached to workhouses and institutions, 1834–1909, MH 12, listed alphabetically by county and then by Poor Law Union, the contents arranged chronologically, with subject indexes, 1836–1920, in MH 15; appointments, resignations and dismissals are also included, 1837–1921, in MH 9; correspondence between the Poor Law Board and

Poor Law School Districts for appointment of teachers, 1848–1910, MH 27. Payments of superannuation and disablement allowances to teachers in England, 1899–1921/2, indexed from 1905, PMG 68, registers of superannuations and annuities, 1899–1934, PMG 68/36–37, withdrawals, 1904–30, PMG 68/38–41, death gratuities, 1919–29, PMG 68/48–49, short service gratuities, 1920–9, PMG 68/50–51, payments of superannuation and disablement allowances to teachers in Scotland, 1903–28, PMG 55; non-effective pensions of Army schoolmasters, 1909–28, PMG 33, and of schoolmistresses, 1909–28, PMG 34/1–5; pensions paid to widows and orphans of Naval schoolmasters, 1889–1929, PMG 19/51–94, 1889–99, ADM 23/115–23, 1899–1914, ADM 23/161–64, and 1899–1932, ADM 23/145–60.
see *Navy, Royal* for Naval Instructors or Schoolmasters

Scotland State Papers, 1509–46, SP 49, 1547–53, SP 50, 1553–8, SP 51, 1558–1603, SP 52, 1688–1783, SP 54, and Border Papers, 1558–1603, SP 59, included in *Calendar of State Papers, Scotland, 1509–1603, Calendar of the State Papers relating to Scotland and Mary, Queen of Scots, 1547–97, Calendar of the Border Papers, 1560–1603, Calendar of Home Office Papers of the reign of George III, 1760–75,* and *Calendar of State Papers, Foreign, 1558–77.* Scotch Rolls, featuring summonses for military service, letters of protection and safe conduct, licences to merchants, grants of estates to Scots, attainders and pardons, 1291–1516, C 71. Rentals of Crown lands, 1832–1954, LRRO 12 (most closed 100 years), with a descriptive list arranged chronologically. Claims to Scottish peerages, 1822–38, HO 80, Scottish peers' Oath Roll, 1837, C 214/21.

Presentation to churches, 1724–1808, SP 56, included between 1760 and 1775 in *Calendar of Home Office Papers of the reign of George III*. First list of justices of the peace, 1708, Entry Book of justices, 1838–75, and registers, 1879–1975, C 193; fiats for justices of Scottish burghs, 1823–1929, and for Scottish counties, 1705–1973, arranged alphabetically by county, C 234; lists of clerks of the peace, *c*.1819–39, HO 94. Petitions in criminal matters, 1782–1853, HO 102, out-letters, 1762–1849, most with indexes, HO 104; legal proceedings in Scotland after the Jacobite Rebellion, 1745, including trials of Scottish peers, lists of rebels and of prisoners, names of witnesses and evidence produced in court, 1745–53, TS 20; reports and surveys on forfeited estates of convicted rebels, 1745–56, T 64. Alphabetical list of persons paying duty on carriages, 1756–62, T 36/7, and on silver plate, 1756–62, T 36/8; letters sent to Surveyors and Distributors of the Board of Stamps, 1809–33, IR 46; Apprenticeship Books, containing the names and addresses of masters and apprentices, date of indenture and period, premium paid and trade to which bound, the duty levied, and the name and residence of the apprentice's father or guardian to *c*.1752, arranged chronologically, 1710–1811, IR 1, to which there are indexes of apprentices to 1774, and to masters to 1762, IR 17, on open access; Death Duty papers, 1839–41, IR 7. Staff lists of Customs officers, 1671–1922, superannuation registers, and widows' pensions showing names and birth dates of children, 1803–1922, CUST 39 (closed 75 years), sporadic returns made to Parliament of Customs staff, giving residences, 1693–1978, with indexes on open access, ZHC 1, pay lists, 1714–1829, T 43, quarter bills of salaries

due, 1829, CUST 19, salary bills and Establishment lists of Customs officers for the collection of Excise and duties on salt, malt and tobacco, 1708–1832, T 45, applications for pensions, made by officers and their widows and dependants, 1671–1921, T 1 (indexed by subject, 1852–1920, in T 108, and in registers of papers, 1777–1920, T 2); names of Commanders of Revenue Cruisers in Scotland, 1822–3, ZHC 1/773. List of civil staff of the Ordnance Survey, 1854–8, ZHC 1/2451. Muster rolls of the Scottish Army in England, 1646, SP 41, noted in *Calendar of State Papers (Domestic Series) of the reign of Charles I*; pensions paid by the Royal Hospitals of Chelsea and Greenwich to retired military, naval and marine personnel, arranged under pay-district, and giving name, rank, regiment and number, date of commencement, amount and nature of pension, and any transfer elsewhere, plus date of death, 1842–62, WO 22/118–40. Warrants for patents for invention, 1774–1847, indexed, HO 106, and 1840–55, HO 105. Payments of superannuation and disablement allowances to teachers, 1903–28, PMG 55. Authenticated registers of birth, baptism and burial of Scottish churches in England to 1858, RG 4. List of passengers sailing from Gravesend to Scotland, 1677, E 157; weekly emigration returns to America of ships leaving Scottish ports, giving name and type of vessel, date of sailing, port of departure and destination, names, ages, residences, occupations and purpose of the journey of those on board with their destinations, 1774–5, T 47/12; list of Scottish settlers in Canada, 1815, CO 385/2, and enrolled at Edinburgh, 1815, for a passage to Canada, AO 3/144; births, marriages and deaths of Scottish passengers at sea, 1854–90, BT 158, births at sea, 1875–91, BT 160, deaths at sea, 1875–88, BT 159.

Scottish Fund List of contributors and their wives, 1780–1852, AO 3/947–48.

Scutage Originally a composition paid by knights to avoid military service in time of war, it became a regular imposition on Knights' Fees. Scutage Rolls, 1214–1328, C 72, and 1217/8–1327, listed alphabetically by county and then by regnal year, E 179.
see *Subsidy, Lay*

Sea Fencibles Musters and pay lists of fishermen and boatmen recruited as part-time coastal defence, and appointments of Naval officers, 1798–1810, ADM 28.

Sedition Miscellaneous papers relating to seditious libel cases, involving various Societies, and mainly consisting of printed pamphlets, 1732–1885, TS 24; prosecutions, 1584–1856, TS 11, to which there is a calendar and nominal index on open access.

Sequestration of Delinquents' Estates, Committee for the Correspondence and Orders of the Commissioners investigating the lands owned by delinquents (Royalists), 1643–60, SP 23, included in *Calendar of Proceedings of the Committee for Compounding, 1643–60*; books and papers, 1643–53, SP 20; names of delinquents and estates sequestrated, arranged alphabetically by county, and giving name, residence, status and date of seizure, including the City of London, (?)1649, C 203/2, and 1656, C 203/3; accounts and papers, 1642–60, SP 28/205–18.
see *Delinquents, Committee for Compounding with*

Sewers, Commissioners of
see *Bedford Level*

Serjeants at Law Barristers of the Order of the Coif, to which they were called under writ of the Great Seal of England, with a right of exclusive audience in the Court of Common Pleas, and from whose ranks all judges of the superior common law courts were drawn until 1875, when supplanted by Queen's Counsel. Admission rolls, temp. William and Mary–1844, C 216, indexed in IND 1/16818; nominal index of appointments and place-name index, 1570–1873, C 202; list of warrants for issue to pay half-yearly wages, thirteenth–nineteenth centuries, to which there is a nominal and place-name index, E 404; Association Oath Roll, 1696, C 213/373.

Sheriffs Election certificates, 1303–1648, listed by borough and county, then by regnal year, C 267; enrolments of lists of persons proposed as sheriffs in England and Wales, and annual 'pricked lists' indicating who was chosen, 1531–1678, C 227, 1700–1841, C 172, 1844–1935, PC 3; nominations and excuses submitted for non-service, and nominal lists, 1774–1950, PC 13; writs of appointment, enrolled on the Fine Rolls, to 1641, C 60, with printed *Calendars* to 1509; references to appointments, in Unbound Papers of the Privy Council, 1481–1946, PC 1, to which there is a chronological descriptive list on open access; warrants of appointment, 1828–56, T 56/17, 47–49; bills, draft patents and other papers, relating to the appointment of sheriffs in the Palatinate of Lancaster, 1684–1876, DL 21; announcements of annual appointments, 1665–1986, in *The London Gazette*, with subject indexes sporadically from 1790, and invariably from 1848, ZJ 1; writs and commissions to receive oaths from sheriffs, 1570–1921, with a nominal and topographical index, C 202; receipts of sheriffs for allowances, 1824–32, E 404/518.

Ship Money A few nominal lists, arranged under county, 1634–40, SP 16, and SP 17, cited in *Calendar of State Papers (Domestic Series) of the reign of Charles I*; proclamations and writs, 1633–40, PC 2, to which there are general indexes on open access.

Ships' Passenger Lists Some survive for Continental, American and West Indian destinations, 1565–1798, E 190, and temp. Elizabeth–1677, including coastal journeys, in E 157; weekly returns of passengers leaving English and Welsh ports, 1773–6, (gaps 13–18 April, 27 April–9 May 1774, and 7–12 November 1775), giving port of departure, date of embarkation, name and type of vessel, its destination, and names, addresses, ages and occupations of passengers, with the purpose of the voyage and ultimate destination, including emigrants, T 47/9–11, to which there is a nominal card index, and weekly emigrations from Scotland to America, 1774–5, T 47/12; both series are published. Inwards lists, of ships arriving from or bound for ports outside Europe and the Mediterranean, arranged by port, chronologically, 1878–88, 1890–1960, and containing information by class of ticket, and for aliens, on name, age, occupation, address in the United Kingdom, destination, and country of origin, and ticket number, BT 26; outwards, 1890–1960, similarly organized, BT 27; registers of Ships' Passenger Lists, 1906–51, arranged under year and then by month, record arrivals and departures from ports, with precise dates from 1921, though until October 1908 returns survive only for Bristol, Southampton and Weymouth BT 32, on open access.

see *Aliens, Licences to pass beyond the Seas, Port Books*

Shipwrecks Correspondence and papers relating to enquiries about wrecks of merchant vessels, 1864–6, 1919–69, including the SS *Titanic*, April 1912, MT 9 (some closed 50 or 75 years), with registers and indexes, 1851–1919, MT 85, and MT 86; out-letters, 1864–6, MT 4, indexed, 1866–7 in MT 5; shipping losses, 1912, reports on enquiries, 1934, 1936–9, and losses from enemy action, 1940–5, MT 15, returns of deaths, 1917–20, MT 15/285; losses and damage, including to fishing vessels, 1914–20, MT 25/83–85, and 1939–45, ADM 199/2073–2194; reports of losses of warships, c.1698–1976, ADM 1, with a nominal and subject index, 1793–1938, ADM 12; reports of naval losses, c.1850–1960, ADM 116, to which there is a subject index; losses, 1914–18, ADM 137/3089–832, and 1939–45, ADM 199; Royal Naval ships lost, arranged alphabetically, some recording date of loss, and number of casualties, others the ship's class and cause and place of loss, 1914–19, ADM 242/6; courts martial of surviving captains and officers, 1680–1839, arranged by year, ADM 1/5253–494. Staff list, 1921, MT 15/309, survey staff, arranged by district, 1922, MT 15/344.

see *Bona Vacantia Division, Coast-guard*

Sierra Leone Registers of emancipated slaves, ships' papers, letters and Minute Books, 1819–68, FO 315, census of liberated Africans, 1831, CO 267/111.

Silver Plate, Duty on 1756–77. Yearly lists of names and abodes of persons paying, 1756–62, and actual and suspected defaulters, 1757–68, 1776,

T 47/5–7, and persons paying in Scotland, 1756–62, T 36/8.

Singapore Births to Britons, 1922, RG 36.

Slaves Royal African Company records of slave trading, including sales in Barbados, Jamaica, Antigua, Montserrat, Nevis and St Christopher, Virginia and South Carolina, giving names of ships, captains, dates and places of sale, names of purchasers, numbers bought and amounts paid, outward invoices, 1683–1816, homeward invoices, 1673–1743, T 70/913–61. The slave trade was abolished in the British colonies by statute in 1807, reinforced by a further Act in 1811: as a consequence surveys of slaves and their owners were undertaken with a view to paying compensation to their former owners. The Slave Compensation Commission was embodied in 1833 under which slaves were converted to apprentice labourers, and made free in 1838, whilst compensation was paid out to their former proprietors. Names of owners and plantations, 1813–34, with registers of negroes lawfully held in slavery in the West Indies, 1832, are organized by Island, and parish, for which there are parochial returns of slaves and slave registers, recording name, age, occupation, colour and country of origin of personal and plantation slaves in Trinidad, 1813–34, Nevis, St Lucia and Virgin Islands, 1815–34, Antigua, 1817–32, Barbados, Dominica, Grenada, Montserrat, St Christopher, and St Vincent, 1817–34, Demerara, 1817–32, Berbice, 1818–34, Tobago, 1819–34, Bermuda, 1821–34, Bahamas, 1822–34, Honduras, 1834, Mauritius, 1817–32, the Cape of Good Hope, 1816–19, and Ceylon, 1818–32, in T 71, together with an incomplete index of slaves in Ceylon, 1819;

census of liberated Africans in Sierra Leone, 1831, CO 267/111; registers of emancipated slaves, correspondence and Minute Books in the same colony, 1819–68, FO 315; alphabetical returns of slaves in Surinam, 1811, CO 278; registers of slaves and slavers at Havana, 1819–69, FO 313; registers of suspected slavers at Cape Town, 1843–70, FO 312; indexed registers of claims for compensation, by parish within each colony, valuers' returns, original certificates of claim and counterclaim, adjudications where the claim was contested, and parochial compensation certificates, lists of awards, 1834–46, including those made under trust, 1837–41, arranged by colony, and with an index to the claimants' registers, 1835–46, T 71; awards, 1835–46, AO 14; awards in the West Indies, including marriage and death certificates of claimants, and affidavits, bearing the signatures of them and their legal representatives, and sums awarded, 1835–42, NDO 4; Slave Trade papers, including proceedings, 1805–77, HCA 30; Slave Trade Commission proceedings in London, relating to the British and Portuguese trade, 1819–24, FO 308; Minute Book of the Court in Jamaica, 1843–51, FO 314; Appeals to the Procurator General from the Vice–Admiralty Courts in the colonies, 1827–62, indexed, TS 15; correspondence about the Slave Trade, 1814–92, arranged by country, FO 84; correspondence and papers from the Consulate in New York, 1834–42, FO 285; drafts and rough library indexes to slave trade registers, 1869–75, FO 96. Correspondence, listed by country, 1814–92, FO 84.

Solicitors Since 1875 the collective term applied to solicitors, attorneys and proctors, before which solicitors were those lawyers specialising in Equity matters. Certificates of admission, 1730–87, giving name, address and date of admission, indexed, C 203/7; affidavits as to due execution of articles of clerkship for five years, 1730–1800, and 1835, C 217/23–39, affidavits of qualification of solicitors, 1800–39 (gaps), affidavits of the execution of articles, 1818–31, and admissions, 1815–42, C 217/186, affidavits of qualification, 1804–34 (gaps), and admissions, 1738–1818, C 217/183; Oath Roll on admission of solicitors in Chancery, 1778–1836, C 217/180/1–3, Oath Roll on admission of Roman Catholic solicitors, 1791–1813, C 217/180/5, Solicitors' Roll, 1859–75, C 216/16, Solicitors' Roll, 1800–42, IND 1/4613; Rolls or Books of Solicitors in the Equity Court of Exchequer, 1729–1841, E 109, Certificate Book, 1785–1843, E 108; Oath Rolls, 1730–1841, E 200; Admission Rolls of solicitors in the Exchequer at Chester, 1750–1806, and the Great Sessions, 1697–1830, articles of clerkship, affidavits of due execution of articles, and Oath Rolls, 1729–1800, CHES 36; admissions of solicitors to the Court of Bankruptcy, January 1832–January 1883, B 2/8; samples of admission papers relating to the Supreme Court of Judicature, 1875, 1876, 1880, 1890, 1900, and 1904, arranged alphabetically, and with affidavits of due execution of articles, 1875, 1880, 1900 and 1903, and applications for practising certificates, 1875, 1880 and 1889, J 89; register of solicitors struck off, 1905–60, C 193/141.

Somaliland (Somalia) Births, 1905–20, RG 36, indexed in RG 43/18.

South Africa Selected claims for compensation presented to Central District Claims Boards in South Africa by civilians for losses and requisitions incurred in the Boer War, with an index of claimants, 1902–3, and of places, 1902–3, and a numerical register of claims over the same period, WO 148. Musters of Cape Levies, 1851–3, WO 13; registers of suspected slavers at Cape Town, 1843–70, FO 312. see *Boer War, Cape Colony, Natal, Slaves, Yeomanry, Imperial*

South Sea Company Annuities payable, 1711–13, E 351/57–58, 1711–1828, AO 1/28–38, unclaimed dividends and lottery prizes, 1786–1828, AO 1; subscribers to the 1720 lottery and annuities, T 38/740; court of record judgments, 1727–8, PRO 30/26.

Spain Deaths of Britons, 1831–1920, RG 35/20–44; Aguilas, births, 1875–1911, deaths, 1874–1911, FO 920/1–2; Balearic Islands, title deeds, deeds for graves, 1773, 1802–94, FO 214; Barcelona, papers concerning British nationality, repatriation and marriage, 1940, FO 637, passports, 1775–1922, FO 639; Bilbao, deaths, 1855–70, FO 729/1; Cartagena, births, 1847–87, marriages, 1858–1904, deaths, 1855–71, FO 920/3–6; Garrucha, births, 1876–90, deaths, 1883–1905, FO 920/7–8; Madrid, marriages, 1846–90, FO 83, indexed in FO 802/239, registers of British subjects, 1835–95, 1906–31, FO 445; Association Oath Roll of the English Factory at Malaga, 1696, C 213/460; Porman, births, 1907, deaths, 1911, FO 920/9–10; Seville, births, marriages and deaths, 1948, FO 332/14–16. Claims for losses sustained by merchants and others inflicted by Spain, 1730–32, listed alphabetically, CO 388/89–93; registers of payments made to British subjects for losses on confiscation of property and sequestration of book debts before the dec-laration of war against Britain in 1804, 1835–53, PMG 64, and 1838–55, T 78, both listed alphabetically and including supporting documents for the claims; claims, 1908–10, FO 227; claims of British and Spanish subjects against seizures of vessels and property after the Peace of 1808, register of claims, 1823–4, and an index, FO 316/64–65, and register of claims, 1790–1823, FO 316/67; allow-ances paid to distressed Spanish refugees, 1828–9, T 50, 1855–1909, PMG 53.

Stamp Distributors Appointed by the Stamp Office (later the Board of Stamps) to collect Stamp Duty on commercial and legal documents, and certain other duties, including Legacy Duty. Appointments, 1796–1810, IR 51, Entry Book of appointments, resignations and dismis-sals, 1832–60, IR 84; letters, memorials and reports, 1800–33, IR 49, and letters from the Board of Stamps to Distributors in England and Wales, 1807–19, IR 43, 1819–33, IR 44, Scottish out-letters, 1809–33, IR 46, and Irish Letter Books, 1807–19, IR 43, 1827–33, IR 47.

Stamps and Taxes, Board of Set up in 1834 on the merger between the Board of Stamps and Board of Taxes, and amal-gamated into the Board of Inland Revenue in 1849 together with the Board of Excise. Appointments of officers, 1833–77, IR 84.

Staple, Constables of the Relating to sea ports from which wool, leather, tin and lead were exported and which were regulated by the Statute of the Staple. Certificates of elections, 1303–1648, C 267, to which there is a nominal index on open access.

Star Chamber, Court of Set up by Henry VII, with summary jurisdiction over unlawful combinations, riots and assemblies, offences committed by local officials, and later widened to deal with offences against Royal Proclamations, and with a civil jurisdiction over mercantile and ecclesiastical disputes, it was abolished in 1642. The records are in English. Bills, answers, and other pleadings, plus deposi-tions of witnesses, temp. Henry VII (1485–1509), STAC 1, temp. Henry VIII (1509–47), STAC 2, temp. Edward VI (1547–53), STAC 3, temp. Mary (1553–8), STAC 4, temp. Elizabeth (1558–1603), STAC 5 and STAC 7, temp. James I (1603–25), STAC 8, and temp. Charles I (1625–42), STAC 9, with an undated collection of material in STAC 10; there are nominal and topo-graphical indexes to 1625, by reign, on open access. No decrees and orders of the Court survive, but records of fines paid by those found guilty, 1596–1641, are in E 159, with a nominal index on open access.

State Paper Office This comprised the collections of papers amassed while in office by Secretaries of State at the Royal Palace of Whitehall in the sixteenth century, which formed the basis of a pri-vate library of confidential material con-cerned with the prosecution of domestic and foreign affairs. A Keeper of State Papers was appointed in 1610, a post which survived until 1782 when its busi-ness was divided between the Home and Foreign Offices. The contents cover a wide variety of topics relating to policy, Royal Proclamations, poor law, merchant trade abroad, taxation, aliens, ecclesiastical, military and naval matters, and touching individuals petitioning for favours, pardons and privileges. Letters and papers, temp. Henry VIII, 1509–47, SP 1, and 1516–39, SP 2, are both included in *Calendar of Letters and Papers (Foreign and Domestic) of the reign of Henry VIII, 1509–47*. Thereafter they are divided into:

(1) State Papers, Domestic, temp. Edward VI, 1547–53, SP 10, temp. Mary, 1553–8, SP 11, temp. Elizabeth, 1558–1603, SP 12 and SP 13, all printed in *Calendar of State Papers (Domestic Series) of the reign of Edward VI, Mary and Elizabeth*; temp. James I, 1603–25, SP 14, included in *Calendar of State Papers (Domestic Series) of the reign of James I*. Addenda, temp. Edward VI–James I, SP 15, for which there is a printed *Calendar*; temp. Charles I, 1625–49, SP 16 and SP 17, printed in *Calendar of State Papers (Domestic Series) of the reign of Charles I*; Interregnum, 1649–60, SP 18, contained in *Calendar of State Papers (Domestic Series), Commonwealth*; the papers accumulated by the various Parliamentary Committees merit classes of their own (see entries); temp. Charles II, 1660–85, SP 29 and SP 30, in *Calendar of State Papers (Domestic Series) of the reign of Charles II*; temp. James II, 1685–8, SP 31, included in *Calendar of State Papers (Domestic Series) of the reign of James II*; temp. William and Mary, 1689–1702, SP 32 and SP 33, printed in *Calendar of State Papers (Domestic Series) of the reign of William and Mary*; temp. Anne, 1702–14, SP 34, for which there is a printed *Calendar of State Papers (Domestic Series) of the reign of Anne* running to 1704, with a manuscript descriptive list for the remainder of her reign on open access, arranged by year; temp. George I, 1714–27, SP 35, to which there are printed descriptive lists, and an index; temp. George II, 1727–60, SP 36; temp. George III, 1760–82, SP 37, with a printed *Calendar of Home Office Papers of the reign of George III* to 1775; after 1782 material formerly filed here is located in HO 42.

(2) State Papers, Ireland and State Papers, Scotland (see **Ireland, Scotland**)

(3) State Papers, Colonial (see **Colonies**, and under individual colonies)

(4) State Papers, Foreign, 1547–53, SP 68, 1553–8, SP 69, 1558–June 1577, SP 70, described in *Calendar of State Papers (Foreign), 1547–77* and *Addenda, 1544–77*; thereafter until *c*.1780 they are organized under country, and consist of general correspondence from ambassadors abroad, SP 71–SP 99, to which there are printed *Calendar of State Papers (Foreign) 1578–89*, and *List and Analysis of State Papers (Foreign) 1589–93*, otherwise some have descriptive lists, nominal or subject indexes; from 1780 they form part of the Foreign Office classes.

see **Advance of Money, Committee for, Both Kingdoms, Committee for, Colonies, Dominions and Dependencies, Commonwealth Exchequer Papers, Council of State, Crown Lands, Delinquents, Committee for Compounding with, Fee–Farm Rents, Foreign Office, Indemnity, Committee and Commissioners for, Ireland, Plundered Ministers, Committee for, Scotland, Sequestration of Delinquents' Estates, Committee for the**

State Trials Temp. Edward IV (fifteenth century)–George III, with a nominal index giving name, residence, occupation, offence charged, names of informers, and sentence, on open access, KB 8; proceedings, 1584–1856, TS 11, with a descriptive list arranged chronologically and a nominal index, both on open access.
see **Jacobite Rebellions**

Stationery Office Printed staff lists of Established and unestablished officers, 1909–April 1945, STAT 13.

Subsidy, Lay A regular tax imposed on the laity, as opposed to clerical subsidies on the clergy, and based on a fraction of the value of a person's moveables to 1523 (though quotas became rigidly fixed from 1334–1522 and were collected from the township and vill at large, the sums apportioned out by the local collectors, so that no nominal lists of payers survive), and thenceforward in addition to the fixed quota of a tenth from towns and cities and a fifteenth from rural areas, a levy on the value of a person's goods, lands or wages over a certain amount was imposed. The main impositions fell between 1290 and 1663, to which were added sporadic aids, scutage, tallage, carucage, and taxes on aliens, grants and loans, benevolences, devotion money, free and voluntary gifts, poll taxes and from 1662, the Hearth Tax, which superseded it. 'Rolls of particulars' (nominal lists of persons assessed to pay), lists of persons in arrears, collectors' accounts and miscellaneous documents relating to appointments of Commissioners, temp. Henry III (thirteenth century)–William and Mary, are in E 179, the class list being arranged alphabetically by county, then by regnal year and outlining the hundreds, wapentakes, cities or boroughs covered by each bundle and the nature of the contents which are organized by township, vill or ward and parish; certificates of residence, granting exemption from double liability and certifying where and how much tax had already been paid, temp. Edward VI–Charles II, E 115, to which there is a nominal index on open access; certificates of election of subsidy collectors, 1303–1648, C 267, with a nominal index on open access; contri-butions to a Loan, 1590, giving names, status, and amount, under county, and for London, some giving parish of residence, and including clergy arranged by diocese, indicating parish, SP 12/236; weekly and monthly assessments, 1642–60, SP 28/148–204, arranged in county bundles, then by hundred and parish, including contributions for a Loan for the relief of the King's distressed subjects in Ireland, 1642, SP 28/191–95, to which there is a parish index on open access, under county; later aids and grants, and poll taxes, temp. William and Mary, are in E 182, in yearly county bundles, and then by parish, and in E 181, though not all counties have nominal lists of taxpayers, some giving totals collected and names of tax collectors, persons in default or arrears, and Papists paying double assessments; other returns for the reign, 1689–97, are in SP 33 Cases B–D. see *Aliens, Residence, Certificates of, Roman Catholics*, individual taxes and *Loans*

Succession Duty Imposed under a statute of 1853 on all gratuitous acquisitions of real and personal property worth £100 or more on a person's death, and on which no Legacy Duty was payable, and abolished in 1949; gifts to spouses were exempt, but those properties descending on their deaths to other persons then attracted Duty. Registers, giving name, occupation and address of deceased, date of demise, date of will and probate or administration, in which court or registry, details of affected estate, to whom it was to pass, and the relationship of the beneficiary to the deceased, and when it vested in a liable party, its value when the original holder died, and when Duty became due, and how much was payable, calculated on the difference, 1853–94, IR 26/4868–6262, with annual indexes, IR 27;

because the registers were kept open for fifty years marriages and deaths of beneficiaries were also entered during the intervening years before Duty was assessed; arrears registers, 1885 for accrued arrears from 1853–65, and 1889 for accrued arrears between 1866–78, IR 26/6263–82, indexed in IR 27; Succession and Probate Duty Case Books, 1853–66, IR 67.
see **Death Duty, Estate Duty, Probate Duty**

Sudan Births to Britons, 1916–50, marriages, 1907–50, deaths, 1917–46, RG 36, indexed, 1904–40, in RG 43/18.

Suffragettes Prisoners in Holloway, 1909, CAB 41/32/29; reports of trials, 1908–14, HO 144, to which there is a descriptive list.
see **Riots and Civil Disturbances**

Superstitious Uses, Lands given to Usually to propagate the rites of Roman Catholics or other faiths not tolerated by the law. Commissions of enquiry, 1552–1744, with a descriptive list and nominal index, FEC 1, 1681–99, C 205; registers of estates given to superstitious uses, 1716, arranged alphabetically by county, or town, then by name, FEC 2/68–69, 120.

Surgeons Registers of qualifications of candidates for commissions in the Army Medical Department, 1825–67, WO 25/3923–44; service records of officers, 1800–40, indexed, WO 25/3896–912; confidential reports on medical officers 1860–61, WO 25/3944; casualty returns, 1809–52, WO 25/265, 2384–85, 2395–2407; Medal Book of the Royal Army Medical Corps, 1879–96, WO 25/3992. Original applications and certificates of Royal Naval surgeons, 1660–1830,

ADM 106; surgeons' lists, 1780–1804, 1805–17, 1820–23, ADM 104; records of Royal Naval surgeons' services, 1774–1886, and of assistant surgeons, 1795–1873, ADM 104, indexed 1774–1886, ADM 104/11, surgeons' services, 1742–1819, 1830–74, and assistant surgeons' services, 1803–16, 1829–78, staff and fleet surgeons, 1859–86, temporary surgeons' services, 1914–16, ADM 104; reports and memoranda regarding surgeons, 1822–3, ADM 105/10–19; Establishment Books of Royal Naval hospitals, 1807–19, Entry Books of surgeons and surgeons' mates, 1790–1823, wages and salary lists of persons employed in the care of prisoners of war, 1803–15, ADM 104; succession book of surgeons in Royal Naval hospitals, 1789–1803, ADM 102/851; appointments of surgeons to emigrant ships, 1891–4, registers of particulars about them, 1854–92, CO 386/186–87; medical journals of emigrant ships, 1825–53, ADM 101/76–79, of convict ships, 1852–71, ADM 101/1–75, 251–63, and selected medical journals of Royal Naval ships, c.1797–1855, listed alphabetically by ship, ADM 101/80–127, and of various stations, 1856–1943, listed by station, ADM 101/128–250, 264–618 (some closed 75 years), with an index to the class list for ADM 101/128–293; medical journals of convict ships, 1858–67, MT 32; surgeons' reports on convicts in prisons and hulks, awaiting transportation, 1802–49, HO 9, sworn and attested quarterly lists of convicts supplying details on health, 1824–76, HO 8; assignments and surgeons' reports on convicts being transported, 1787–1867, HO 11/1–19. Letters from surgeons of hospitals and hospital ships, 1702–1862, ADM 97, with an index to correspondents, giving registered number, 1832–62, ADM 133; selected registers of

letters, 1832–62, giving date received, ADM 132; accounts of surgeons of London hospitals, 1810–22, ADM 100.
see *Hospitals, Medical Officers, Royal Naval*

Surinam (Dutch Guiana) Births, marriages and deaths of Britons, 1889–1966, and Paramaribo, births, 1941–51, and deaths, 1943, all in FO 907/1–32; return of slaves, and alphabetical returns of whites and slaves, population returns of free, coloured and black inhabitants, 1811, CO 278/15–25.

Surveyors, District Correspondence concerning expenses incurred by Highway Boards, 1879–1900, arranged alphabetically by Board, MH 21; registers of correspondence, 1879–1900, MH 22.

Sweden Deaths of Britons, 1831–1920, RG 35/20–44; Gothenburg, baptisms, 1881–90, FO 818/15, marriages, 1845–91, RG 33/153, indexed in RG 43/7; Hudiksvall, deaths, 1884, FO 730/1; Os-

karshamn, deaths, 1887, FO 731/1; Stockholm, births, marriages and deaths, 1920–45, wills and estate deeds, FO 748/6–101, marriages, 1847–90, FO 83, indexed in FO 802/239.

Switzerland Marriages of Britons, 1816–32, FO 194/1, indexed in FO 194/2, deaths, 1831–1920, RG 35/20–44; Berne, marriages, 1846–90, FO 83, indexed in FO 802/239; Geneva, Association Oath Roll of English merchants, 1696, C 213/461, births, 1850–1934, marriages, 1850–1933, deaths, 1850–1923, FO 778/13–22; Lausanne, births, 1886–1948, marriages, 1887–1947, deaths, 1887–1948, FO 910/1–20; Montreux, births, 1902–39, marriages, 1927–33, deaths, 1903–41, FO 911/1–3.

Syria Aleppo, baptisms, marriages and burials of Britons, 1756–1800, SP 110/70; Damascus, births, 1934–5, marriages, 1935, FO 684/16–17.

T*t*

Tahiti Papeete, births to Britons, 1818–1941, marriages, 1845–1941, deaths, 1845–1936, FO 687/23–32, indexed in FO 687/33.

Taiwan (Formosa) Births, marriages and deaths of Britons, 1866, FO 681/57, deaths, 1873–1901, FO 721/1.

Tallage A medieval tax on the Royal demesne, including cities and boroughs.
see *Subsidy, Lay*

Tasmania (Van Diemen's Land) Incomplete lists of settlers and convicts, 1808–49, ledger returns of convicts, 1846, 1849, and pardons, 1834–8, 1840–59, HO 10.
see *Australia, Convicts, Transportation of, Emigrants*

Taverns Drinking houses which sold wine, and with less spacious accommodation than inns. Licences, certificates and presentments of taverns and cookshops in the City of London, to ensure they adopted and followed prevailing regulations for the sale of food and drink, temp. James I and Charles I, C 203/1.
see *Alehouse Recognizances, Lenten Certificates, Victuallers' Recognizances, Vintners' Fines, Wine Licences*

Tax Officers Oaths of office of Tax Commissioners, 1815, E 169; some appoint-ments of Commissioners, and tax assessors (also serving as collectors), may be found in the assessment lists, or as indicated in the class list, temp. Henry II (twelfth century)–William and Mary, organized alphabetically by county, then by regnal year, E 179; later nominal records are the returns of parish totals made by collectors of Land Tax and other Assessed Taxes, 1689–1830, arranged in annual county bundles, and then by parish listing, and signed receipts for salaries and expenses, E 182 and E 181; tax officers of the Board of Stamps and Taxes, 1796–1860, IR 51, and 1833–77, IR 84; appointments, 1929–69, LCO 34 (most closed 50 years).

Telegraphic Engineers and Electricians, Society of Journals, 1872–88, including a list of officers and members, 1883, ZLIB 23.

Territorial Army In 1908 the Volunteers and Yeomanry were absorbed into the Territorial Force, which was styled the Territorial Army from 1920. Musters of some Middlesex and County of London regiments, 1908–12, WO 70; service medals of officers, 1908–32, WO 330.
see *Volunteers, Yeomanry*

Testamentary Causes 1324–1515, with a descriptive list, C 270; cases in the Prerogative Court of Canterbury, Court of Probate and Probate, Divorce and

Admiralty Division, 1845–78, TS 15; cases referred by ecclesiastical courts to the Court of King's Bench (Crown Side), 1329–1843, on the Controlment Rolls, and in Latin to 1733, KB 29, and on the Crown Rolls, 1702–1857, KB 28. Appeals from ecclesiastical courts to the High Court of Delegates and Judicial Committee of the Privy Council, 1652–1859, DEL 9, indexed in DEL 11, wills and affidavits filed with the appeals, 1636–1857, DEL 10, indexed in DEL 11, Case Books, 1796–1834, DEL 7; proceedings on appeal to the Judicial Committee of the Privy Council, 1834–58, PCAP 1, and Case Books, 1834–58, PCAP 3.

see *Administration, Letters of, Canterbury, Prerogative Court of, Chancery (Equity), Court of, Chancery Division of the High Court of Justice, Delegates, High Court of, Ecclesiastical Causes, King's Bench (Crown Side), Court of, Privy Council, Judicial Committee of the, Probate, Court of, Probate, Divorce and Admiralty Division of the High Court of Justice, Star Chamber, Court of, Wills*

Test Oath
see *Oath Rolls*

Thailand Register of mortgages, and land transactions of Britons, 1865–1941, FO 628.

Theatres General letters from the Lord Chamberlain's Department contain references to grants of letters patent, 1719–1902, LC 1; warrants for patents, registers of licences, inspection reports, plans of theatres, 1660–1901, LC 7, and 1660–1820, LC 5/137–64, with a descriptive list in *Theatrical References in the Lord Chamberlain's Office*, two volumes; the patents are enrolled on the Patent Rolls in C 66.

Tithes A tenth of a person's annual produce from his land (predial tithes from fruits of the soil, mixed tithes from farm stock, and personal tithes from personal industry), taken in kind by the parson or lay impropriator, was commuted to an annual rent charge in 1836. From 1918 it could be redeemed by purchase of annuities of up to fifty years, extended to sixty years in 1925. In 1936 all tithe rent charges were abolished and replaced by redemption annuities for sixty years, or lesser period if redeemed, or otherwise were extinguished, and the tithe-owners were compensated with Government Stock. The annuities were abolished in 1977. Tithe suits, temp. Edward IV (fifteenth century)–George III, E 13, temp. Henry VIII–1841, E 112; Commissions of enquiry, temp. Elizabeth–Victoria, E 178, and in the Forest of Dean, 1781–1891, F 16. Awards and agreements between tithe- and landowners, containing signatures, 1836–66, TITH 2, Boundary Awards, defining ancient parochial boundaries, and drawing new ones to resolve disputes between landowners before commutation, and including plans and schedules of property, listing landowners and occupiers, 1839–60, TITH 1; Special Awards, where there was no apportionment because the new rent charge was extinguished by merger or redemption, 1836–86, IR 106; declaration of merger, where the landowner was also the titheowner, 1837–1936, TITH 3, the merger number being identified in IR 29, containing the apportionments made in English and Welsh parishes, 1836–*c*.1846, which give details of owner, occupier, nature and extent of property, and the rent charge, with any later amendments to 1936, plus the plot number, which is then related to accompanying maps in IR 30, both classes being listed alphabetically by parish; later amendments, and orders for apportionment, many with maps or plans annexed to them, and marking out boundaries of the original tithe plots, and in colour the sub-divisions created by subsequent alterations, 1936–77, IR 94; original and draft maps, c.1840, are in IR 77. Ordnance Survey maps used to establish the boundaries of Tithe Districts, 1846–1915, of six inches to the mile, IR 93, and of one inch to the mile, 1805–97, IR 105. Annual certificates of the capital value of lands under cultivation for crops, fruit or market gardening used as the basis of assessment of the rent charge, under a statute of 1886, 1886–1936, IR 95. Extinguishment of tithes by Enclosure Act and Award, 1836–c.1870, IR 18; registers of certificates of redemption of tithe rent charges by lump sum payments, 1847–1938, indexed to 1928, IR 10; registers of confirmations of annuities for up to fifty years, 1919–65, IR 118, and certificates of redemption by annuities, 1918–69, IR 102; lists of owners and rent charges in 1936, arranged alphabetically by county, Tithe District, and whose numbers correspond with those in IR 29, IR 110; Tithe District maps, c.1956, using the original tithe maps, IR 90; certificates of redemption for the City of London, arranged by parish, and address, 1886–1947, MAF 8; Vicar's Rate in Halifax, certificates of redemption, 1873–1926, MAF 16, and Kendal Corn Rent certificates of redemption, 1931–64, MAF 28, both classes listed by address; out-letters concerning the Extra–Parochial Tithe Commission, 1849–52, CRES 24.

Titles, British and Foreign Correspondence, 1745–1905, FO 83, to which there is a descriptive list, and a selection, 1906–60, FO 371, with a card index, 1906–19, and index, 1920–51, in FO 409; creations of titles, and writs of summons to Parliament, 1783–1921, indexed, HO 116; claims to titles, 1820–40, 1862–84, HO 80; Entry Books of petitions, 1784–1898, HO 56; sign manual warrants relating to foreign titles, 1777–1864, HO 37. Announcements of creations and successions to titles are made in *The London Gazette*, 1665–1986, with subject indexes sporadically from 1790 and invariably from 1848. ZJ 1.

see **Baronets, Knighthood, Peers**

Tontines A loan to the government, the proprietors of which received an annuity during the lifetime of named nominees (sometimes themselves, or relatives or friends), with the benefit of survivorship, the annuity increasing for remaining proprietors as the nominees died. The annuity could be assigned or willed to others for the duration of the life of the nominee. There were three English State Tontines, in 1693, 1766 and 1789, and three Irish State Tontines, in 1773, 1775 and 1777. Certificates of sums invested by existing subscribers to the 1693 tontine, and new subscribers, for ninety-six-year annuities, giving the names and relationship to them of nominees, and the amounts invested, plus annual yield, 1698, E 403/2379; signed receipts of annuities, including the 1766 and 1789 tontines, 1706–1832, E 404/520–24; ledger of the 1766 tontine, offering a life annuity and entry into a lottery, dividing contributors into classes according to date of application, giving names and addresses of proprietors, amount subscribed, and in return for what annuity, and names and addresses of nominees, their dates of death and names of proprietors' assignees, NDO 2/1; Posting Book, giving names of nominees, indexed, NDO 2/2, and account book, NDO 2/3, both containing half-yearly lists of payments of annuities, and recording deaths and defaulters; ledgers containing lists of contributors and nominees, divided into six classes according to age-bands, and including six classes of Government nominees drawn from specified social and professional groups, giving dates of nominees' deaths, and annuities paid out, 1789–1888, for the 1789 tontine, NDO 2/10–14, printed lists 1792, giving ages of nominees, their parentage, and residence, and date and age at death, 1792, according to class, NDO 2/15–17, and 1809, 1818, 1865, 1873 and 1878, NDO 2/18, 25–29; life certificates proving survival of contributors' nominees, signed by the minister and churchwardens of the parish, or by affidavit of a justice of the peace, or British consul if overseas, 1831, NDO 1/11, and of government nominees, 1832, 1840, NDO 1/13, 107; indexed birth, marriage and death certificates of nominees, NDO 2/46–51; Tontine and Annuity Dead Orders, of original debentures, payment orders, deaths of nominees, NDO 1/128–501; extracts from wills, and administration grants, and assignments of annuities, 1802–78, NDO 2/53–58; payment of annuities, 1789, T 60/44. Irish Tontine Ledgers, and payment books, marriage and death certificates of nominees, and declarations of identity of nominees, 1773–1870, NDO 3/32.

see *Annuities, Loans, Lotteries, Million Bank, South Sea Company*

Trained Bands Armed men aged between sixteen and sixty, mustered from 1573, and trained four times a year at parish expense, under the direction of paid county officers. Association Oath Roll of officers, 1696, C 213/163.

see *Militia*

Traitors Extents of lands and goods, 1554–8, E 387. Estate deeds of persons attainted during the 1715 Jacobite Rebellion and including claims and legal proceedings, 1715–44, FEC 1, to which there is a descriptive list and subject index. Precedents of treason cases, seventeenth–nineteenth centuries, KB 33.

see *Attainder, Central Criminal Court, Forfeitures and Escheats, Jacobite Rebellions, State Trials*

Trans-Jordan Index of births, marriages and deaths of Britons, 1936–40, RG 43/18; Amman, births, 1946, marriages, 1927, RG 36.

Treasure Trove Evidence and papers, 1825–1909, TS 18, to which there is a descriptive list, arranged under subject (some later files are closed 75 or 100 years); Royal warrants and Treasury Solicitor's authority for payments, 1804–1925, TS 30.

see *Bona Vacantia Division, Treasury Solicitor*

Treasury Salary lists of staff, 1794–1856, T 41/1; 'Property Tax' assessments on staff, 1803–16, T 95.

Treasury Solicitor This office dates from at least 1655, and was originally responsible for cases in the Exchequer affecting the King's revenue, extended in 1696 to political prosecutions. From 1876 the office became a corporation with sole power to hold real and personal property, and with power to sue and be sued. The Treasury Solicitor thenceforward has acted as the Crown's nominee in intestacy matters, and from the same date has also held the office of Procurator General, and between 1884 and 1908, functioned as the Director of Public Prosecutions. Since 1950 the Procurator General has dealt with matrimonial causes with a power to

intervene in divorce or nullity proceedings when asked by the court, or where information suggests collusion. Staff appointments, 1804–1936, TS 30 (some files closed 75 or 100 years). Legal proceedings of State trials, escheats, administration of estates cases, and preservation of the public peace, 1584–1856, TS 11; selected *bona vacantia* cases, including pedigrees, letters of administration to 1857 of intestates and testators failing to dispose of residuary estates, or dying without a lawful heir, 1698–1955, TS 17, and 1517–1953, TS 18 (some closed 75 or 100 years), and to which there is a nominal card index to pedigrees in TS 33, cross-referencing this class, on open access; letter books relating to administration of estates and to lunatics, 1813–1924, TS 3.
see *Procurator General, Her Majesty's, State Trials*

Trinity House Certified requests to arm ships in the Thames, giving ship's name, builder, owner, master, detailed description of layout, and intended destination, 1630–8, SP 16/17.

Tristan da Cunha Marriages of Britons, 1871–1951, deaths, 1892–1949, PRO 30/65.

Trust Deeds, Charitable Enrolled on the Close Rolls to 1903, C 54, with a pasted-up topographical index 1736–1870, and card index 1871–1903, on open access; later enrolments, 1903–1987, J 18, to which there is a topographical card index, 1903–5, on open access; memorials of charities, arranged in county bundles, 1812–75, J 19; files of the Bona Vacantia Division include details of property belonging to trusts, 1824–1955, TS 17.
see *Bona Vacantia Division*

Tunisia Bizerta, deaths, of Britons, 1898–1931, FO 870/1; Djerba, deaths, 1925, FO 871/1; Gabes, deaths, 1925, FO 872/1; Goletta, births, 1885–8, FO 878/1–2; Monastir, deaths, 1905–8, FO 873/1; Sfax, deaths, 1896–1931, FO 874/1; Susa, deaths, 1894–1931, FO 875/1.

Turkey Deaths of Britons, 1831–1920, RG 35/20–44; Adana, marriages, 1913, 1942, 1946, FO 609/1–3; Ankara and Konya, births, 1895–1909, FO 732/1; Bucharest, births, 1851–1931, baptisms in the British chaplaincy, 1858–1948, deaths, 1854–1929, FO 625/2–4, 6, marriages, 1870–90, FO 83, indexed in FO 802/239; Constanta (Kustendje), births and deaths, 1862–73, FO 887/1–2; Constantinople (Istanbul), marriages, 1846–90, FO 83, indexed in FO 802/239, marriages, 1885–1958, RG 33/154, indexed in RG 43/7, 11–12, marriage affidavits, 1895–1924, and registers of deeds, 1914–43, FO 441; Cyprus, register of deeds, 1829–39, FO 329; Dardanelles, births, 1900–14, FO 733/1; Edirne (Adrianople), births, 1888–1912, marriages, 1887–1905, 1913–14, FO 783/3–4, 7; Jaffa, births, 1900–14, FO 734/1; Jassy Consular District, Moldavia, register of British subjects, 1844–59, FO 786/119, and 1851–1948, FO 625/2–4; Jerusalem, births, 1850–1914, 1920–21, and deaths, 1851–1914, FO 617/3–5; Lower Danube, baptisms in the British Chaplaincy, 1869–1907, FO 625/5, marriages, 1868–1914, RG 33/143, indexed in RG 43/7, and burials, 1869–70, FO 786/120; Rustchuk, births, 1867–1908, and deaths, 1867–1903, FO 888/1–2; Smyrna (Izmir), baptisms, marriages and burials, 1833–49, RG 33/155, indexed in RG 43/1, 7 and 3 respectively, wills, with numerical and nominal in dexes, 1820–1929, FO 626; Sulina, births 1861–1932, deaths, 1860–1931, FO 728/1–2, births, 1870–77, and deaths, 1866–77, FO 886/1–2; Trebizond (Trabzon), registers of British subjects, 1836–1913, FO 526.

U u

Uganda Births, marriages and deaths of Britons, 1905–18, RG 36, indexed in RG 43/18.

Upper Bench Used to describe the Court of King's Bench during the Interregnum see *King's Bench, Court of*

Uruguay Montevideo, marriages of Britons, 1870–90, FO 83, indexed in FO 802/239.

Under-Sheriffs, County Lists, *c.*1819–39, HO 94.

Vv

Vaccination Details relating to vaccination of inmates of Union workhouses, 1834–1909, MH 12, listed alphabetically by county and then by Union, and the contents chronologically, to which there are subject indexes, 1836–1920, MH 15.

Vagrants
see *Poor Law Unions*

Valuation Office Record sheet plans, being Ordnance Survey maps of various dates, *c*.1886–1912, and scales, usually 1:2500, but often bigger in urban areas, and 1:10,560 for moorland, marking out District boundaries and containing assessment numbers of valued properties as the key to the Field Books in IR 58, organized by administrative region and then alphabetically by Valuation District Office and constituent civil parishes: London Region, IR 121, South Eastern Region, IR 124, Wessex, IR 125, Central, IR 126, East Anglia, IR 127, Western, IR 128, West Midland, IR 129, East Midland, IR 130, Wales, IR 131, Liverpool, IR 132, Manchester, IR 133, Yorkshire, IR 134, Northern, IR 135. The Field Books, arranged alphabetically by civil parish within each Valuation District, contain entries corresponding to plot numbers on the maps, and set out a description of the construction of buildings, the number and purpose of rooms in each property, details of outbuildings, their condition, land acreage, estimated gross market value with and without buildings and timber, the name of the owner and occupier and responsibility for rates, Land Tax and other outgoings, annual rent if any, and date of any recent sale, *c*.1910–*c*.1914, IR 58; 'Domesday Books' of the City of London and Paddington, containing similar information, but without detailed descriptions of property layout, 1910, IR 91. Sample appeals against the Valuation Act, 1910–20, and registers of proceedings, 1938–47, LT 5.

Van Diemen's Land
see *Tasmania*

Venezuela Marriages of Britons, 1836–8, RG 33/155, indexed in RG 43/7; claims against Venezuela for seizure of property, 1903, FO 310.

Verderers Forest officers appointed to protect growing trees, shrubs and deer. Certificates of election, 1283–1633, C 242; Rolls of Verderers, temp. John (thirteenth century)-Charles II, E 32; appointments, 1570–temp. Charles II, with a nominal index, C 202. Proceedings of the Verderers' Court in the Forest of Dean, 1846–1907, F 16.

Verge, Court of the
see *Marshalsea, Court of the, Palace Court*

Veterinary Surgeons Selected appeals to the Veterinary Surgeons' Tribunal for exemption from military service, 1915–18, MH 47.

Vice-Admiralty Courts With jurisdiction similar to the High Court of Admiralty, in British possessions overseas, and sometime in maritime counties of England and Wales. Appeal lay to the King in Council or to the High Court of Admiralty, and after 1834 to the Judicial Committee of the Privy Council. Appointments of Court officers, temp. James I–1873, HCA 50, indexed in HCA 51, which includes an index by office; proceedings of the Court, 1636–1875, including the Cape of Good Hope, 1795–1805, Cape Nicholas Mole, 1797–99, Guadaloupe, 1811–15, Jamaica, 1662–3, 1747–48, Minorca, 1799–1902, New York, 1777–83, Sierra Leone, 1808–17, and in Lancashire and Cheshire, 1636–9, piracy proceedings in America, Africa and the West Indies, and the Channel Islands, 1723–39, HCA 49; some colonial proceedings to 1849, HCA 1, with nominal indexes, 1740–1860, HCA 30. Notes on proceedings in appeals to the Procurator General, 1827–78, TS 15.
see *Admiralty, High Court of, Privy Council, Judicial Committee of the, Procurator General, Her Majesty's*

Victoria Cross Instituted in 1856 for acts of conspicuous bravery, and awarded retrospectively from 1854, it was extended in 1920 to staff of the Nursing Services and to civilians under orders or direction of the Armed Forces. Citations listed in *The London Gazette*, to 1986, with annual or half-yearly subject indexes, ZJ 1; original Royal Warrant, 29 January 1856, and correspondence and papers, 1856–1953, including recommendations for awards, 1856–63, with a descriptive list, WO 98, and Register of the Victoria Cross, 1856–1900, containing additional notes about recipients to 1952, and annotated with dates of death to 1956, WO 98/3–4, alphabetical list of recipients, 1914–20, and 1856–1952, WO 98/6–7; recommendations, 1856–1954, arranged chronologically by campaign or war, WO 32 code 50M, and for the Boer War, 1901–2, WO 108; military pensions for recipients, 1857–95, WO 23; gratuities to warrant officers, 1873–1941, PMG 35; recommendations for the Royal Navy and Royal Marines personnel, 1857–1972, ADM 171, 1944–50, ADM 116 Code 85; naval and marine pensions, 1857–1920, PMG 16; allowances, 1857–1902, and pension books, 1866–9, 1886–9, ADM 23; Royal Air Force recommendations (World War I), AIR 1, 1918–55, AIR 30, and 1939–60, AIR 2 Code B 30; list of recipients, including citations, 1940–6, CAB 106/312. see *Medals*

Victuallers' Recognizances Victualler is the generic term applied to inn-, tavern-, and alehousekeepers. Bonds that they would not kill, dress or eat flesh during Lent, keep gaming-houses, suffer unlawful games to be played on their premises, or harbour rogues and vagabonds, and would observe the regulations relating to keeping alehouses and retailing food and drink, temp. Elizabeth–Charles II, listed alphabetically by county, date and place, E 180, and temp. James I–Charles I, C 203; bonds in the Palatinate of Durham, 1583–84, DURH 8.
see *Alehouse Recognizances, Lenten Certificates, Taverns, Vintners' Fines, Wine Licences*

Vintners' Fines Indentures made between the Crown patentee and tavernkeepers and sellers of wine for compositions for offences against the statute of 1552 concerning wine retail, 1569–72, listed nominally by regnal year, and including place of residence, and informations, 1566/7, 1569/70, and 1583–9, listed by legal term and groups of counties, E 176.

see *Alehouse Recognizances, Lenten Certificates, Taverns, Victuallers' Recognizances, Wine Licences*

Virgin Islands St Croix, deaths of Britons, 1849–70, RG 35/4; St John, deaths, 1849–72, RG 35/4; St Thomas, deaths, 1849–70, RG 35/4–7. Registers of slaves, 1815–34, T 71.

Volunteers Musters in Britain, arranged by title of regiment, and giving names, ages and abodes, 1797–1814, 1873–8, Canadian Volunteers, 1837–50, WO 13; musters of some Middlesex and County of London regiments, 1860–1912, including from 1908 the Territorial Force of which the Volunteers then became part, WO 70/1–6, Lists of commissions, appointments and warrants, 1758–1855, HO 51, commissions and returns, 1782–1840, HO 50; fees for commissions, 1782–1880, HO 88; allowances paid to Volunteers, 1798–99, 1837–1927, PMG 13; records of services, 1804–5, WO 44/704–13; service medals of officers, 1892–1908, WO 330.

see *Fencibles, Territorial Army, Yeomanry*

W w

Wales, Principality of Many of the sources described in this book are applicable to both England and Wales. The following relate to material peculiar to the Principality, much of which is in Latin to 1733. Association Oath Roll, arranged by county, 1696, C 213/168. Court rolls of manors and Honours and other local jurisdictions, *c*.1200–*c*.1900, SC 2, to which there is a topographical index on open access; rentals and surveys of manors and Honours, temp. Henry III (thirteenth century)–William IV, SC 11 and SC 12; court rolls of Crown manors, 1441–1950, CRES 5; out-letters concerning Crown rents, 1825–47, CRES 24; estates and manors sold by the Crown, 1685–1940, CRES 34; rentals of Crown lands, 1832–1961, LRRO 12 (most closed 100 years), indexed to 1902 in LRRO 65; Enrolment Book of grants, leases and warrants of Crown lands, temp. Henry VIII–1834, LR 1. Plea Rolls, Anglesey, 1509–16, WALE 16/1, Carnarvon, 1386–99, 1530, and 1533, WALE 20/1–3; Ruthin Lordship records, 1343, 1634–1808, including presentments to the Court, 1722–98, and papers in Causes, 1713–92, lists of freeholders and inhabitants, 1343 and 1742–97, WALE 15/8–13, manorial court rolls, 1294–1654, SC 2. Ancient Deeds, Series F, temp. Edward I (thirteenth century)–Elizabeth I, WALE 29, Series FF, *c*.1507–1633, WALE 30; Modern Welsh Deeds, temp. James II–

nineteenth-century, WALE 31. Fiats for justices of the peace of Welsh counties, arranged alphabetically by county, 1705–1973, and of Welsh boroughs, 1837–1973, C 234; Entry Book of justices of the peace, 1937–66, and of Welsh boroughs, 1851–1937, C 193. Returns by county clerks of the peace of names and estates of Papist recusants, 1715, FEC 1. Staff lists of Customs officers, 1671–1922, and superannuation registers, including widows' pensions citing names and dates of children's births, 1803–1922, CUST 39 (closed 75 years); sporadic Parliamentary returns of Customs officers, ZHC 1, to which there is an index on open access; quarter bills of salaries due to Customs officers, 1673–89, PRO 30/32/15–29, 1675–1813, CUST 18, 1716–1847, T 42, 1814–29, CUST 19; applications by staff and their dependants for pensions, 1671–1920, T 1, with registers of them, 1777–1920, T 2, to which subject indexes, 1830–1920, T 108, on open access, are the key. Pensions paid by the Royal Hospitals of Chelsea and Greenwich to retired military, naval and marine personnel, giving rank, regiment and number, address, date of commencement, amount and nature of pension, arranged by pay-district, adding information on transfers elsewhere and date of death, 1842–62, WO 22/114–117.

Wards and Liveries, Court of Established in 1541 and abolished in 1660, it dealt with incidents of tenure by knight service and wardship over lands of infant heirs, idiots and lunatics, held as tenants-in-chief from the Crown, and granted livery of seisin (possession) of them on reaching full age or restoration of sanity, administering in the meantime the profits attached to them, and exercising the power to sell the wardship or arrange the marriage of the under-age heir. Inquisitions post mortem, temp. Henry VIII–Charles I, to which there is a nominal index arranged by reign, giving the county and regnal year of the inquisition into lands held on the death of the former tenant-in-chief, to establish the name, age and relationship of the next heir to the deceased, or when a person lost lucidity, WARD 7. Pleadings, temp. Edward VI–Charles I, WARD 13, temp. Henry VIII–Commonwealth, WARD 14, and temp. Henry VIII–Charles I, WARD 15; depositions and some exhibits, temp. Henry VIII–Charles I, WARD 3; deeds and evidences, c.1200–Charles I, WARD 2; affidavits, decrees and orders, temp. Henry VIII–Charles I, including some depositions, WARD 1; indentures of wardship, including marriages and leases, temp. Henry VIII–Charles I, WARD 6, particulars for leases, temp. Henry VIII–Charles I, WARD 12; liveries of seisin, decrees, indentures, surveys, bargains of sale of wardships, leases, petitions, inquisitions and affidavits, temp. Henry VIII–1652, WARD 9; valuations and extents of lands, including particulars for dower, temp. Henry VIII–Charles I, WARD 4, and temp. Elizabeth–Charles I, WARD 5, both listed by county.

see *Age, Proofs of, Idiots and Lunatics, Inquisitions post mortem*

Wardship To 1660 the Crown had power of wardship over heirs of tenants-in-chief who were under twenty-one, or idiots or lunatics; during this time the Crown administered their lands, collected the rents and used the profits to maintain and educate the heir, and had the right to sell wardship or arrange the marriage of the minor. On reaching maturity or if lucidity returned the lands were restored to the heir by livery of seisin. Enrolments of grants of wardship of heirs under twenty-one, and of livery of seisin in the lands held as tenant-in-chief of the Crown on reaching maturity, are on the Fine Rolls, temp. John (thirteenth century)–1641, C 60, with printed *Calendars*, 1272–1509; inquisitions post mortem, recording the age, date of birth and relationship of the next heir, and a recital of lands held in any county at the time of death of the previous tenant-in-chief, temp. Henry III (thirteenth century)–Charles I, C 132–C 142, and temp. Henry III–James I, E 149–E 150, E 152, including some proofs of age on reaching maturity; there are printed *Calendars* to 1405, and for the reign of Henry VII, 1485–1509, while the rest are listed by reign in the Chancery series, or up to 1484 in a manuscript index for the Exchequer series, and thereafter included with the Chancery listing; duplicates in the Court of Wards and Liveries, 1541–c.1641, WARD 7, listed with the other two series. Indentures of wardship, including marriages of wards, and leases of their lands, temp. Henry VIII–Charles I, listed by regnal year, WARD 6; valuations and extents of lands, including particulars for dower, temp. Henry VIII–Charles I, WARD 4, temp. Elizabeth–Charles I, WARD 5, both arranged under county.

see *Age, Proofs of, Idiots and Lunatics, Infants, Inquisitions post mortem, Wards and Liveries, Court of*

Wards of Court When legal action was instituted in the Chancery Division relating to a minor or his property under the care of a guardian, he became a ward of court; since 1949 an order of the court has been necessary. Until 1970 the Chancery Division of the High Court dealt with cases concerning wards of court, but since then they have been dealt with by the Family Division. Deeds and evidences, 1517–1953, relating to wards of court on whose behalf action was taken to 1970 in the Chancery Division, TS 18, with a descriptive list, and to which there is a nominal card index on open access where related material is also found in TS 33.
see *Chancery Division of the High Court of Justice*

War Pensions Pensions paid to widows and allowances for children of Army officers, 1812–1914, PMG 10; selected war pensions to widows and disablement awards to other ranks in the Army and Royal Navy, arising from service before 1914, listed by category of applicant, giving effective dates of pension, and the papers containing details of name, rank, regiment, circumstances of injury or death, age, date and place of birth, occupation, address, annual income, parentage and parental status, siblings, marital status, date and amount of pension awarded, and with subsequent material attached to the original signed application, 1854–1977, PIN 71; pension applications, awards and payments for service in the Boer War, 1899–1902, World War I and World War II, including those made under Personal Injuries (Civilians) Schemes, 1901–82, PIN 15 (closed 75 years); selected World War I pension award files, covering all types of disability, 1920–72, PIN 26 (most closed 50 years),

and selected payments, from 1917, PIN 45 (closed 75 years); temporary retired pay and gratuities to invalided officers of all three Services, and to nurses for disabilities, 1917–20, PMG 42; interim payments at pension rates to relatives of Army officers posted missing, 1915–20, PMG 47; on notification or presumption of death the entries were then transferred to the registers of payments of pensions to relatives of deceased officers, 1916–20, PMG 44, to widows of Army officers, 1917–19, PMG 45, and to registers of allowances to their offspring, 1916–20, PMG 46; allowances to widows, children and dependent relatives of specially entered mercantile crew and crews of merchant ships commissioned as Royal Naval ships and Auxiliary Craft, and of other civilians killed or incapacitated, 1914–28, PMG 56.

Waterloo, Battle of Waterloo Medal Book, recording corps and regiments and the names and ranks of officers and men, MINT 16/112; lists of officers killed or wounded, 16 and 18 June 1815, MINT 16/111, and in *The London Gazette*, 1 July 1815, ZJ 1/138; returns of officers, June 1815, WO 1/206, and of officers and men of the Royal Artillery entitled to prize money, WO 30/111.

Wesleyan Methodist Metropolitan Registry, Paternoster Row, London Founded in 1818, it relates to English, Welsh, Irish, Scottish, Guernsey and overseas entries of births, registered by dissenters until its closure in 1838, and containing details of parents recording their own births with those of their progeny; authenticated registers of births and baptisms, 1773–1838, RG 4, indexed in RG 4/4680.

West Indies Colonial Papers, General Series, include references to early settlers and planters, in charters, letters, memorials and petitions, 1574–1757, CO 1, printed in *Calendar of State Papers, Colonial, America and West Indies, 1574–1738*; Treasury out-letters, 1763–1838, T 28; Original Correspondence relating to emigration, 1817–96, CO 384; sales of slaves in the West Indies by the Royal African Company, 1673–1816, T 70; slave registers, *c*.1813–*c*.1834, listed under Island and parish, and relating to personal and plantation slaves, T 71; Minute Books of the Court of the British and Portuguese Slave Trade Commission in Jamaica, 1843–51, FO 314; West Indies Slave Compensation Commission awards, including marriage and death certificates and affidavits of claimants or their legal representatives, in Jamaica, Dominica, Grenada, and Trinidad, and setting out the amount awarded and when, 1835–42, NDO 4. Antigua, baptisms and burials, 1733–4, 1738–45, marriages, 1745, CO 152/21, 25; Barbados, baptisms and burials, 1678–9, CO 1/44, and RG 33/156, Association Oath Roll, 1696, C 213/465–67; Bermuda, Association Oath Roll, 1696, C 213/471; Case Book of the Royal Naval Hospital, 1832–6, 1840–44, 1850–62, 1870–83, ADM 104; Cuba, baptisms, 1847–8, marriages, 1842–9, RG 33/155, indexed in RG 43/7, registers of slaves and slavers in Havana, 1819–69, FO 313; Curaçao, births, 1897–1966, marriages, 1922–9, deaths, 1889–1965, FO 907/1–32; Dominican Republic, births, 1868–1932, marriages, 1921–8, deaths, 1874–89, burials, 1849–1910, FO 683/2–6; Guadaloupe, deaths, 1836–71, RG 35/16; Haiti, births, 1833–50, marriages, 1833–93, deaths, 1833–50, FO 866/14, 21–22, births, 1870–1907, FO 376/1–2, deaths, 1836–71, RG 35/16; Leeward Islands, Association Oath Roll, 1696, C 213/472; Martinique, deaths, 1836–71, RG 35/16; Montserrat, baptisms and burials, 1721–9, 1739–45, marriages, 1721–9, CO 152/18, 25; Nevis, baptisms and burials, 1726–7, 1733–4, 1740–5, CO 152/16, 21, 25; St Christopher (St Kitts), baptisms and burials, 1721–30, 1733–4, 1738–45, marriages, 1733–4, 1738–45, CO 152/18, 21, 25.

see *Colonies, Dominions and Dependencies, Licences to pass beyond the Seas, Slaves* and individual islands

West New Jersey Society Formed about 1691 for the 'Hereditary Government of West Jersey in America', tracts of land in West and East New Jersey, Pennsylvania, New England and elsewhere were divided into 1,600 parts as shares for adventurers, on whose death they passed to their heirs, or assigns, under will or letters of administration. The Society was wound up in 1921, and any remaining unclaimed shares became *bona vacantia*. Surviving deposited records include Minute and Entry Books, indexed Share Ledgers, 1692–1876, accounts, registers of shareholders, 1692–1819, share transfers, 1692–1876, unclaimed shares, 1763–1837, and division of dividends, 1885–1915, maps, plans, original deeds, charters, and claims, 1658–1921, TS 12.

Wey Navigation Claims of persons interested in navigation of the River Wey, 1671, after an enabling statute of the same year, E 177/1.

Wills Disposing of a person's real property, and usually combined with a testament relating to his personal goods (including leases), it took effect on that person's death. Until 11 January 1858

wills relating to estates in England and Wales were proved in ecclesiastical courts, although the Court of Chancery (Equity) and later the Chancery Division had jurisdiction over disposal of real estate and any disputes relating to this or to the validity or interpretation of a will was brought there. The ecclesiastical courts could refer their judgments to the Court of King's Bench (Crown Side) for reinforcement and to lend greater authority against defaulting executors. The chief ecclesiastical court was the Prerogative Court of Canterbury; from 1858 probate became the responsibility of civil Probate Registries, and the Court of Probate dealt with disputes, until absorbed into the Probate, Divorce and Admiralty Division of the High Court of Justice in 1875, and on reorganization of which probate cases were transferred to the Chancery Division in 1970; the records of the Prerogative Court have been deposited (see entry). Since 1796 legacies in wills, and since 1805 real estate, have attracted Death Duty (see entry). Wills located among Ancient Deeds, Series DD, 1100–1645, listed by document, date, names of parties and places, or subject, E 211; enrolled for safe-keeping on the Close Rolls, C 54; in relation to Crown lands, temp. Henry VIII–1834, LR 1, indexed; enrolled in the Court of King's Bench (Plea Side), 1656–1760, KB 122, indexed; probates relating to public officers, 1622–1834, indexed, E 406/45–80, 1784–1804, E 407/106/4; Entry Books of wills of members of the Royal Household, 1750–84, LC 5/104–6; wills relating to assigned board wages in the Office of the Clerk of the Kitchen in the Royal Household, 1712–26, LS 13; wills effecting share and annuity transfers arising from the 1677 Goldsmiths' and Bankers' Loan to the Crown, 1677–1704, indexed, E 406/27–44; wills of shareholders in the Royal African Company, 1721–52, and of personnel at Cape Coast Castle, 1718–22, T 70, and wills of Company members, 1710–21, indexed, C 113/292; wills of Roman Catholics enrolled under 1716 statute, 1716–1836, C 54, and CP 43; wills proved in the Palatinate of Chester, 1307–1830, CHES 2; wills of Army officers, 1755–1908, WO 42, to which there is a nominal index on open access; soldiers' wills, 1809–72, WO 25/1359–2410, 3251–471; Royal Naval seamen's wills, 1786–1882, ADM 48, indexed, 1786–1861, 1862–1909, recording date of death, ADM 142; seamen's effects papers, 1800–60, ADM 44, to which there are alphabetical registers, 1802–24, 1825–48 and 1849–61, in ADM 141, and officers' and civilians' effects papers, 1830–60, ADM 45; registers of wills at the Royal Naval Hospital, Gibraltar, 1809–15, ADM 105/40; wills of Royal Marines, 1702–1831, ADM 96; probate registers of all three Services, 1836–1915, PMG 50. Court copies of wills where the Prerogative Court of Canterbury cancelled the original probates or administrations with will annexed, 1660–1827, PROB 23; wills declared invalid, 1600–1827, PROB 20, 1833, LR 1; wills produced in appeals against judgments in ecclesiastical courts made to the High Court of Delegates, 1636–1833, and to the Judicial Committee of the Privy Council, 1834–57, DEL 10, indexed in DEL 11 to 1833 and thereafter in PCAP 1; copies of wills produced in the Court of Chancery (Equity), 1669–1799, listed alphabetically, C 100; Chancery Masters' exhibits, C 103–C 114, to which there is a typescript index; pedigrees relating to administration of wills produced to the Chancery Division, 1852–1974, indexed by earliest antecedent and giving abode and date of birth, marriage or death, and

by Cause title, J 68 (closed 30 years); 7% sample of law suits, 1858–1960, listed alphabetically by year, J 121; memorials concerning cases referred by the Treasury to the Procurator General, indexed, 1804–15, TS 8, and 1815–44, TS 9; selected case papers where the estate was deemed *bona vacantia*, 1698–1964, TS 17, and 1517–1953, TS 18 (some closed 75 or 100 years) to which there is a nominal card index of pedigrees in TS 33 with cross-references to related material in this class, on open access.
see *Canterbury, Prerogative Court of, Chancery (Equity), Court of, Chancery Division of the High Court of Justice, Close Rolls, Death Duty, Delegates, High Court of, Ecclesiastical Causes, King's Bench (Crown Side), Court of, London, Commissary Court of, London, Consistory Court of, Privy Council, Judicial Committee of the, Probate, Court of, Probate, Divorce and Admiralty Division of the High Court of Justice, Testamentary Causes*

Window Tax 1696–1851.
see *Land Tax and Assessed Taxes*

Windsor, Poor Military and Naval Knights of Retired senior officers, formerly twenty-four helpless and indigent knights when embodied at the institution of the Order of the Garter in 1348 to attend the Knights Companion of the Order and perform religious duties in return for food and lodging; they are housed within the walls of Windsor Castle. Appointments, 1782–1877, indexed, HO 38, 1828–1969, indexed, HO 115; military appointments, 1792–1833, HO 44/50, applications for Naval appointments, 1812–21, ADM 106/3535.
see *Almsmen*

Wine Licences Parts of printed indentures issued by Sir Walter Raleigh under his monopoly granted in 1583, and renewed in 1588, of granting licences to keep taverns, 1583–1602, listed alphabetically by county and regnal year, C 238, 1605, E 163/17/21; the Wine Licence Office was established in 1679, responsibility passing to the Board of Stamps in 1757, and to the Board of Excise in 1790; accounts of agents and commissioners, including names of defaulters and those persons in arrears, giving addresses, 1682–1757, AO 3/1194–1242.
see *Alehouse Recognizances, Taverns, Victuallers' Recognizances, Vintners' Fines*

Women's Land Army Set up in 1916, and reintroduced, 1938–50. Minutes of county committees, collections of photographs and recruiting posters, 1916–50, MAF 59.

Wool, Grant of 1338, 1341, 1347, listed alphabetically by county, then by regnal year, indicating the hundreds for which nominal lists survive, E 179.
see *Subsidy, Lay*

Workhouses
see *Poor Law Unions*

Workmen's Compensation Payments made under Workmen's Compensation Acts 1897 and 1907 for injuries sustained in the workplace: appeals to the Court of Appeal from County Courts, most including a copy of the notes taken by judges, and a copy of the original order, 1910–50, J 71; alphabetical Order Books are arranged by number, corresponding to those in J 71, 1911–26, J 72; Orders, 1897–1906, KB 25, 1907–10, J 70; com-

pensation paid to staff in public departments, 1897–1924, PMG 28.
see *Railways*

Works, Ministry of Accounts and payments to tradesmen and others engaged at Royal Palaces and other buildings, 1660–1703, 1709–88, 1778–1814, and salaries, 1727–1832, WORK 5.
see *Offices, Royal and Public*

World War I 1914–18. Despatches, campaign reports, casualty lists, citations for awards and decorations, in *The London Gazette*, to which there are annual or half-yearly subject indexes, ZJ 1. Minute Books, and selected case papers of Central and Middlesex Military Tribunals, Veterinary Tribunals and Appeal Tribunals, relating to appeals for exemption from military service, and by non-attested men, and conscientious objectors, 1916–18, MH 47; representative medical records for German and Belgian sick and wounded, arranged by field ambulance, admission and discharge registers from hospitals and casualty clearing stations, field ambulances, an ambulance train and hospital ship, samples of records showing the range of injuries, diseases contracted and treatments offered, medical cards for soldiers in the Leicestershire Regiment and Royal Field Artillery, 1912–21, MH 106 (some closed 75 years); incomplete alphabetical collection of death certificates of British and Dominion military in French and Belgian hospitals away from the War Zone, 1914–21, RG 35/45–69; card index to Naval officer casualties, giving name, rank, date, place and cause of death, and the name and address of the next of kin, 1914–20, ADM 242/1–5, and alphabetical War Graves Roll, 1914–19, ADM 242/7–10; consideration, award and

payment of pensions and allowances, to 1982, PIN 15 (some closed 75 years); selected war pensions award files, covering all types of disability, 1920–72, PIN 26 (most closed 50 years), and selected payments from 1917, PMG 45 (closed 75 years); temporary retired pay and gratuities awarded to invalided officers of all three Services, and to nurses for disabilities, 1917–20, PMG 42/1–12; supplementary allowances and special grants to officers of the three Services, their widows and dependants, 1916–20, PMG 43; payments of pensions to relatives of deceased offices of the three Services, 1916–20, PMG 44; pensions to widows of Army officers, 1917–19, PMG 45, and allowances to progeny, 1916–20, PMG 46; interim payments at pension rates to relatives of Army officers reported missing, 1915–20, PMG 47; allowances to widows, children and dependants of specially entered mercantile crew and crews of merchant vessels commissioned as Royal Naval ships, and Auxiliary Craft, and to other civilians killed or incapacitated, 1914–28, PMG 56; sample claims made by British subjects in the African Dominions and Far East for losses, listed by name, CO 348.
see *Air Force, Royal, Army, British, Marines, Royal, Medals, Naval Reserve, Royal, Navy, Royal, Prisoners of War, War Pensions*

World War II 1939–45. Despatches, campaign reports, casualties, and citations for awards and decorations, are in *The London Gazette*, with annual or half-yearly subject indexes, ZJ 1. Army Roll of Honour, 1939–45, listing servicemen and servicewomen who died, rank, regiment, birthplace, residence, where the fatality or death occurred, arranged in code, WO 304, with a key in WO 304/1;

Extracts from reports of pilots, August–September 1940, AIR 20/229, air crew casualties, January 1940–April 1945, AIR 20/888–90, air crew casualties, July–October 1940, AIR 16/609, daily summaries of Royal Air Force casualties, 1939–43, AIR 22/99–100; some notifications of death in all Services, prisoners of war, internees and aircraft lost in flight, RG 32; deaths in Hong Kong from enemy action, 1941–5, RG 33/11, indexed in RG 43/14; consideration, award and payment of pensions and allowances, including under Personal Injuries (Civilians) Scheme, to 1982, PIN 15 (some closed 75 years); War Damage (Valuation Appeals) Panel case files, 1941–5, LT 1, indexed in registers of appeals, 1946–61, LT 2; general claims under Compensation (Defence) Act 1939 for loss of business, property damage, requisition of land, buildings and food, 1940–58, LT 6, with registers and in-dexes, 1940–62, LT 7; in 1940 the Children's Overseas Reception Board was set up for the care of children, including orphans, accompanied or otherwise leaving the European War Zone for the British colonies: case files, 1940–46, registers of child applicants to go to Australia, Canada, New Zealand and South Africa, 1940, survivors and casualties of the *City of Benares*, 1940, DO 131/106–12, casualties among children going to New Zealand, 1941–5, DO 131/17–18, list of mothers and children evacuated to America, now in the United Kingdom, 1942–4, DO 131/31. War Crimes papers, listed by case or camp, giving name and date of trial, 1939–45, to which there is a nominal index, WO 325.

see *Air Force, Royal, Army, British, Evacuees, Marines, Royal, Medals, Navy, Royal, Prisoners of War, War Pensions*

Y*y*

Yeomanry Merged with the Volunteers into the Territorial Force in 1908. Musters of Yeomanry Cavalry in Great Britain, 1803–53, arranged alphabetically by county, WO 13; commissions, appointments and warrants, 1758–1855, HO 51, fees for appointments, 1782–1880, HO 88; allowances paid to Yeomanry, 1789–99, 1830–1927, PMG 13; records of services, 1804–55, WO 44/704–13; pensions paid by the Royal Hospital at Chelsea, giving age, length of service, how invalided out, and date of death, 1821–9, WO 23.

see *Territorial Army, Volunteers*

Yeomanry, Imperial Soldiers' documents, giving birthplace, age at enlistment, and occupation, service record and conduct sheet, arranged under regimental number, 1899–1902, WO 128, to which there is an index, plus casualty books, 1900–2, and a nominal roll of officers serving in South Africa, 1899–1902, in WO 129; casualties, 1899–1902, WO 108/89–91, 338.

see *Boer War*

Zz

Zanzibar Births to Britons, 1916–18, marriages, 1917–19, deaths, 1916–19, RG 36, indexed in RG 43/18.

Glossary

abjuration: denial of Jacobite claim to the Crown.

administration *de bonis non* (Admon. d.b.n.): grant of letters of administration of an unadministered estate where the original administrator has died leaving part of the estate unadministered.

administration with will annexed (Admon. *cum testatmento annexo*): where the Court has appointed an administrator in the absence of an executor being named in the will or where he has renounced.

advowson: right of presentation to an ecclesiastical benefice.

aetate probanda, de, writ of: used to prove the age of majority of an heir at law.

affidavit: written statement made voluntarily under oath.

amercement: pecuniary payment by an offender 'at the mercy' or discretion of the court.

Annates: first year's profits of a benefice, payable until 1532 to the Pope. They were then suspended and three years later were granted to the King together with an annual pension of a tenth of all the temporal and spiritual possessions of the Church. All benefices were subjected to valuation, leading to the *Valor Ecclesiasticus*. From 1704 the moneys were paid to the Commissioners of Queen Anne's Bounty. By the First Fruits and Tenths Measure 1926 they were extinguished or redeemed.

attainder: deprivation of rights including those of heirs after conviction of treason or felony.

attorney: person admitted to practise in the superior common law courts. Known as 'Solicitors of the Supreme Court' since the Judicature Act 1873.

attorney, warrant of: written authority by a defendant to a suit to enable a person to enter an appearance in an action and allow judgment to be entered for the plaintiff or to suffer judgment by default. Usually given to secure payment of a sum of money by a certain date, and if not paid then the warrant is put into force.

bill of sale: deed witnessing transfer of property as security for a debt.

bushel: four pecks; eight bushels make a quarter.

calendar: summary of contents of a series of documents in their original language or in translation.

Calendar, Gregorian (New Style or N.S.): introduced by Pope Gregory XIII in a Papal Bull in 1582 to replace the Julian Calendar, it was adopted in Europe at varying dates, Catholic countries generally using it before Protestant. It was instituted in England, Wales and Ireland in 1752, when the New Year began on 1 January. In that year too, 2 September was followed by 14 September. The Calendar was assumed in Scotland from 1 January 1600.

Calendar, Julian (Old Style or O.S.): the 365 ¼ day year was introduced by Julius Caesar in 45 BC. In England the New Year began on 25 March from at least the eleventh century, until replaced by the Gregorian Calendar in 1752.

carucage: tax on ploughland.

catalogue: enumeration of documents of a particular nature often dispersed among a variety of classes.

certiorari, writ of: directed to an inferior court commanding it to 'certify' some matter of a judicial character, and used to remove civil causes or indictments to a superior court. Issued out of the Court of King's Bench to 1875, thereafter by Queen's Bench Division.

chantry: endowment for the singing of masses for the souls of the dead.

codicil: an addition or alteration to, explanation or confirmation of a will already made by the testator, and executed in the same way, reciting the date of the will to which it is to be attached.

cognovit: written acknowledgement of a debt, authorizing summary recovery in default of a specific performance.

company, exempt private: to 1967 one which was not obliged to file its accounts.

constat: certificate of a matter on record.

contumace capiendo, de: writ ordering commitment to lay custody of a person pronounced 'contumacious' by an ecclesiastical court.

co-parceny: tenants inheriting jointly (usually sisters).

corrody: allowance of food and clothing for the maintenance of a retired servant made by a religious house and granted to the Crown or other benefactor.

covenant: an agreement creating an obligation contained in a deed.

covenant, writ of: used to claim damages for a breach of a covenant. Abolished by the Real Property Limitation Act 1833.

cursitor: clerk in the Chancery Office making out all original writs and processes returnable to the Court of King's Bench and elsewhere. Abolished in 1835.

curtilage: courtyard adjoining a messuage.

debenture: legal instrument, usually under seal, issued by a company or public body as evidence of a debt or as security for a loan of a fixed sum of money at interest, and containing a promise to pay the amount mentioned in it.

defeasance: a condition relating to a deed contained in a separate instrument on which being performed renders the deed void.

demesne: land held by a feudal or manorial lord for his own use.

demesne, ancient: land held in demesne by the Crown in the time of Edward the Confessor as recorded in Domesday Book.

diem clausit extremum, **writ of:** used to order an enquiry about the lands held by a tenant-in-chief of the Crown on information that 'he has closed his last day'; abolished in 1660.

dismissal/dismission: decree whereby a Chancery bill is dismissed out of court.

distress: act of taking a person's moveables and of retaining them until compensation was made, usually for a debt.

docket: (**a**) abstract of a judgment, decree or order etc.; (**b**) index slip used as a means of reference to a registered file; (**c**) note of action taken; (**d**) abstract of a warrant for a grant.

Dormant Funds: cash and securities under the control of the Supreme Court in England and Wales, standing to the credit of accounts which have not been dealt with for more than five years. There are published lists running from 1890 up to 1974.

dorse: back, underside.

dower: portion of lands or tenements belonging to a wife or widow for her lifetime. Abolished by Administration of Estates Act 1925.

en ventre sa mère: a child in its mother's womb.

essoin: excuse for absence.

estreat: extract from or copy of a record.

excommunication: exclusion from Communion of the Church and used as a means of enforcing ecclesiastical judgments.

excommunicatum, capias ad, **writ of:** issued for the arrest of an excommunicate.

exemplification: sealed office copy of a document.

fee: (**a**) hereditary tenement held by feudal service; (**b**) payment due to an official.

fee-farm rent: perpetual rent imposed on grantee of land held in fee simple.

felony: criminal offence entailing to 1870 forfeiture of goods and escheat of lands, as well as the death penalty.

fême covert: married woman.

fême sole: unmarried woman.

fiat: (**a**) authorization especially by the Attorney General or the Lord Chancellor for certain action to be taken; (**b**) note of making the authorization.

fieri facias (fi. fa.): writ ordering levy of a specified sum from a debtor's goods to pay off a debt. The goods were seized and sold by the sheriff at auction.

First Fruits: (see Annates).

free warren: privilege of keeping and killing hares and rabbits on a piece of ground, abolished in 1971.

fugitive: a person fleeing to escape trial for felony.

gallon: eight pints.

gestation: time elapsing from conception to birth of a child, usually about nine months of thirty days each. The time is added where necessary to the period allowed under the rule against perpetuities.

guardian *ad litem:* person appointed to defend an action on behalf of a minor or person under a disability.

habeas corpus, unit of: directing a person detained in custody to be produced before the court.

hawker: travelling seller of goods.

hereditament: real property which can be inherited.

holograph: deed or will handwritten by the grantor or testator.

Honour: several manors held by one lord.

imparl: confer with, discuss.

index, alphabetical: arranged strictly alphabetically by surname.

index, initial: arranged by initial letter of a surname only.

infant: a child under seven years.

inferior courts: any court other than the Supreme Court, and subject to Orders of Certiorari, Mandamus and Prohibition.

information: step by which certain civil and criminal proceedings were instituted.

inspeximus: exemplification of a record.

interlocutory: provisional or incidental decree or order.

levari facias, **writ of:** order for a levy of a specified sum from lands and goods of a debtor by seizure and sale, and receipt of the rents and profits of the land until the debt was settled.

libel: (a) defamation; (b) first written plea or complaint in proceedings in civil or canon law.

librate: a piece of land worth a pound a year.

list, descriptive: one in which the items are described more fully.

list, numerical: enumeration of items within a class or part of it, usually giving the dates covered by each.

livery: (a) handing over; (b) allowance for maintenance, usually in the form of dress.

mandamus, writ of: directed to a person or body ordering performance of a public duty, and issued by the Court of King's Bench to 1875 and thereafter by the Queen's Bench Division.

mark: 13*s*. 4*d*.

marriage *ab initio:* a void marriage, where the parties went through a ceremony and where some necessary ingredient of a valid marriage was missing, rendering it void '*ab initio*' (from the beginning) as if the marriage had not taken place.

marriage, voidable: a valid subsisting marriage until a decree of nullity was pronounced e.g. for non-consummation.

merger: where the right of a person by reason of its coinciding with an even greater right of the same person is extinguished.

messuage: house, including gardens, courtyard, orchard and outbuildings.

minor: person over seven and under twenty-one (lowered to eighteen by the Family Law Reform Act 1969).

modus decimandi: payment of tithes other than by a tenth of the yearly increase of the land, and rendered in money or in kind.

moiety: half.

Mortality, Weekly Bills of: commenced in the late sixteenth century to contrast normal levels of mortality with plague levels, and extending to the late-eighteenth century, covering London and other towns. They record totals, by age-band, and sometimes giving causes, under parish. In 1636 London was deemed to extend from Stepney to Westminster and included the square mile of the City. By 1682 it ran from Limehouse to Whitehall North of the Thames, and from Rother-hithe to Southwark South of the River, and included the East and West Ends.

mortmain, alienation in: grant of land to a religious house or other corporation to deprive the Crown or other feudal lord of incidents due on a tenant's death. It could be done only by a licence from the Crown or under statute. The law of mortmain was abolished by the Charities Act 1960.

motion: application to a court or judge for an order for something to be done in the applicant's favour.

outlawry, judgment in: a person put outside the protection of the law and liable to capital punishment or imprisonment and forfeiture. Used as the final means of compelling appearance in court or compliance with a court order. It was abolished by Administration of Justice (Miscellaneous Provisions) Act 1938.

Palatinate: area where an earl or bishop exercised administrative and judicial authority elsewhere exercised by the Crown.

peck: two gallons; four pecks make a bushel.

pedlar: travelling salesman of small goods, usually in a pack.

perch: in long measure 5½ yards, four of which make a chain.

per stirpes: distribution of property amongst those equally entitled to it, e.g. children, and the descendants of deceased children taking the parent's share equally.

pole: (a) in long measure 5½ yards, four making a chain; (b) in square measure 30¼ square yards, forty making a rood.

Postea: formal note of subsequent proceedings, endorsed on the original entry of a case.

***praecipe quod reddat,* writ of:** writ of right in real actions for the recovery of fee simple land.

process: (a) entire course of procedure in legal action; (b) writ or summons to appear in court.

proctor: civil and canon equivalent of an attorney acting in ecclesiastical courts or the High Court of Admiralty. Called 'Solicitors of the Supreme Court' since Judicature Act 1873.

prohibition, writ of: used to restrain an inferior court from extending its powers, and may be absolute, temporary or partial. Issued out of the Court of King's Bench to 1875 and thereafter from the Queen's Bench Division.

prothonotary: chief clerk of various courts e.g. Common Pleas, and in the Palatinates of Chester, Durham and Lancaster and in the Principality of Wales.

quarter: (a) eight bushels; (b) twenty-eight pounds avoirdupois weight. Four quarters make a hundredweight (cwt).

quietus est: auditor's note at the foot of a document that the party concerned is discharged free of debt.

quire: twenty-four sheets of paper.

quit-rent: paid by tenants to manorial lord in lieu and in discharge of services.

quo warranto, writ of: issued by the Crown against a person claiming an office, franchise or liberty, requiring by what authority it was done.

rack-rent: highest annual rent a tenement can fetch on the open market.

ragman: parchment document with many pendant seals.

ream: twenty quires.

recognizance: formal acknowledgement of debt or other obligation, usually with sureties and subject to specific penalties for default of performance of a specified act, and enrolled in a court of record.

recorders: barristers of five years' standing appointed by the Crown to act as justices of the peace and sole judge in a Borough Court of Quarter Sessions, 1882–1971. Since 1972 Recorders of London, Liverpool and Manchester have served as circuit judges, the Recorder of London being the judge of the Central Criminal Court. Other recorders may be appointed as part-time judges of the Crown Court.

recto: top-side, or right hand page.

recusant: a person denying the Sovereign's ecclesiastical supremacy or refusing to attend services of the Established Church.

rent charge: rent payable on land to a person with no possession or reversion in it and with a right of distress for default granted by express agreement between the parties.

residue: remainder of a deceased person's estate after payment of debts, funeral and probate expenses, legacies and annuities.

rod: in long measure 5½ yards, four rods making a chain.

rood: in square measure, forty poles make a rood and four roods an acre.

scire facies, writ of: ordering a matter to be brought to the notice of someone so that he may if he wishes appear and defend his rights therein.

seisin, livery of: delivery of feudal possession of freehold land.

solicitor: lawyer practising in courts of Equity; since Judicature Act 1873 used as a generic term for attorneys, proctors and solicitors. Has a right of audience in the inferior courts and employed to advise on legal matters.

stone: fourteen pounds.

supersedeas: writ ordering stay or end of proceedings.

tallage: tax especially on land of unfree tenants and the Crown's ancient demesne.

tally: rectangular stick on which notches were made at each payment to the Exchequer or elsewhere, and which was cut lengthwise, one half being retained by the creditor and the other given to the debtor as proof of payment. Replaced by indented check receipts in 1826.

tenement: (**a**) land; (**b**) house especially one divided up into apartments.

Tenths: (**a**) tenth part of annual profit of an ecclesiastical benefice; (**b**) tax on personal property imposed by the Crown.

tenancy in common: where two or more persons are entitled jointly to a piece of land and none to it exclusively. On the death of one that person's share passes to his devisee.

tenancy, joint: where two or more persons are entitled jointly to a piece of land and on the death of one his share vests in the survivors.

terrier: survey of land.

Tithe, Great: payable to the Rector and including corn, hay and wood, and produce of soil tilled with the plough.

Tithe, Small: payable to the Vicar and including produce of soil tilled with the spade.

tontine: annuity increasing for the survivors as the nominees of the subscribers entitled to it die.

transcript: (**a**) an official copy of court proceedings; (**b**) exact copy of an original document in another hand.

trust: an association between one person and at least one other whereby property is held as trustee(s) for the benefit of the other. It replaced the 'use' after the Statute of Uses 1535.

ulnage or alnage: duty imposed on an ell (forty-five inches in length) of cloth.

use: an association between one person and at least one other whereby property was held as feoffee(s) to uses for the benefit or 'use' of the other. It was abolished by the Statute of Uses 1535.

verso: the reverse or left-hand of a page.

victualler: supplier of food to the public or to ships or troops.

virgate: usually thirty acres of arable land in the common fields of a manor, but varied from ten up to eighty acres depending on the part of the country.

warranty: guarantee or assurance; covenant by feoffor or donor of land to the feoffee or donee in possession of it that he would defend his title to it, and give him land of equal value if he was evicted from it.

waste, impeachability for: liability for commission or omission of an act on uncultivated or other land by a tenant for life or for term of years which alters it, such as felling certain trees, conversion of arable to pasture, pulling down buildings.

will, nuncupative: declaration by a testator without writing and made before witnesses.

yardland: about thirty acres (see virgate).